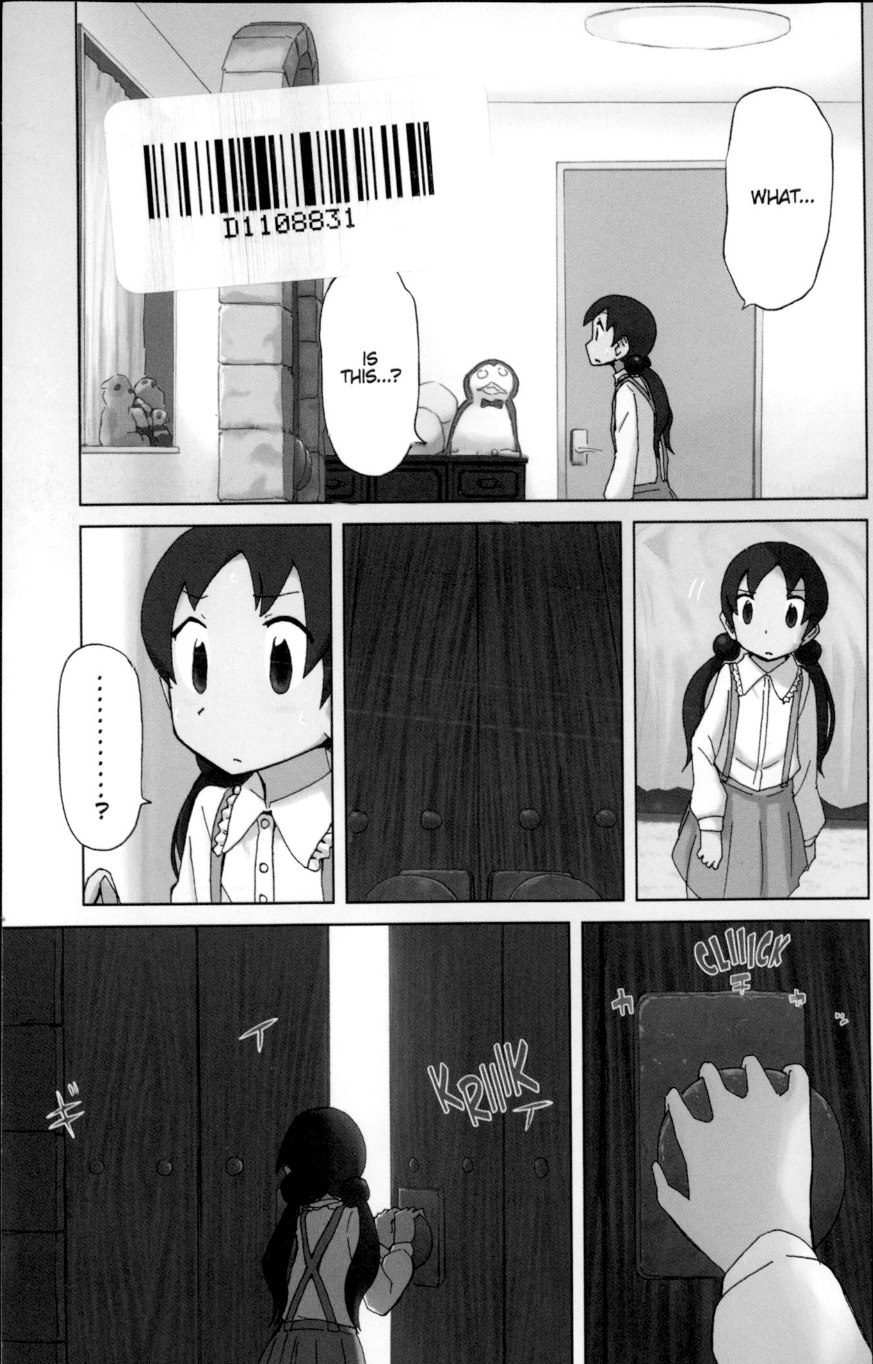
WHAT...
IS THIS...?
..........?
CLIIICK
KRIIK

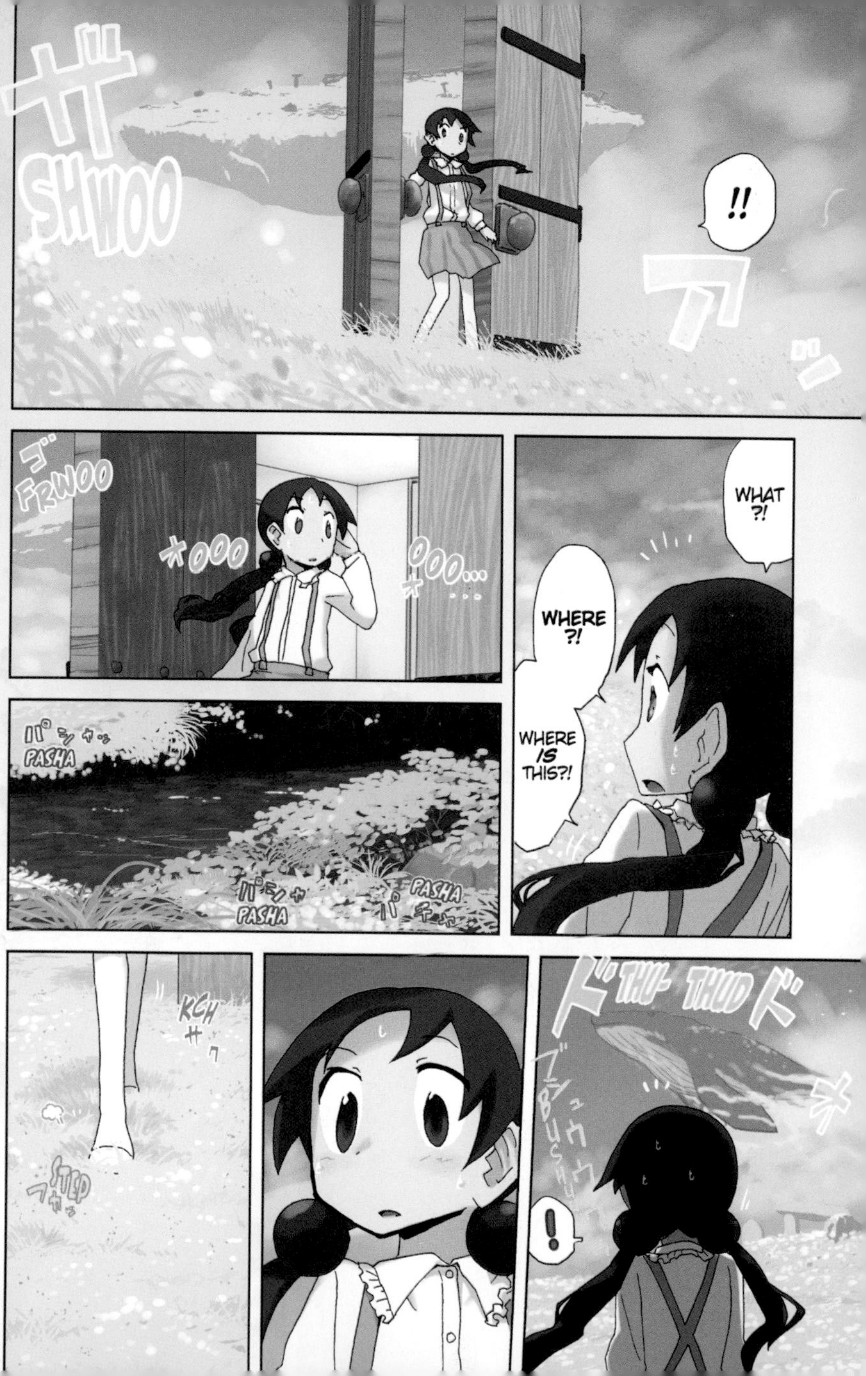
!!
SHWOO
WHAT ?!
WHERE ?!
WHERE IS THIS?!
FRWOO
OOOO
OOO...
PASHA
PASHA
PASHA
THU- THUD
BUSHUU
!
KCH
STEP

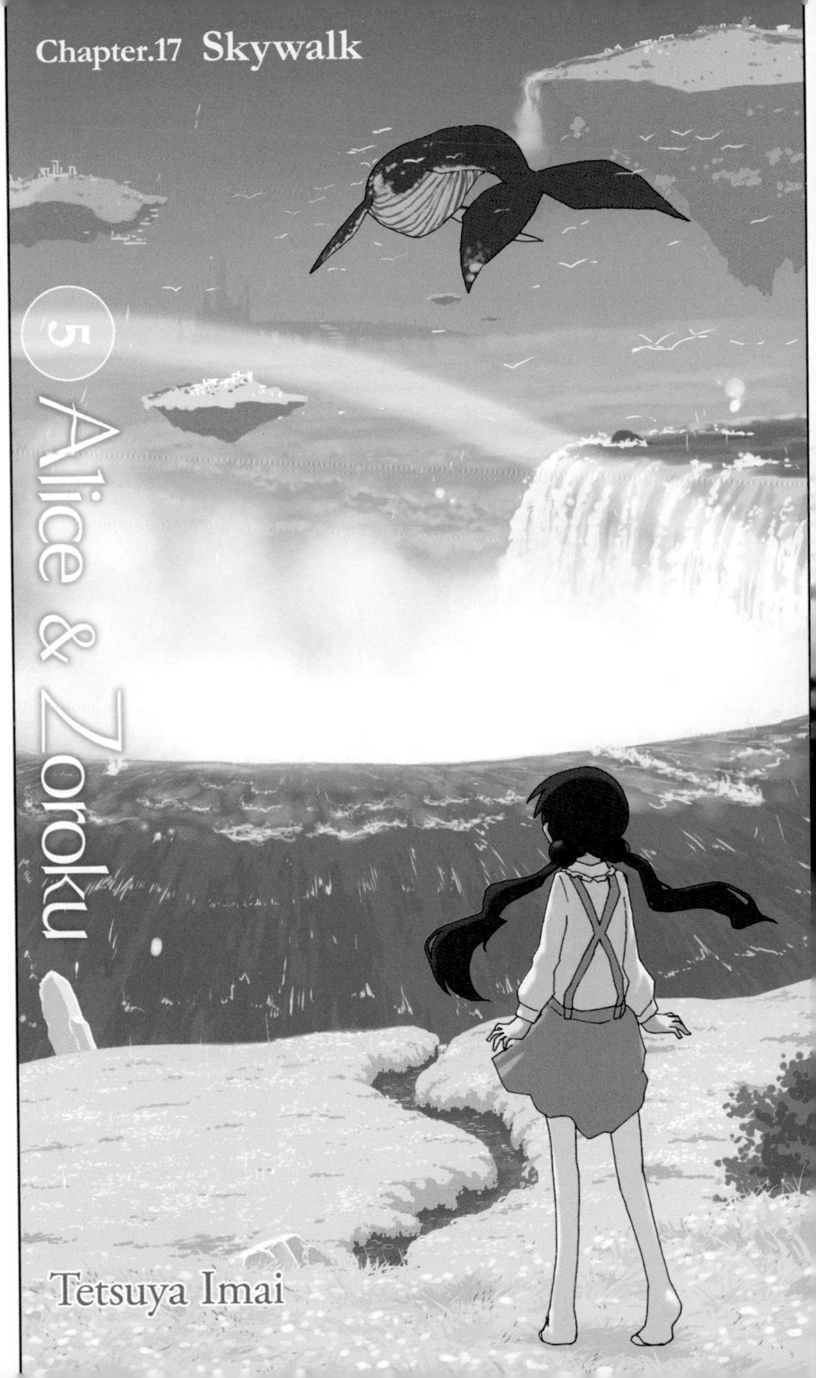
Chapter.17 Skywalk
5
Alice & Zoroku
Tetsuya Imai

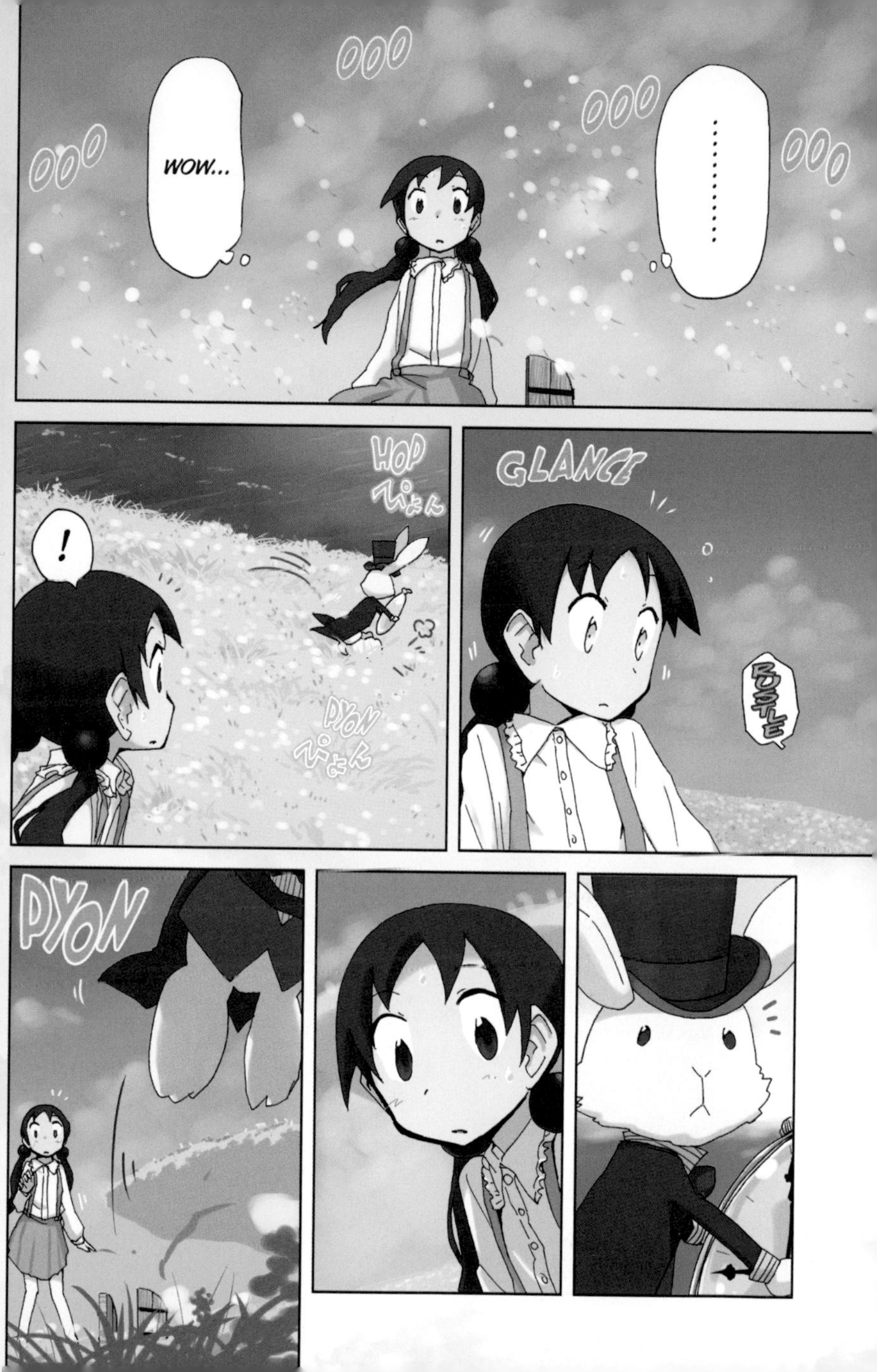
OOO
OOO
OOO
......
WOW...
OOO
GLANCE
RUSTLE
HOP ぴょん
!
PYON ぴょん
PYON

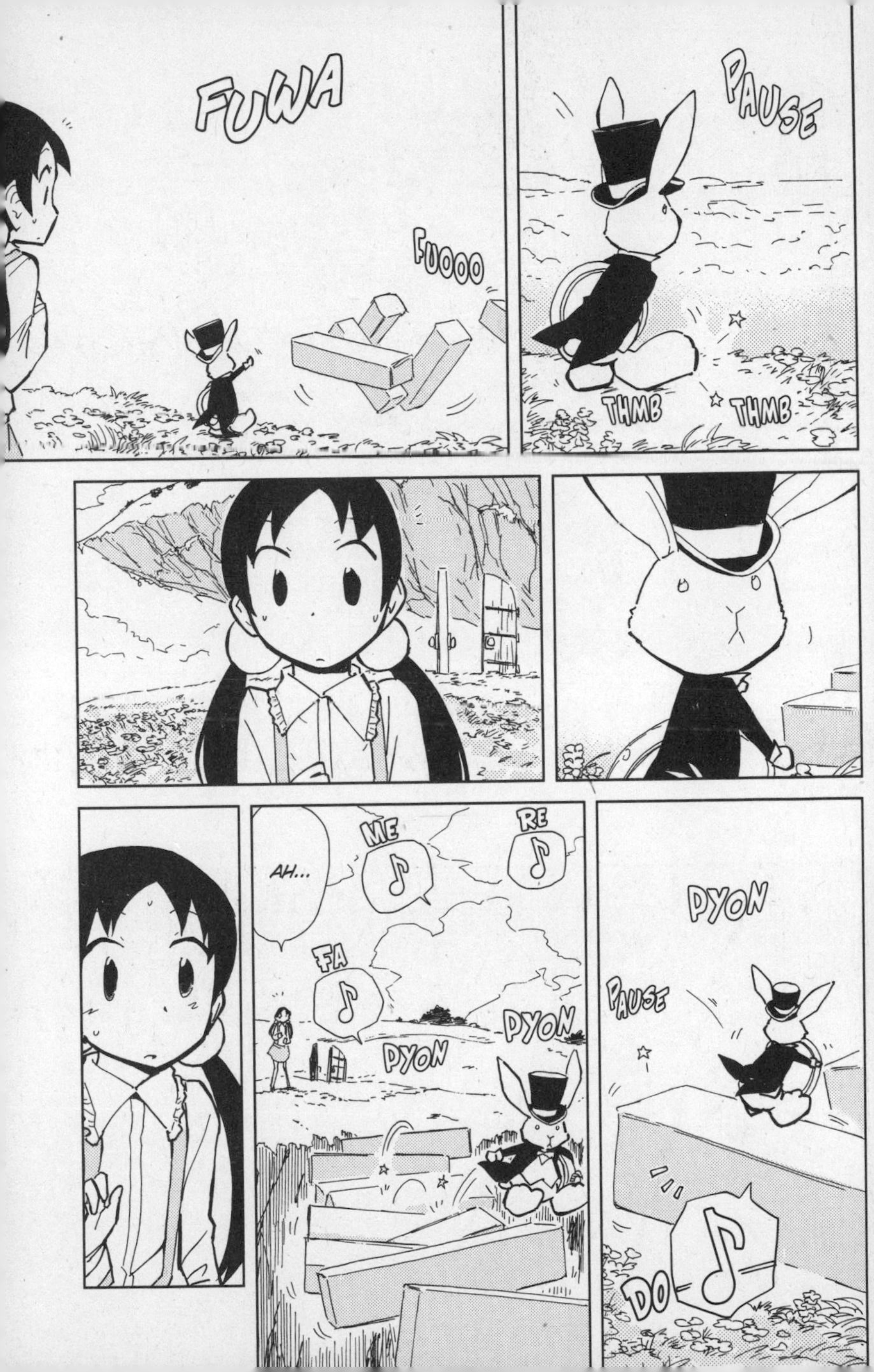
PAUSE
THMB
THMB
FUWA
FUOOO
PYON
PAUSE
DO
RE
ME
AH...
PYON
FA
PYON

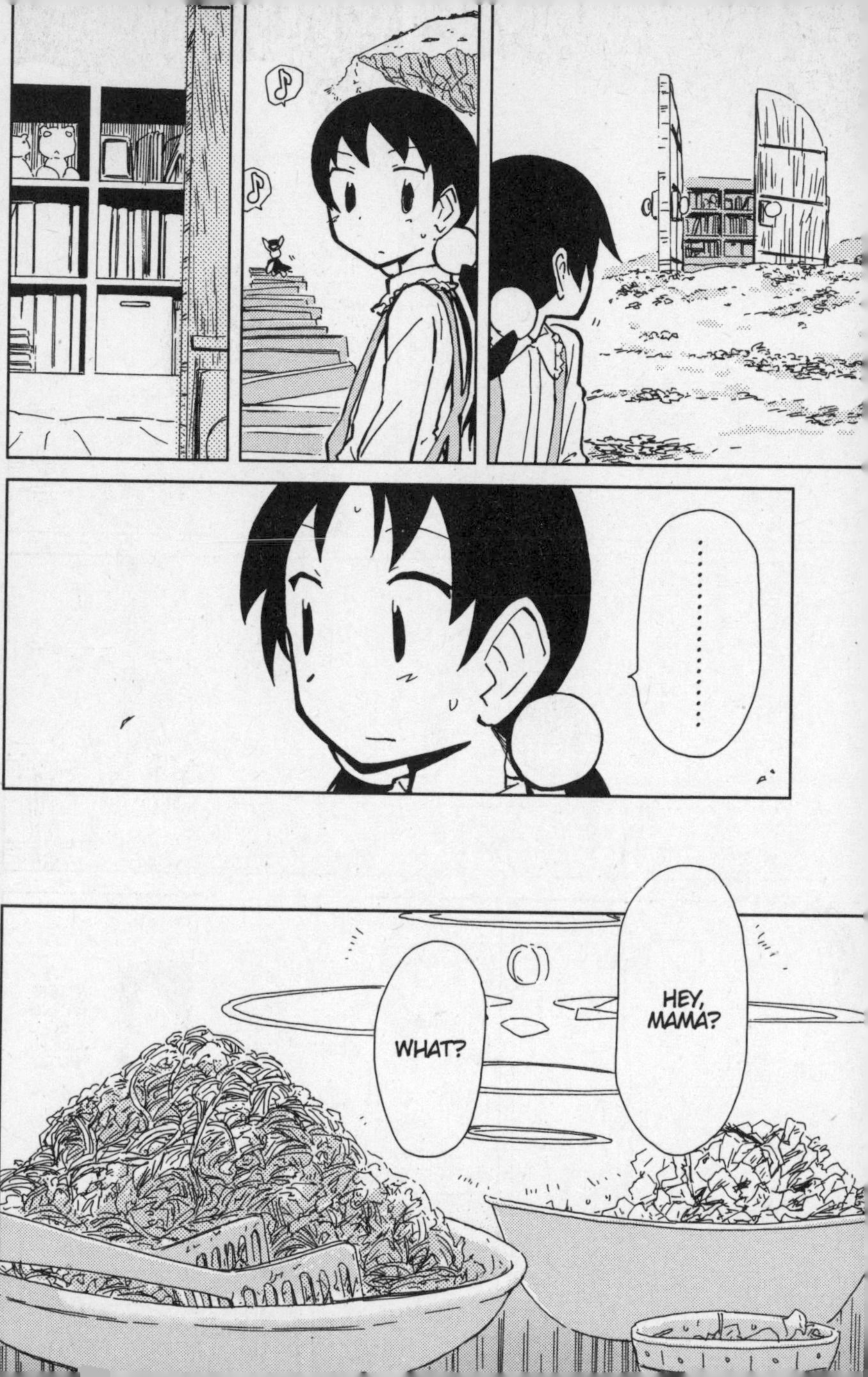

......
HEY, MAMA?
WHAT?

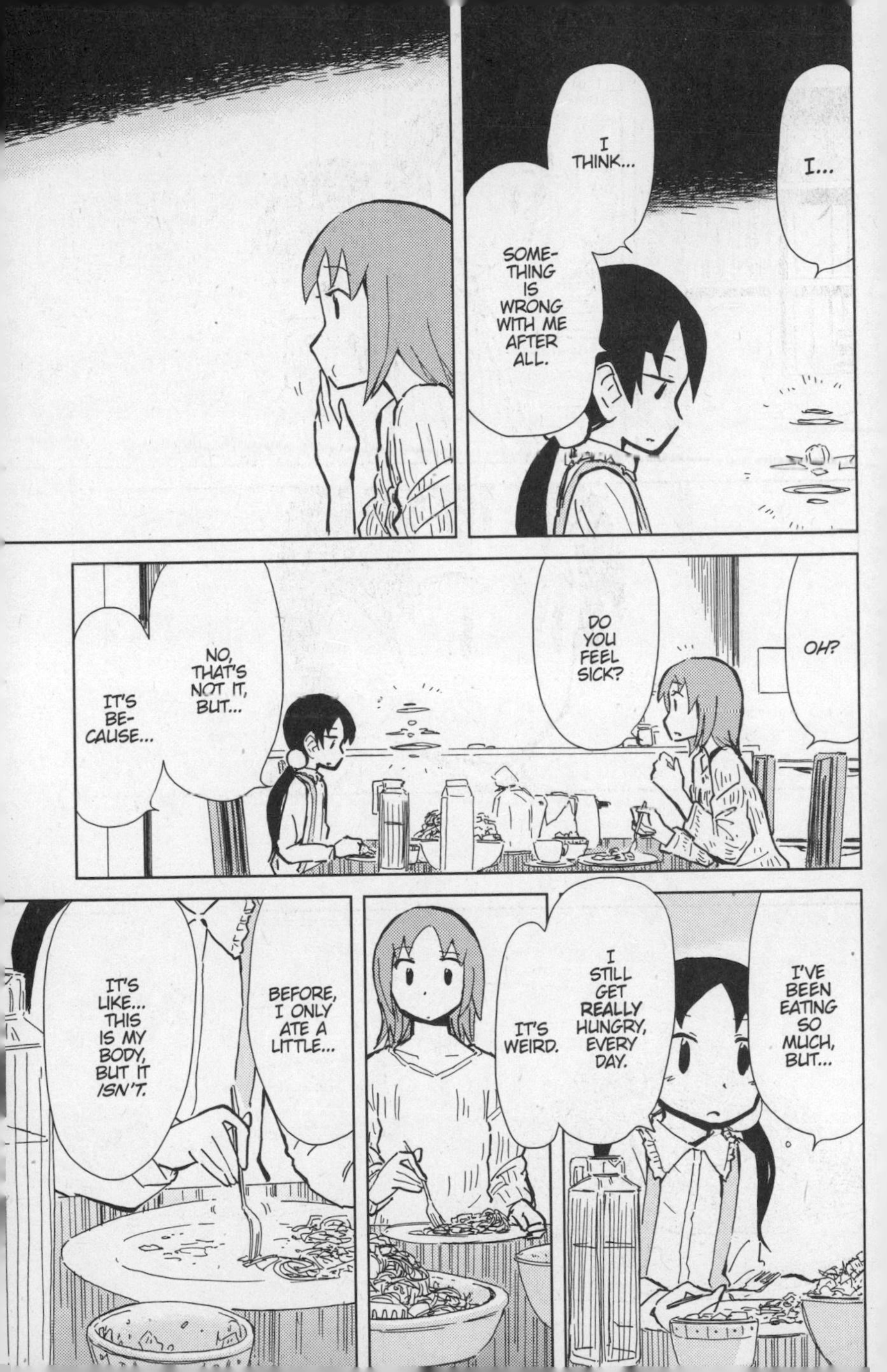
I...
I THINK...
SOMETHING IS WRONG WITH ME AFTER ALL.
OH?
DO YOU FEEL SICK?
NO, THAT'S NOT IT, BUT...
IT'S BECAUSE...
I'VE BEEN EATING SO MUCH, BUT...
I STILL GET REALLY HUNGRY, EVERY DAY.
IT'S WEIRD.
BEFORE, I ONLY ATE A LITTLE...
IT'S LIKE... THIS IS MY BODY, BUT IT *ISN'T.*

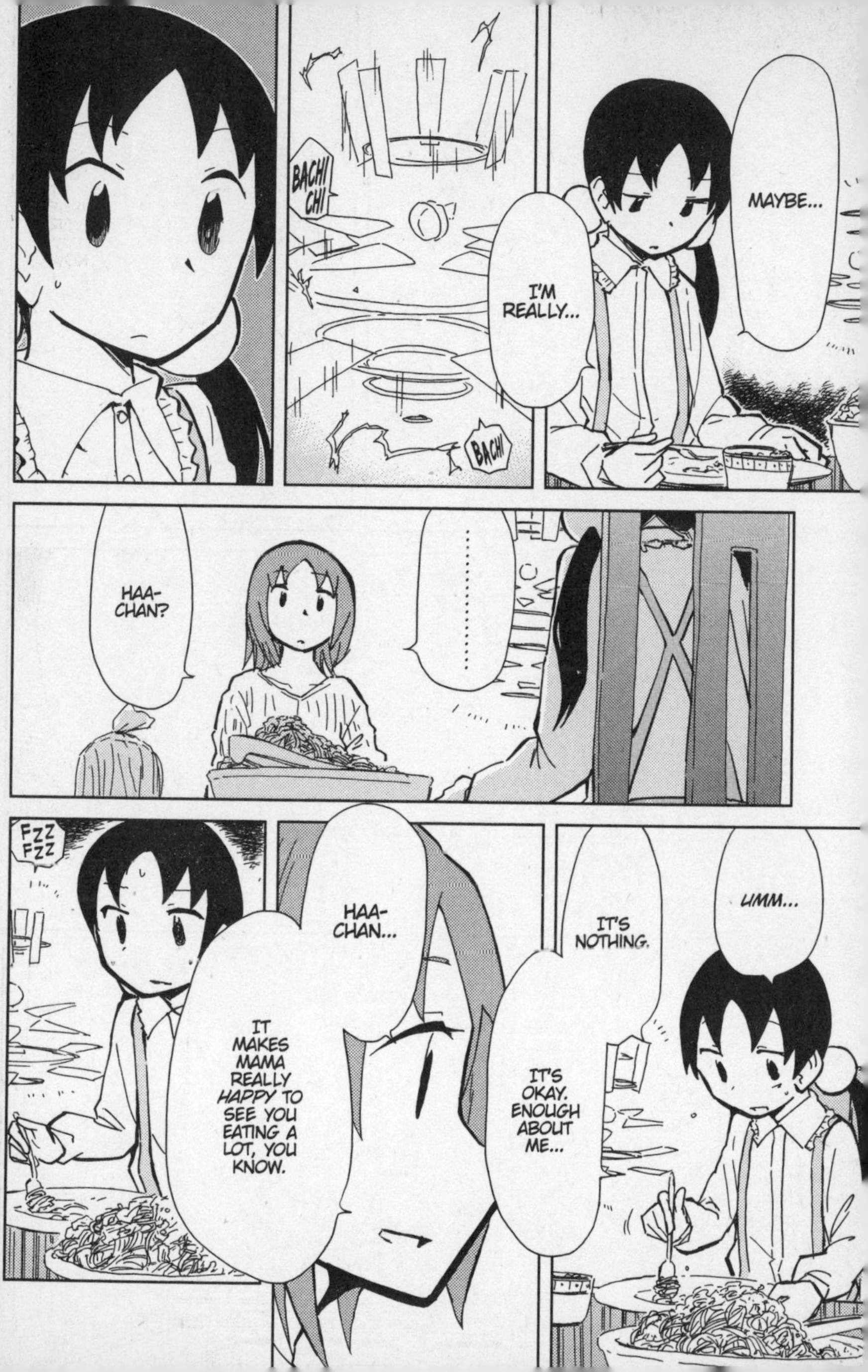
MAYBE...
I'M REALLY...
BACHI CHI
BACHI
......
HAA-CHAN?
UMM...
IT'S NOTHING.
IT'S OKAY. ENOUGH ABOUT ME...
HAA-CHAN...
IT MAKES MAMA REALLY *HAPPY* TO SEE YOU EATING A LOT, YOU KNOW.
FZZ FZZ

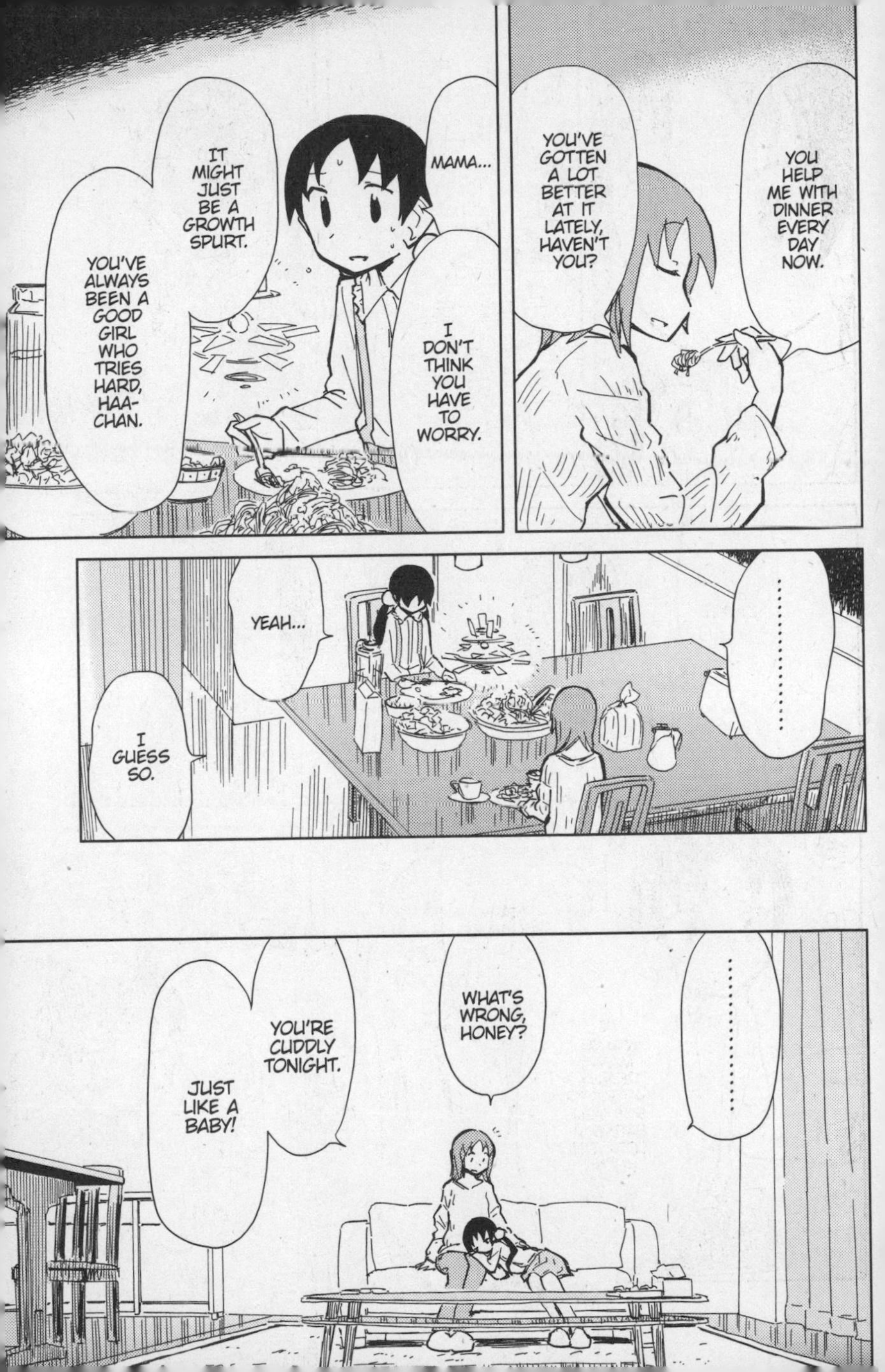
YOU HELP ME WITH DINNER EVERY DAY NOW.
YOU'VE GOTTEN A LOT BETTER AT IT LATELY, HAVEN'T YOU?
MAMA...
I DON'T THINK YOU HAVE TO WORRY.
IT MIGHT JUST BE A GROWTH SPURT.
YOU'VE ALWAYS BEEN A GOOD GIRL WHO TRIES HARD, HAA-CHAN.
......
YEAH...
I GUESS SO.
......
WHAT'S WRONG, HONEY?
YOU'RE CUDDLY TONIGHT.
JUST LIKE A BABY!

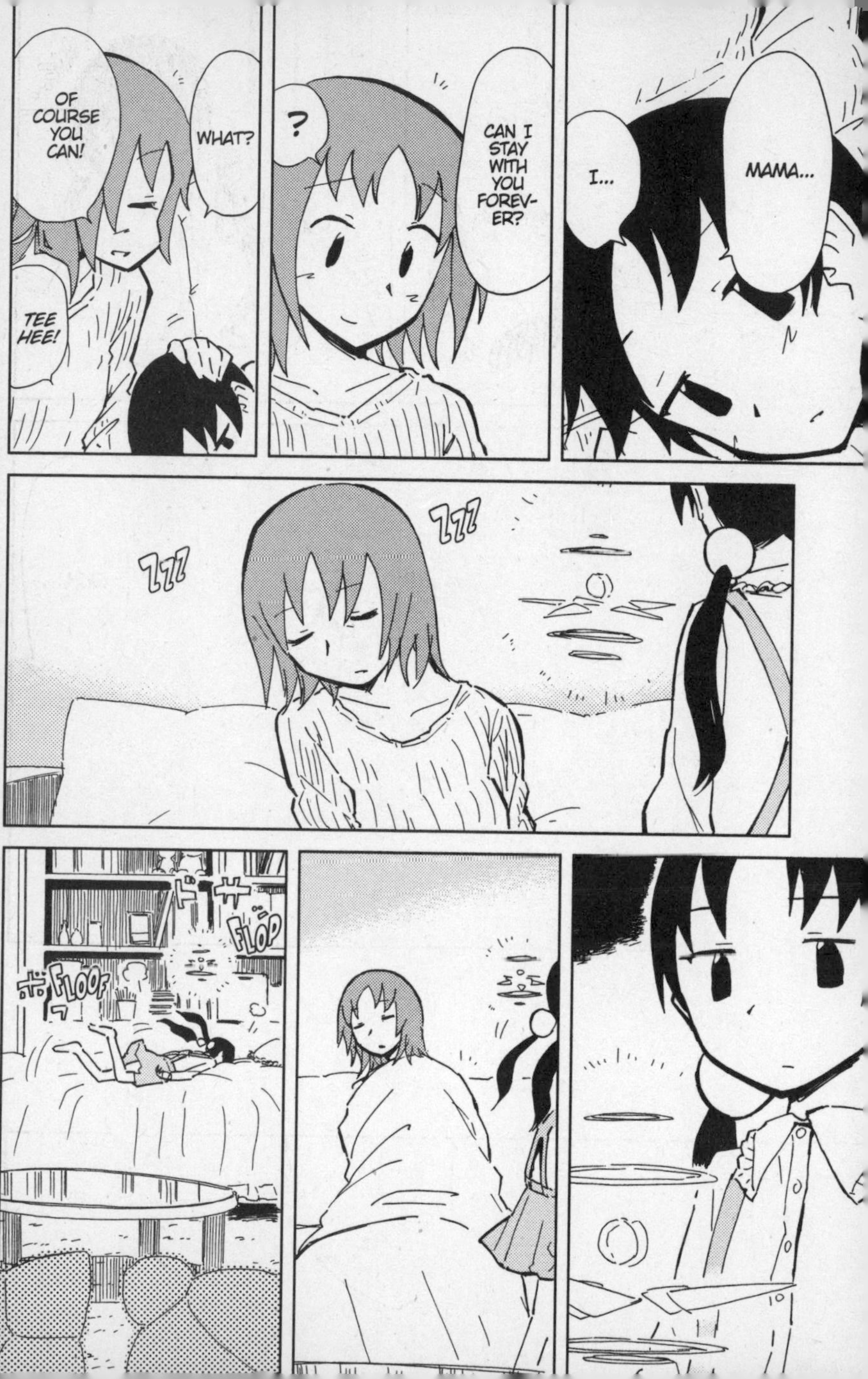
MAMA...
I...
CAN I STAY WITH YOU FOREVER?
?
WHAT?
OF COURSE YOU CAN!
TEE HEE!
ZZZ
ZZZ
FLOP
FLOOF

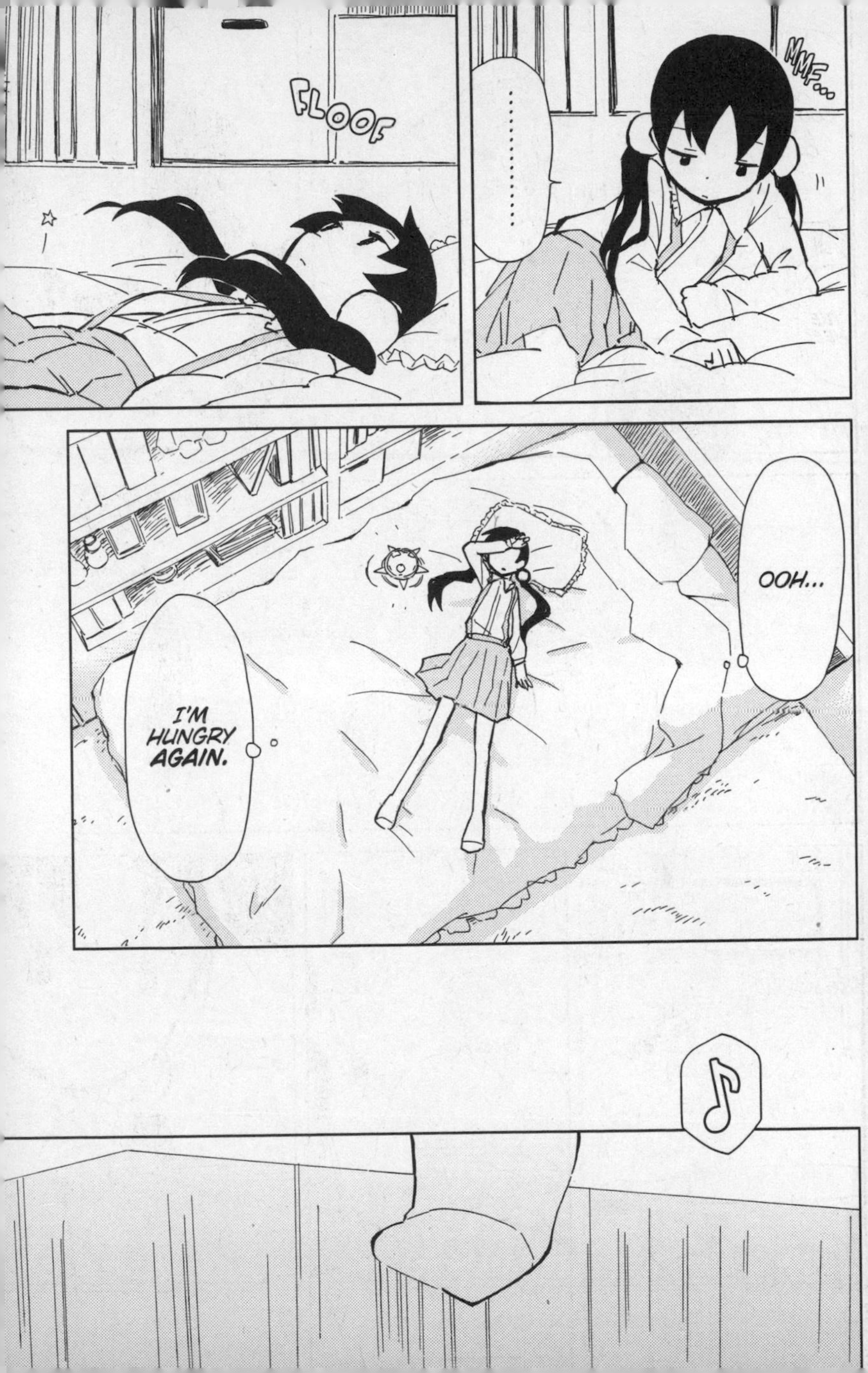
MMF...
......
FLOOF
OOH...
I'M HUNGRY AGAIN.
♪

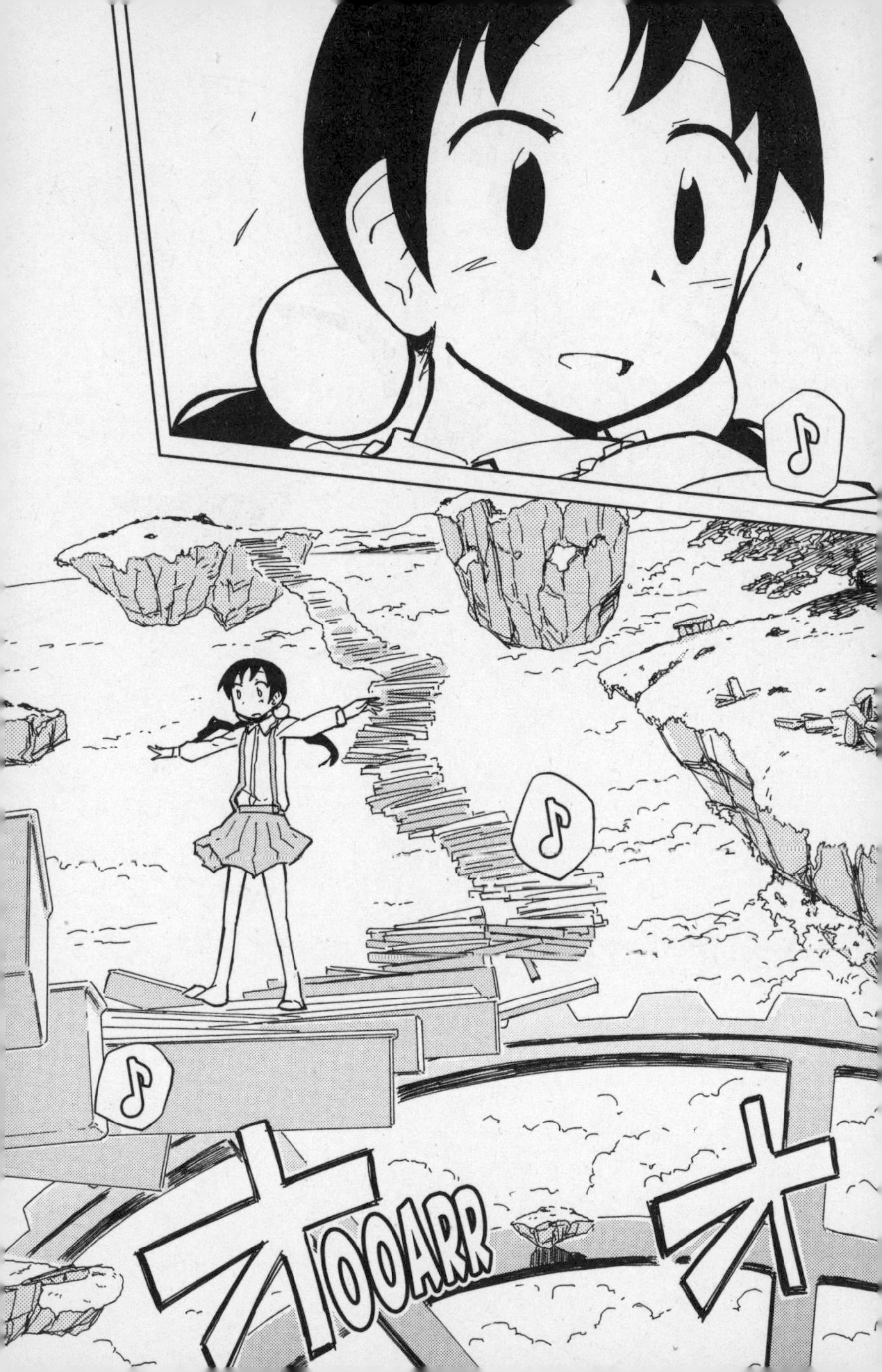
OOARR

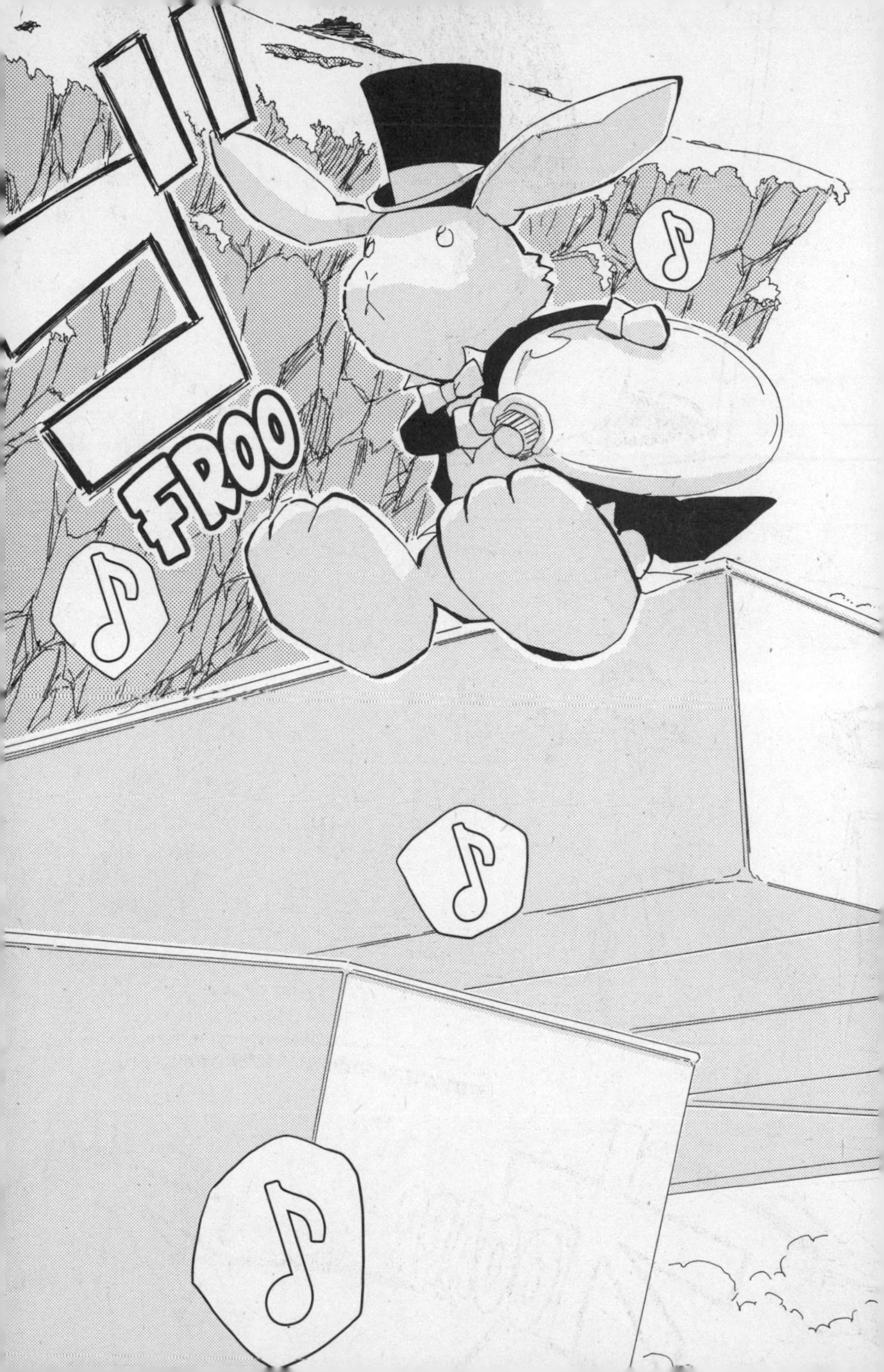
FROO

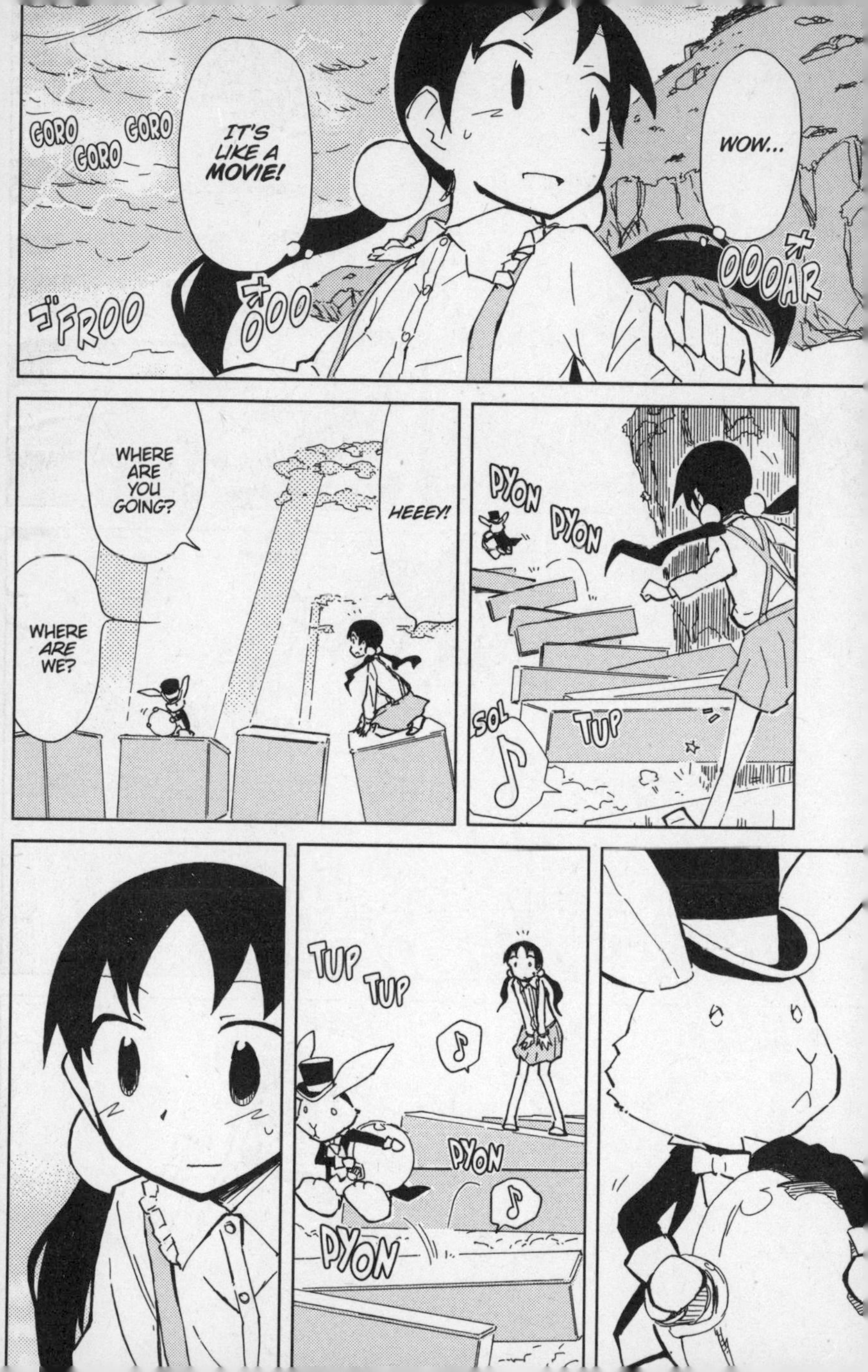
WOW...
OOOAR オ
IT'S LIKE A MOVIE!
GORO GORO GORO
ゴ FROO
オ OOO
PYON PYON
SOL
TUP
HEEEY!
WHERE ARE YOU GOING?
WHERE ARE WE?
TUP TUP
PYON
PYON

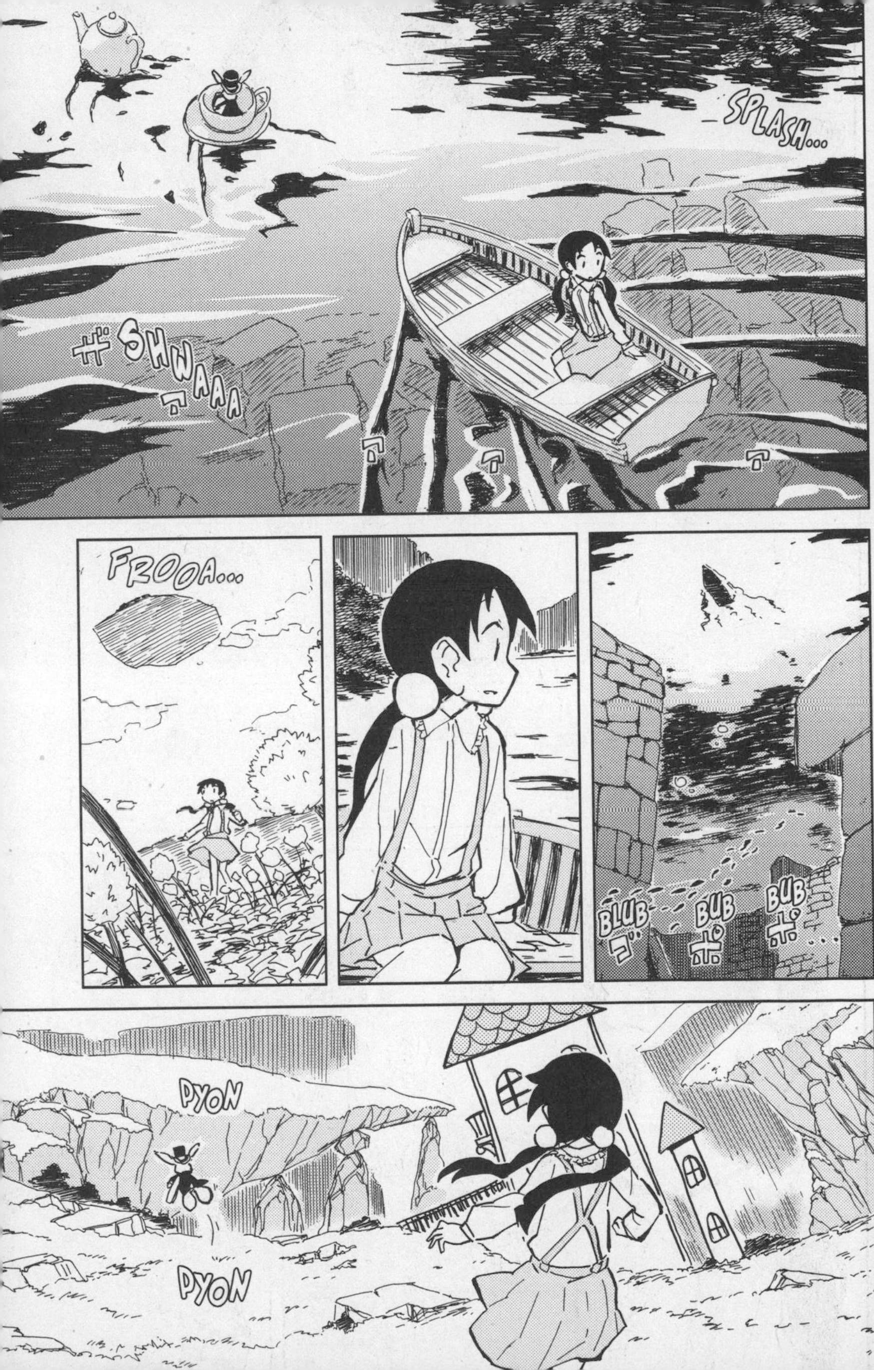
SPLASH...
SHWAAA
BUB
BUB
BLUB
FROOA...
PYON
PYON

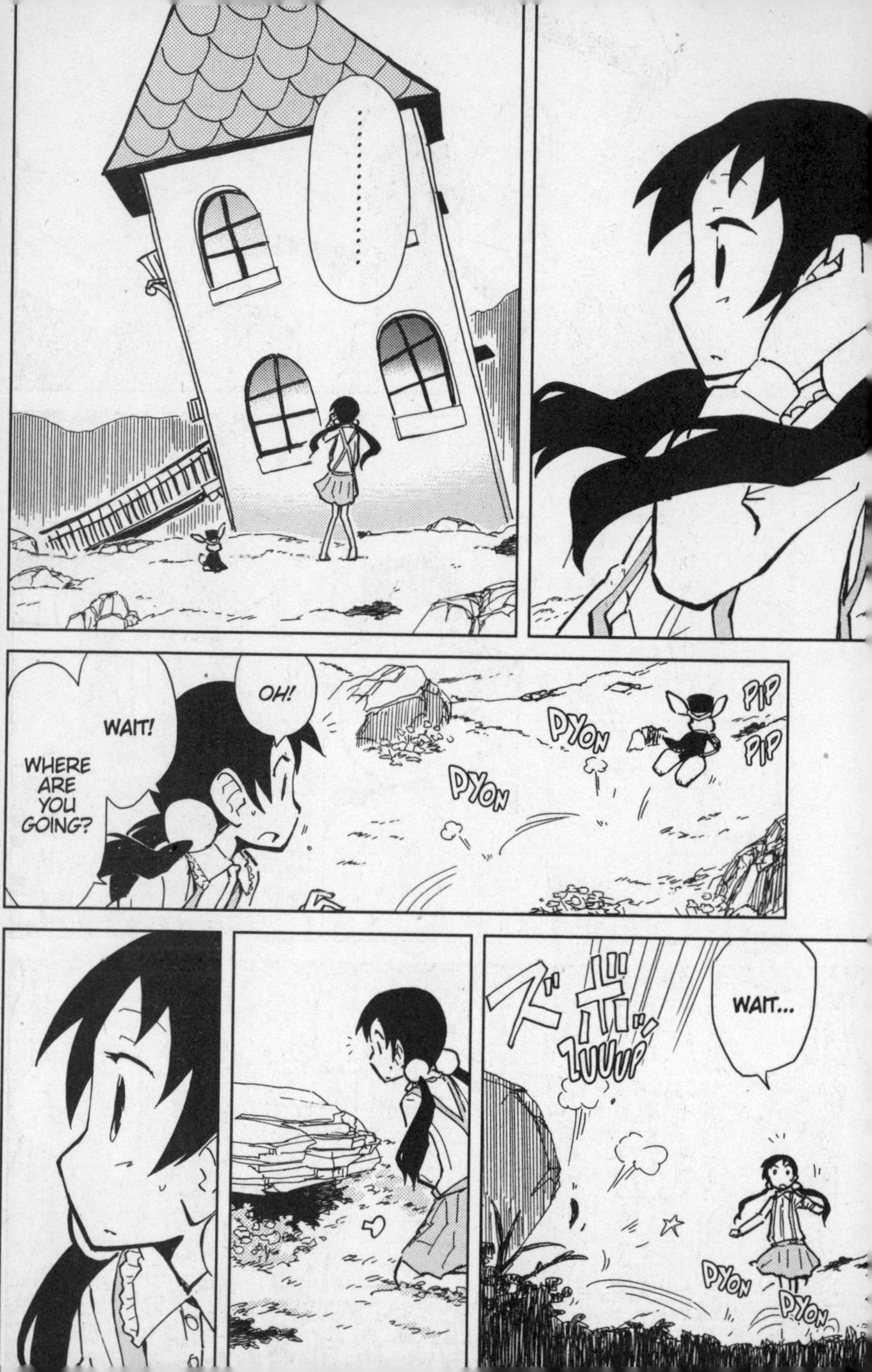

……
PIP PIP
PYON
PYON
OH!
WAIT!
WHERE ARE YOU GOING?
WAIT...
ZUUUP
PYON
PYON

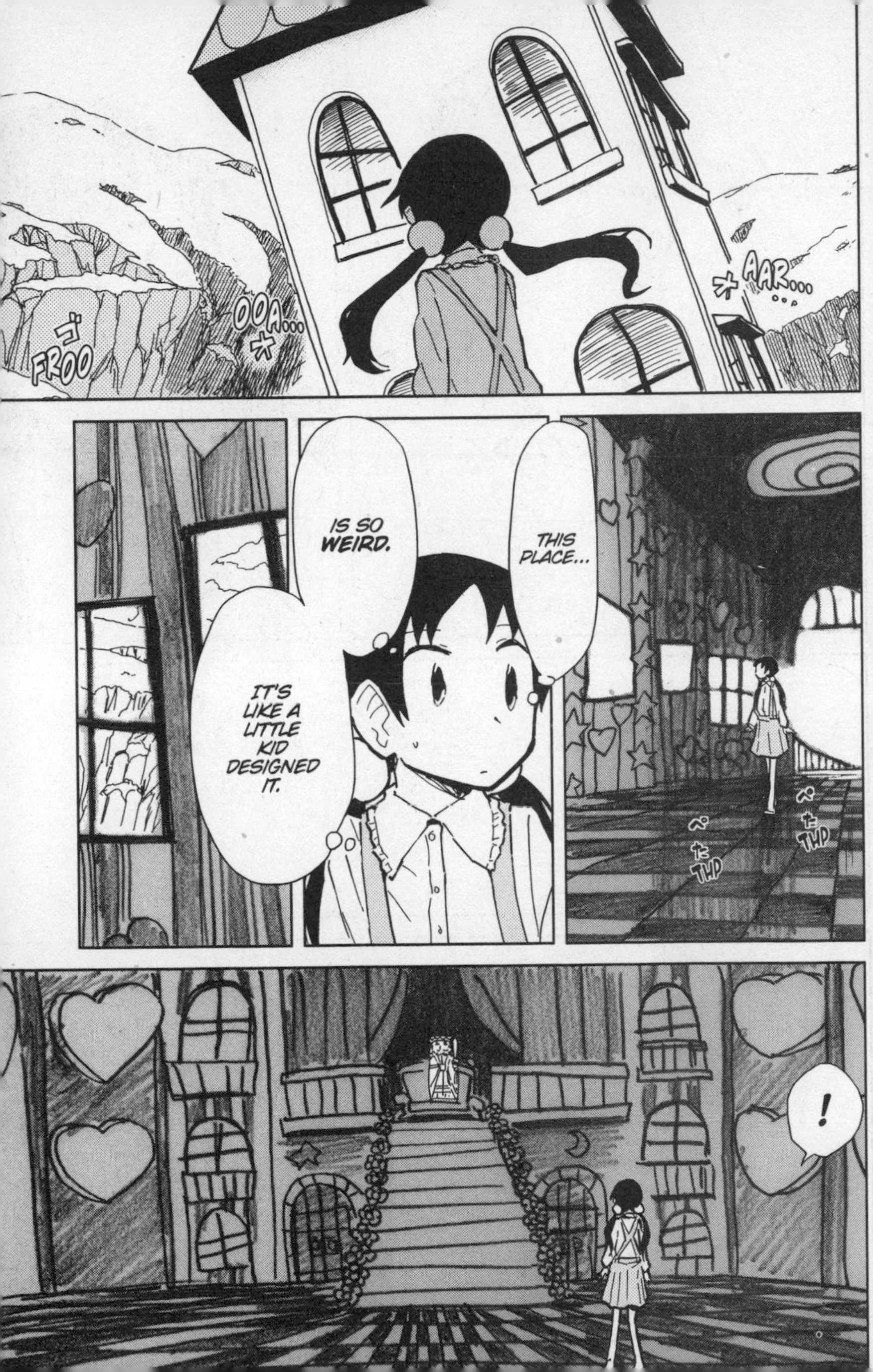

オ AAR...
オ OOA...
ゴ FROO
ぺた THP
ぺた THP
THIS PLACE...
IS SO WEIRD.
IT'S LIKE A LITTLE KID DESIGNED IT.
!

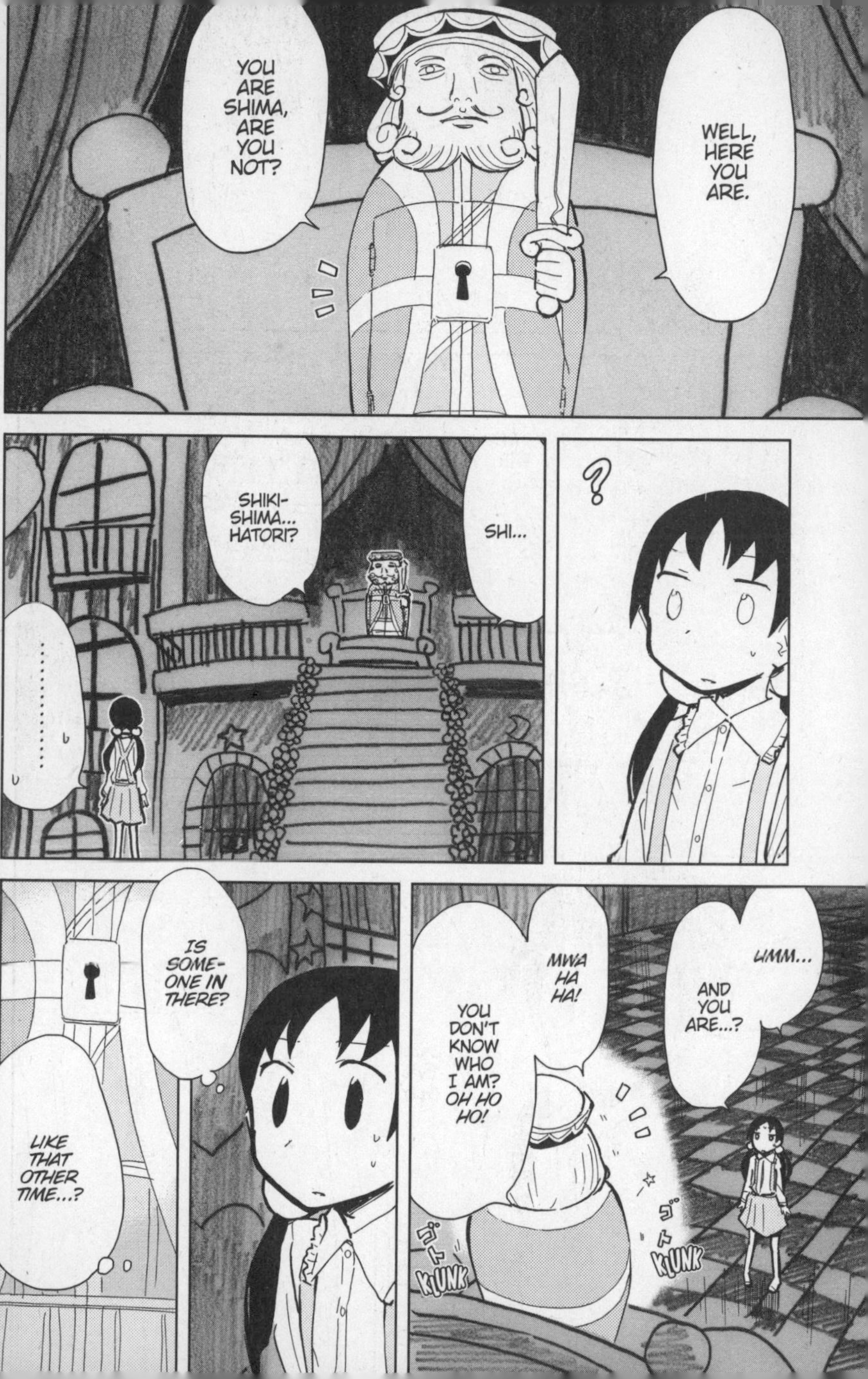
WELL, HERE YOU ARE.
YOU ARE SHIMA, ARE YOU NOT?
?
SHI...
SHIKI-SHIMA... HATORI?
......
UMM... AND YOU ARE...?
MWA HA HA!
YOU DON'T KNOW WHO I AM? OH HO HO!
ゴト KLUNK
ゴト KLUNK
IS SOME-ONE IN THERE?
LIKE THAT OTHER TIME...?

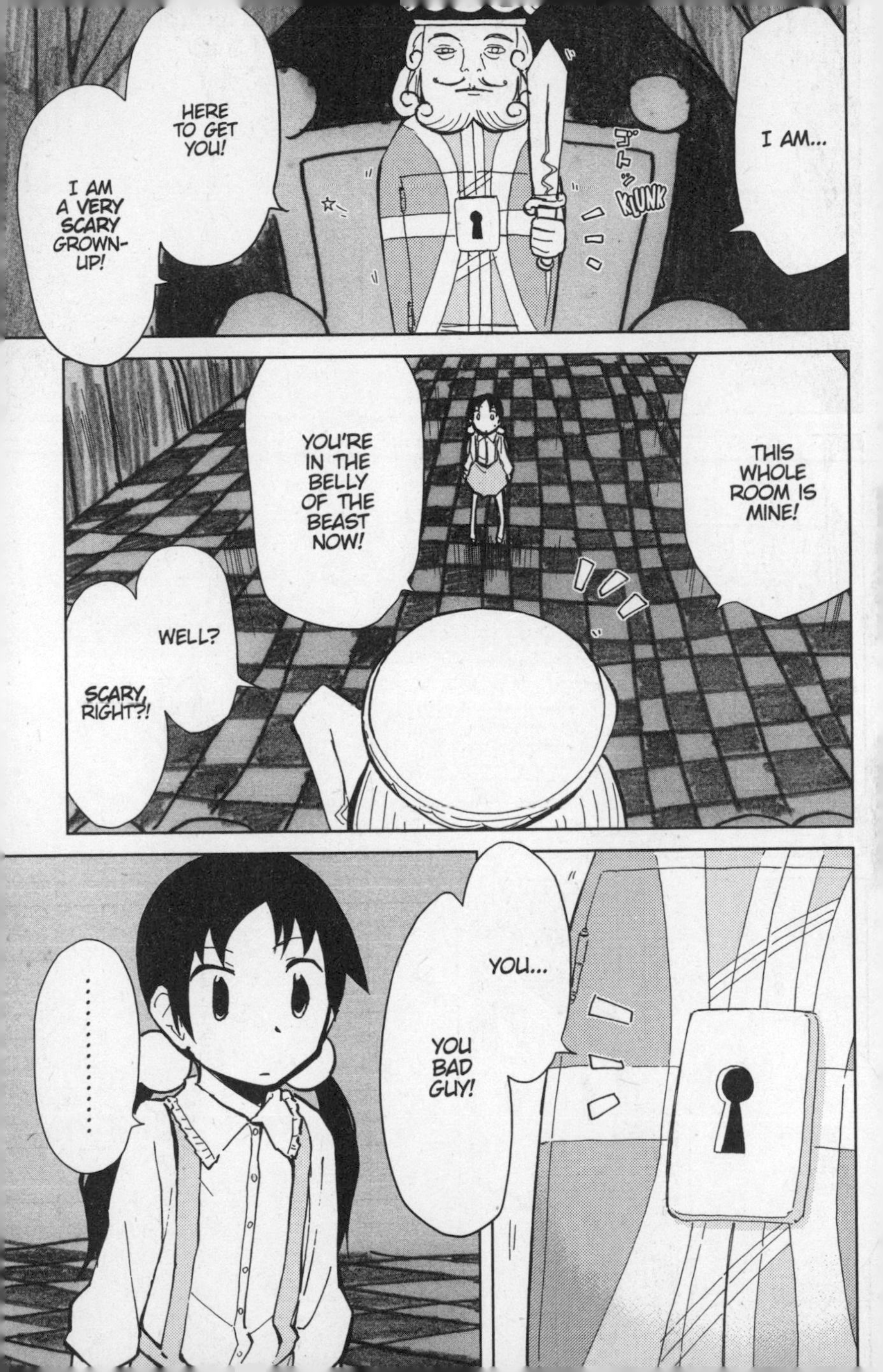
I AM...
ゴトッ
KLUNK
HERE TO GET YOU!
I AM A VERY SCARY GROWN-UP!
THIS WHOLE ROOM IS MINE!
YOU'RE IN THE BELLY OF THE BEAST NOW!
WELL?
SCARY, RIGHT?!
YOU...
YOU BAD GUY!
....

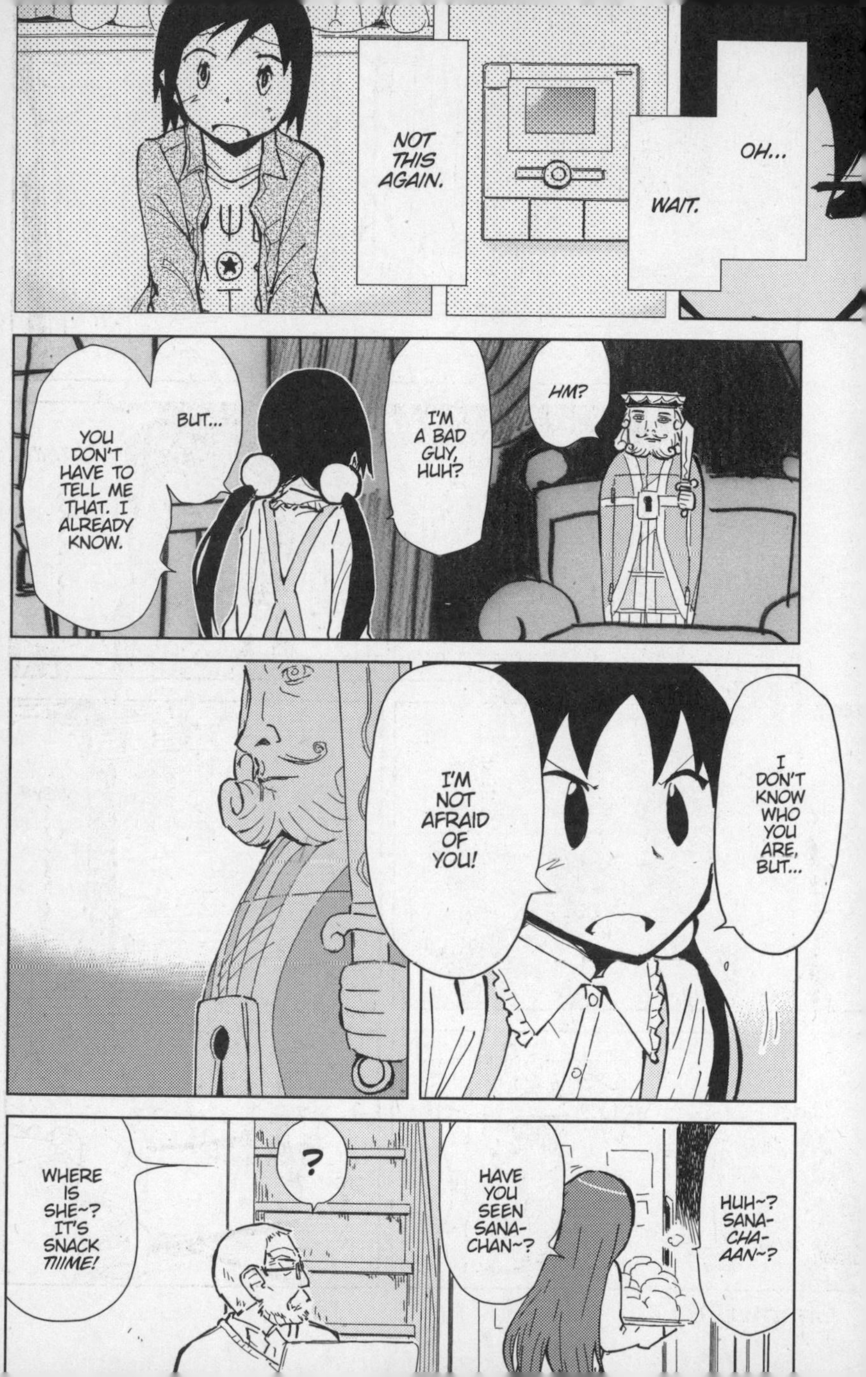
OH...
WAIT.
NOT THIS AGAIN.
HM?
I'M A BAD GUY, HUH?
BUT...
YOU DON'T HAVE TO TELL ME THAT. I ALREADY KNOW.
I DON'T KNOW WHO YOU ARE, BUT...
I'M NOT AFRAID OF YOU!
HUH~? SANA-CHA-AAN~?
HAVE YOU SEEN SANA-CHAN~?
?
WHERE IS SHE~? IT'S SNACK TIIIME!

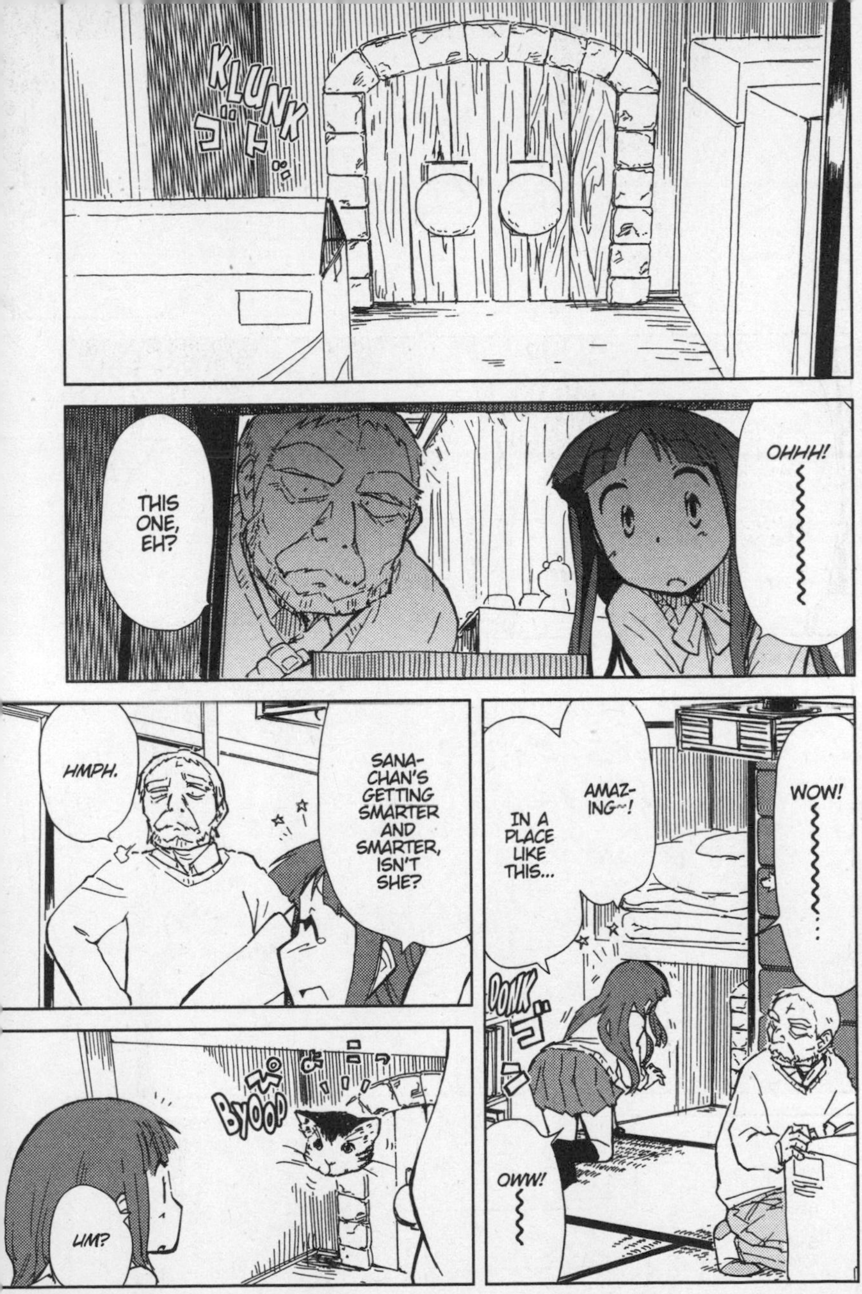
KLUNK
ゴトッ
OHHH!
THIS ONE, EH?
WOW!
AMAZ-ING~!
IN A PLACE LIKE THIS...
SANA-CHAN'S GETTING SMARTER AND SMARTER, ISN'T SHE?
HMPH.
OWW!
BYOOP
UM?

Chapter.18

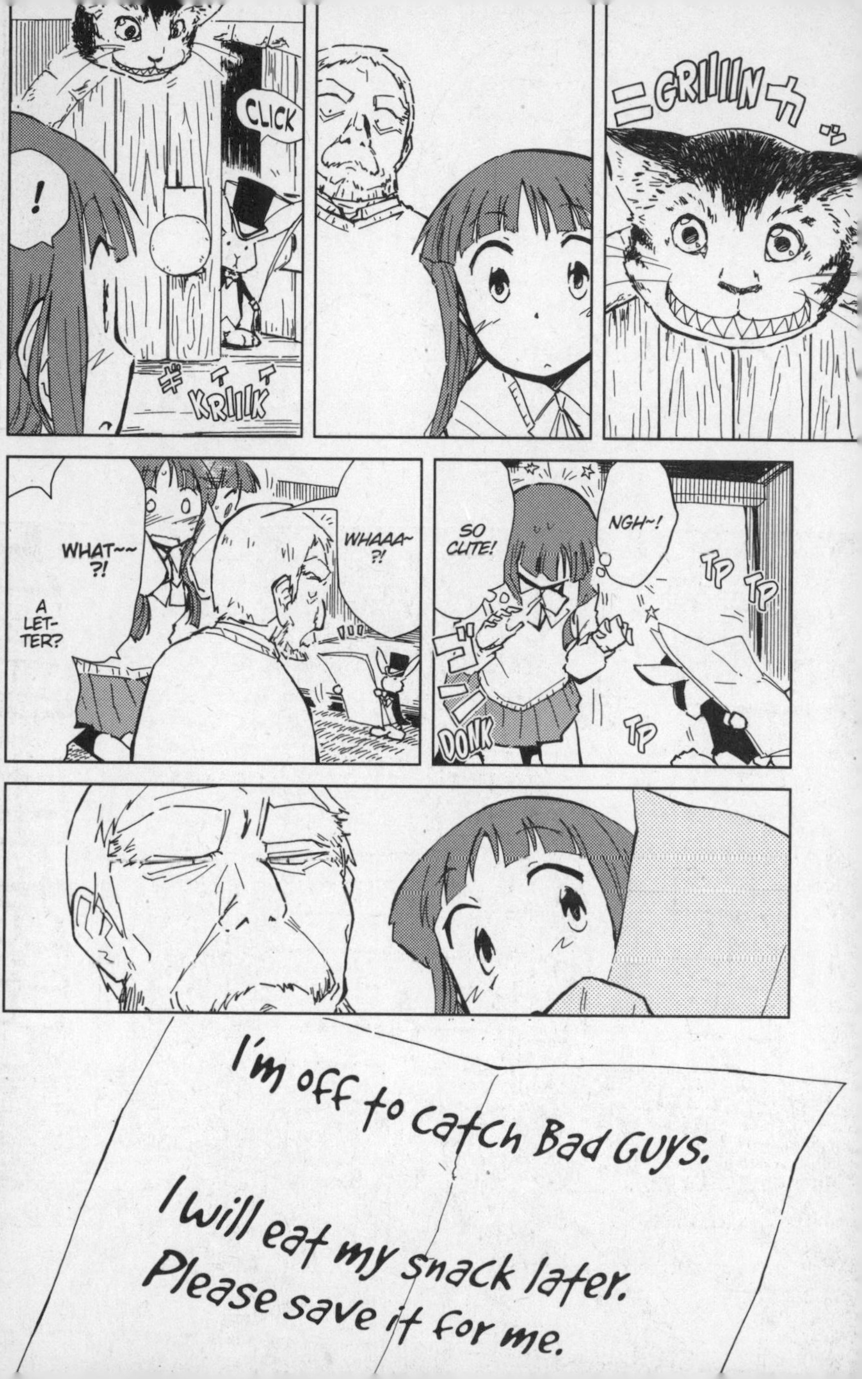
GRIIIIN
CLICK
!
KRIIIK
NGH~!
SO CUTE!
TP TP
DONK
TP
WHAAA~?!
WHAT~~?!
A LETTER?
I'm off to catch Bad Guys.
I will eat my snack later.
Please save it for me.

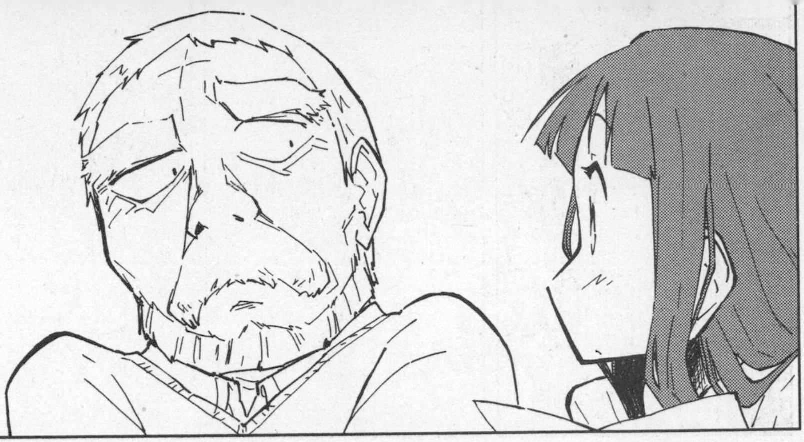

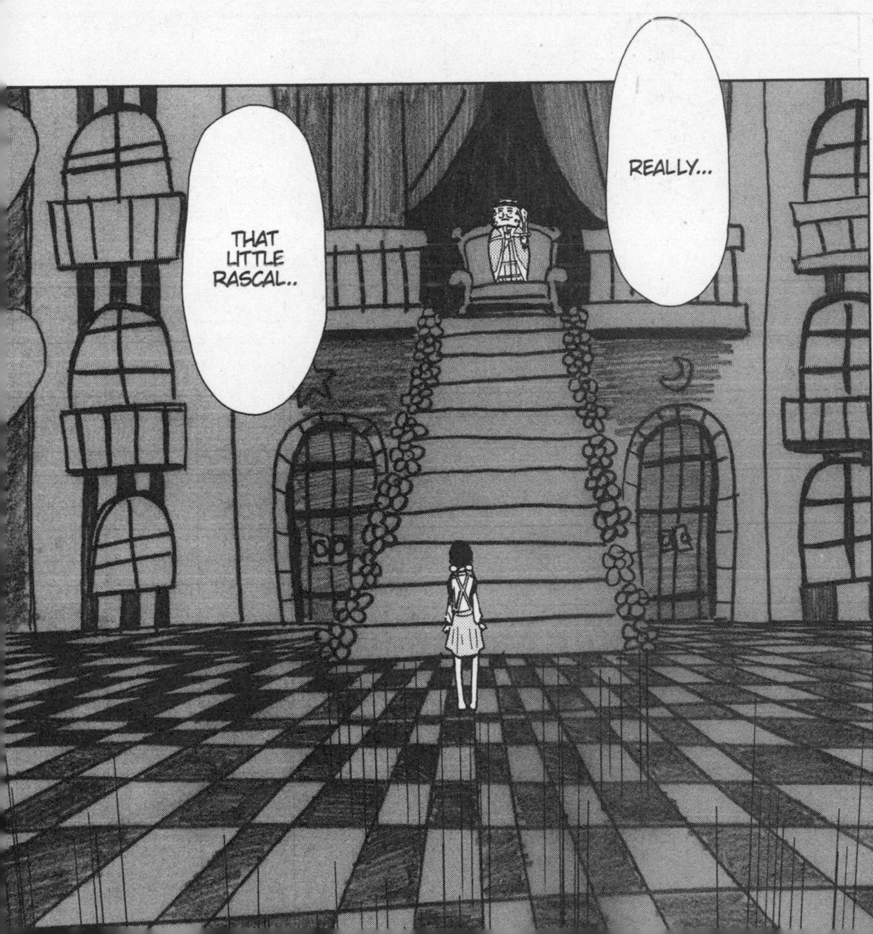
REALLY...
THAT LITTLE RASCAL..

Chapter.18
Two Queens and the Wardrobe

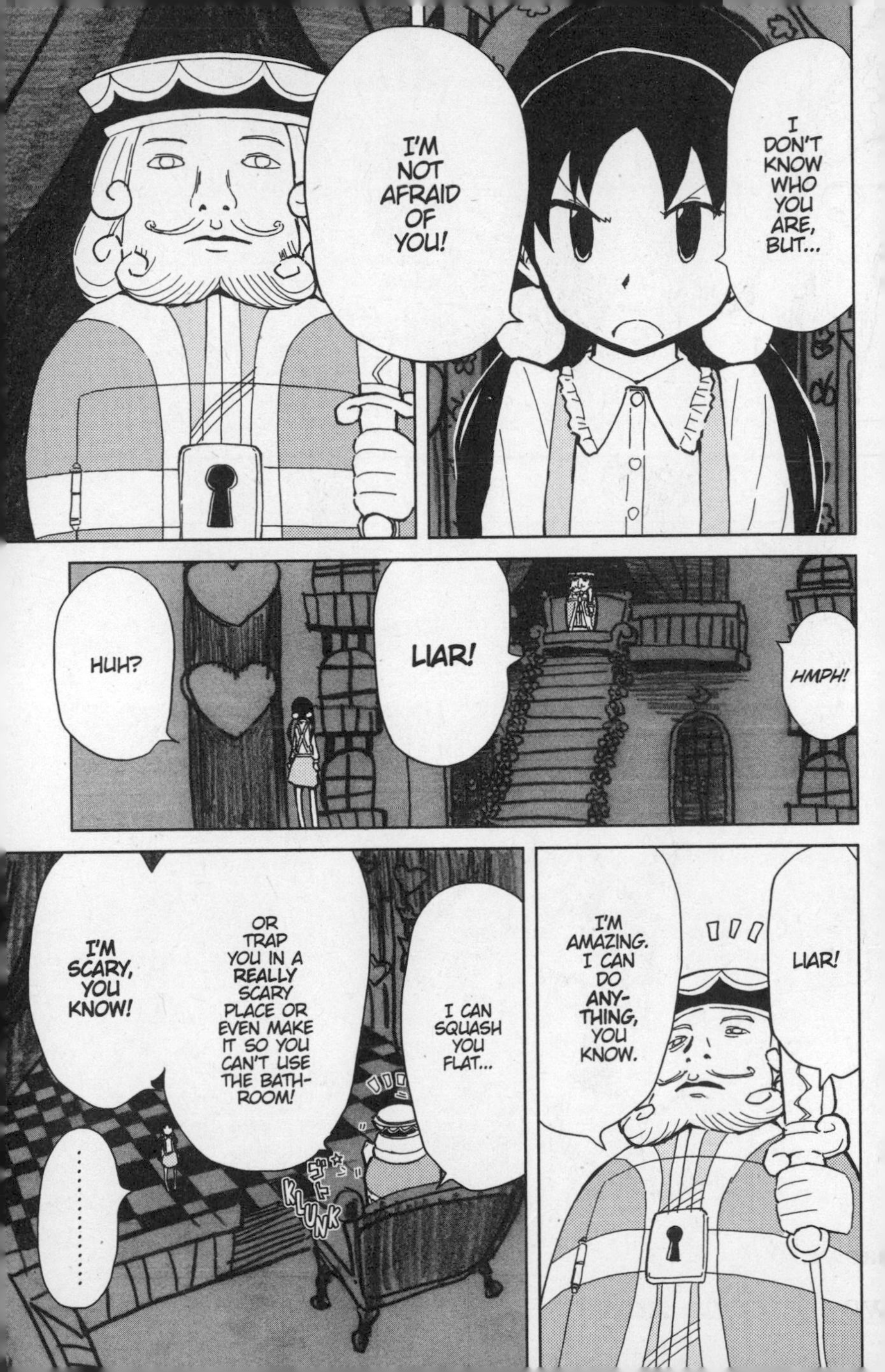
I DON'T KNOW WHO YOU ARE, BUT...
I'M NOT AFRAID OF YOU!
HMPH!
LIAR!
HUH?
LIAR!
I'M AMAZING. I CAN DO ANY-THING, YOU KNOW.
I CAN SQUASH YOU FLAT...
OR TRAP YOU IN A REALLY SCARY PLACE OR EVEN MAKE IT SO YOU CAN'T USE THE BATH-ROOM!
I'M SCARY, YOU KNOW!
......
KLUNK

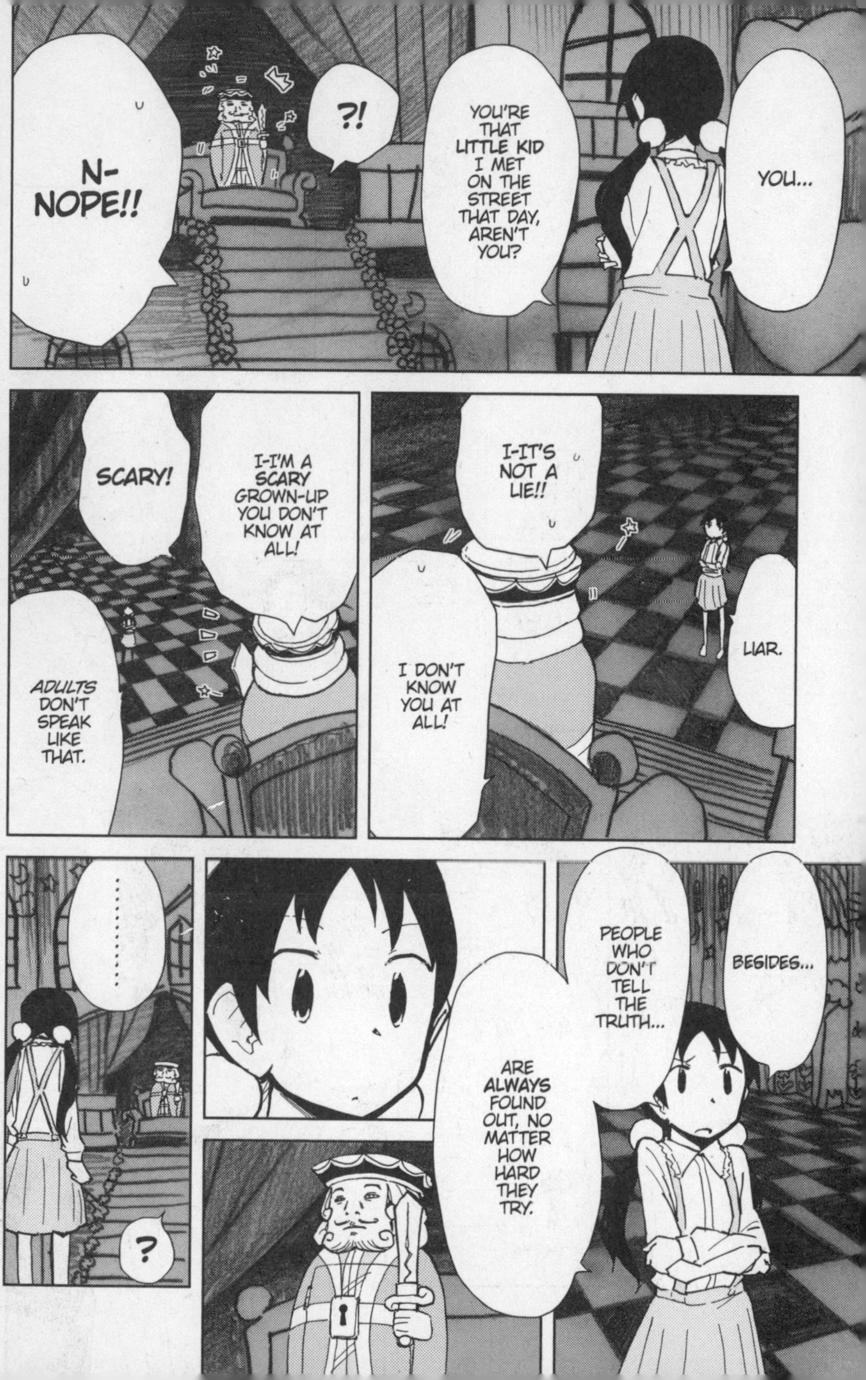
YOU...
YOU'RE THAT LITTLE KID I MET ON THE STREET THAT DAY, AREN'T YOU?
?!
N-NOPE!!
LIAR.
I-IT'S NOT A LIE!!
I DON'T KNOW YOU AT ALL!
I-I'M A SCARY GROWN-UP YOU DON'T KNOW AT ALL!
SCARY!
ADULTS DON'T SPEAK LIKE THAT.
BESIDES...
PEOPLE WHO DON'T TELL THE TRUTH...
ARE ALWAYS FOUND OUT, NO MATTER HOW HARD THEY TRY.
......
?

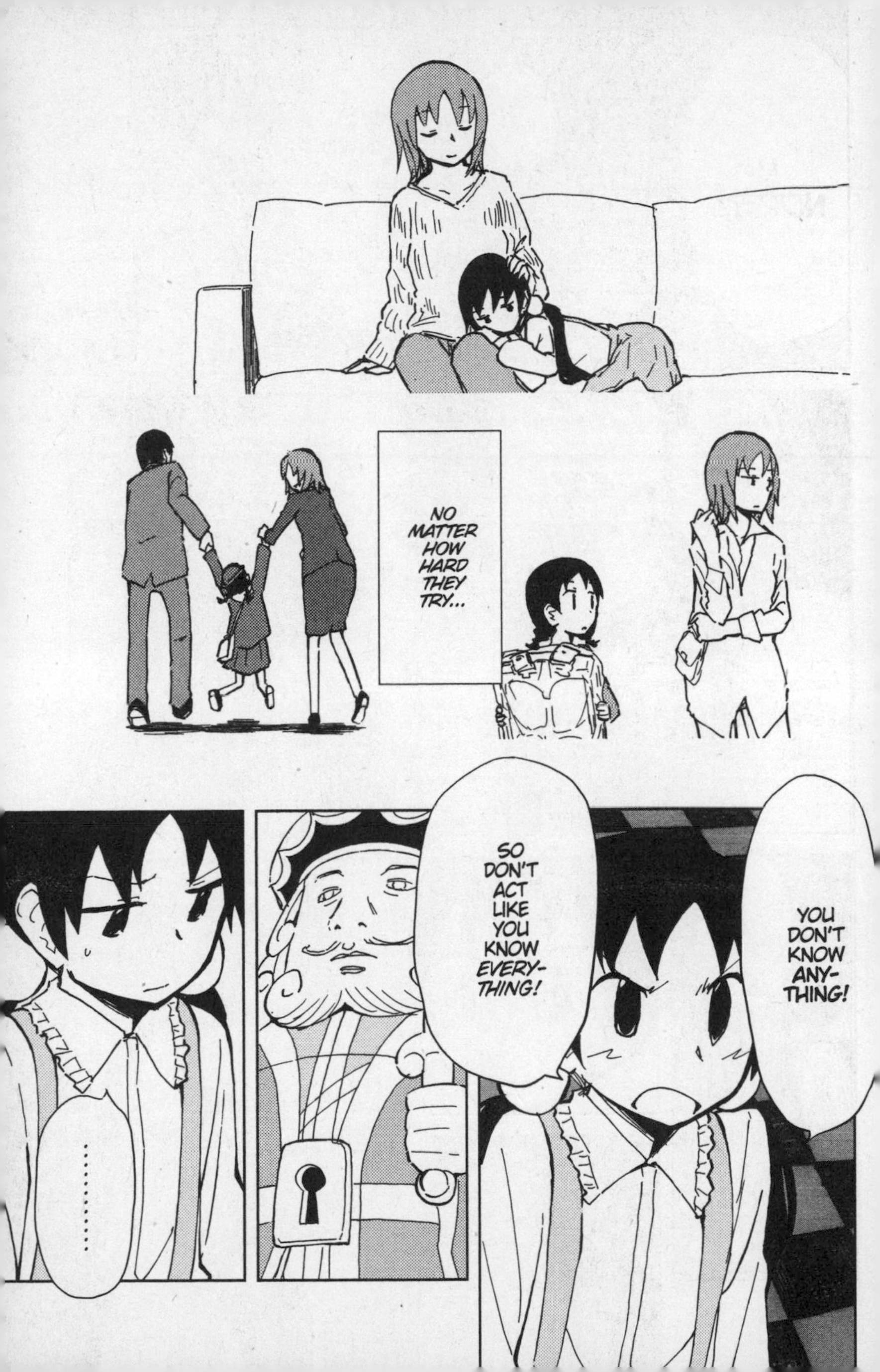
NO MATTER HOW HARD THEY TRY...
YOU DON'T KNOW ANYTHING!
SO DON'T ACT LIKE YOU KNOW EVERYTHING!
……

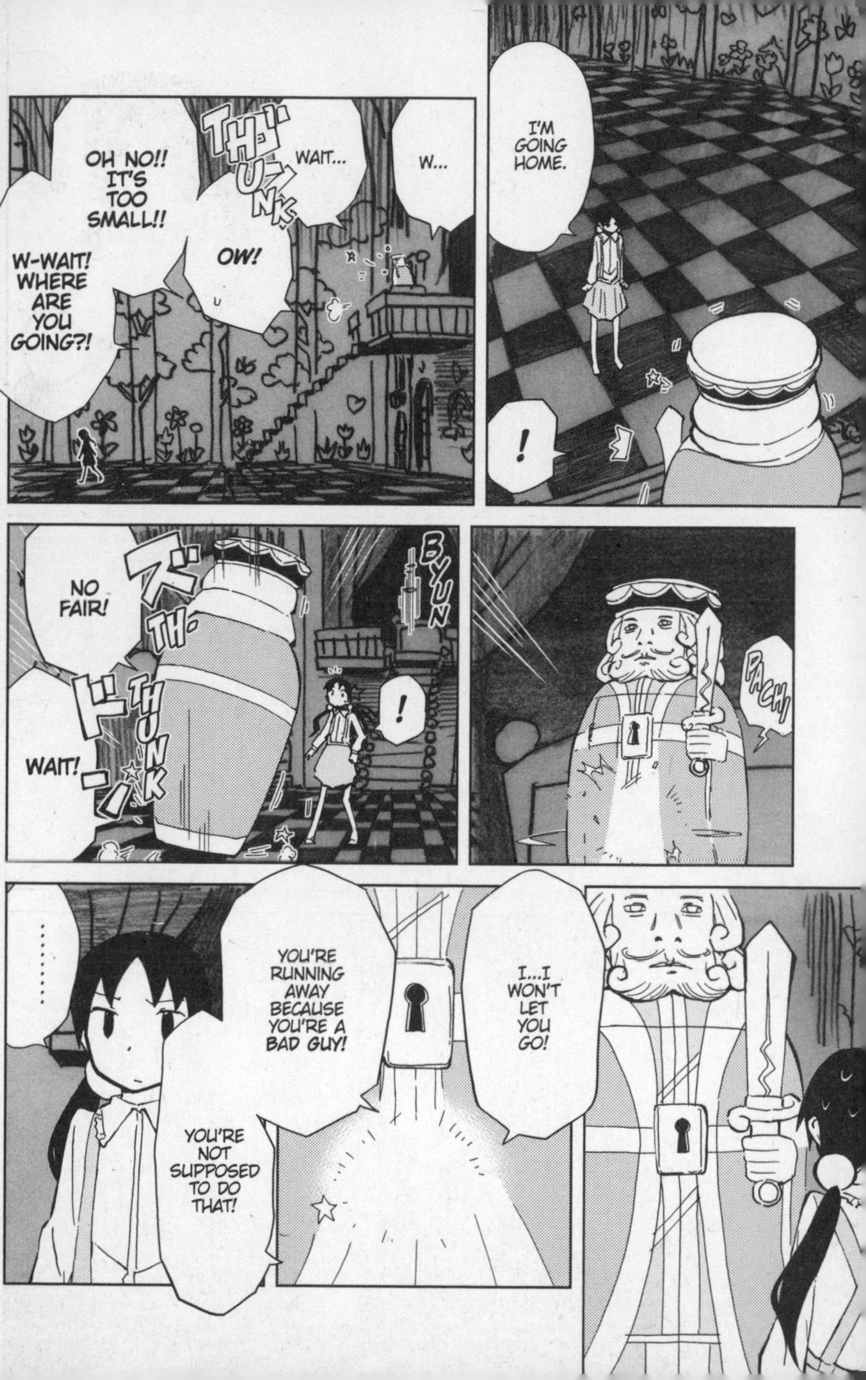

I'M GOING HOME.
!
W...
WAIT...
THUNK
OW!
OH NO!! IT'S TOO SMALL!!
W-WAIT! WHERE ARE YOU GOING?!
PACHI
BYUN
!
NO FAIR!
TH-
THUNK
WAIT!
I...I WON'T LET YOU GO!
YOU'RE RUNNING AWAY BECAUSE YOU'RE A BAD GUY!
YOU'RE NOT SUPPOSED TO DO THAT!
......

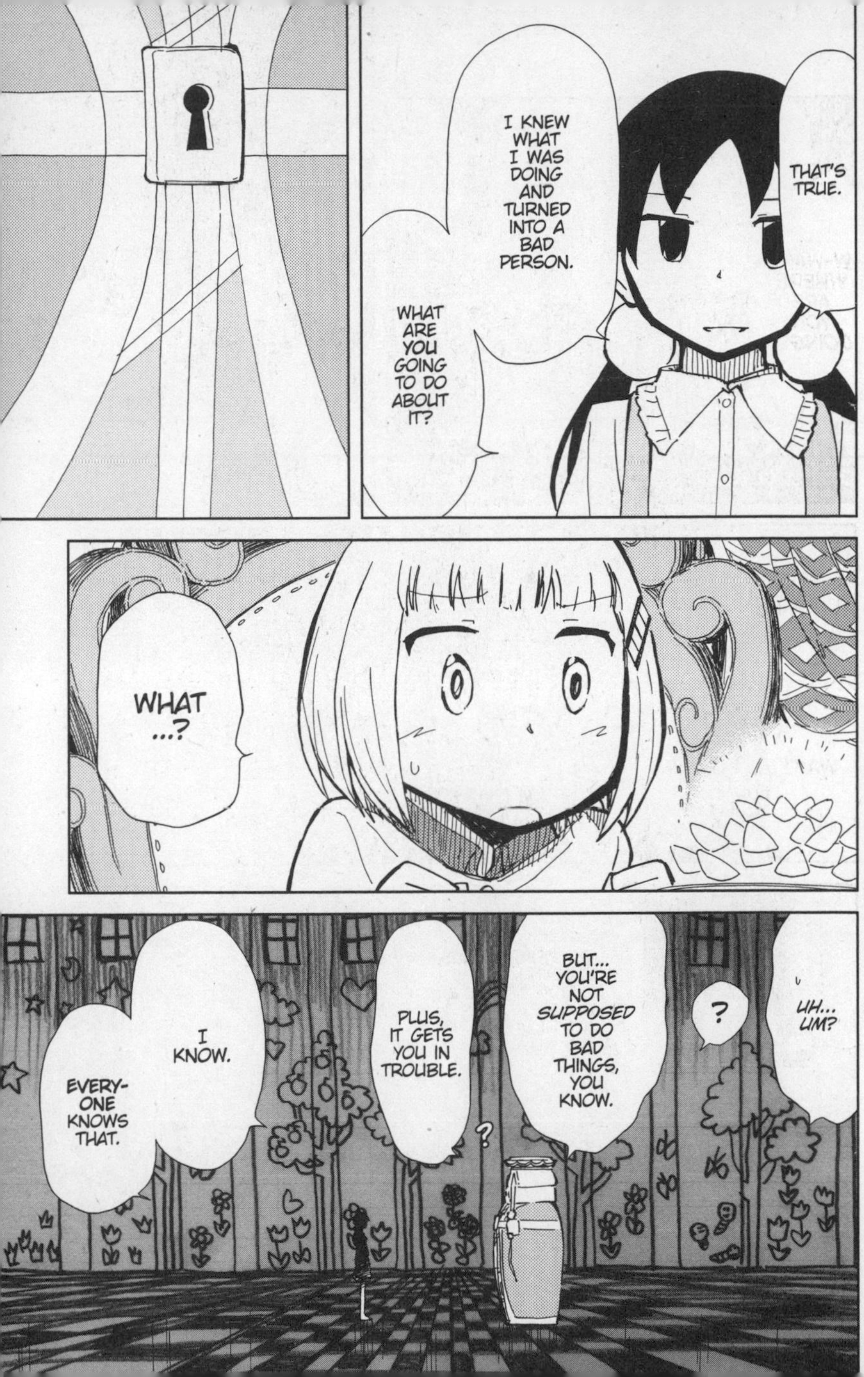
THAT'S TRUE.
I KNEW WHAT I WAS DOING AND TURNED INTO A BAD PERSON.
WHAT ARE YOU GOING TO DO ABOUT IT?
WHAT ...?
UH... UM?
?
BUT... YOU'RE NOT SUPPOSED TO DO BAD THINGS, YOU KNOW.
?
PLUS, IT GETS YOU IN TROUBLE.
I KNOW.
EVERY-ONE KNOWS THAT.

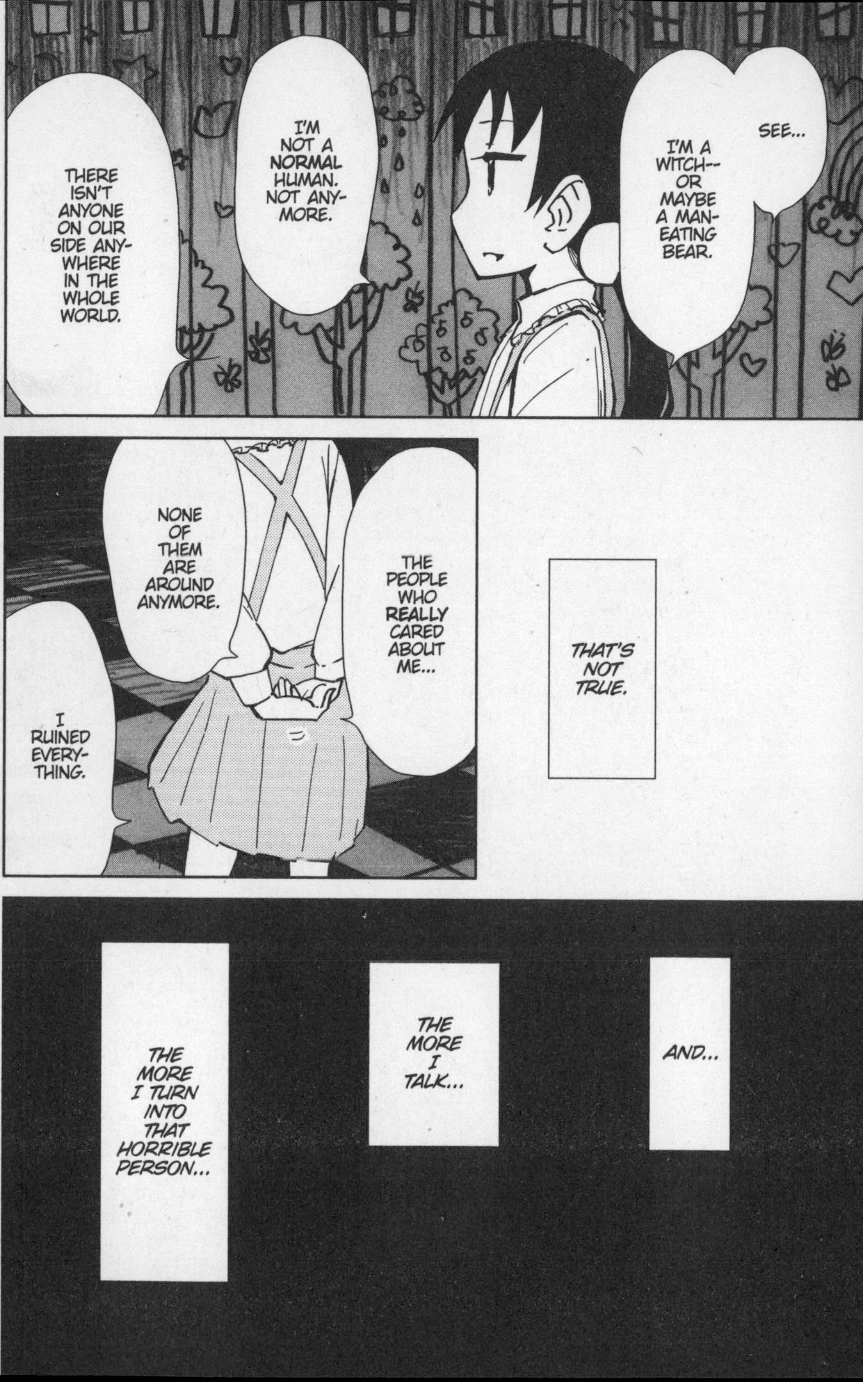
SEE...
I'M A WITCH--OR MAYBE A MAN-EATING BEAR.
I'M NOT A NORMAL HUMAN. NOT ANYMORE.
THERE ISN'T ANYONE ON OUR SIDE ANYWHERE IN THE WHOLE WORLD.
THAT'S NOT TRUE.
THE PEOPLE WHO REALLY CARED ABOUT ME...
NONE OF THEM ARE AROUND ANYMORE.
I RUINED EVERYTHING.
AND...
THE MORE I TALK...
THE MORE I TURN INTO THAT HORRIBLE PERSON...

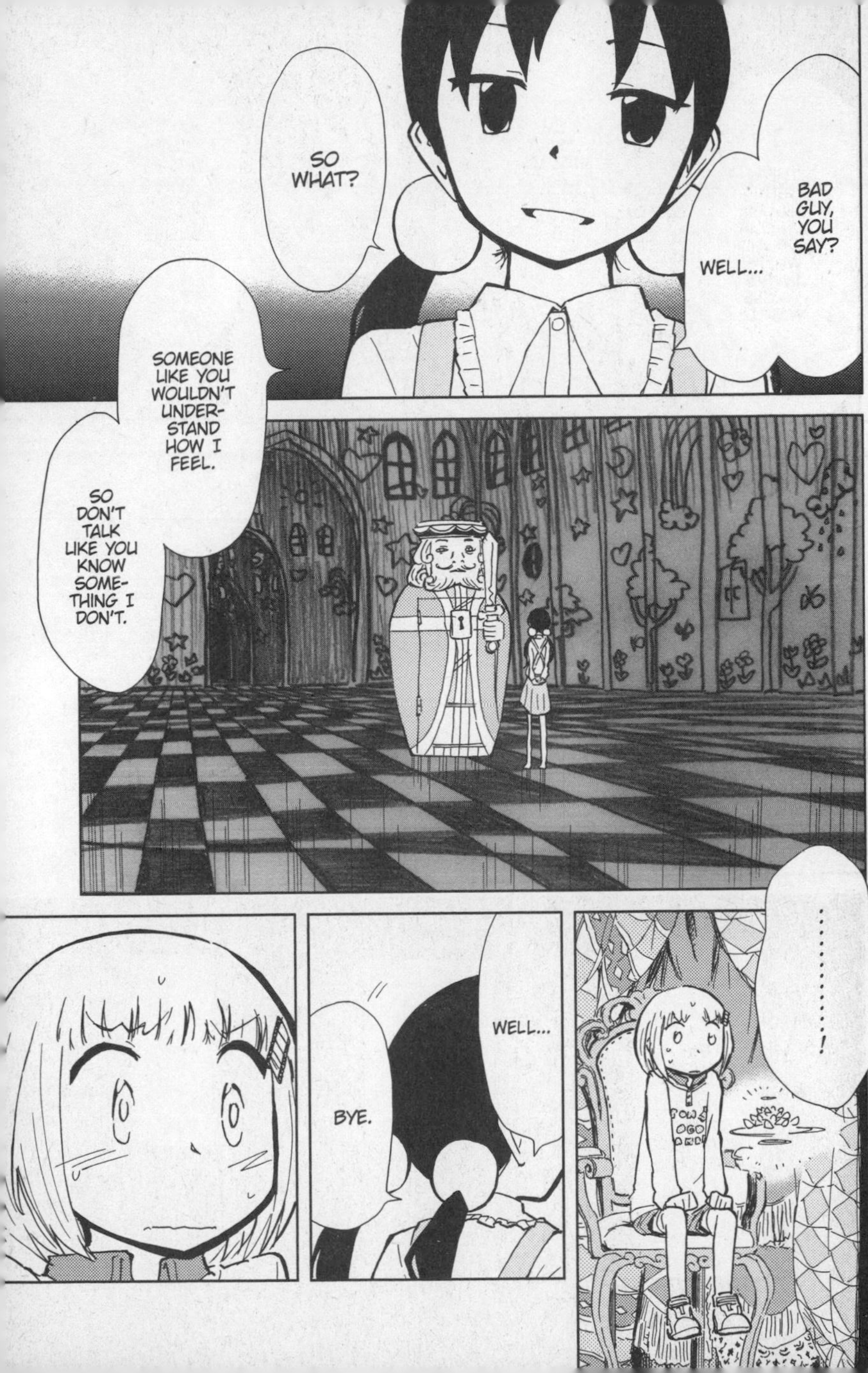
BAD GUY, YOU SAY? WELL...
SO WHAT?
SOMEONE LIKE YOU WOULDN'T UNDER-STAND HOW I FEEL.
SO DON'T TALK LIKE YOU KNOW SOME-THING I DON'T.
......!
WELL...
BYE.

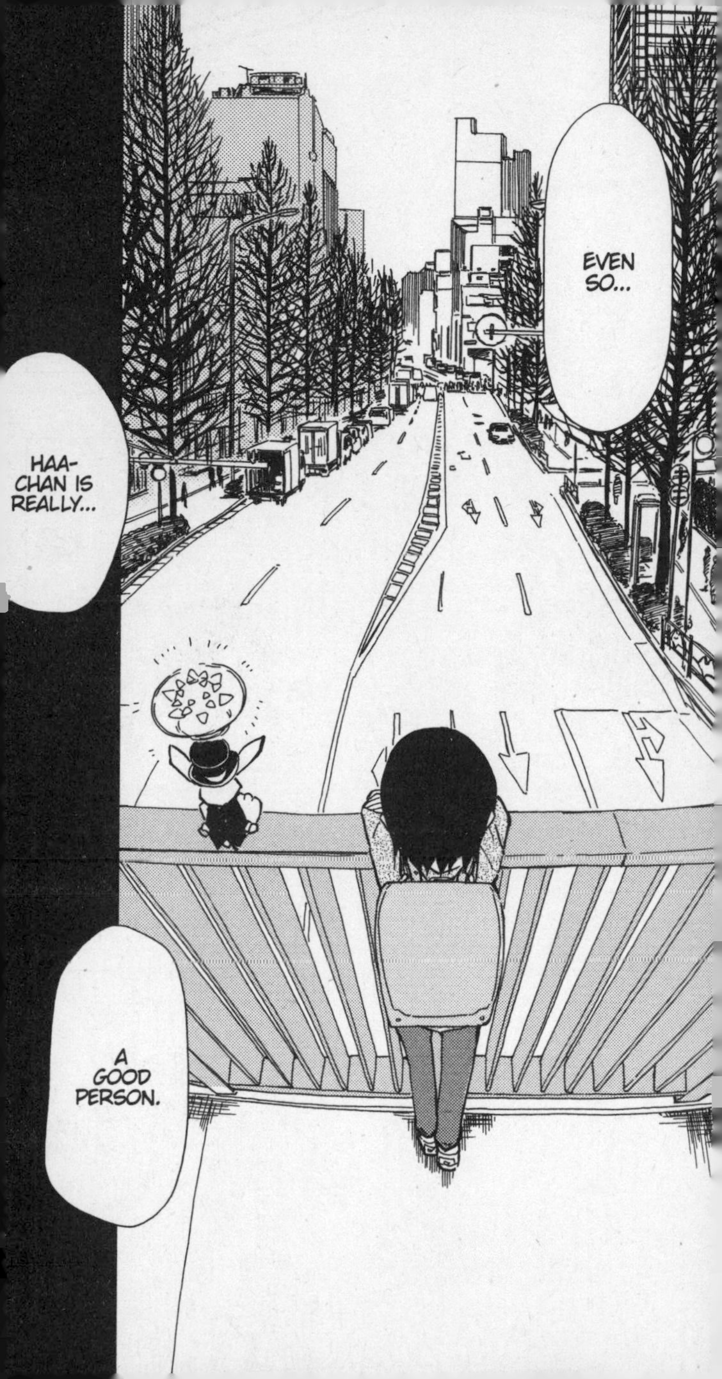
EVEN SO...
HAA-CHAN IS REALLY...
A GOOD PERSON.

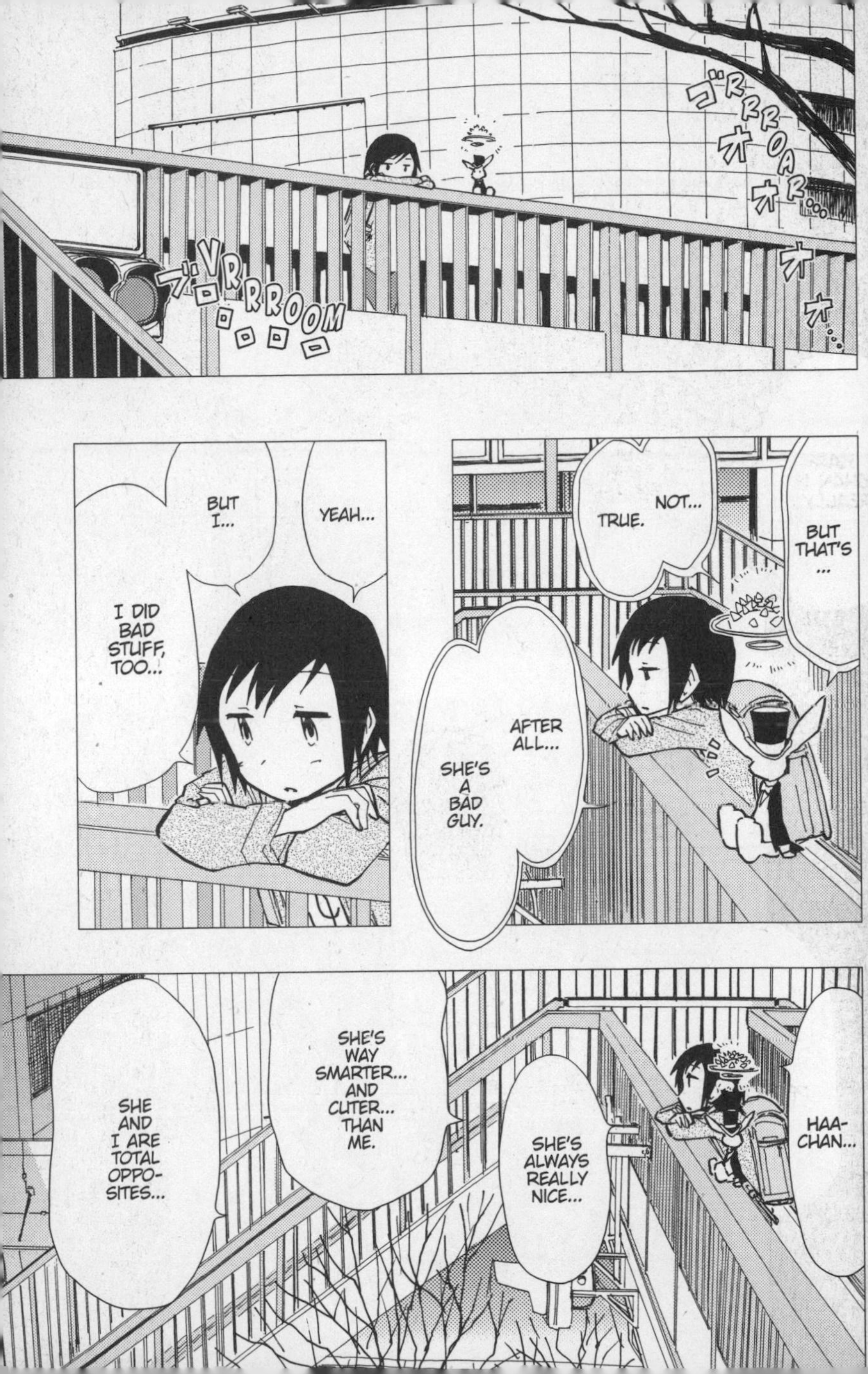
RRROAR...
VRRROOM
BUT THAT'S...
NOT... TRUE.
AFTER ALL... SHE'S A BAD GUY.
YEAH...
BUT I...
I DID BAD STUFF, TOO...
HAA-CHAN...
SHE'S ALWAYS REALLY NICE...
SHE'S WAY SMARTER... AND CUTER... THAN ME.
SHE AND I ARE TOTAL OPPO-SITES...

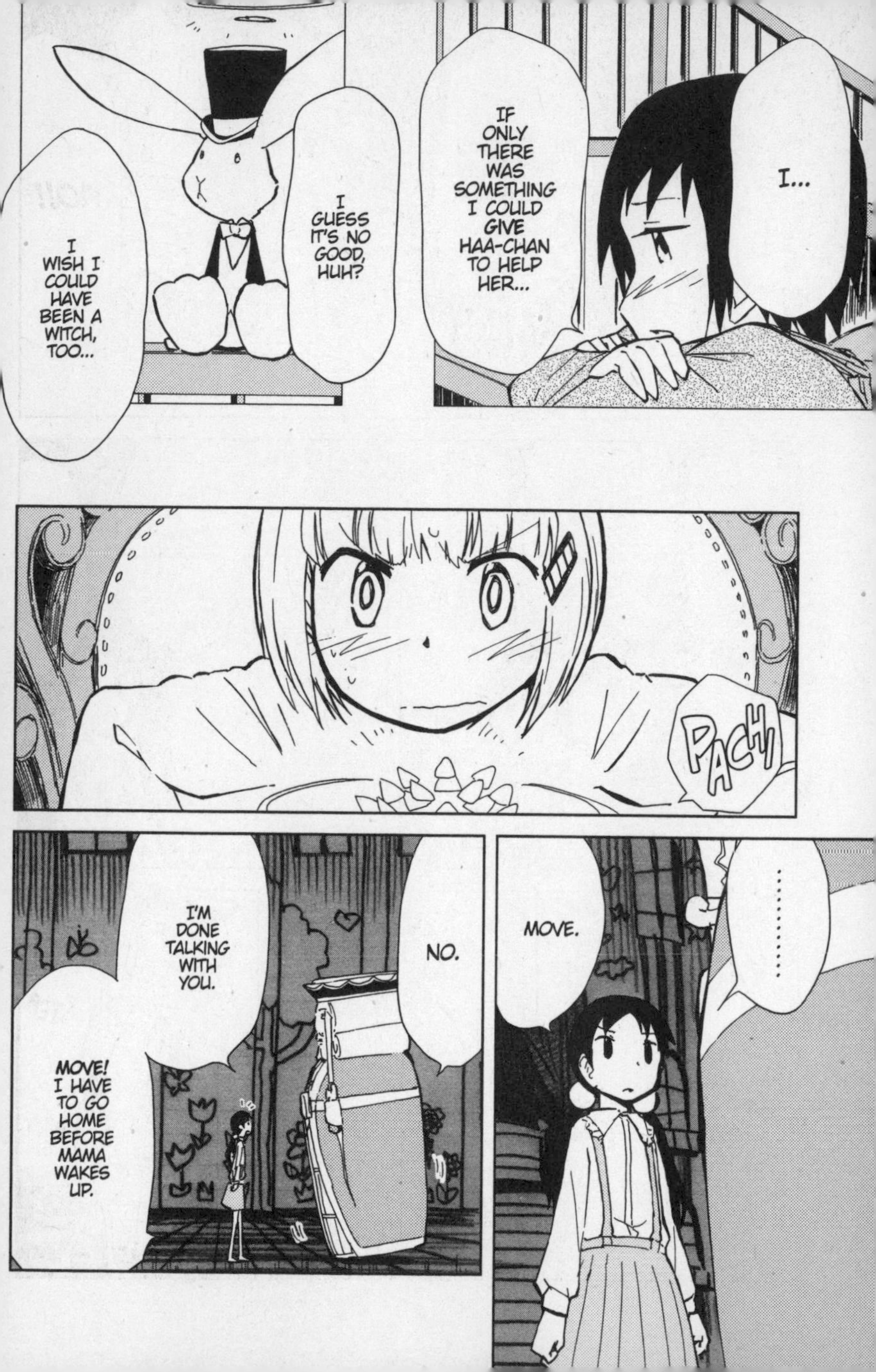
I...
IF ONLY THERE WAS SOMETHING I COULD GIVE HAA-CHAN TO HELP HER...
I GUESS IT'S NO GOOD, HUH?
I WISH I COULD HAVE BEEN A WITCH, TOO...
PACHI
......
MOVE.
NO.
I'M DONE TALKING WITH YOU.
MOVE! I HAVE TO GO HOME BEFORE MAMA WAKES UP.

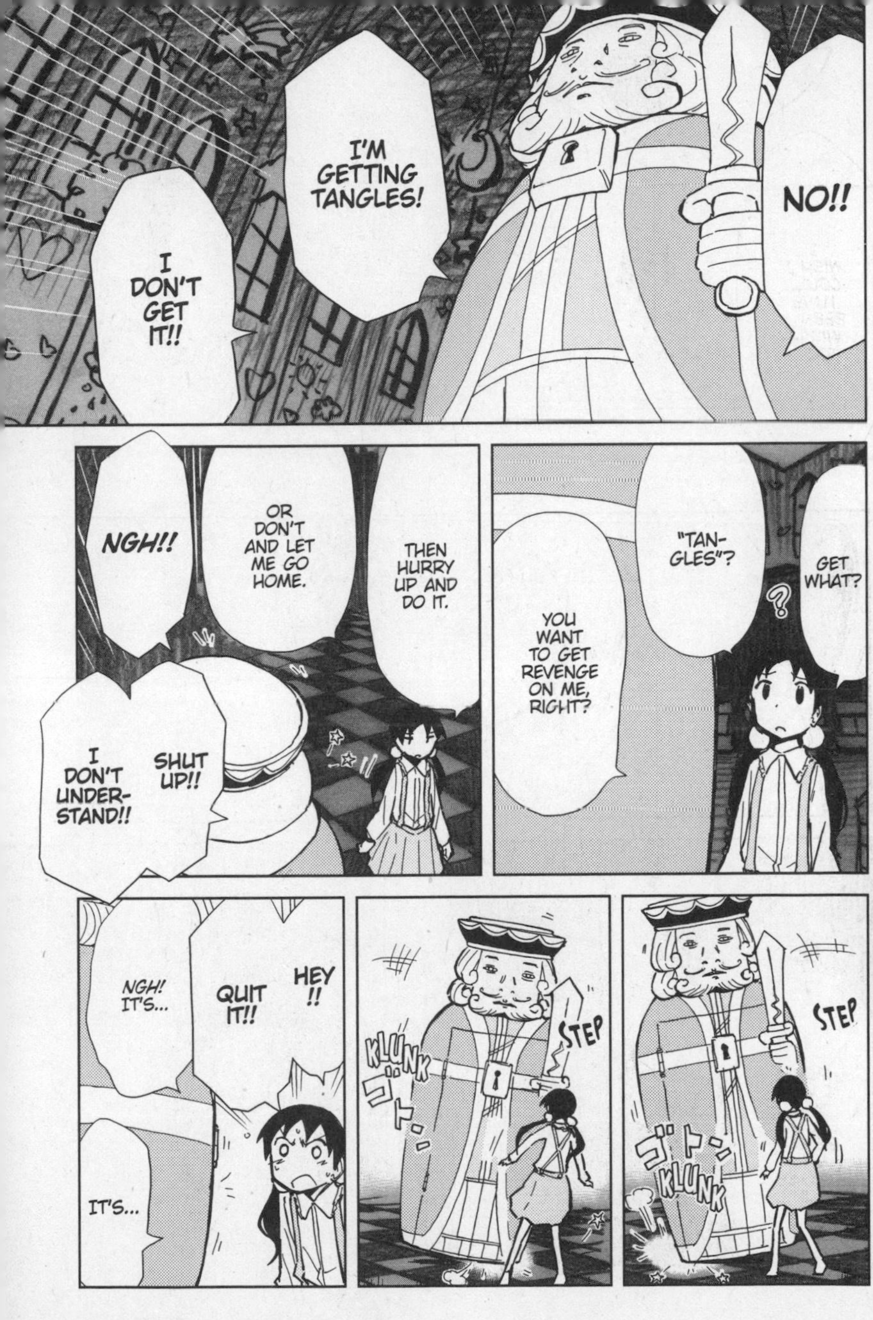
NO!!
I'M GETTING TANGLES!
I DON'T GET IT!!
GET WHAT?
"TAN-GLES"?
YOU WANT TO GET REVENGE ON ME, RIGHT?
THEN HURRY UP AND DO IT.
OR DON'T AND LET ME GO HOME.
NGH!!
SHUT UP!!
I DON'T UNDERSTAND!!
STEP
ゴトーン
KLUNK
STEP
KLUNK
ゴトーン
HEY!!
QUIT IT!!
NGH! IT'S...
IT'S...

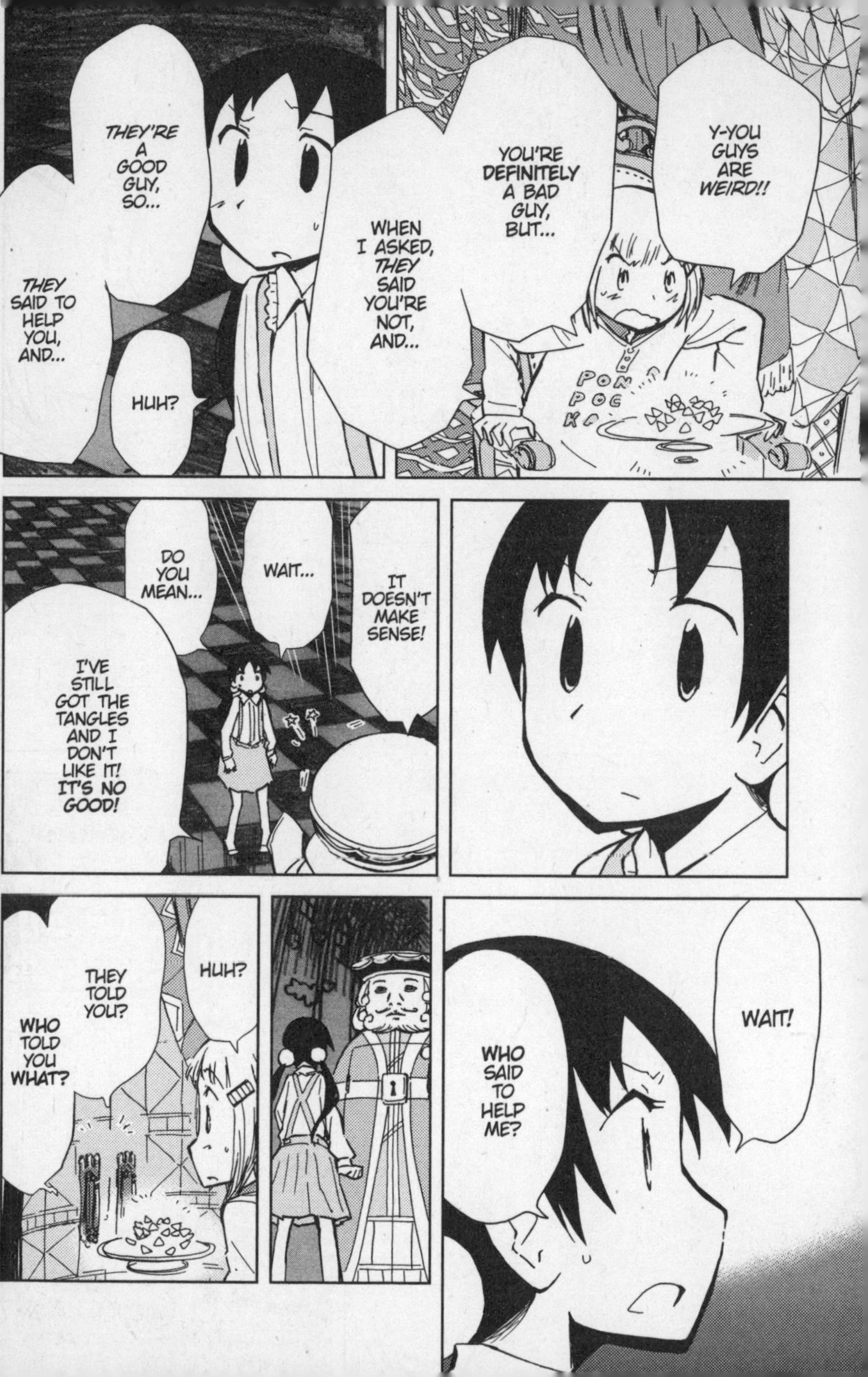
Y-YOU GUYS ARE WEIRD!!
YOU'RE DEFINITELY A BAD GUY, BUT...
WHEN I ASKED, THEY SAID YOU'RE NOT, AND...
THEY'RE A GOOD GUY, SO...
THEY SAID TO HELP YOU, AND...
HUH?
IT DOESN'T MAKE SENSE!
WAIT...
DO YOU MEAN...
I'VE STILL GOT THE TANGLES AND I DON'T LIKE IT! IT'S NO GOOD!
WAIT!
WHO SAID TO HELP ME?
HUH?
THEY TOLD YOU?
WHO TOLD YOU WHAT?

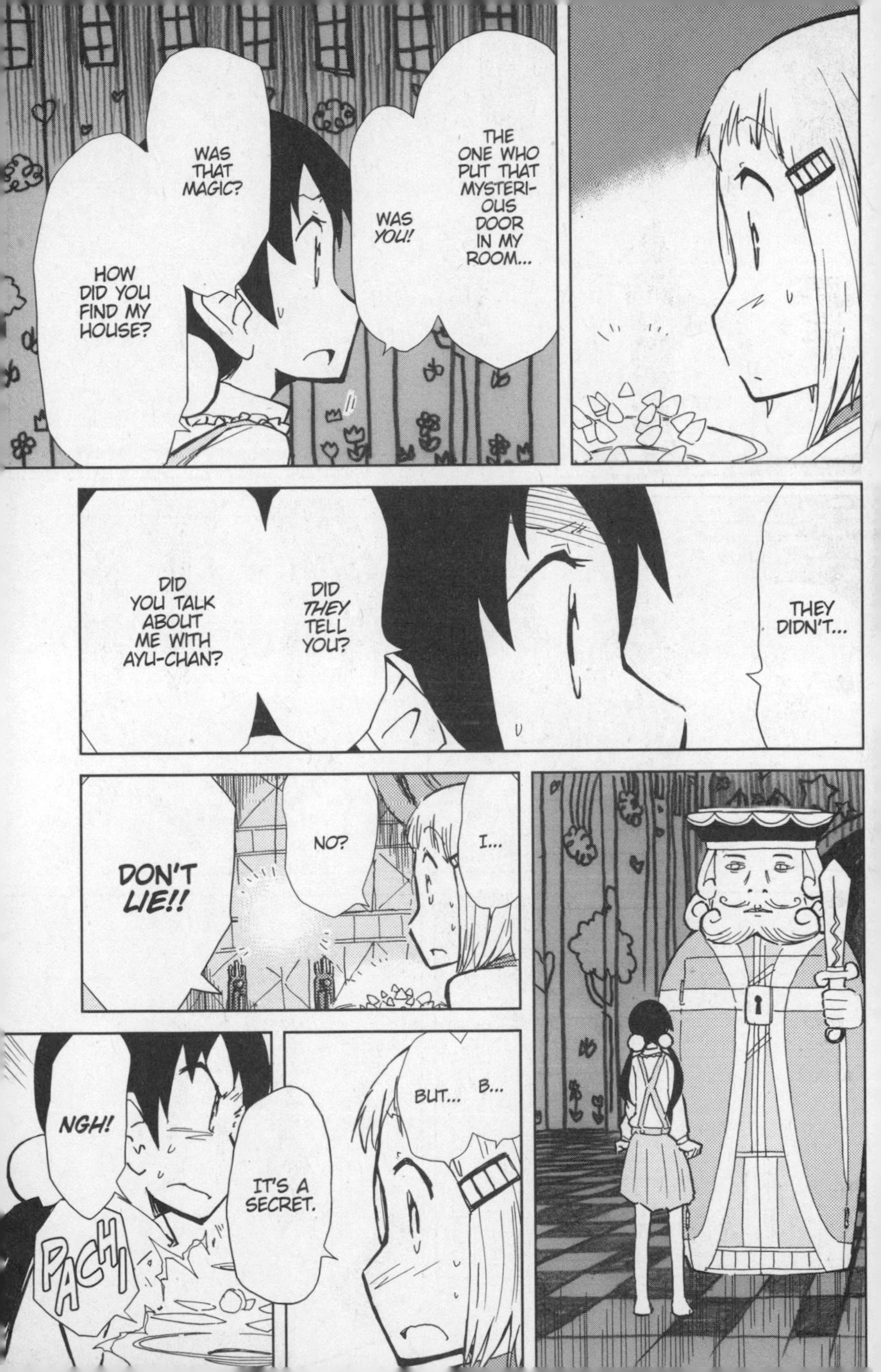
THE ONE WHO PUT THAT MYSTERIOUS DOOR IN MY ROOM...
WAS *YOU!*
WAS THAT MAGIC?
HOW DID YOU FIND MY HOUSE?
THEY DIDN'T...
DID *THEY* TELL YOU?
DID YOU TALK ABOUT ME WITH AYU-CHAN?
I...
NO?
DON'T LIE!!
BUT... B...
IT'S A SECRET.
NGH!
PACHI

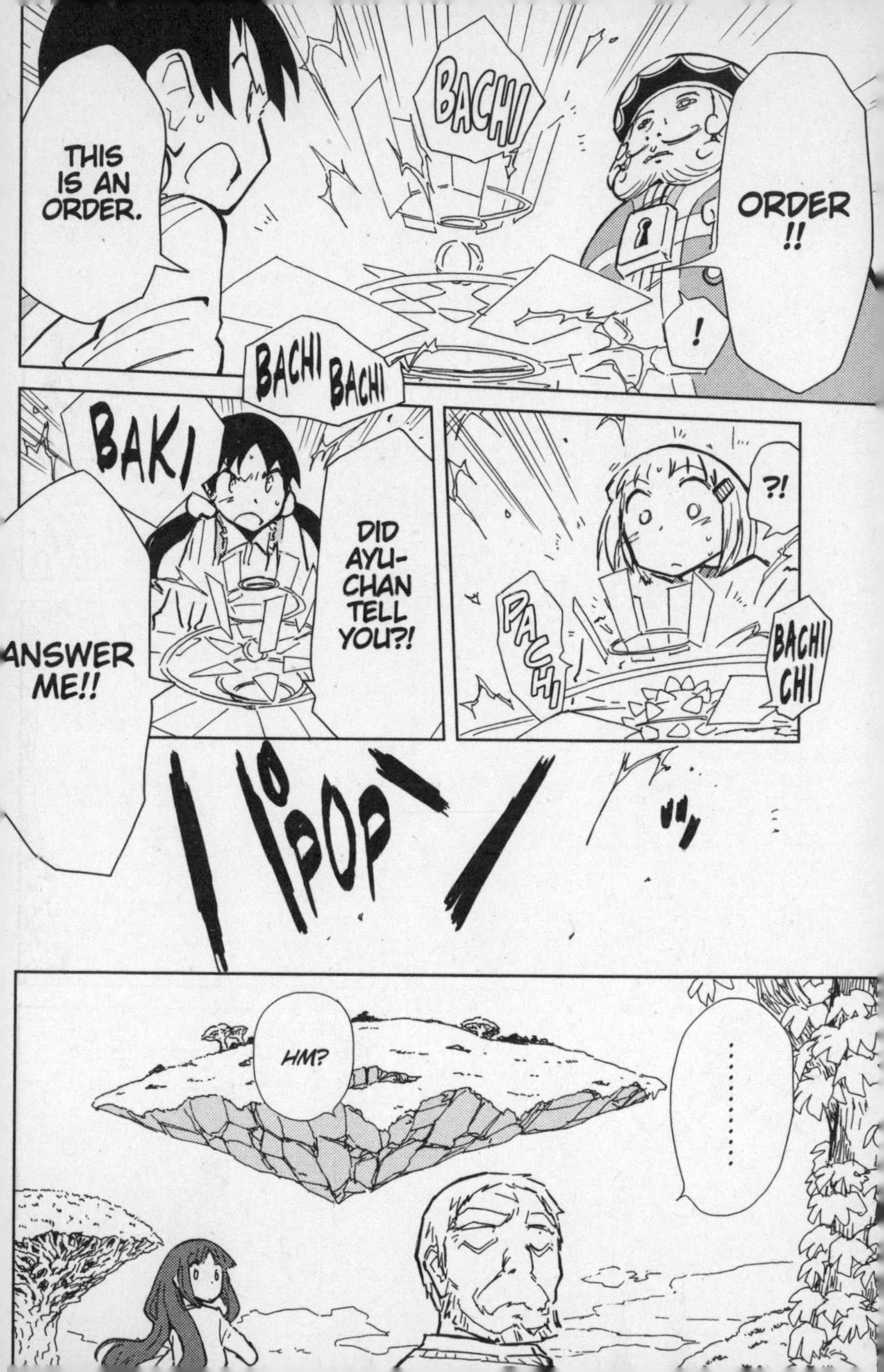
ORDER !!
BACHI
!
THIS IS AN ORDER.
BACHI BACHI
?!
PACHI
BACHI CHI
DID AYU-CHAN TELL YOU?!
BAKI
ANSWER ME!!
POP
......
HM?

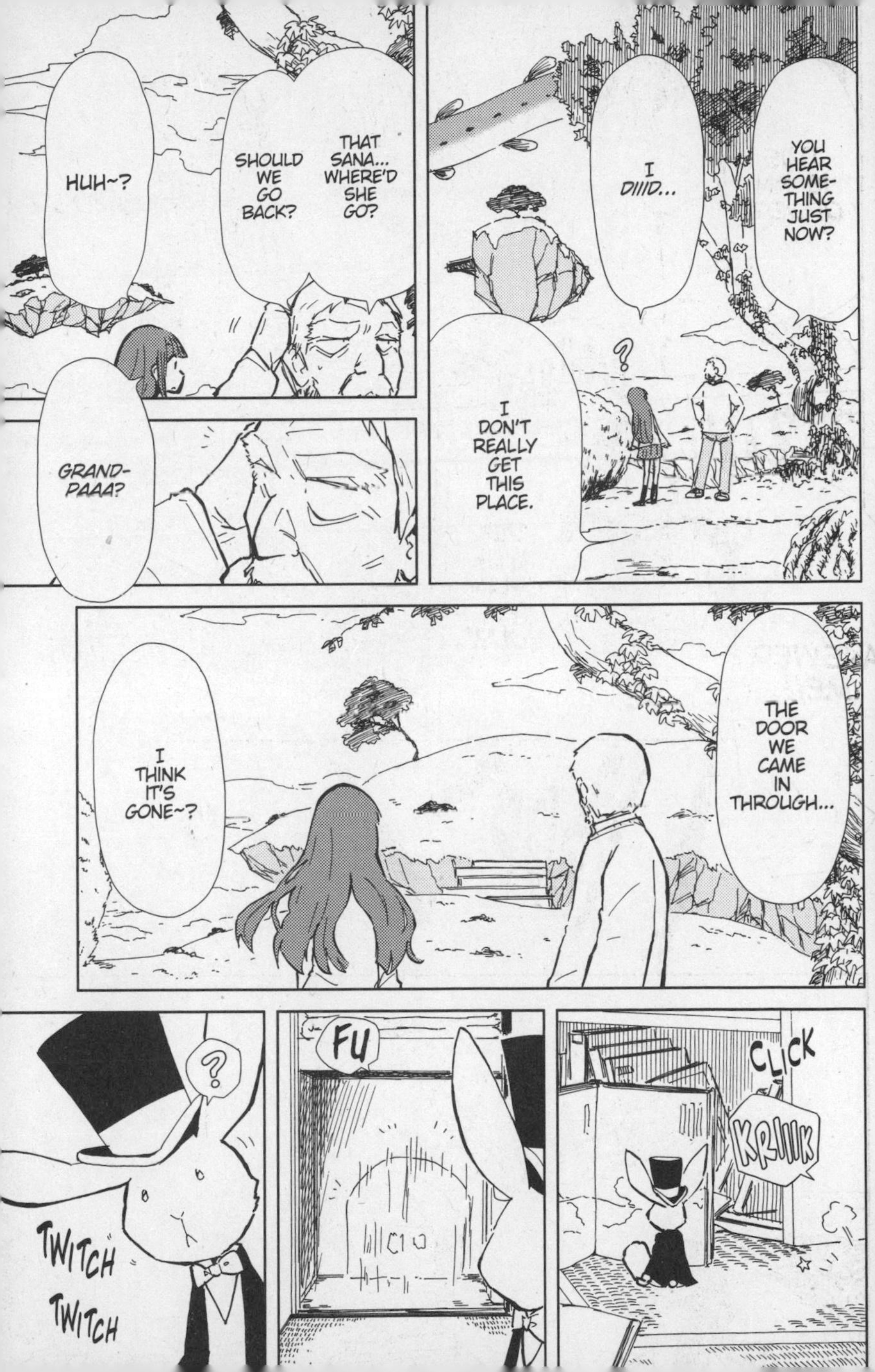
YOU HEAR SOMETHING JUST NOW?
I DIIID...
I DON'T REALLY GET THIS PLACE.
THAT SANA... WHERE'D SHE GO?
SHOULD WE GO BACK?
HUH~?
GRAND-PAAA?
THE DOOR WE CAME IN THROUGH...
I THINK IT'S GONE~?
CLICK
KRIIIK
FU
?
TWITCH
TWITCH

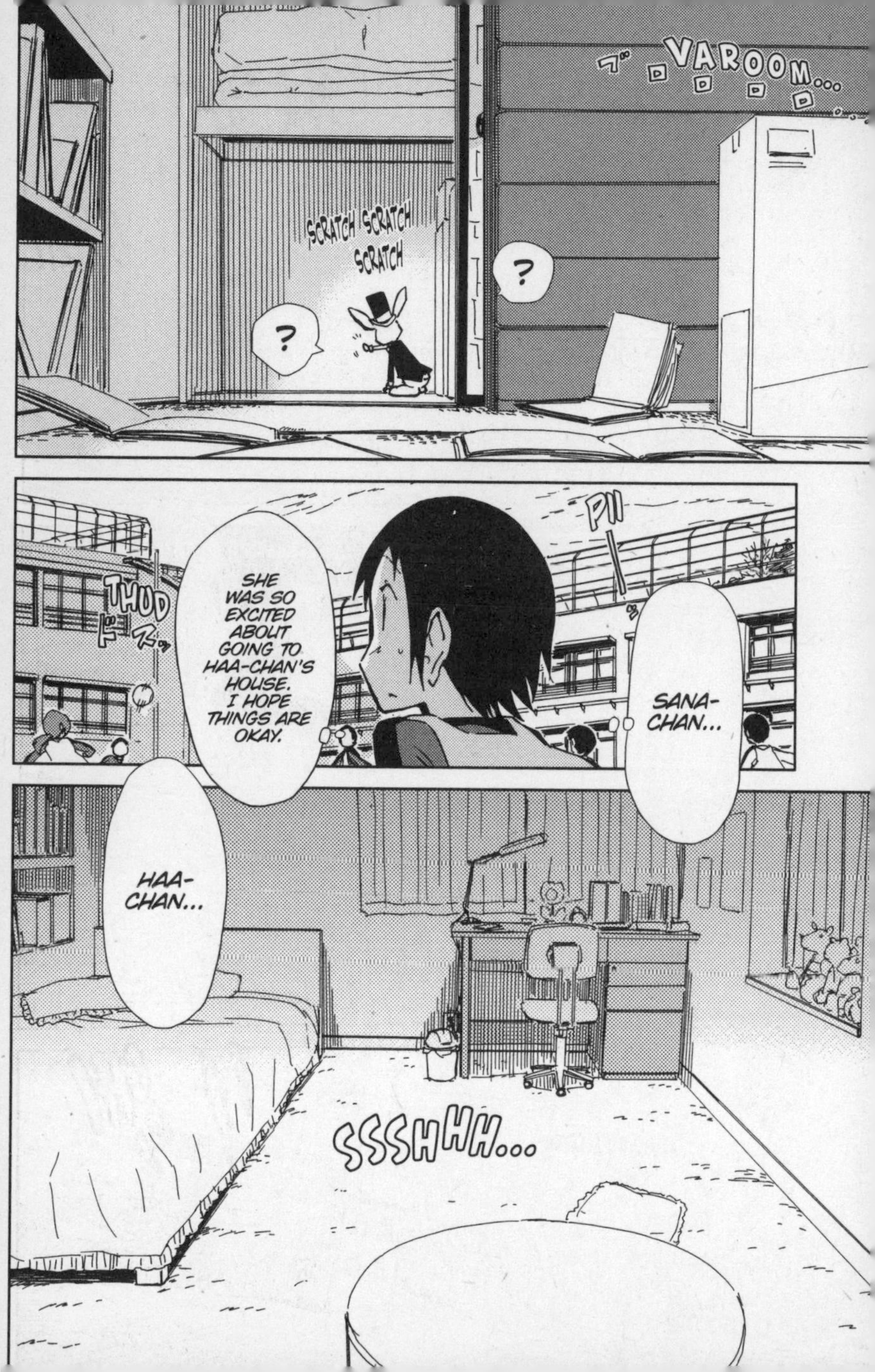
VAROOM...
?
SCRATCH SCRATCH SCRATCH
?
PII
SANA-CHAN...
SHE WAS SO EXCITED ABOUT GOING TO HAA-CHAN'S HOUSE. I HOPE THINGS ARE OKAY.
THUD
HAA-CHAN...
SSSHHH...

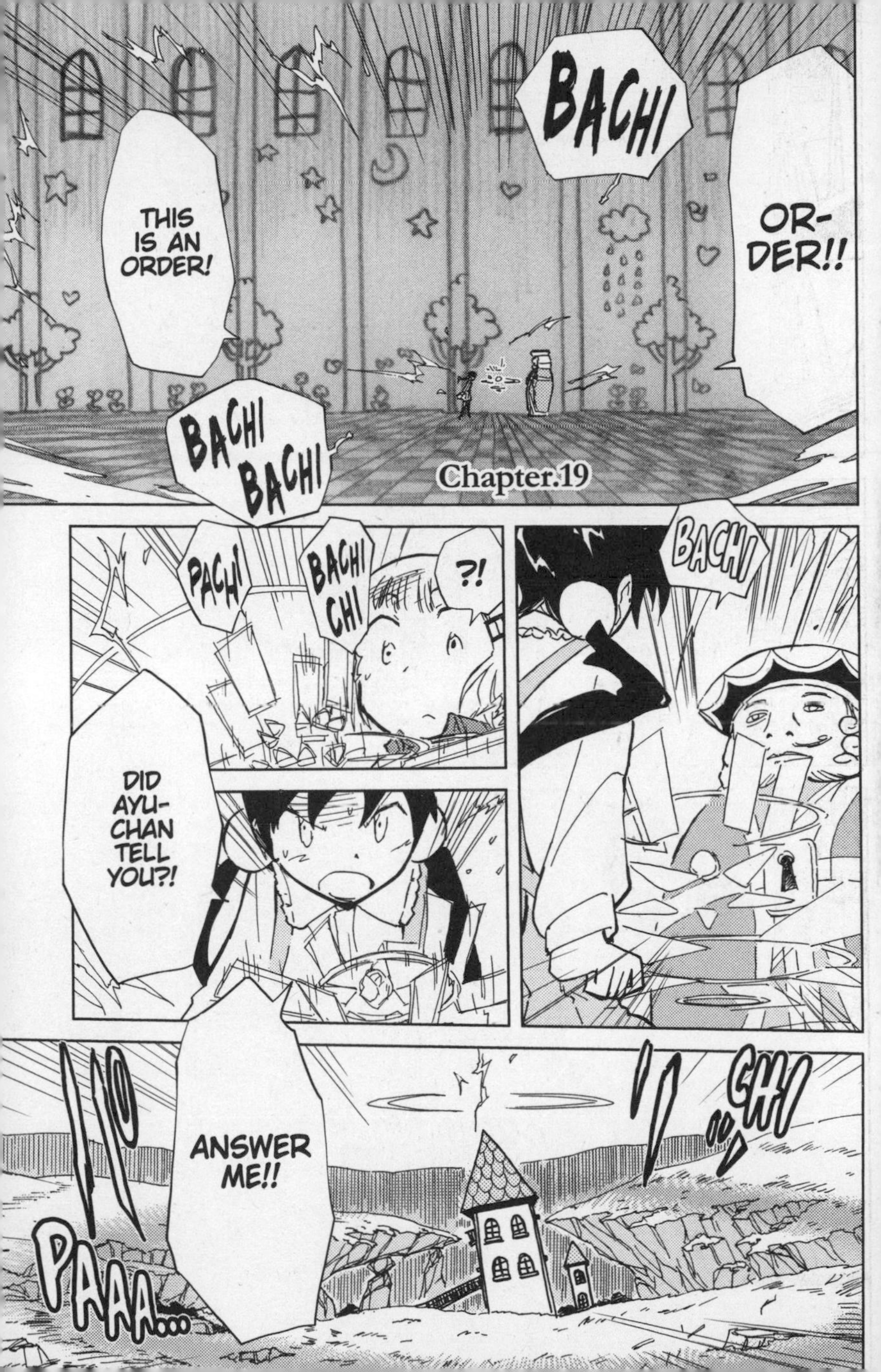
OR-DER!!
BACHI
THIS IS AN ORDER!
BACHI BACHI
Chapter.19
BACHI
?!
BACHI CHI
PACHI
DID AYU-CHAN TELL YOU?!
..CHI
ANSWER ME!!
PAAA...

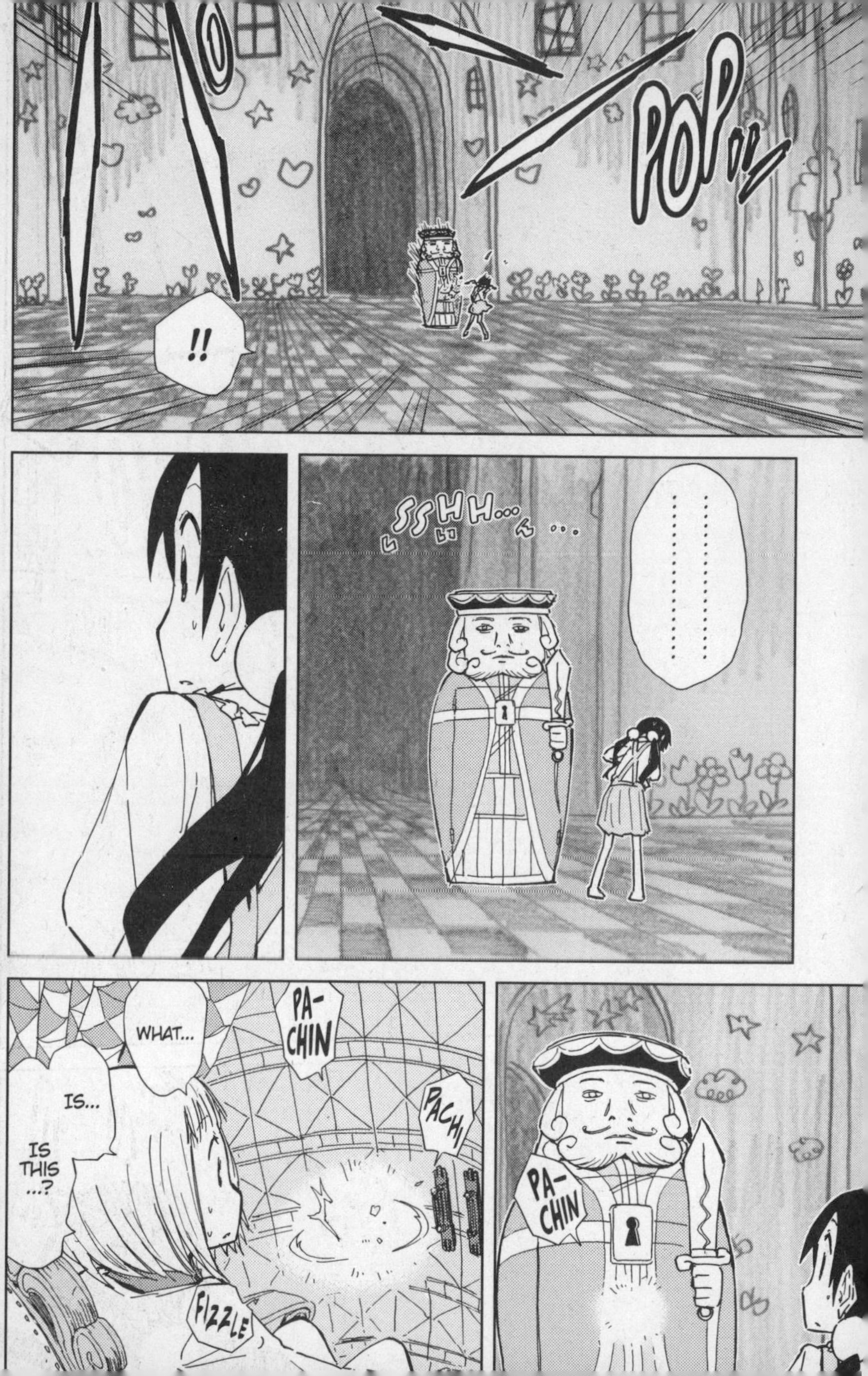
POP
!!
SSHH...
......
PA-CHIN
WHAT...
PA-CHIN
PACHI
IS...
IS THIS ...?
FIZZLE

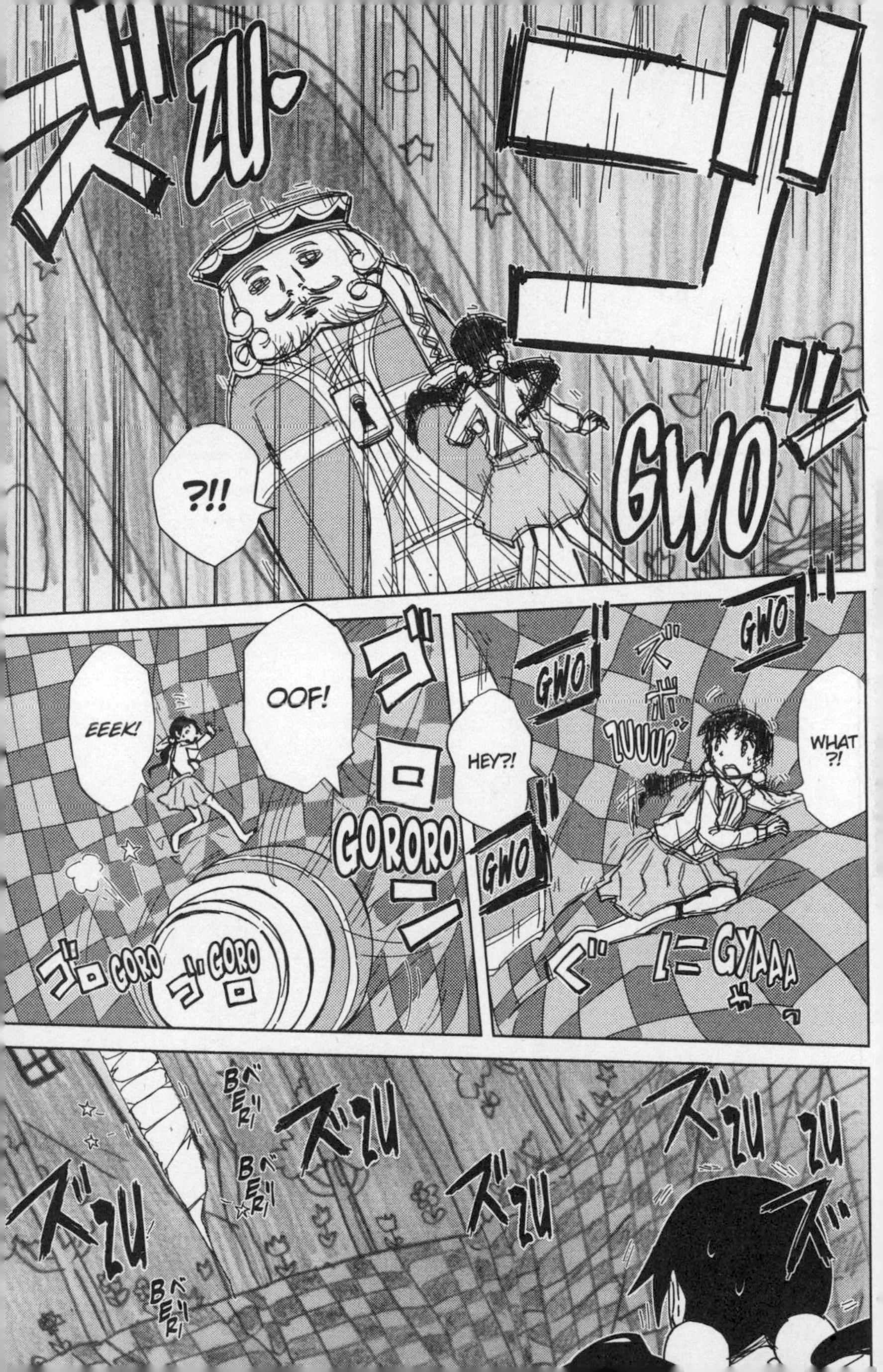
GWO
ZU-
?!!
GWO
WHAT ?!
ZUUUP
GWO
HEY?!
GWO
GYAAA
OOF!
GORORO
EEEK!
GORO
GORO
ZU
ZU
ZU
ZU
BERI
BERI
ZU
BERI

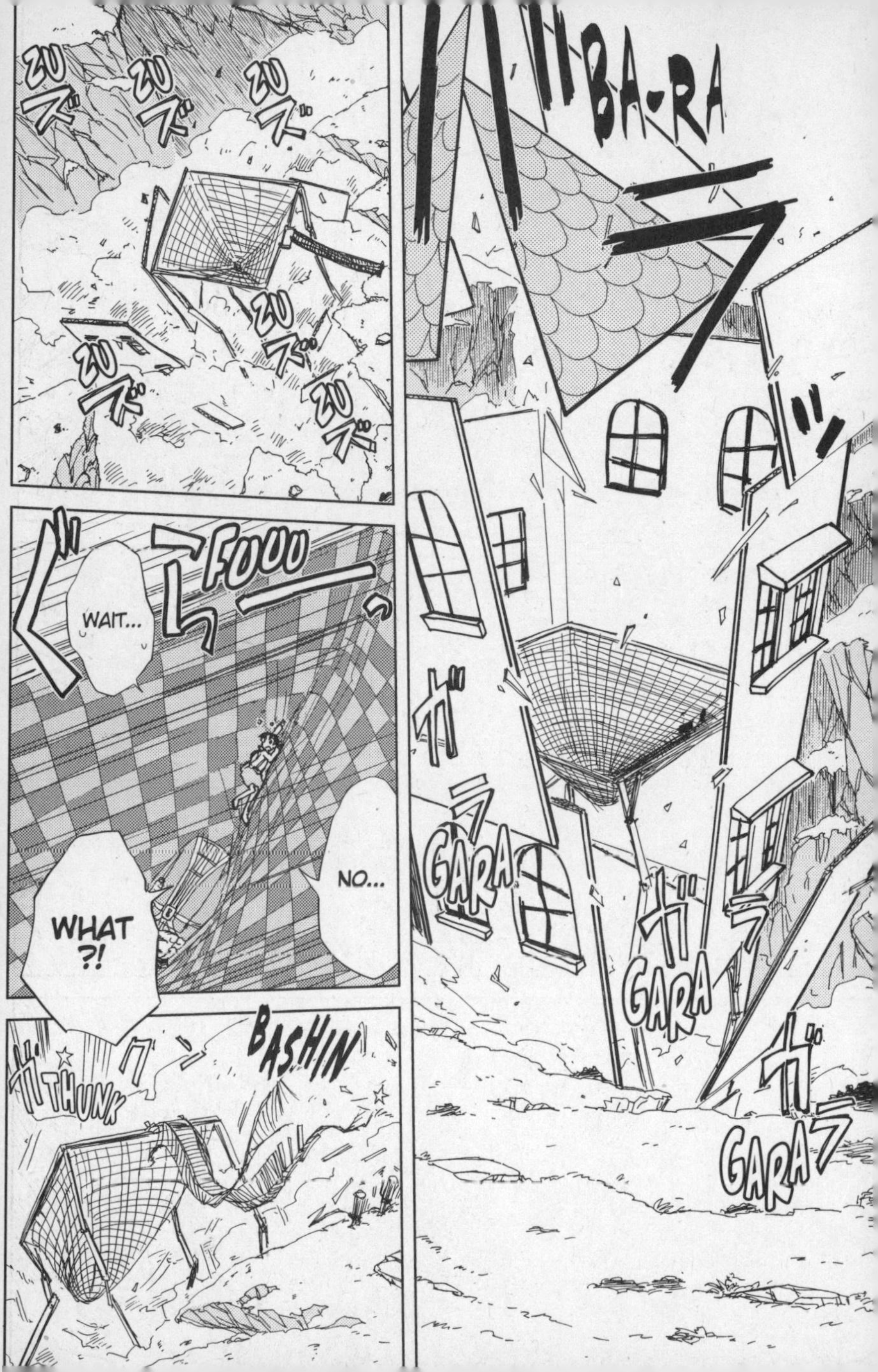
BA-RA
GARA
GARA
GARA
ZU
ZU
ZU
ZU
ZU
ZU
FOUU
WAIT...
NO...
WHAT ?!
BASHIN
THUNK

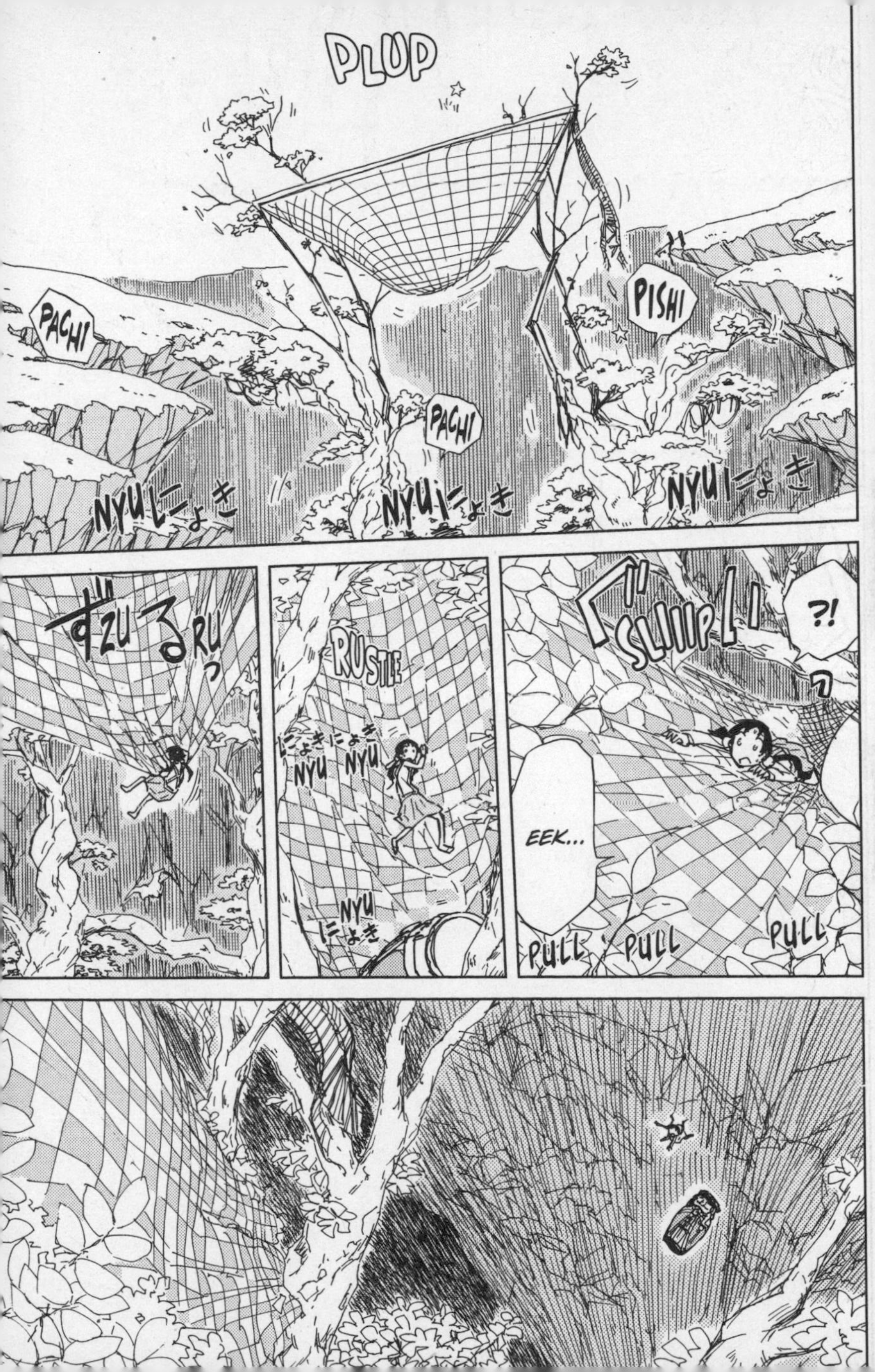

PLUP
PISHI
PACHI
PACHI
NYU にょき
NYU にょき
NYU にょき
SLIIIP
?!
EEK...
PULL
PULL
PULL
RUSTLE
にょきにょき
NYU NYU
NYU
にょき
ず ZU る RU っ

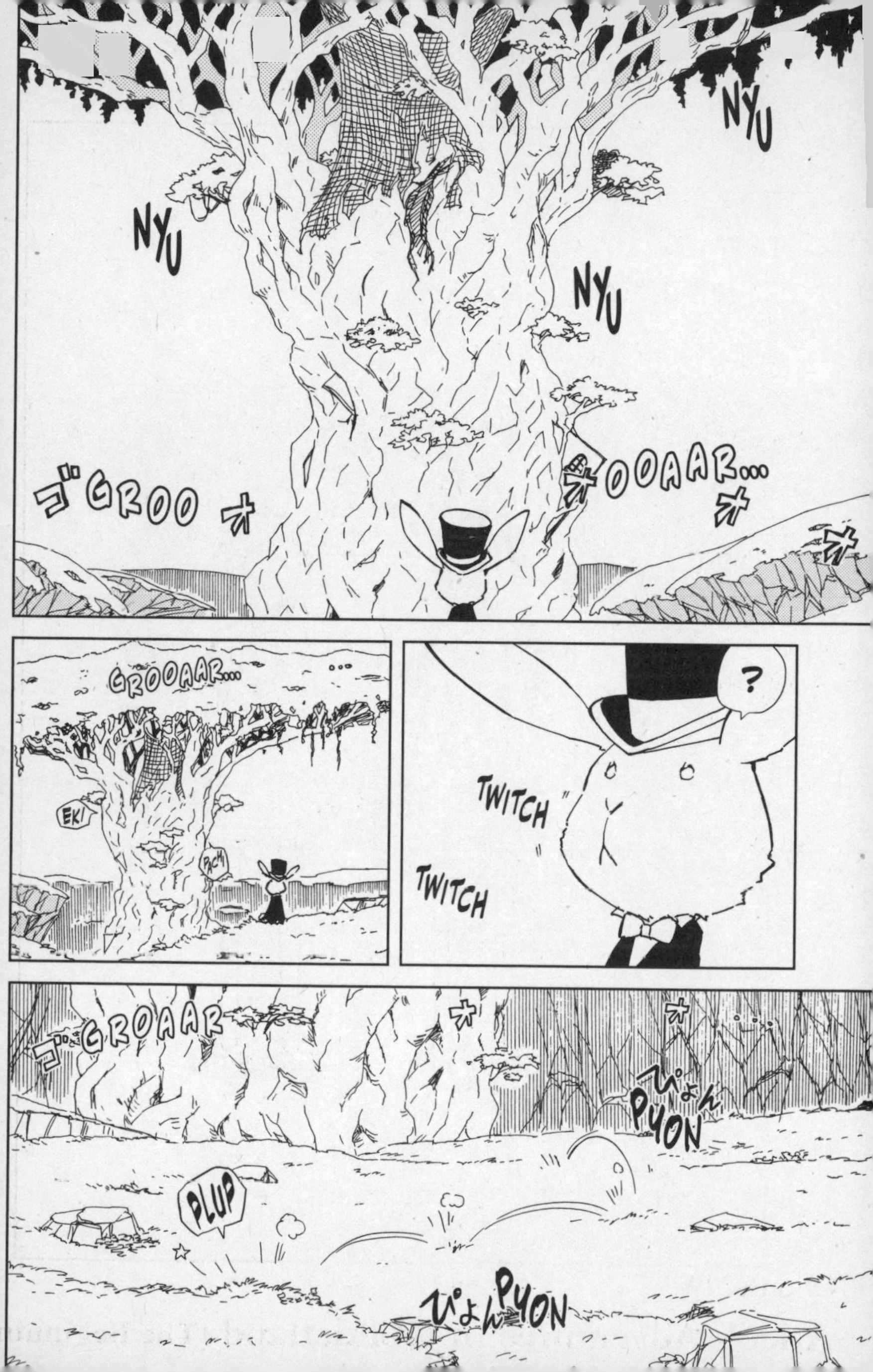

NYU
NYU
NYU
オOOAAR...オ
オ
ゴGROOオ
?
TWITCH
TWITCH
GROOAAR...
...
EKI
PACH
オ
...
ぴょんPYON
オ
ゴGROAAR
PLUP
ぴょんPYON

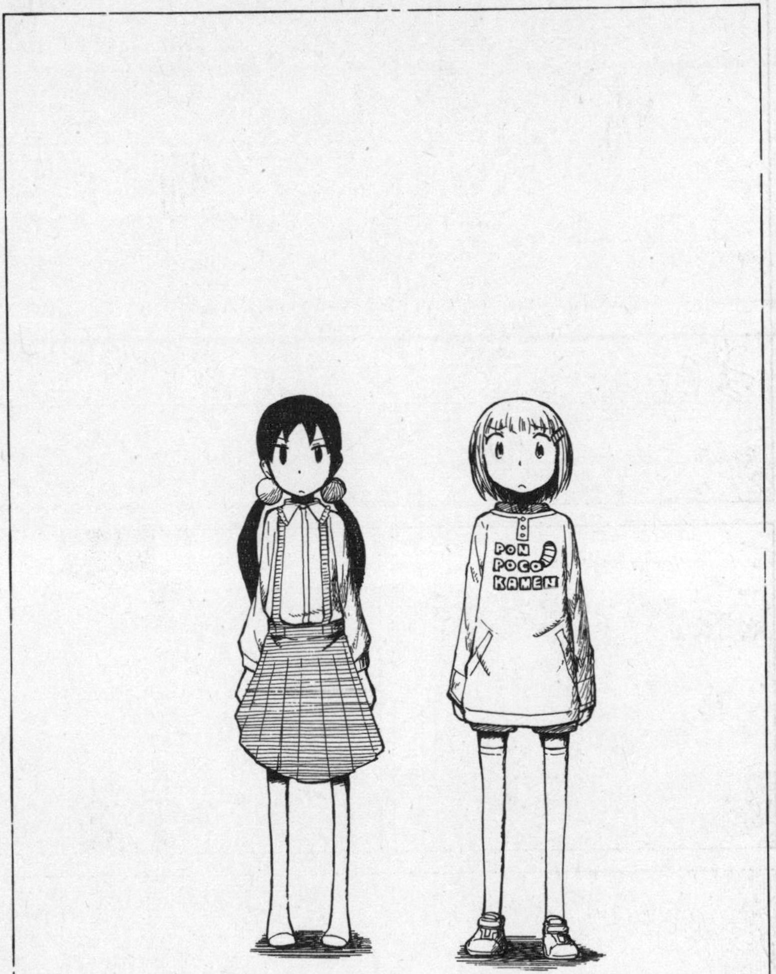
PON
POCO
KAMEN

Chapter.19

Alice's Adventures in Wonderland (The Beginnin

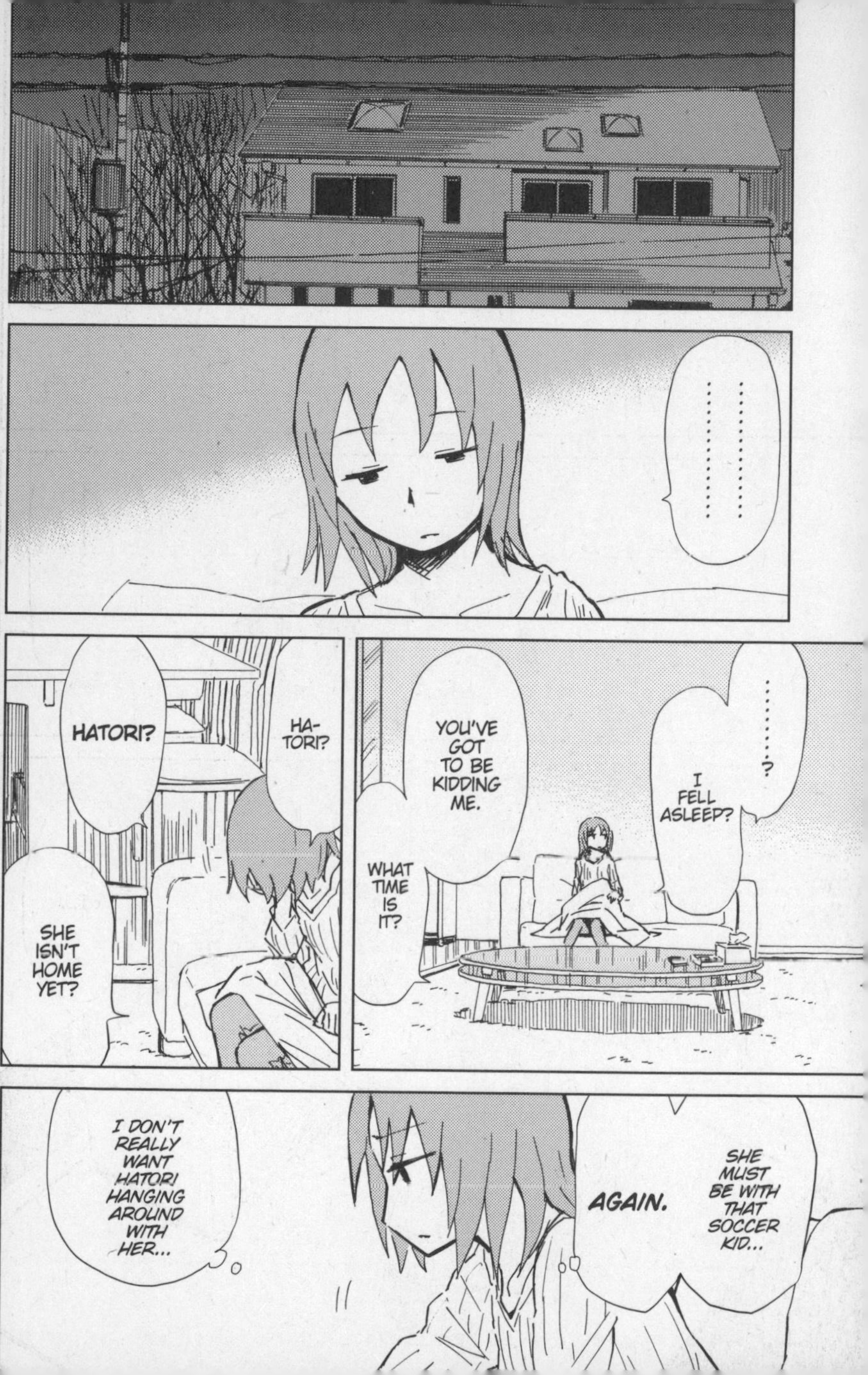
......
......?
I FELL ASLEEP?
YOU'VE GOT TO BE KIDDING ME.
WHAT TIME IS IT?
HA-TORI?
HATORI?
SHE ISN'T HOME YET?
SHE MUST BE WITH THAT SOCCER KID...
AGAIN.
I DON'T REALLY WANT HATORI HANGING AROUND WITH HER...

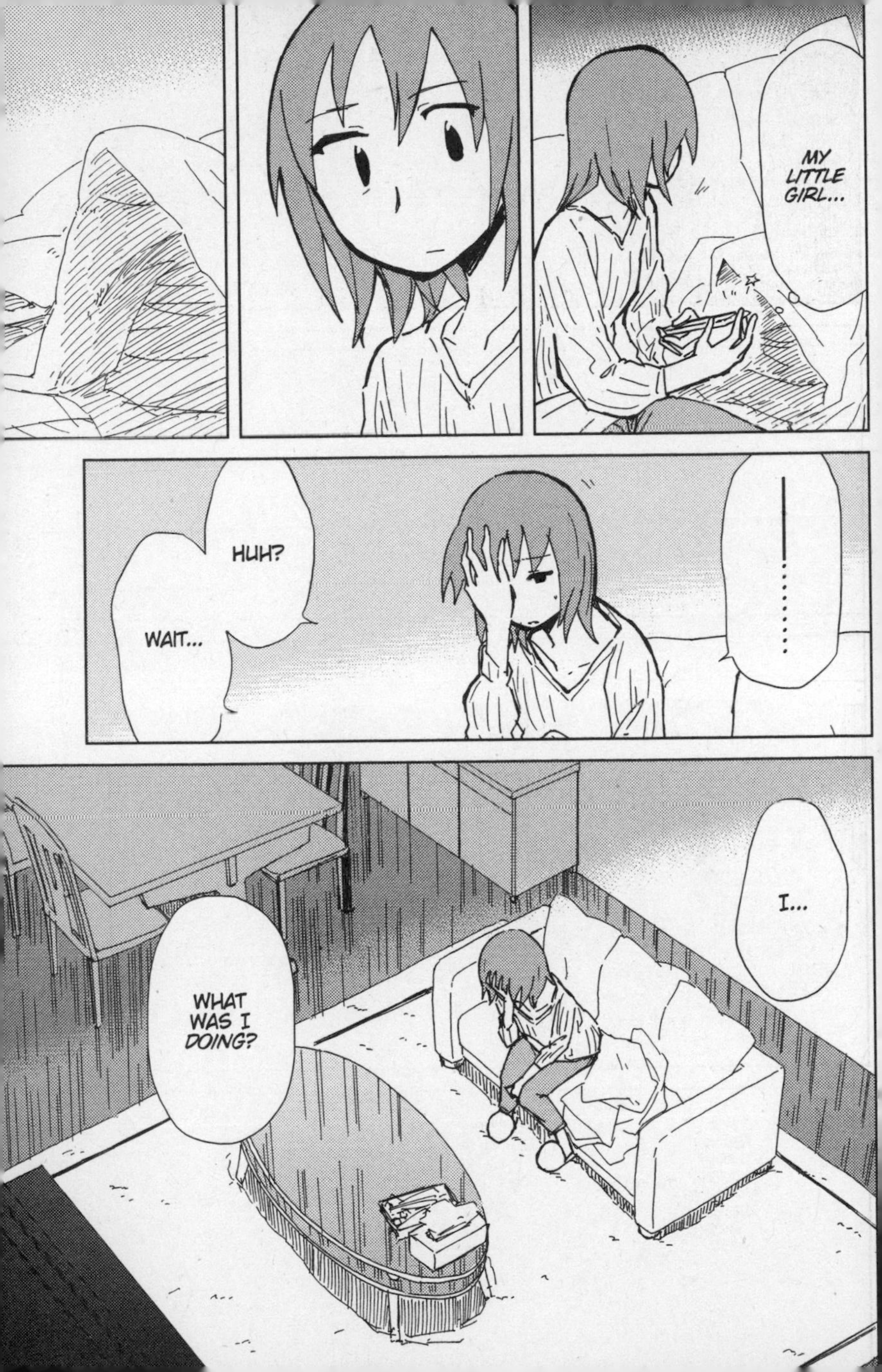
MY LITTLE GIRL...
—......
HUH?
WAIT...
I...
WHAT WAS I DOING?

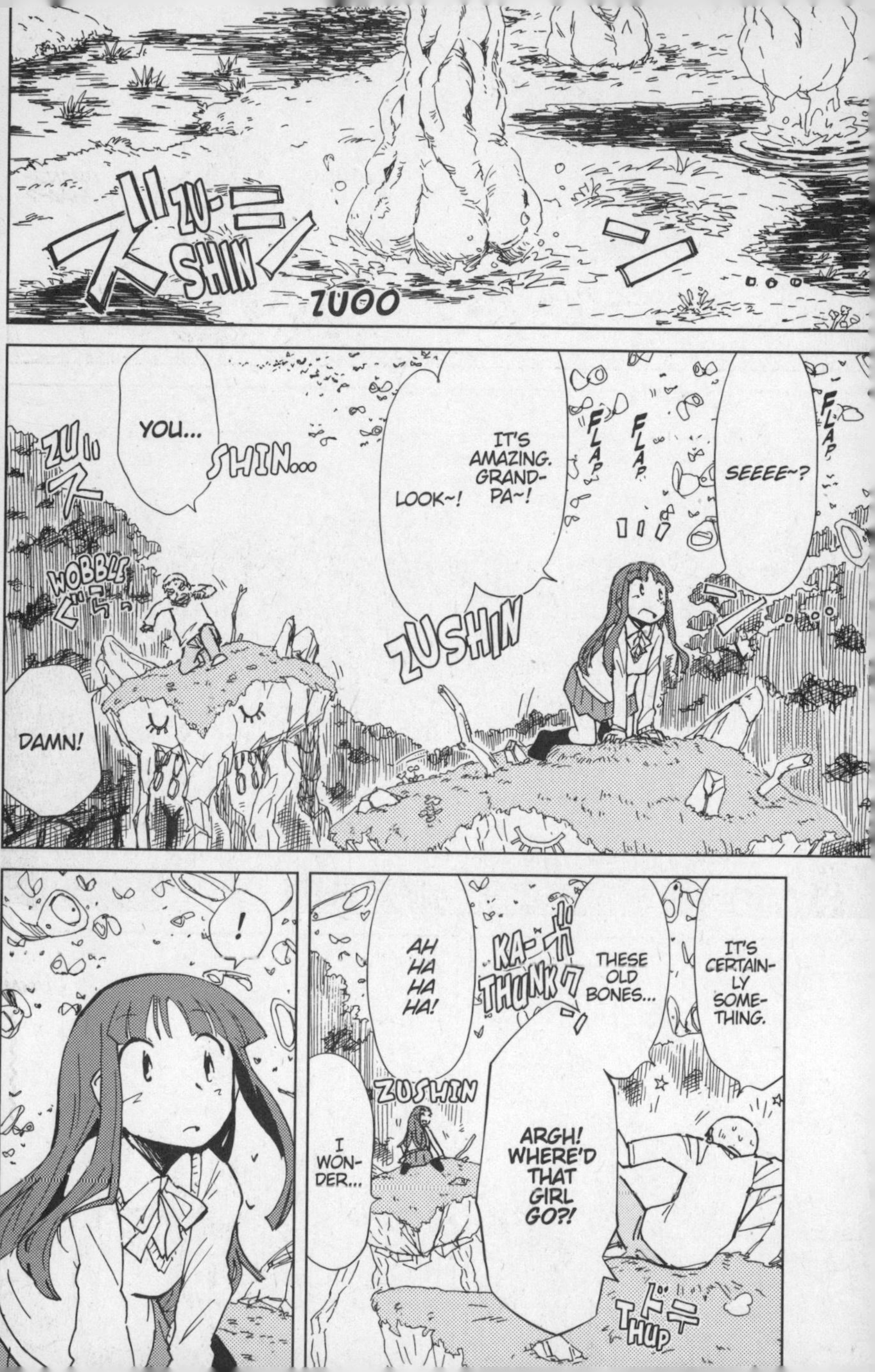
ZU-SHIN
ZUOO
SEEEE~?
FLAP
FLAP
FLAP
IT'S AMAZING. GRAND-PA~!
LOOK~!
ZUSHIN
YOU...
SHIN...
ZU
WOBBLE
DAMN!
IT'S CERTAIN-LY SOME-THING.
THESE OLD BONES...
KA-THUNK
AH HA HA HA!
ARGH! WHERE'D THAT GIRL GO?!
THUP
ZUSHIN
I WON-DER...
!

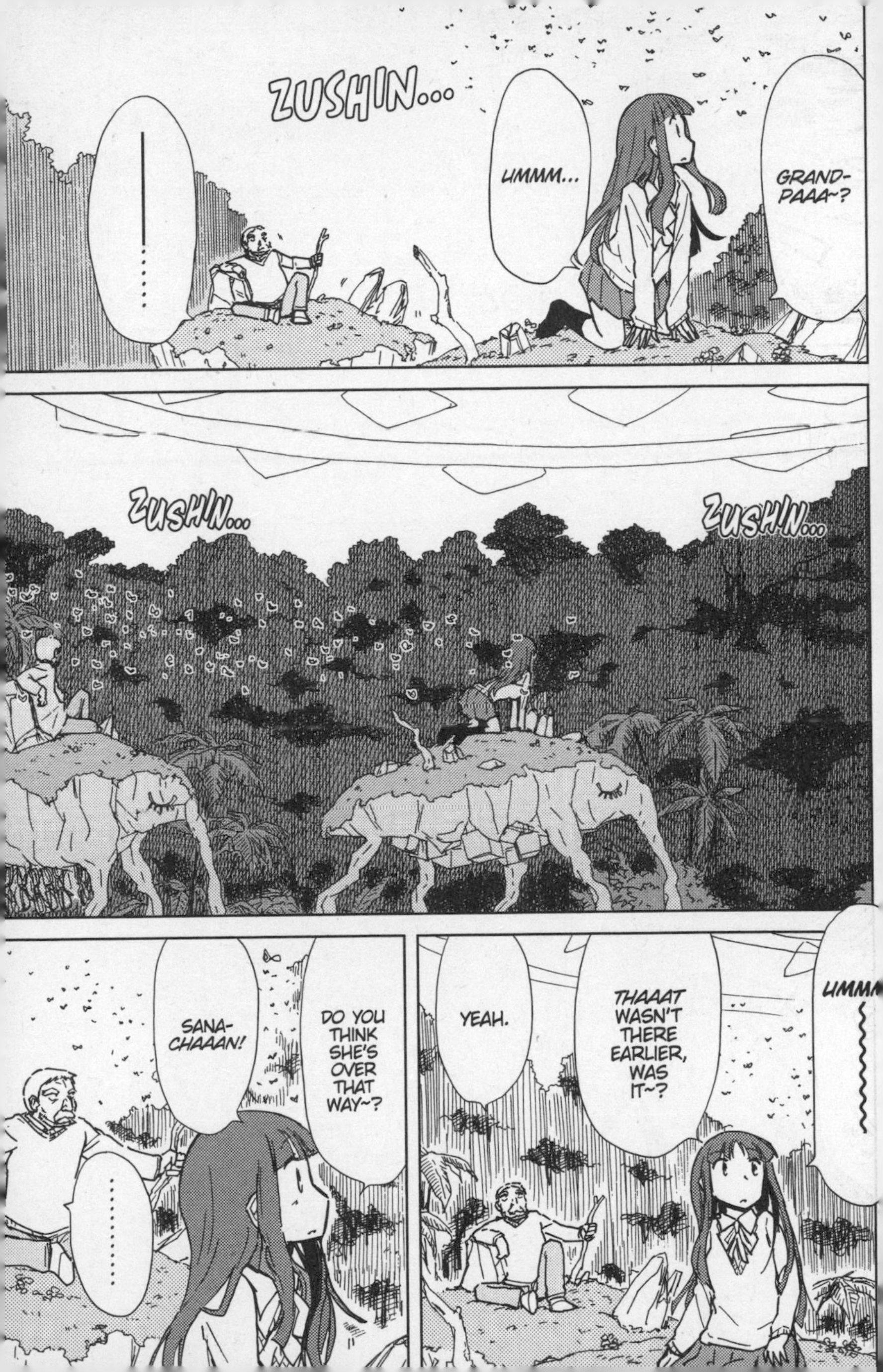
GRAND-PAAA~?
UMMM...
ZUSHIN...
ZUSHIN...
ZUSHIN...
UMMM
THAAAT WASN'T THERE EARLIER, WAS IT~?
YEAH.
DO YOU THINK SHE'S OVER THAT WAY~?
SANA-CHAAAN!
......

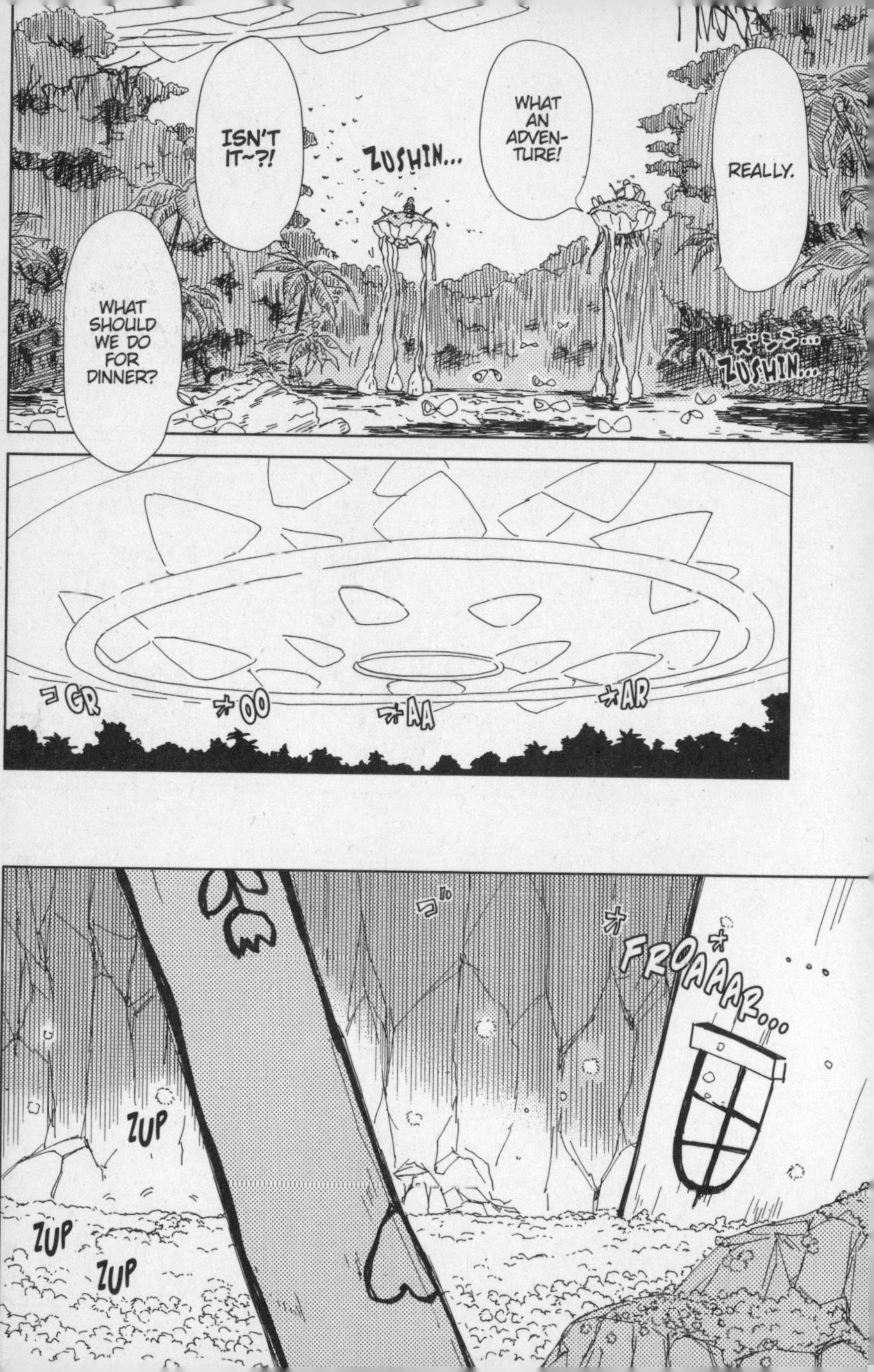
REALLY.
WHAT AN ADVENTURE!
ズシン…
ZUSHIN...
ZUSHIN...
ISN'T IT~?!
WHAT SHOULD WE DO FOR DINNER?
GR OO AA AR
FROAAAAR...
ZUP
ZUP
ZUP

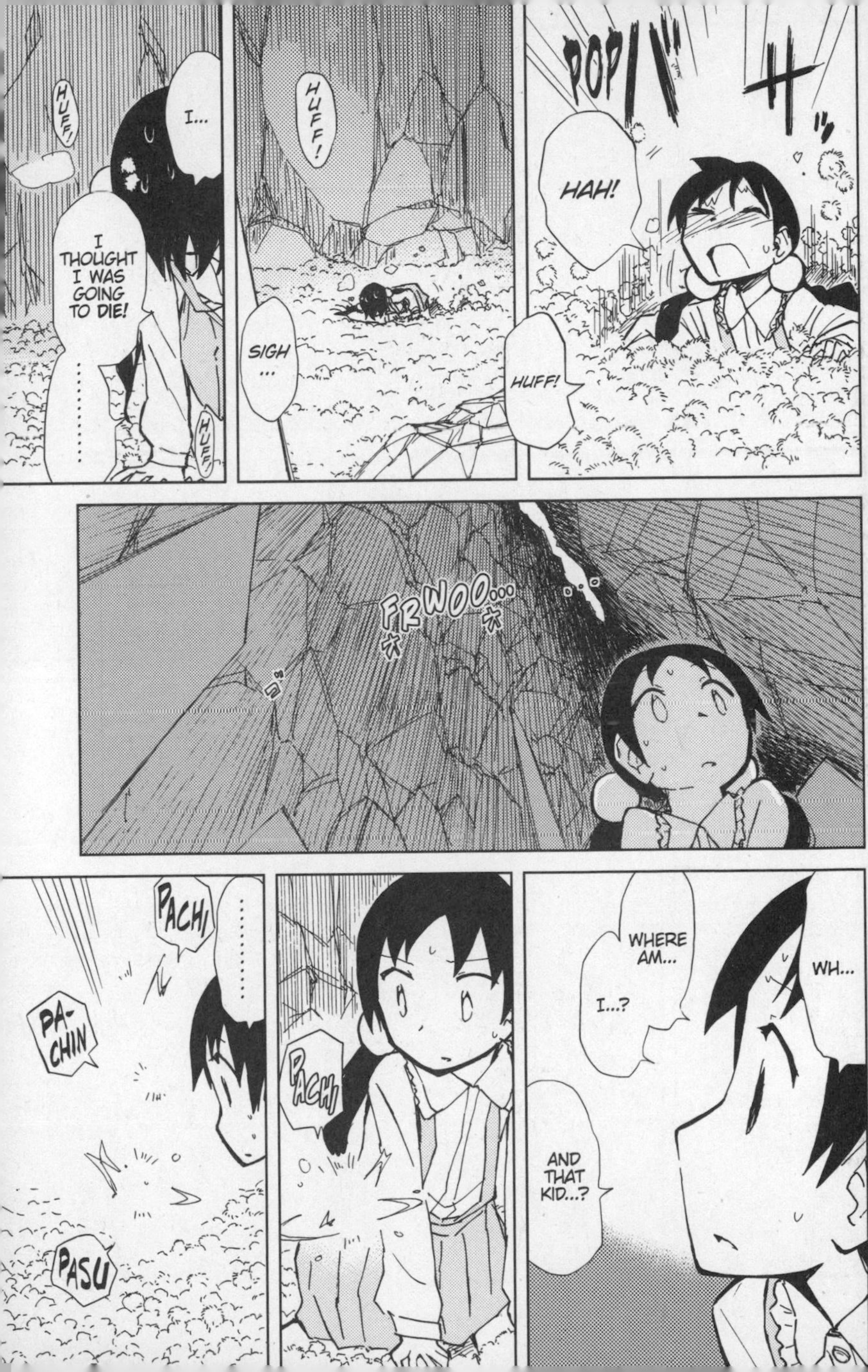
POP
HAH!
HUFF!
HUFF!
SIGH...
I...
HUFF!
I THOUGHT I WAS GOING TO DIE!
......
HUFF!
FRWOO...
WH...
WHERE AM... I...?
AND THAT KID...?
PACHI
......
PACHI
PA-CHIN
PASU

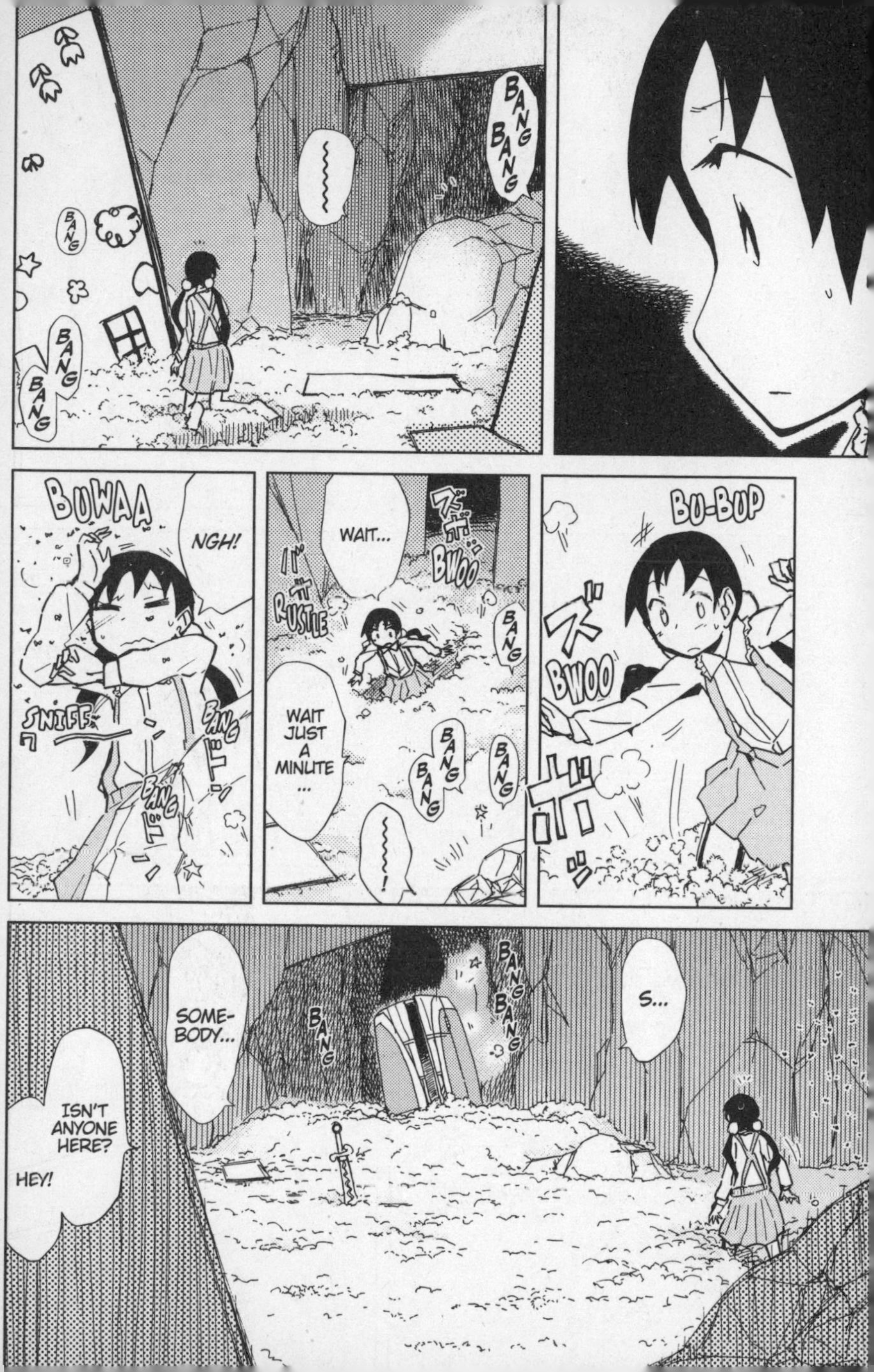
BANG BANG
BANG
BANG BANG
BU-BUP
BWOO
WAIT...
BWOO
RUSTLE
BANG
WAIT JUST A MINUTE...
BANG BANG
BANG
BUWAA
NGH!
SNIFF
BANG
BANG
S...
BANG BANG
SOMEBODY...
BANG
ISN'T ANYONE HERE?
HEY!

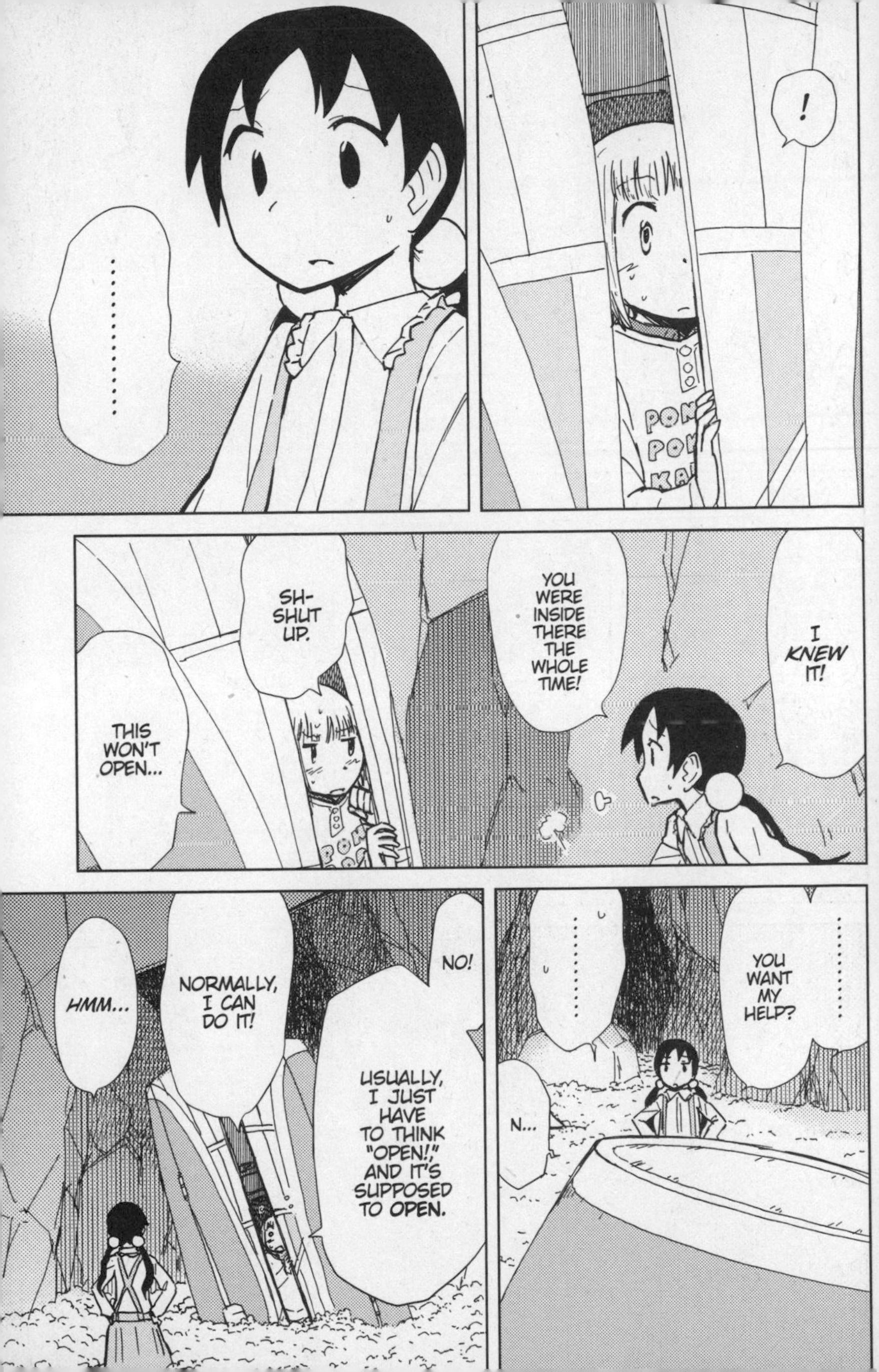
!
......
I KNEW IT!
YOU WERE INSIDE THERE THE WHOLE TIME!
SH-SHUT UP.
THIS WON'T OPEN...
......
YOU WANT MY HELP?
......
N...
NO!
NORMALLY, I CAN DO IT!
HMM...
USUALLY, I JUST HAVE TO THINK "OPEN!," AND IT'S SUPPOSED TO OPEN.

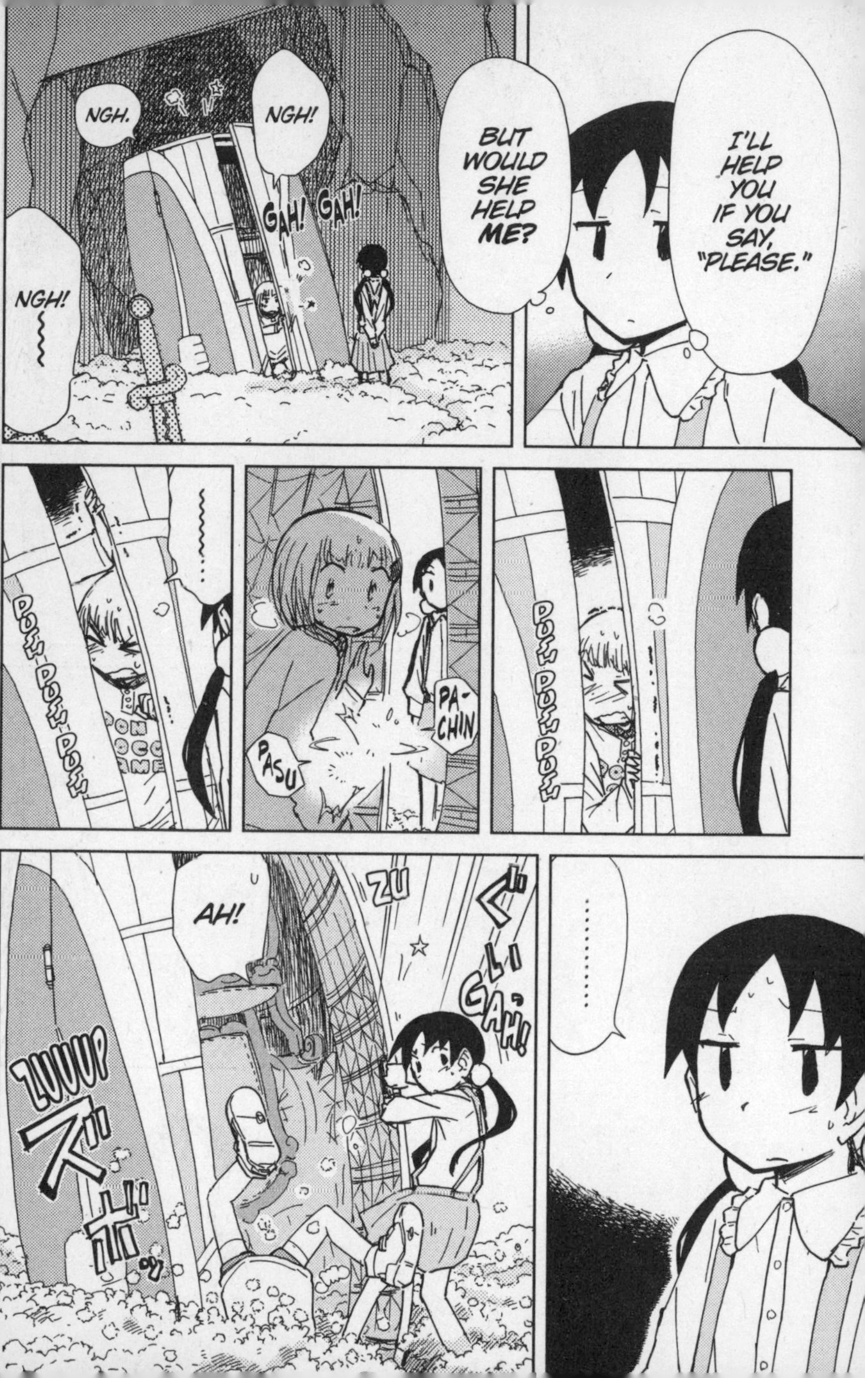

I'LL HELP YOU IF YOU SAY, "PLEASE."
BUT WOULD SHE HELP ME?
NGH!
GAH! GAH!
NGH.
NGH!
POSH POSH POSH
PA-CHIN
PASU
......
POSH POSH POSH
......
ZU
GLI GAH!
AH!
ZUUUP
ズボッ

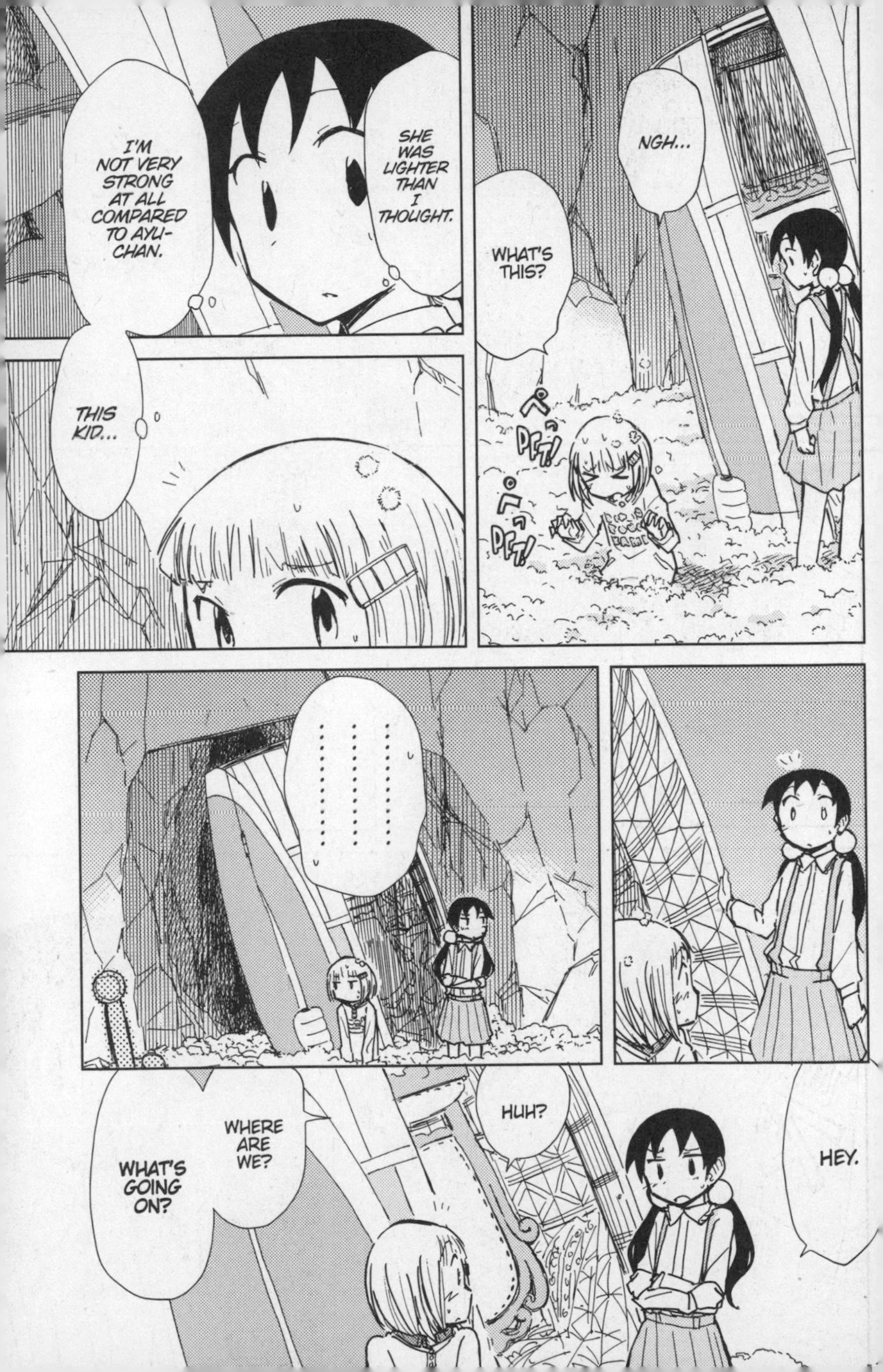
NGH...
WHAT'S THIS?
ペ PFFT!
ぷ PFFT!
SHE WAS LIGHTER THAN I THOUGHT.
I'M NOT VERY STRONG AT ALL COMPARED TO AYU-CHAN.
THIS KID...
......
HEY.
HUH?
WHERE ARE WE?
WHAT'S GOING ON?

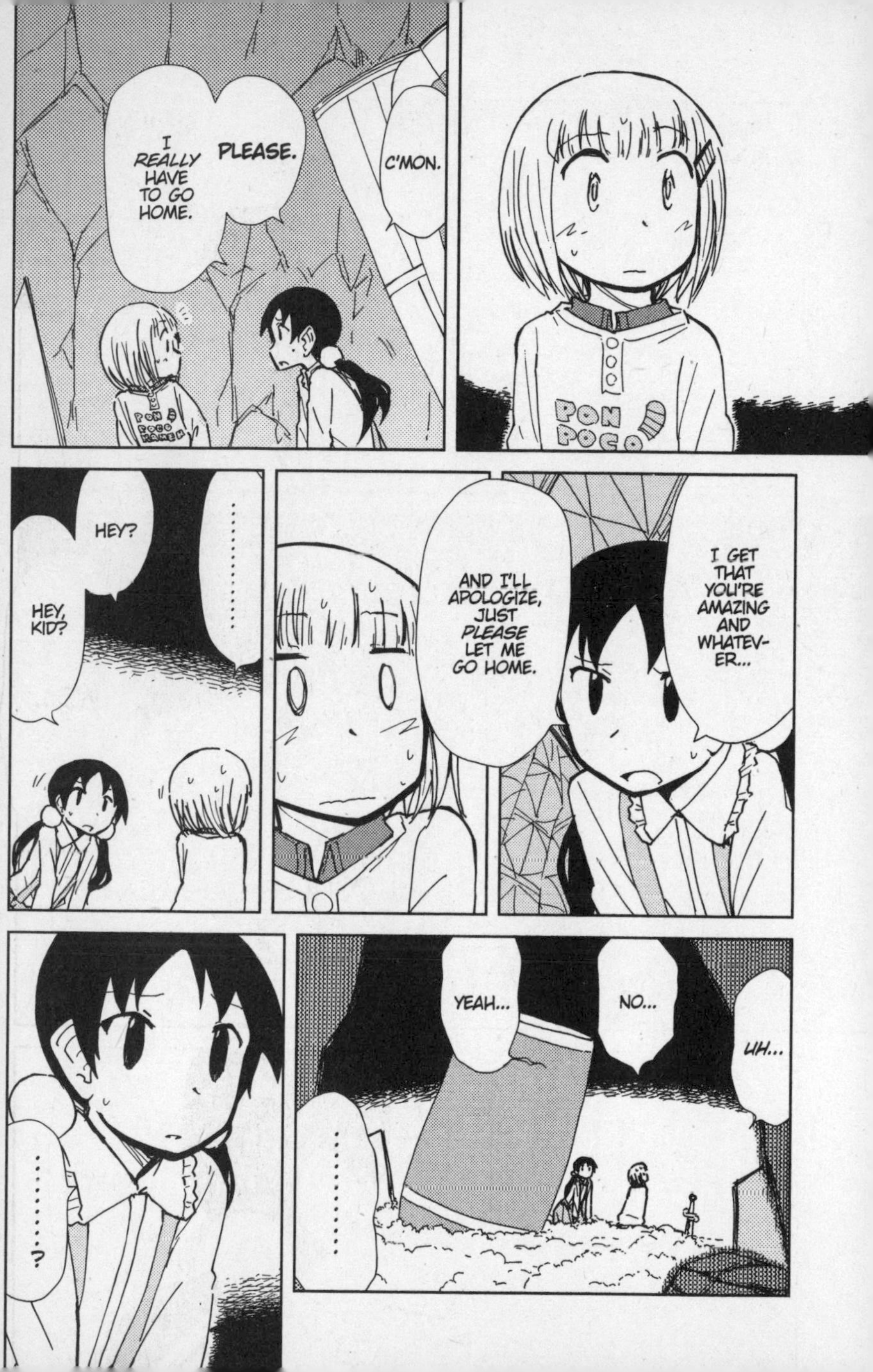
C'MON.
PLEASE.
I REALLY HAVE TO GO HOME.
I GET THAT YOU'RE AMAZING AND WHATEVER...
AND I'LL APOLOGIZE, JUST PLEASE LET ME GO HOME.
......
HEY?
HEY, KID?
UH...
NO...
YEAH...
......
......?

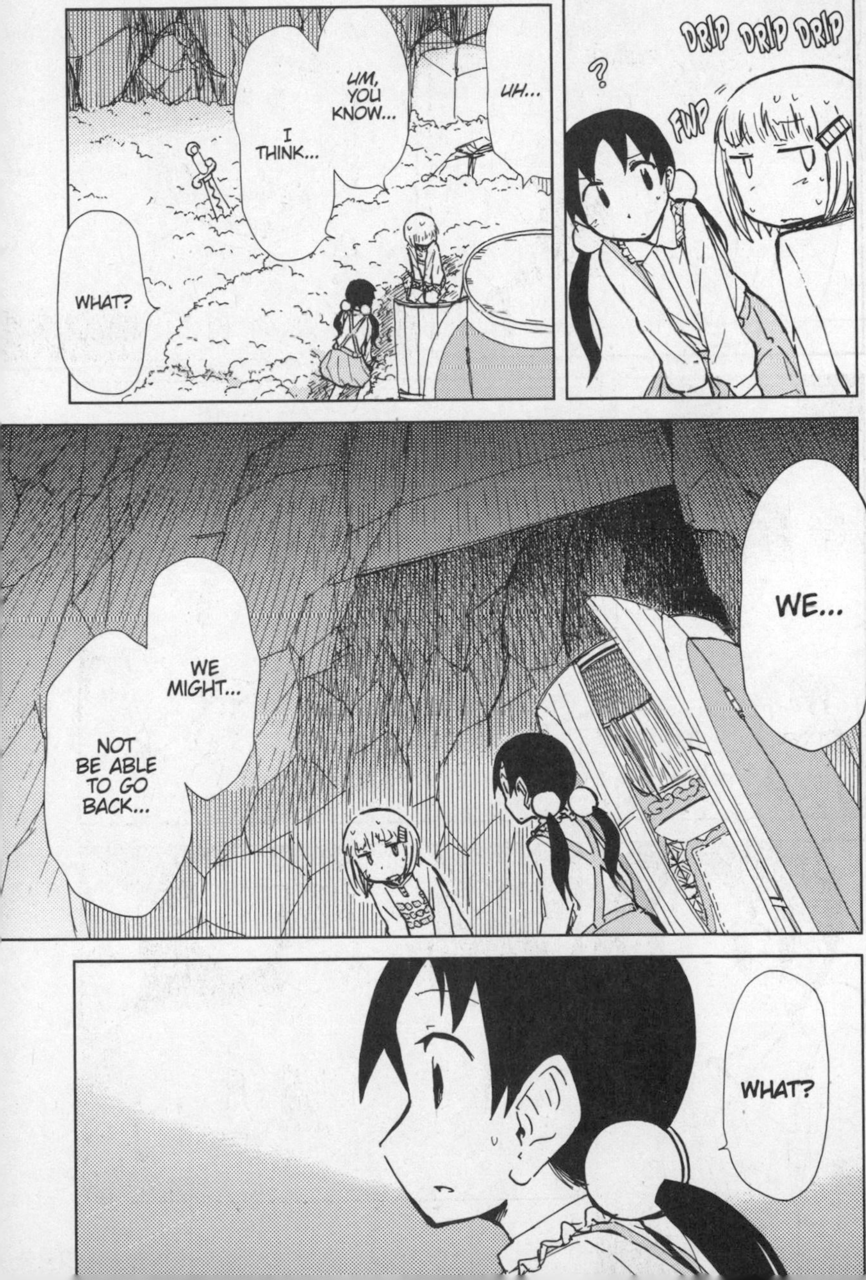
DRIP DRIP DRIP
?
FWP
UH...
UM, YOU KNOW... I THINK...
WHAT?
WE...
WE MIGHT... NOT BE ABLE TO GO BACK...
WHAT?

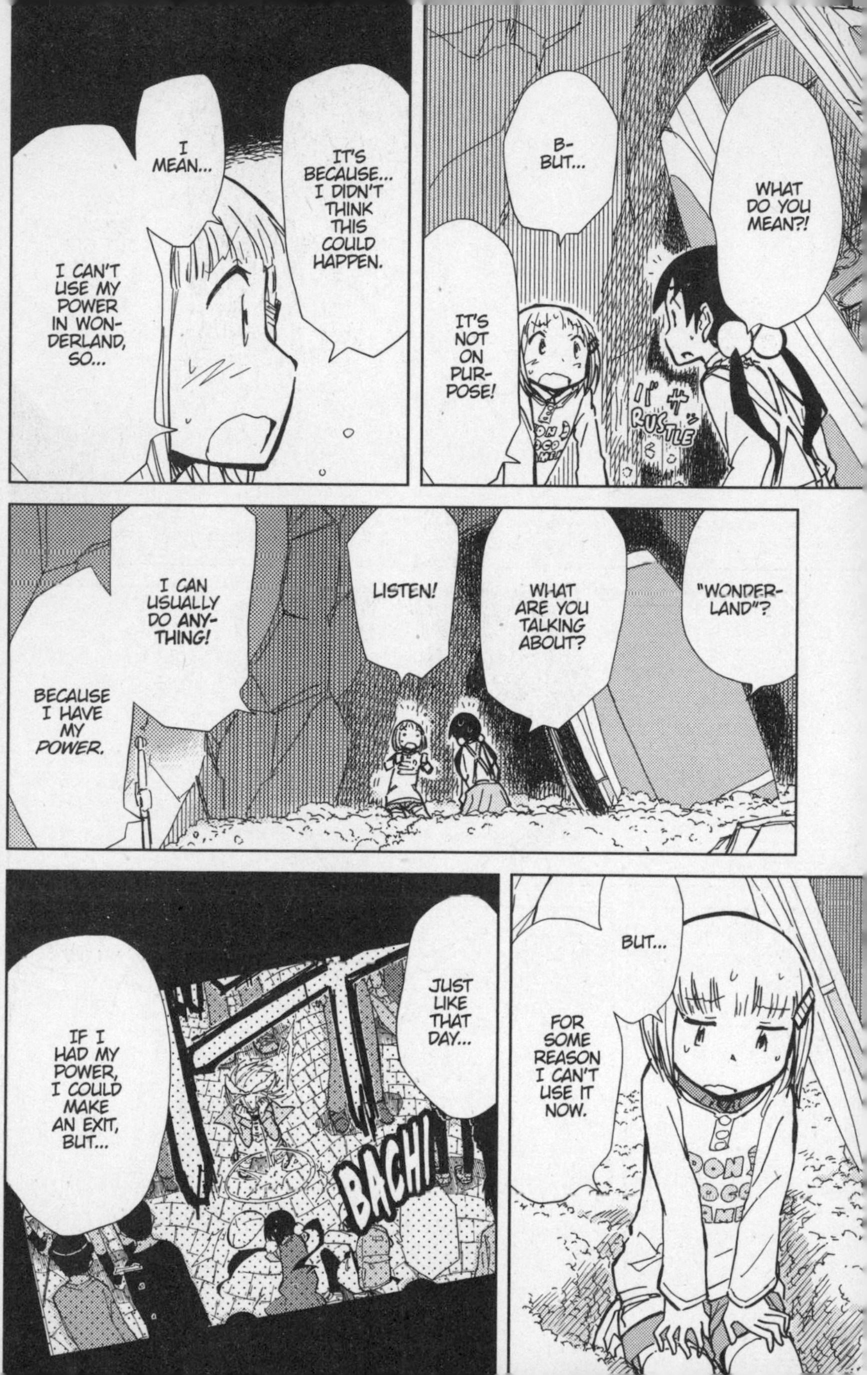
WHAT DO YOU MEAN?!
B- BUT...
IT'S NOT ON PUR- POSE!
バサ
RUSTLE
IT'S BECAUSE... I DIDN'T THINK THIS COULD HAPPEN.
I MEAN...
I CAN'T USE MY POWER IN WON- DERLAND, SO...
"WONDER- LAND"?
WHAT ARE YOU TALKING ABOUT?
LISTEN!
I CAN USUALLY DO ANY- THING!
BECAUSE I HAVE MY POWER.
BUT...
FOR SOME REASON I CAN'T USE IT NOW.
JUST LIKE THAT DAY...
IF I HAD MY POWER, I COULD MAKE AN EXIT, BUT...
BACHI

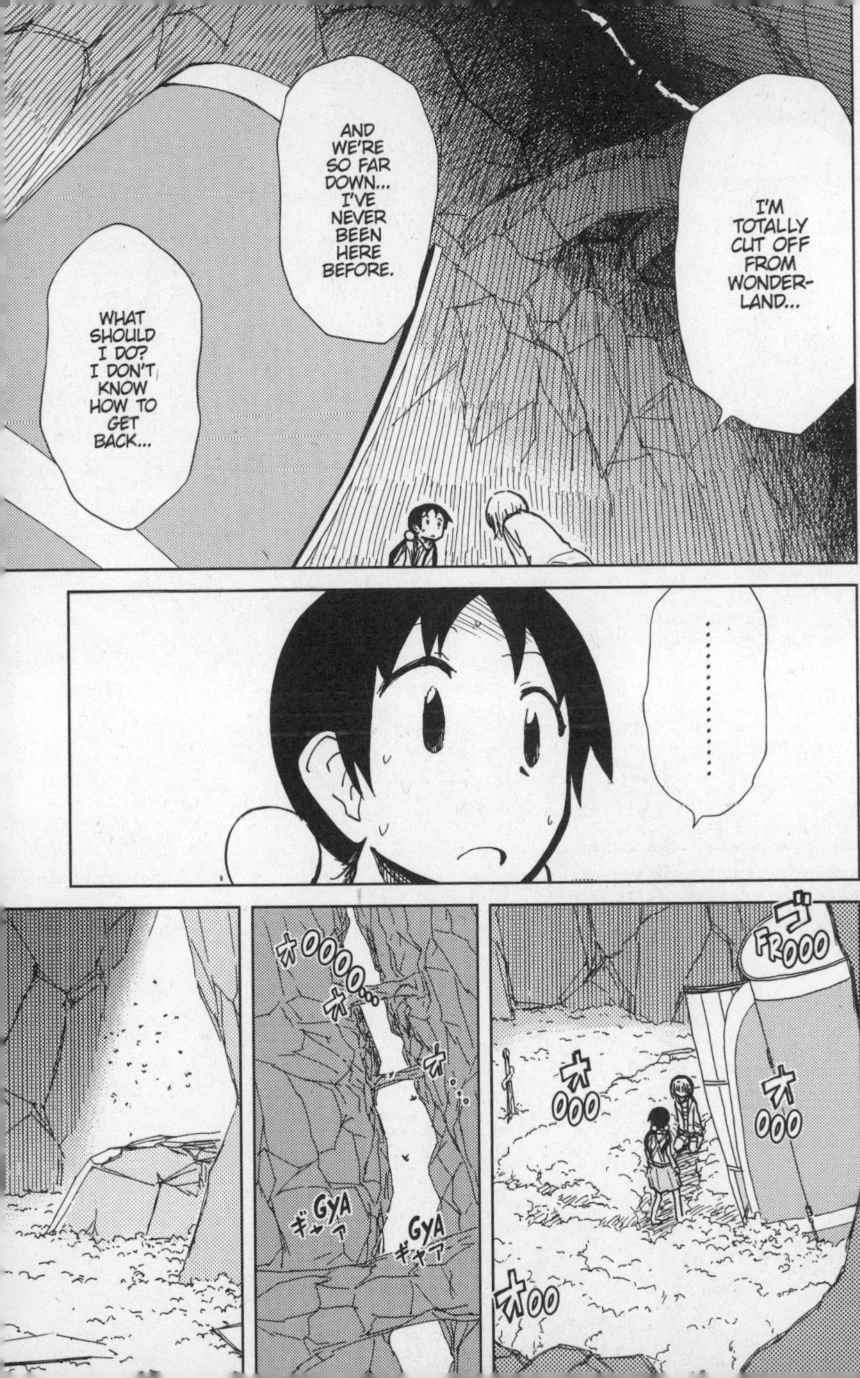
I'M TOTALLY CUT OFF FROM WONDER-LAND...
AND WE'RE SO FAR DOWN... I'VE NEVER BEEN HERE BEFORE.
WHAT SHOULD I DO? I DON'T KNOW HOW TO GET BACK...
......
ゴ FROOO
オ OOO
オ OOO
オ OO
オ OOOO...
オ
オ...
GYA ギャア
GYA ギャア

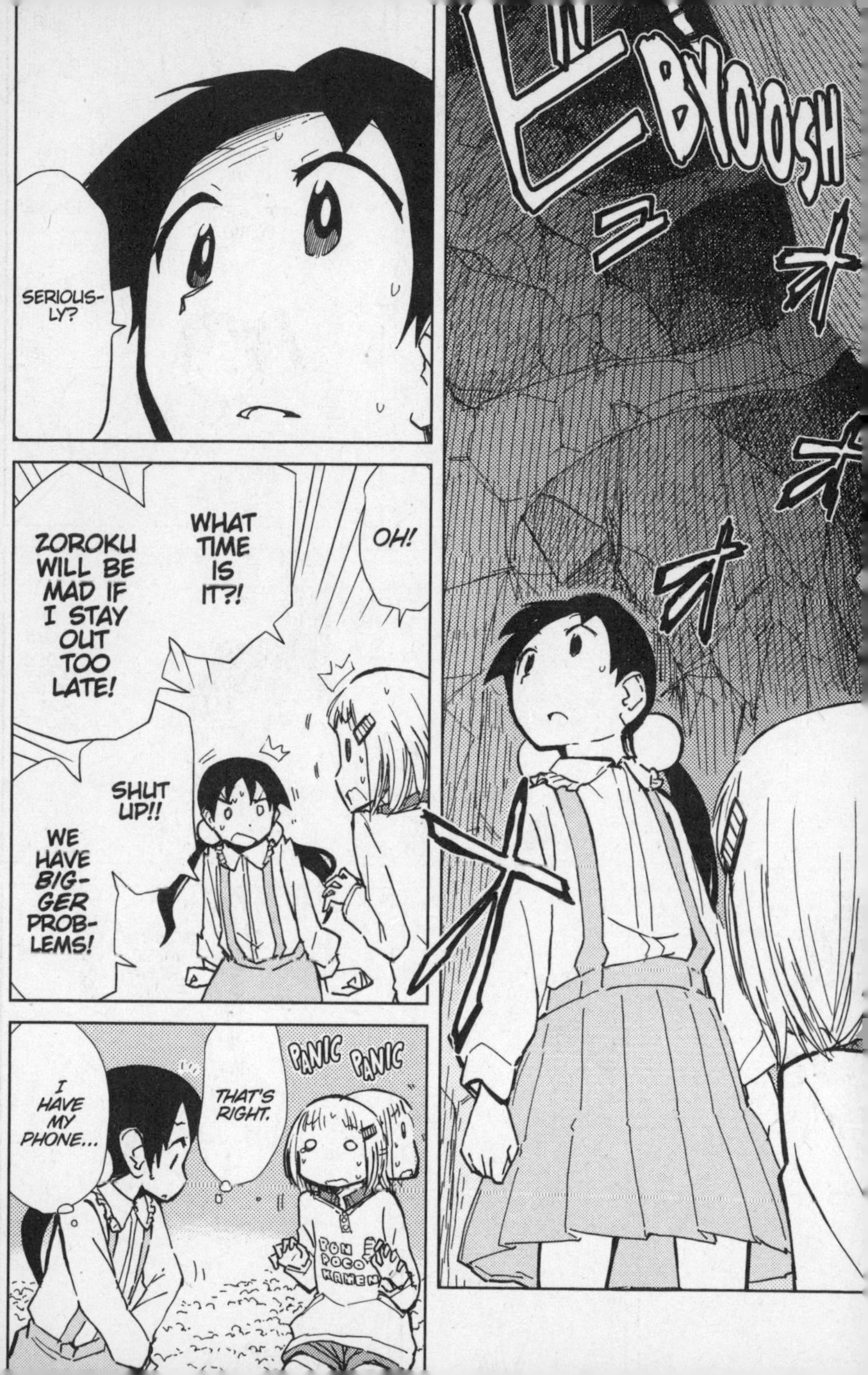
BYOOSH
SERIOUSLY?
OH!
WHAT TIME IS IT?!
ZOROKU WILL BE MAD IF I STAY OUT TOO LATE!
SHUT UP!!
WE HAVE BIGGER PROBLEMS!
PANIC PANIC
THAT'S RIGHT.
I HAVE MY PHONE...
PON POCO KAMEN

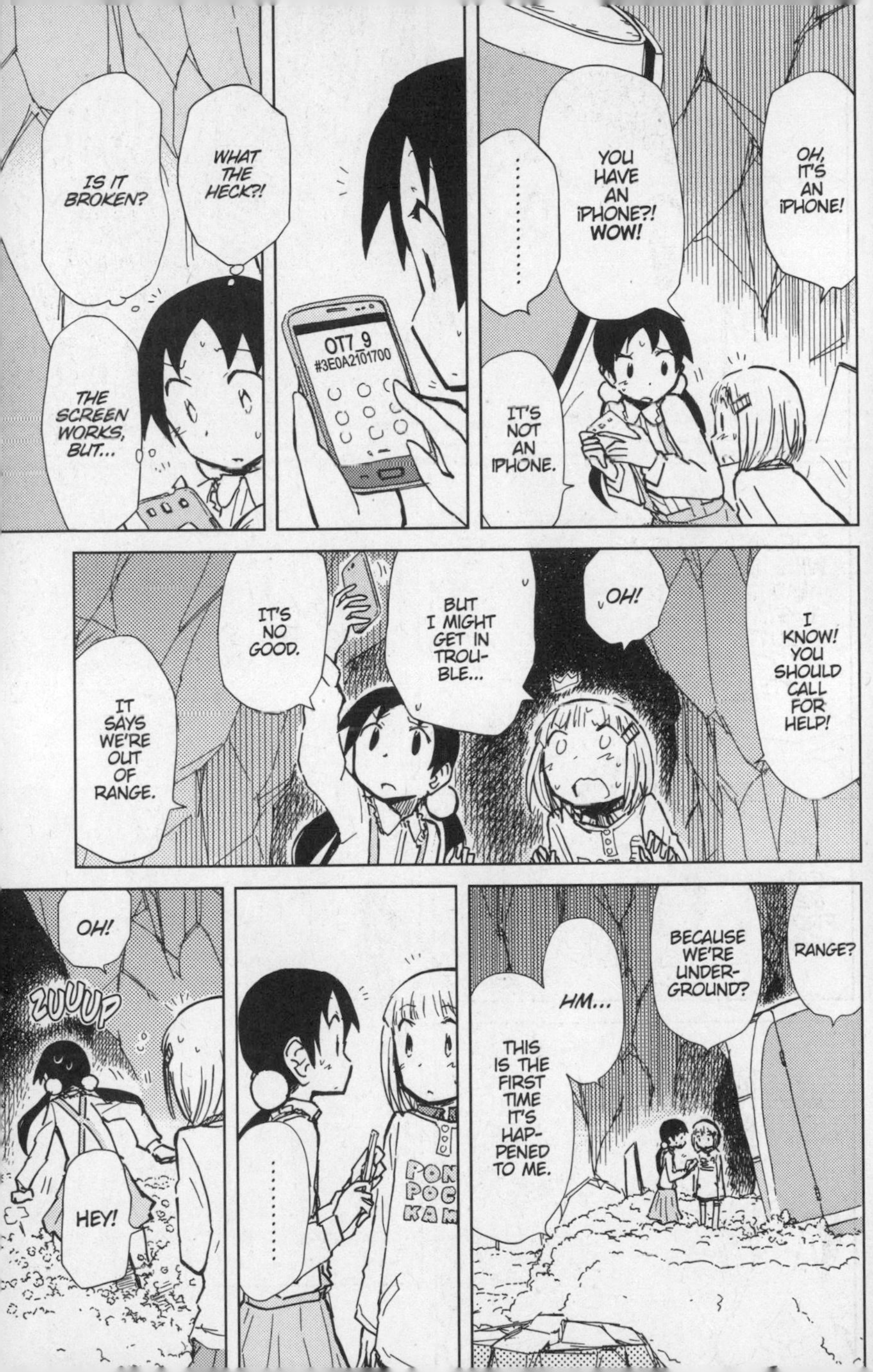
OH, IT'S AN iPHONE!
YOU HAVE AN iPHONE?! WOW!
......
IT'S NOT AN IPHONE.
OT7_9
#3E0A2101700
WHAT THE HECK?!
IS IT BROKEN?
THE SCREEN WORKS, BUT...
I KNOW! YOU SHOULD CALL FOR HELP!
OH!
BUT I MIGHT GET IN TROU-BLE...
IT'S NO GOOD.
IT SAYS WE'RE OUT OF RANGE.
RANGE?
BECAUSE WE'RE UNDER-GROUND?
HM...
THIS IS THE FIRST TIME IT'S HAP-PENED TO ME.
......
OH!
ZUUUP
HEY!

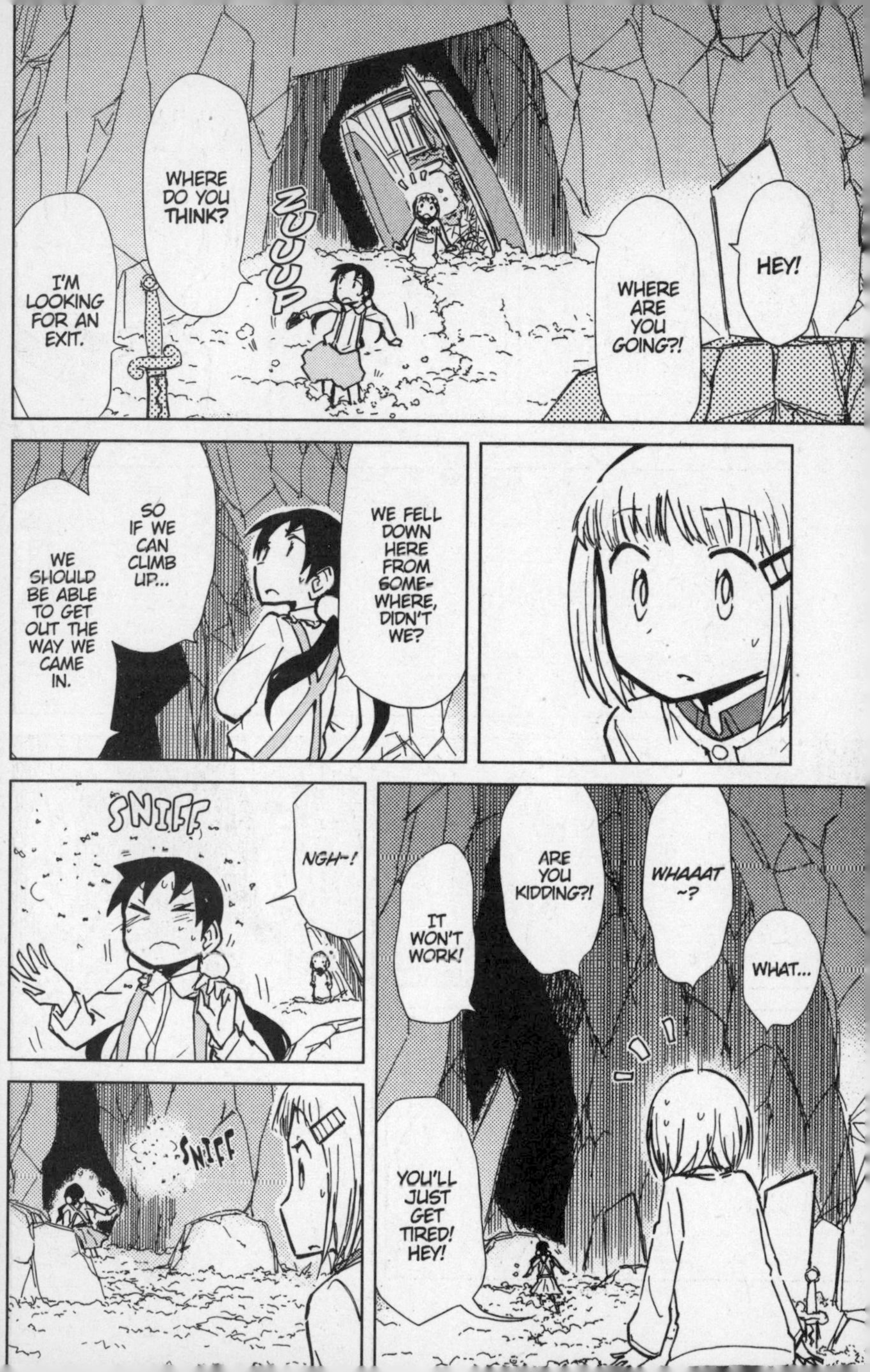
HEY!
WHERE ARE YOU GOING?!
ZUUUP
WHERE DO YOU THINK?
I'M LOOKING FOR AN EXIT.
WE FELL DOWN HERE FROM SOME-WHERE, DIDN'T WE?
SO IF WE CAN CLIMB UP...
WE SHOULD BE ABLE TO GET OUT THE WAY WE CAME IN.
WHAAAT ~?
ARE YOU KIDDING?!
WHAT...
IT WON'T WORK!
YOU'LL JUST GET TIRED! HEY!
NGH~!
SNIFF
SNIFF

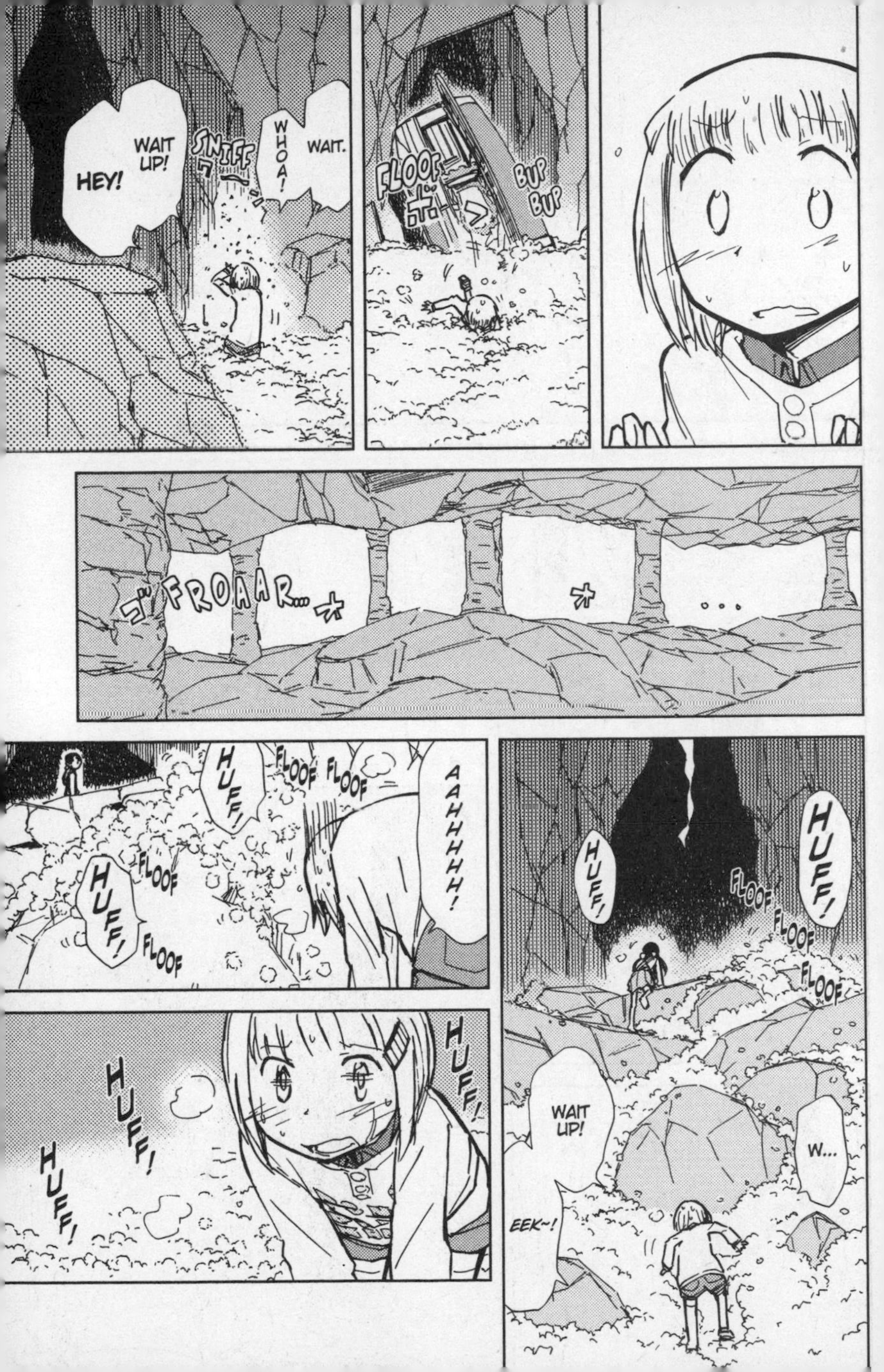
BUP BUP
FLOOF
WAIT.
WHOA!
SNIFF
WAIT UP!
HEY!
...
FROAAR...
HUFF!
HUFF!
FLOOF FLOOF FLOOF
W...
WAIT UP!
EEK~!
AAHHHHH!
FLOOF FLOOF
HUFF!
FLOOF
HUFF!
FLOOF
HUFF!
HUFF!
HUFF!

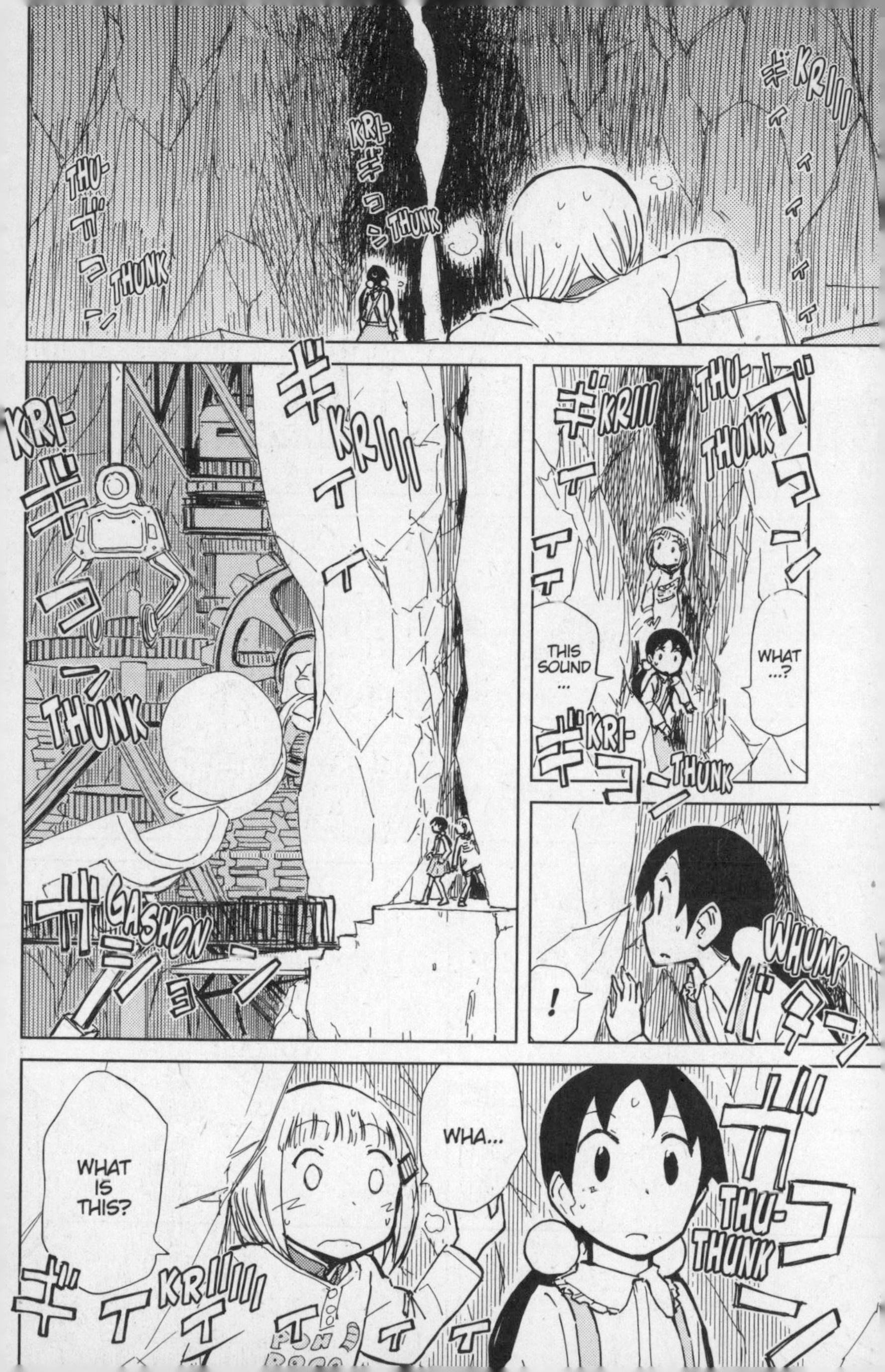
KRIIII
KRI- THUNK
THU- THUNK
THU- THUNK
KRIIII
WHAT ...?
THIS SOUND ...
KRI- THUNK
WHUMP
!
KRIIII
KRI- THUNK
GASHON
THU- THUNK
WHA...
WHAT IS THIS?
KRIIIIII

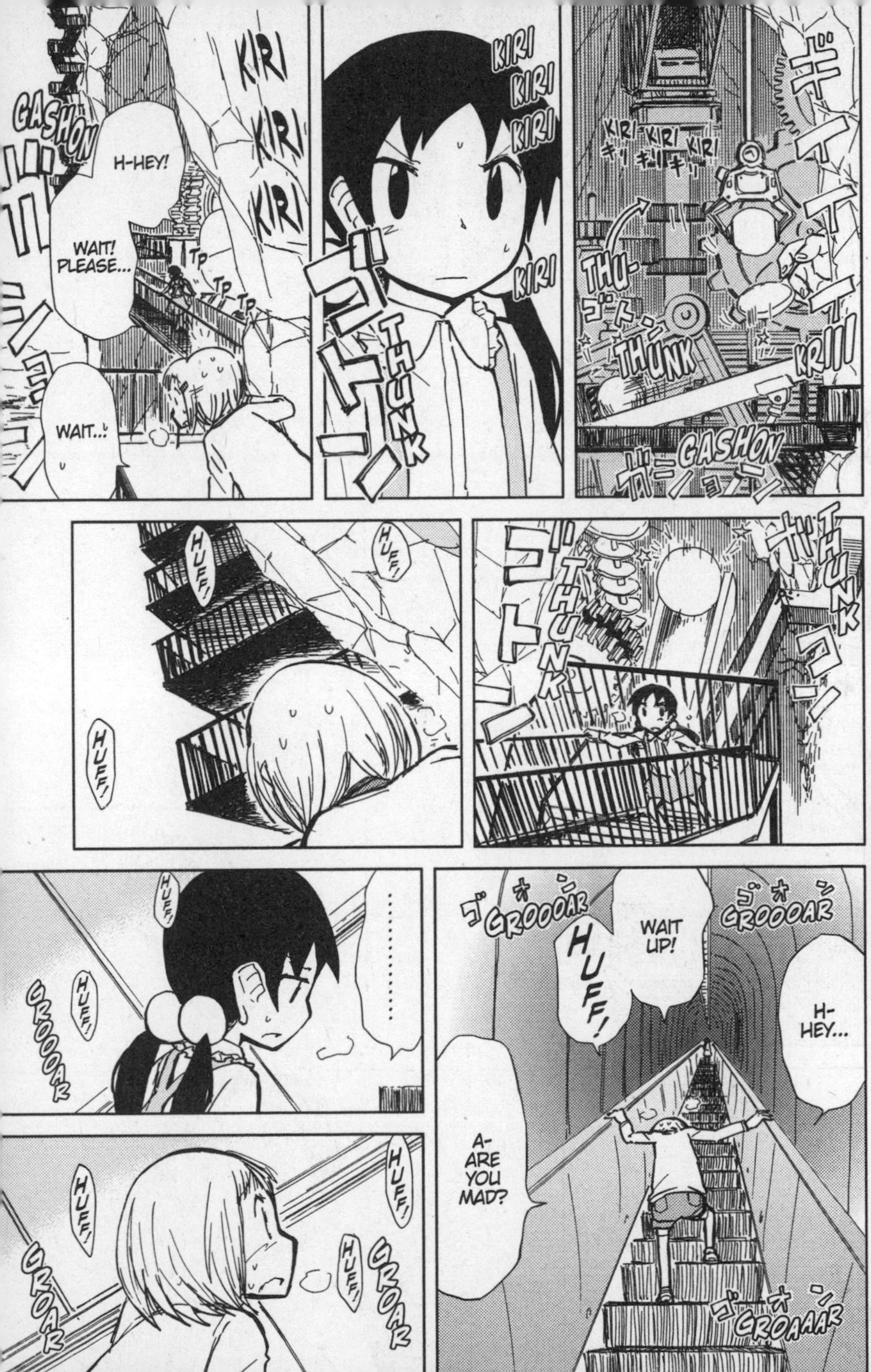
KIRI KIRI KIRI
THU-
THUNK
KRIII
GASHON
KIRI KIRI KIRI
KIRI
THUNK
KIRI KIRI KIRI
GASHON
H-HEY!
WAIT! PLEASE...
TP TP TP TP
WAIT...!
THUNK
THUNK
HUFF!
HUFF!
HUFF!
GROOOAR
WAIT UP!
HUFF!
GROOOAR
H-HEY...
A-ARE YOU MAD?
GROAAAR
HUFF!
......
HUFF!
GROOOAR
HUFF!
HUFF!
HUFF!
HUFF!
GROAR
GROAR

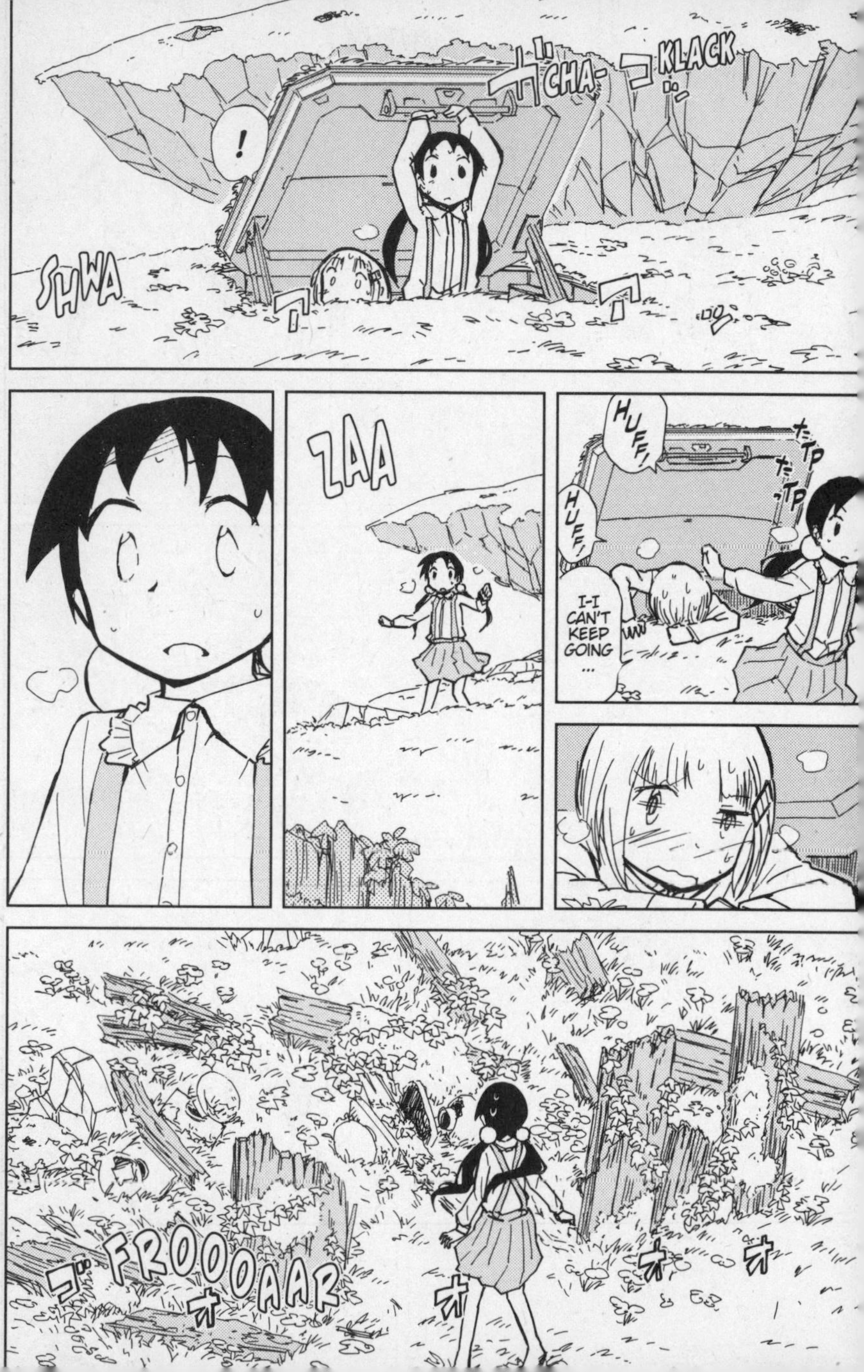

CHA-
KLACK
!
SHWA
TP
TP
HUFF!
HUFF!
I-I CAN'T KEEP GOING ...
ZAA
FROOOAAR

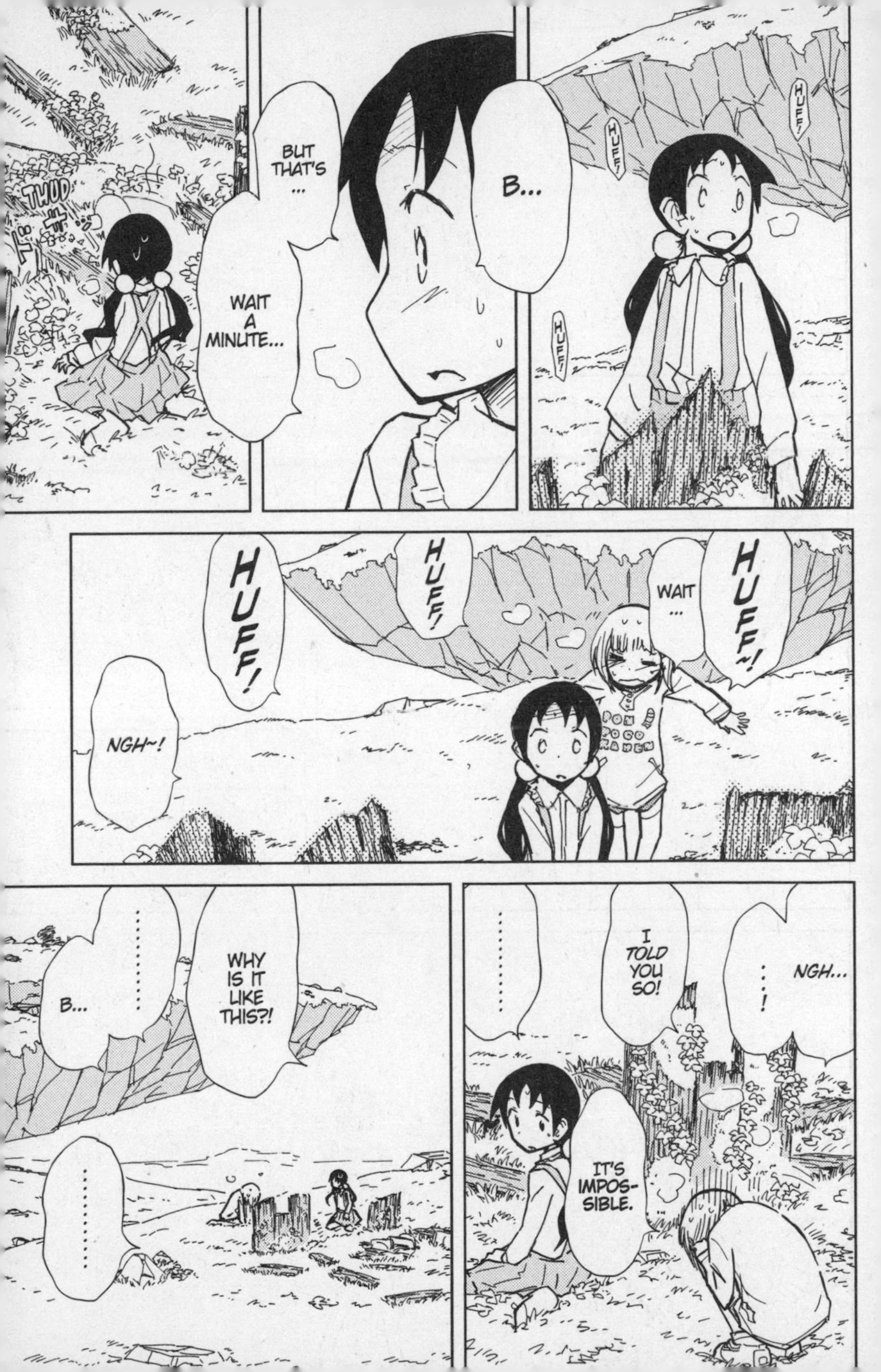
HUFF!
HUFF!
HUFF!
B...
BUT THAT'S ...
WAIT A MINUTE...
THUD
HUFF~!
WAIT ...
HUFF!
HUFF!
NGH~!
NGH...
...!
I TOLD YOU SO!
......
IT'S IMPOSSIBLE. ...
WHY IS IT LIKE THIS?!
......
B...
......

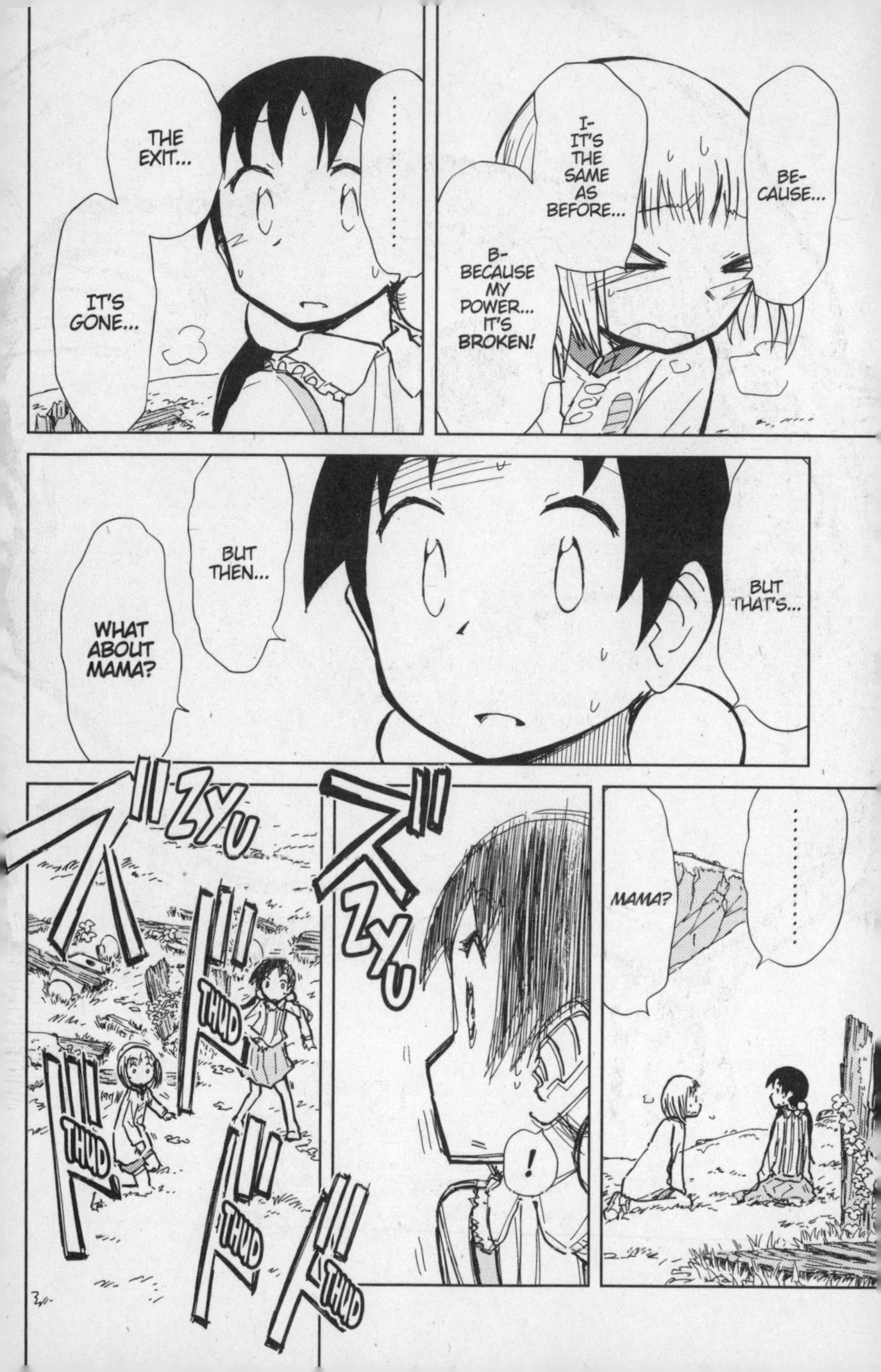
BE-CAUSE...
I- IT'S THE SAME AS BEFORE...
B-BECAUSE MY POWER... IT'S BROKEN!
......
THE EXIT...
IT'S GONE...
BUT THAT'S...
BUT THEN...
WHAT ABOUT MAMA?
......
MAMA?
ZYU
!
ZYU
THUD
THUD
THUD
THUD

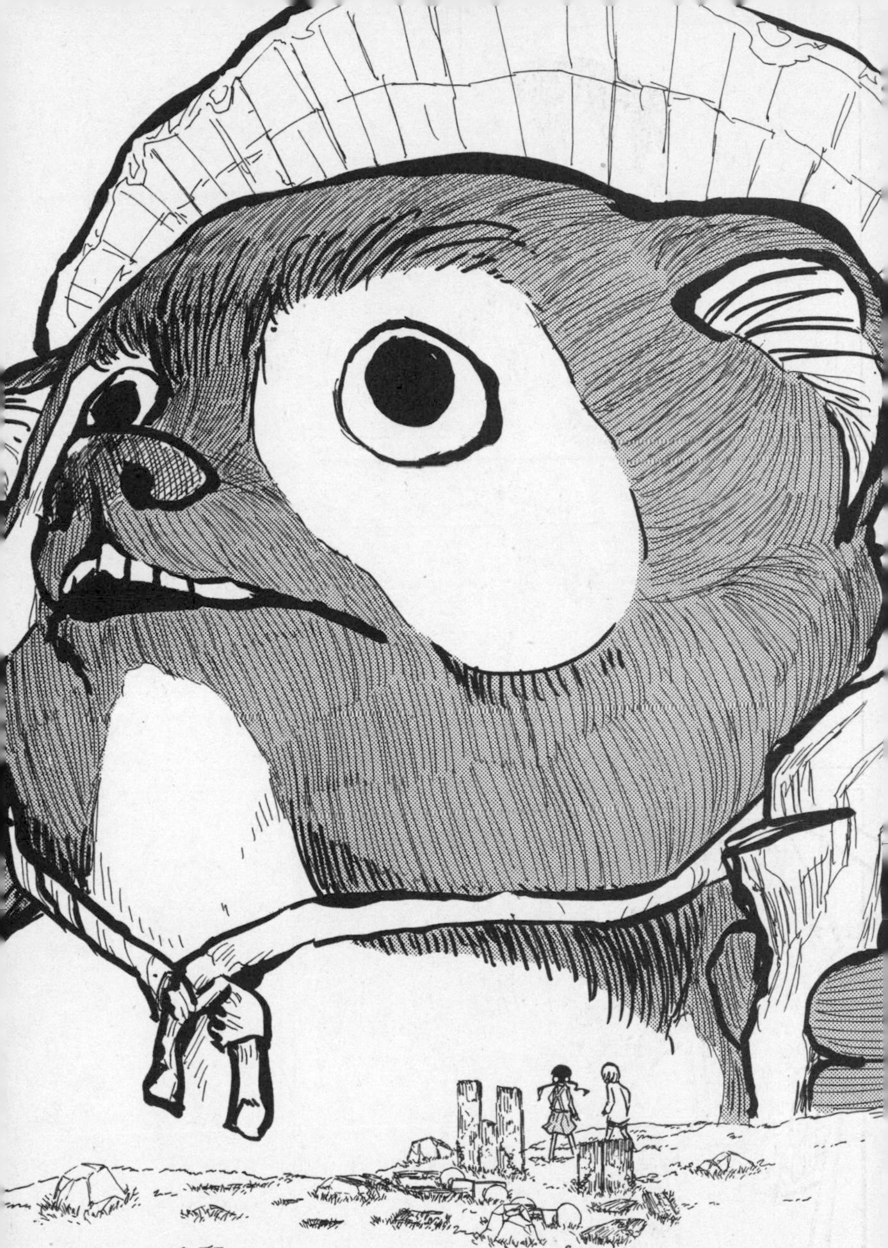

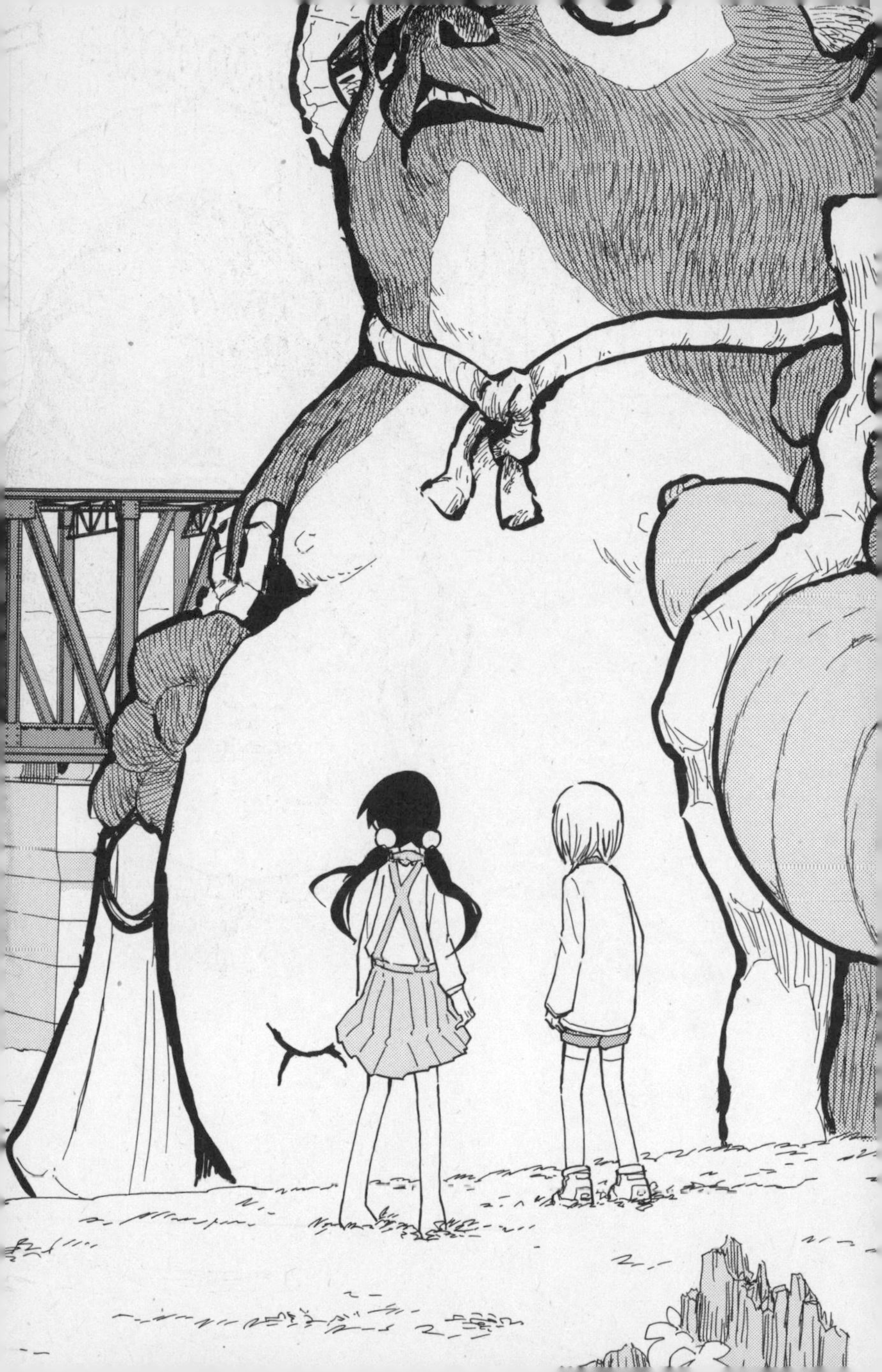

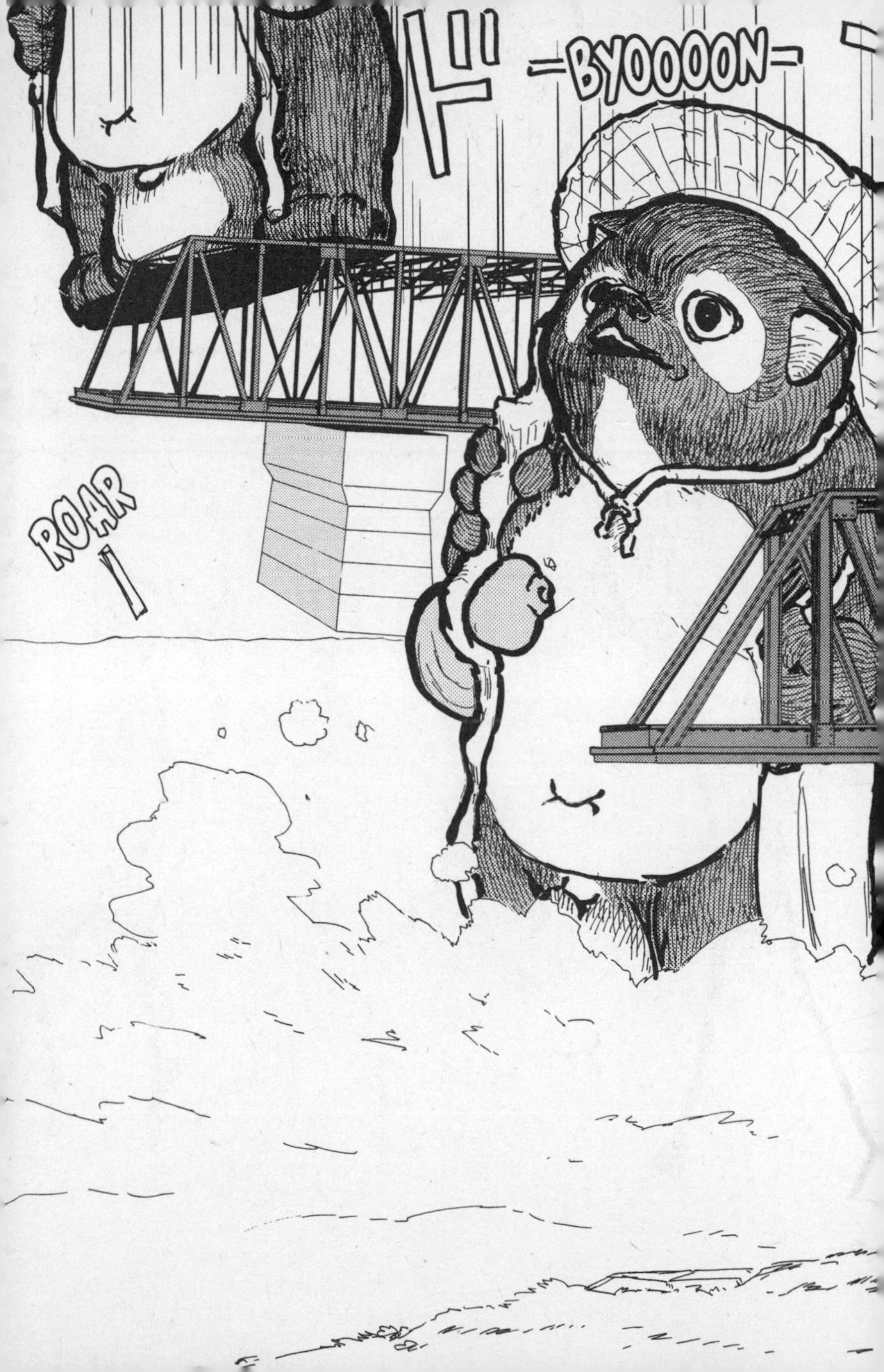
=BYOOOON=
ROAR

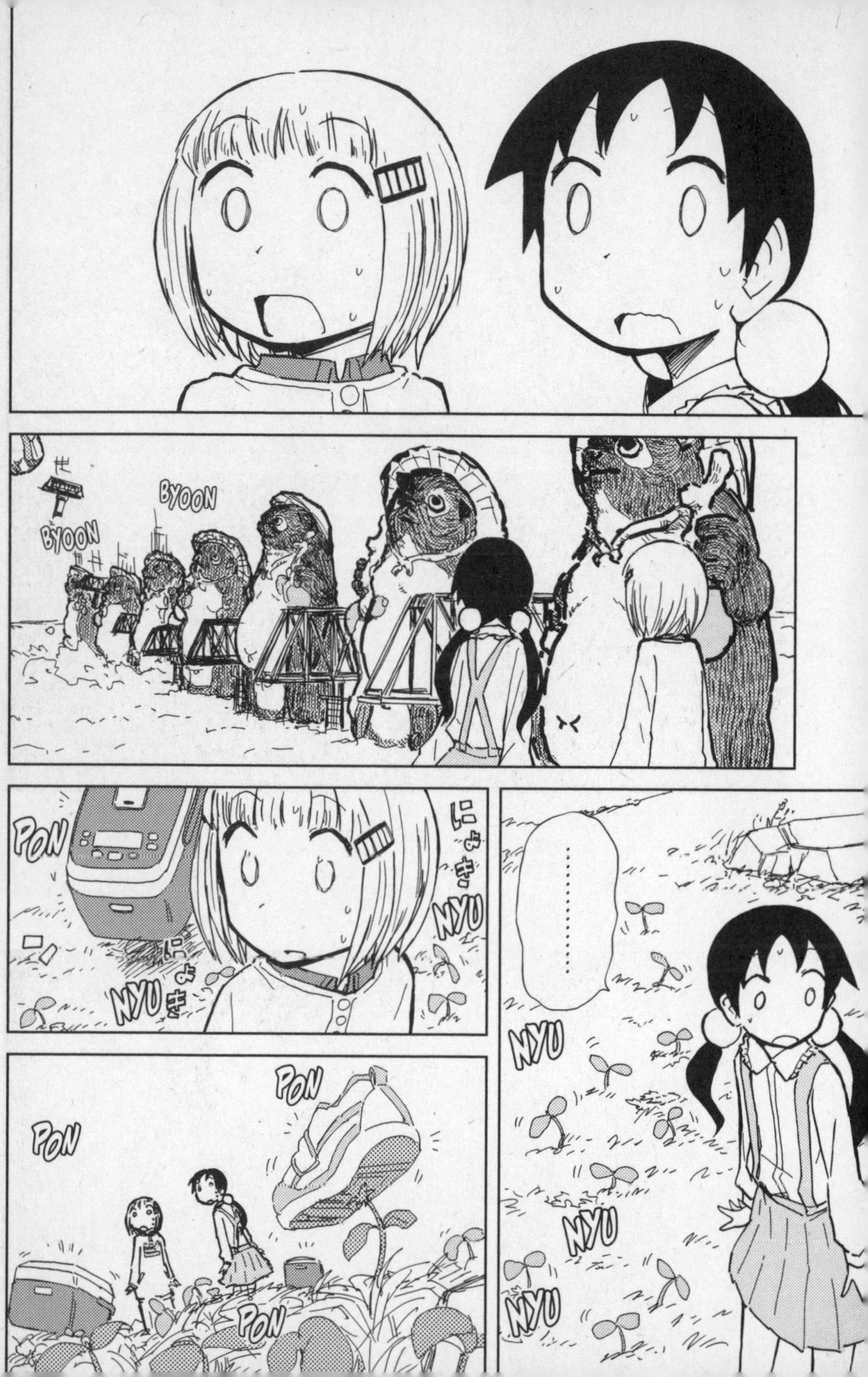
BYOON
BYOON
……
NYU
NYU
NYU
にょき
NYU
PON
にょき
NYU
PON
PON
PON

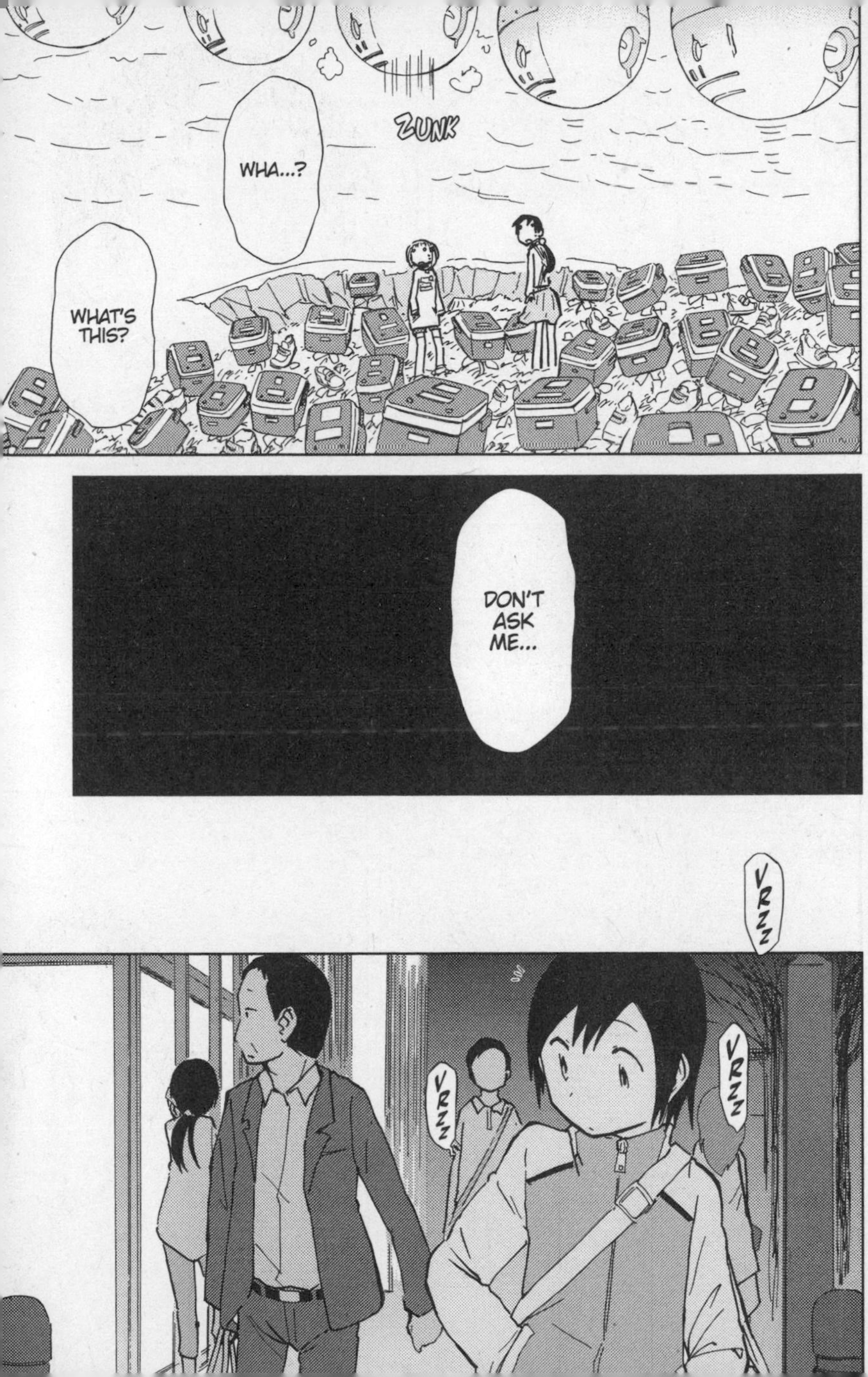
ZUNK
WHA...?
WHAT'S THIS?
DON'T ASK ME...
VRZZ
VRZZ
VRZZ

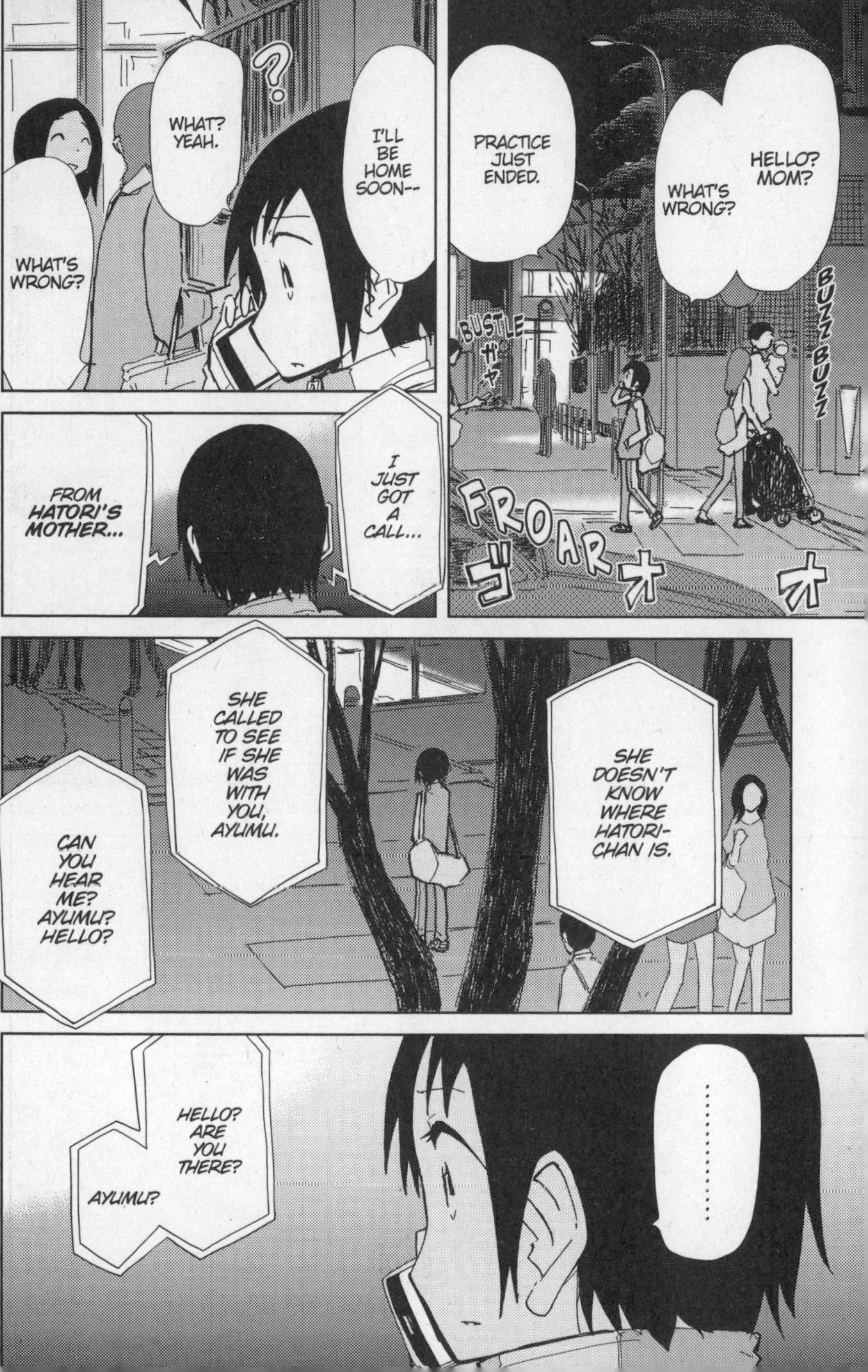
HELLO? MOM?
WHAT'S WRONG?
PRACTICE JUST ENDED.
BUZZ BUZZ
BUSTLE ガヤ
FROAR ゴオオ
I'LL BE HOME SOON--
?
WHAT? YEAH.
WHAT'S WRONG?
I JUST GOT A CALL...
FROM HATORI'S MOTHER...
SHE DOESN'T KNOW WHERE HATORI-CHAN IS.
SHE CALLED TO SEE IF SHE WAS WITH YOU, AYUMU.
CAN YOU HEAR ME? AYUMU? HELLO?
......
HELLO? ARE YOU THERE?
AYUMU?

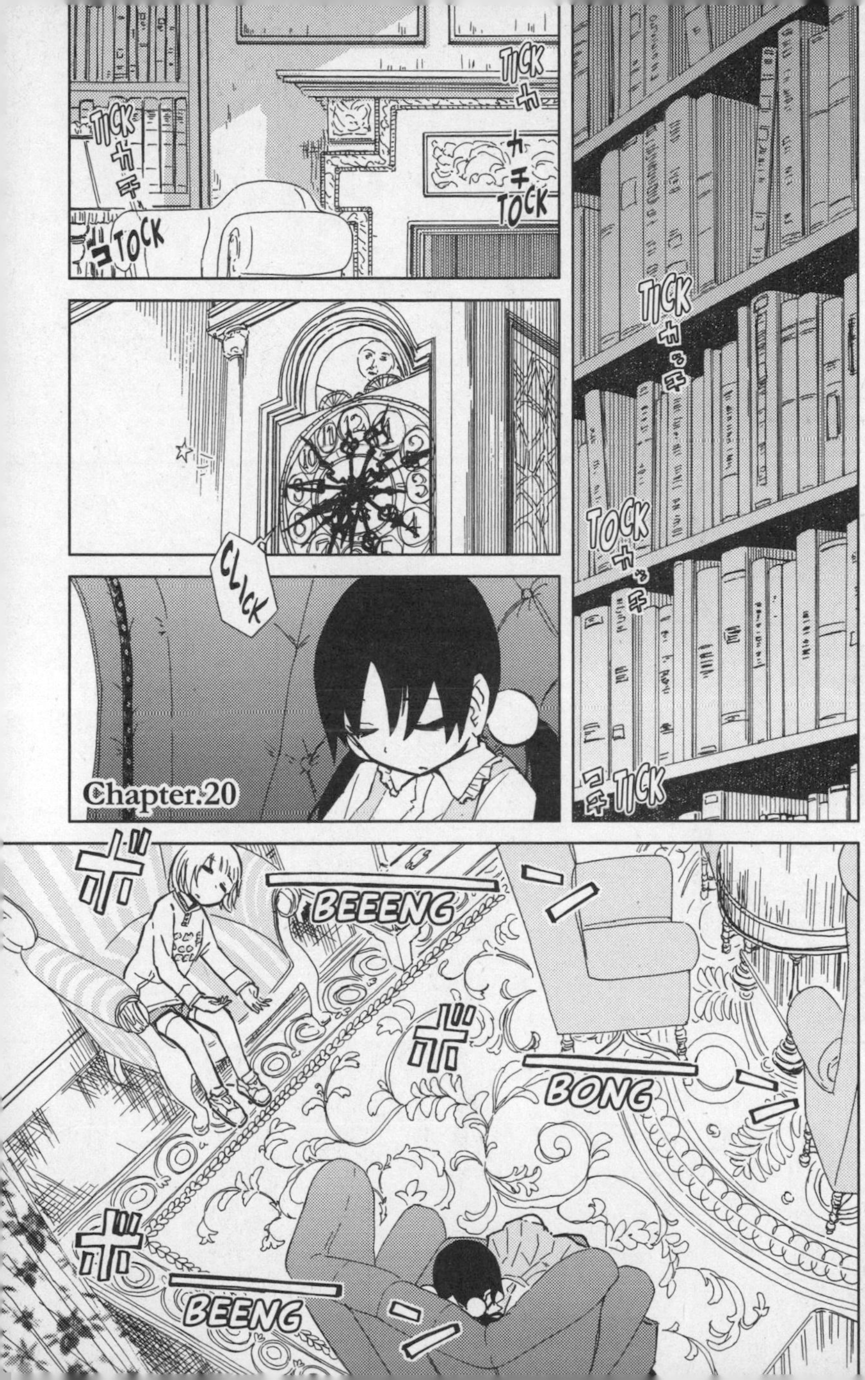
TICK
カチ
TOCK
カチ
TICK
TICK
カチ
TOCK
TICK
カチ
TOCK
CLICK
Chapter.20
ボーン
BEEENG
ボーン
BONG
ボーン
BEENG

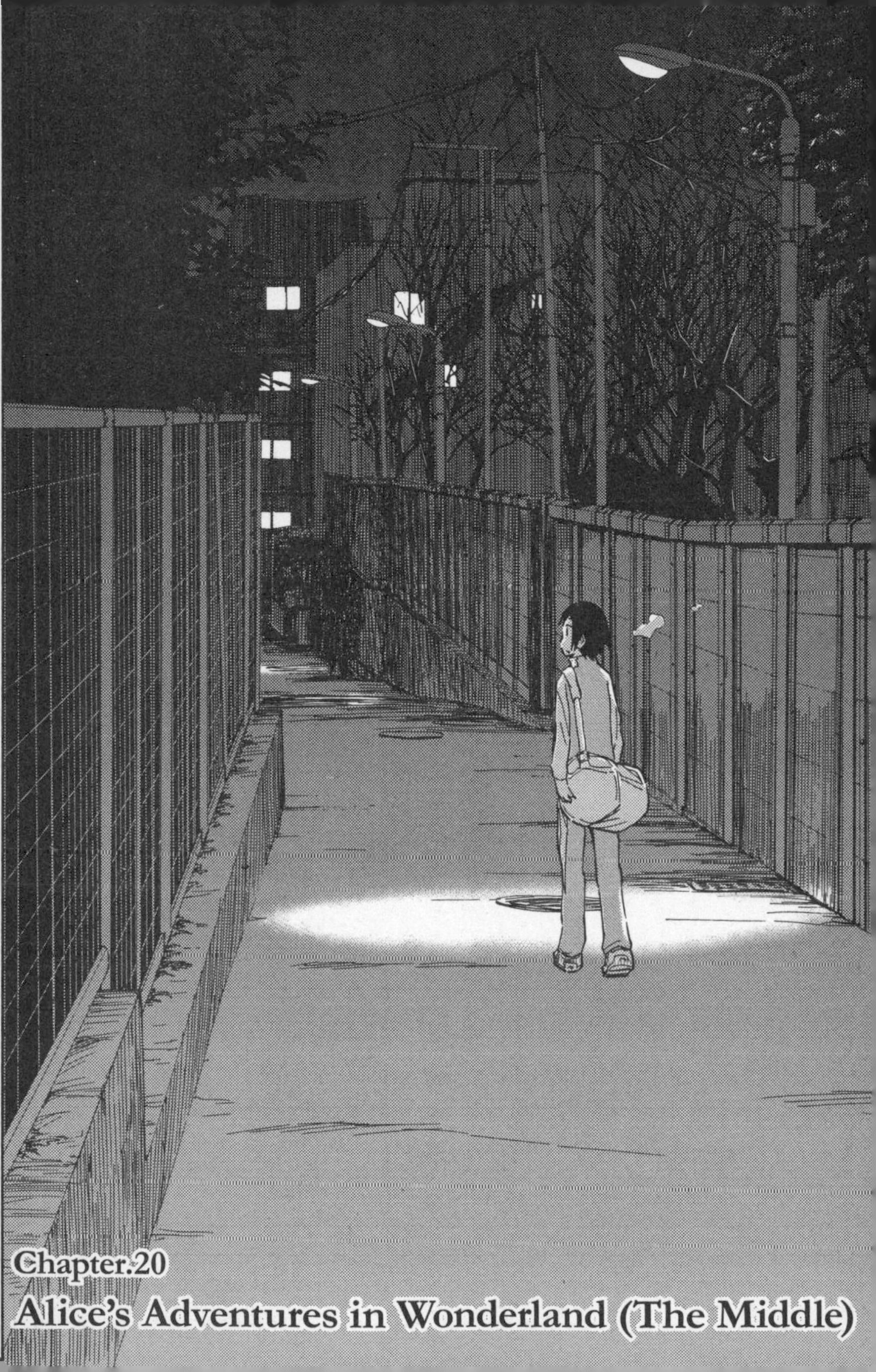
Chapter.20
Alice's Adventures in Wonderland (The Middle)

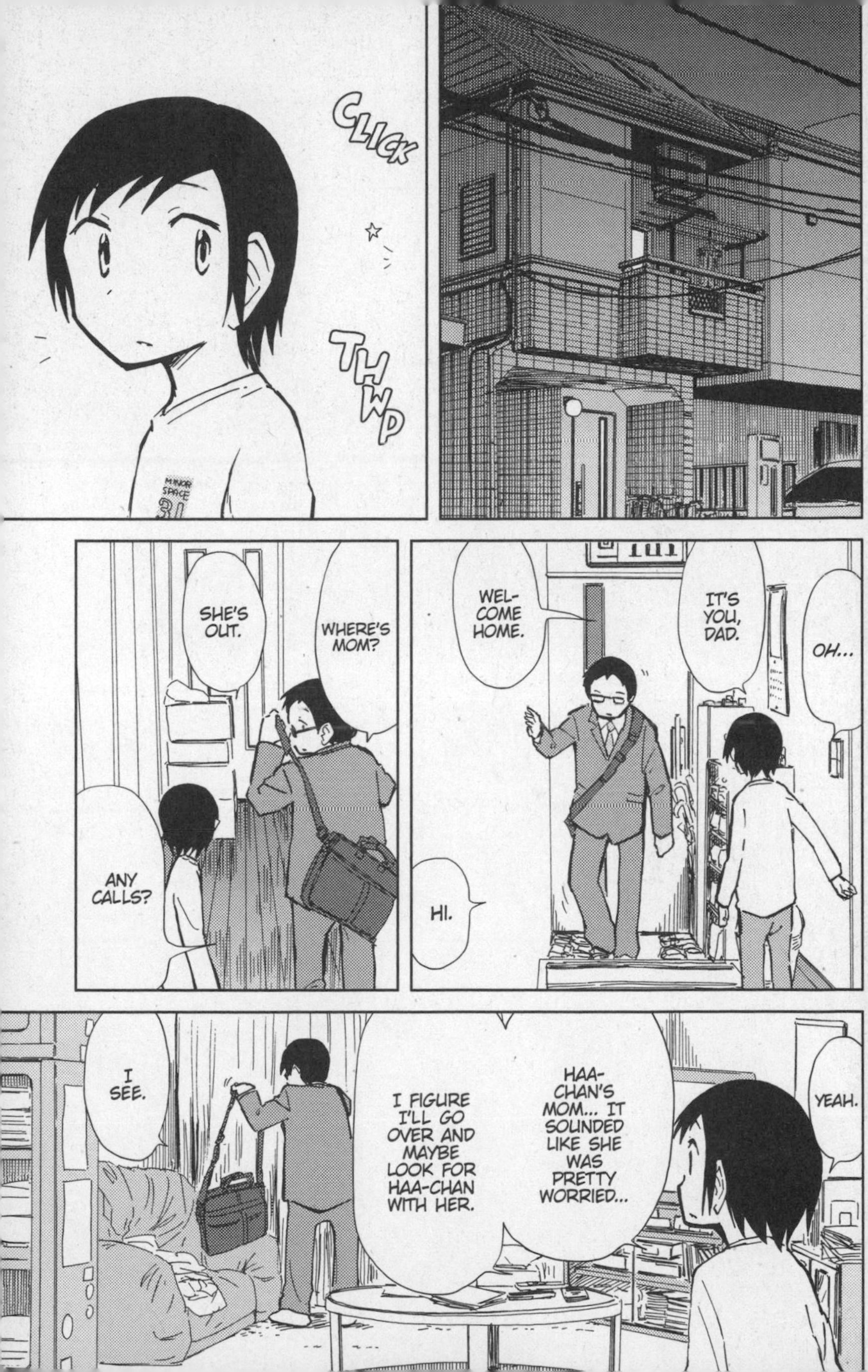
CLICK
THWP
OH...
IT'S YOU, DAD.
WEL-COME HOME.
HI.
WHERE'S MOM?
SHE'S OUT.
ANY CALLS?
YEAH.
HAA-CHAN'S MOM... IT SOUNDED LIKE SHE WAS PRETTY WORRIED...
I FIGURE I'LL GO OVER AND MAYBE LOOK FOR HAA-CHAN WITH HER.
I SEE.

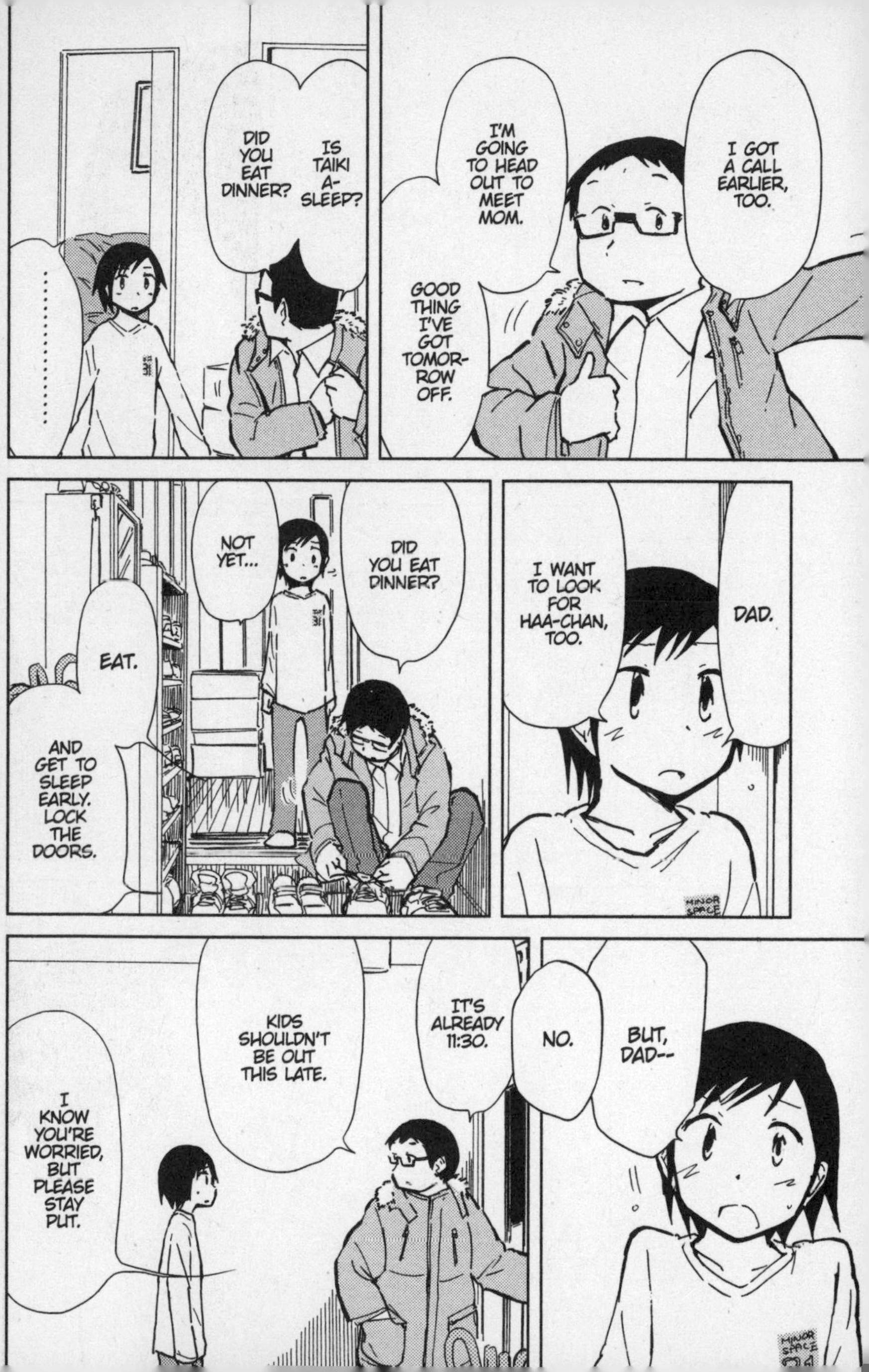
I GOT A CALL EARLIER, TOO.
I'M GOING TO HEAD OUT TO MEET MOM.
GOOD THING I'VE GOT TOMORROW OFF.
IS TAIKI ASLEEP?
DID YOU EAT DINNER?
......
DAD.
I WANT TO LOOK FOR HAA-CHAN, TOO.
DID YOU EAT DINNER?
NOT YET...
EAT.
AND GET TO SLEEP EARLY. LOCK THE DOORS.
BUT, DAD--
NO.
IT'S ALREADY 11:30.
KIDS SHOULDN'T BE OUT THIS LATE.
I KNOW YOU'RE WORRIED, BUT PLEASE STAY PUT.

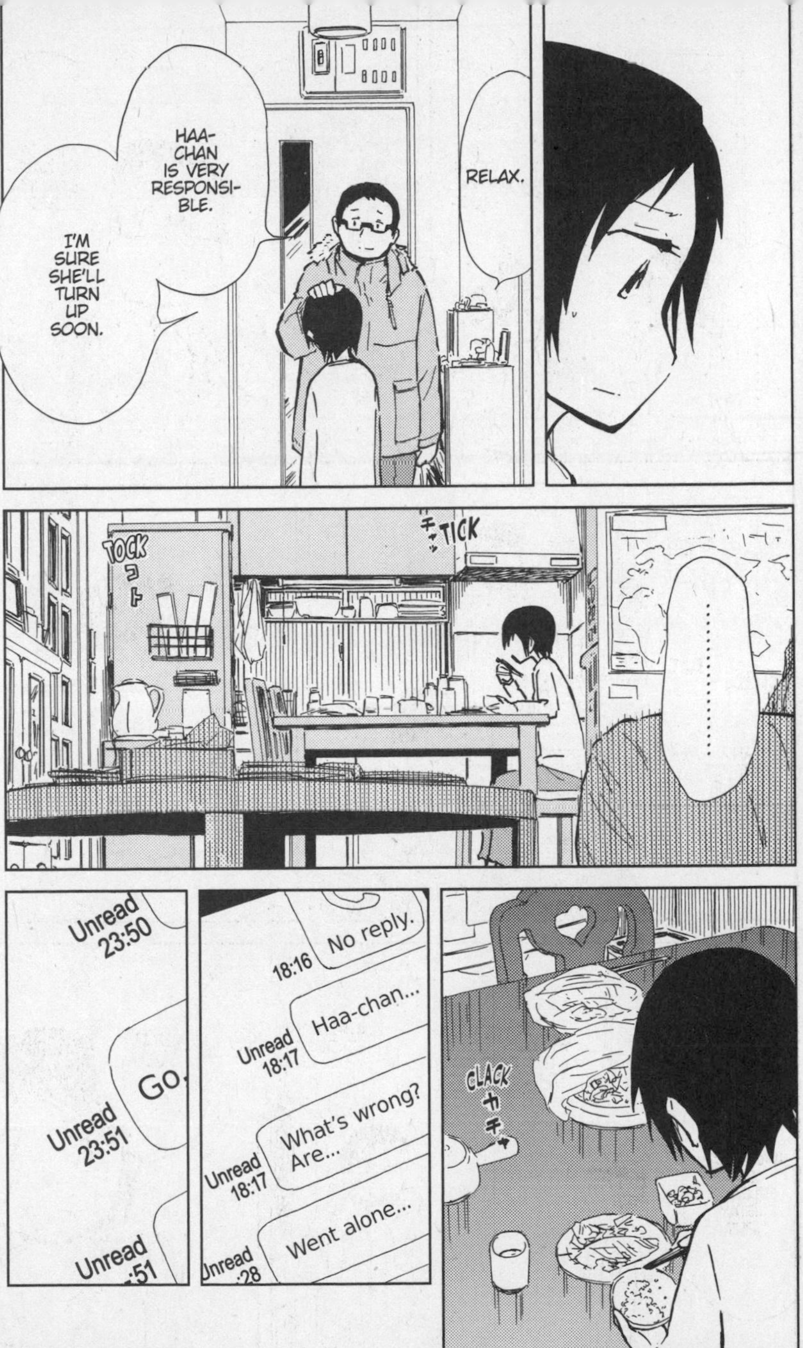
RELAX.
HAA-CHAN IS VERY RESPONSIBLE.
I'M SURE SHE'LL TURN UP SOON.
TICK
チッ
TOCK
コト
......
CLACK
カチャ
No reply.
18:16
Haa-chan...
Unread
18:17
What's wrong? Are...
Unread
18:17
Went alone...
Unread
:28
Unread
23:50
Go.
Unread
23:51
Unread
:51

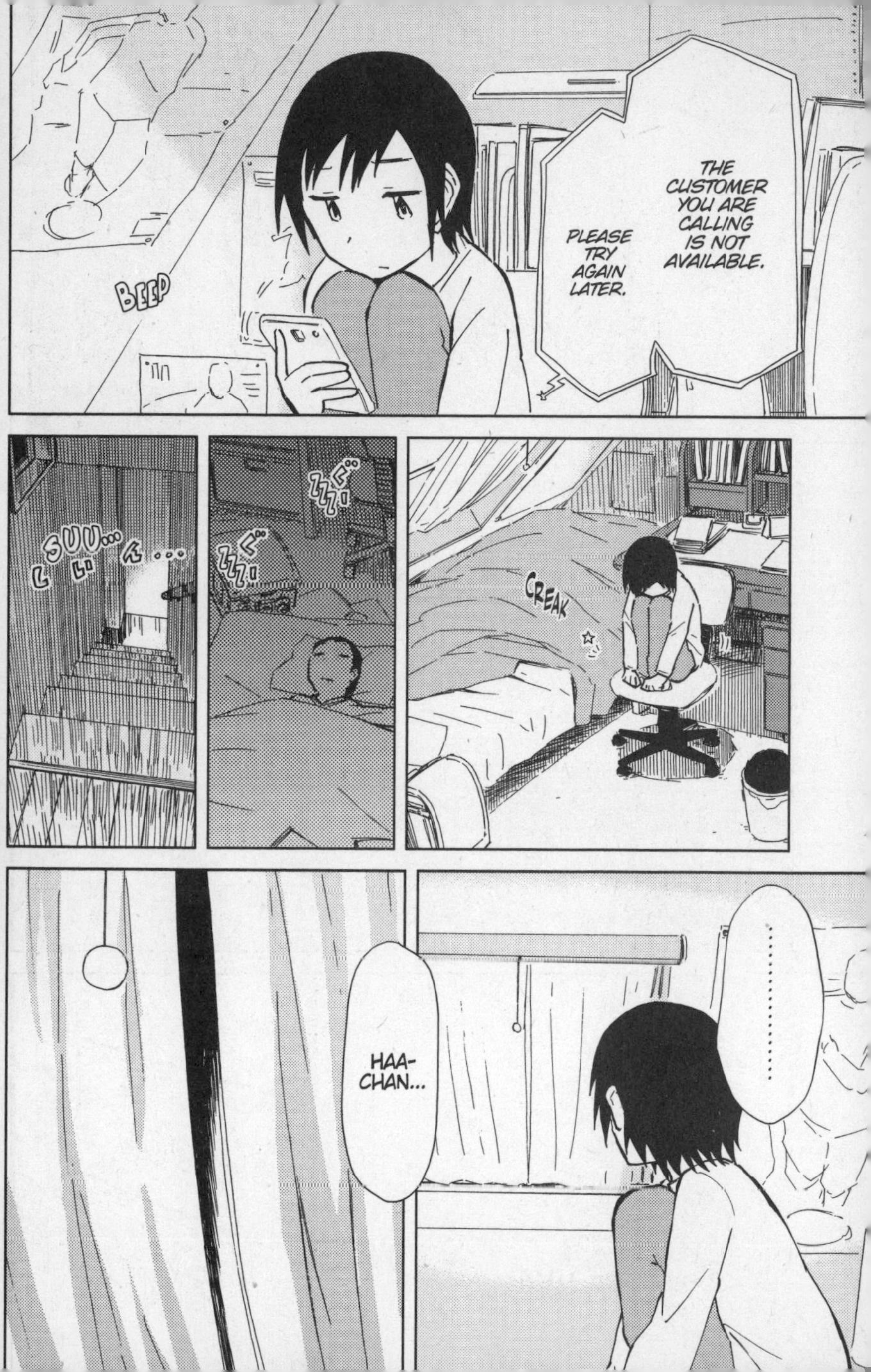
THE CUSTOMER YOU ARE CALLING IS NOT AVAILABLE.
PLEASE TRY AGAIN LATER.
BEEP
CREAK
ぐ ZZZ!
ぐ ZZZ!
SUU...
しぃん...
......
HAA-CHAN...

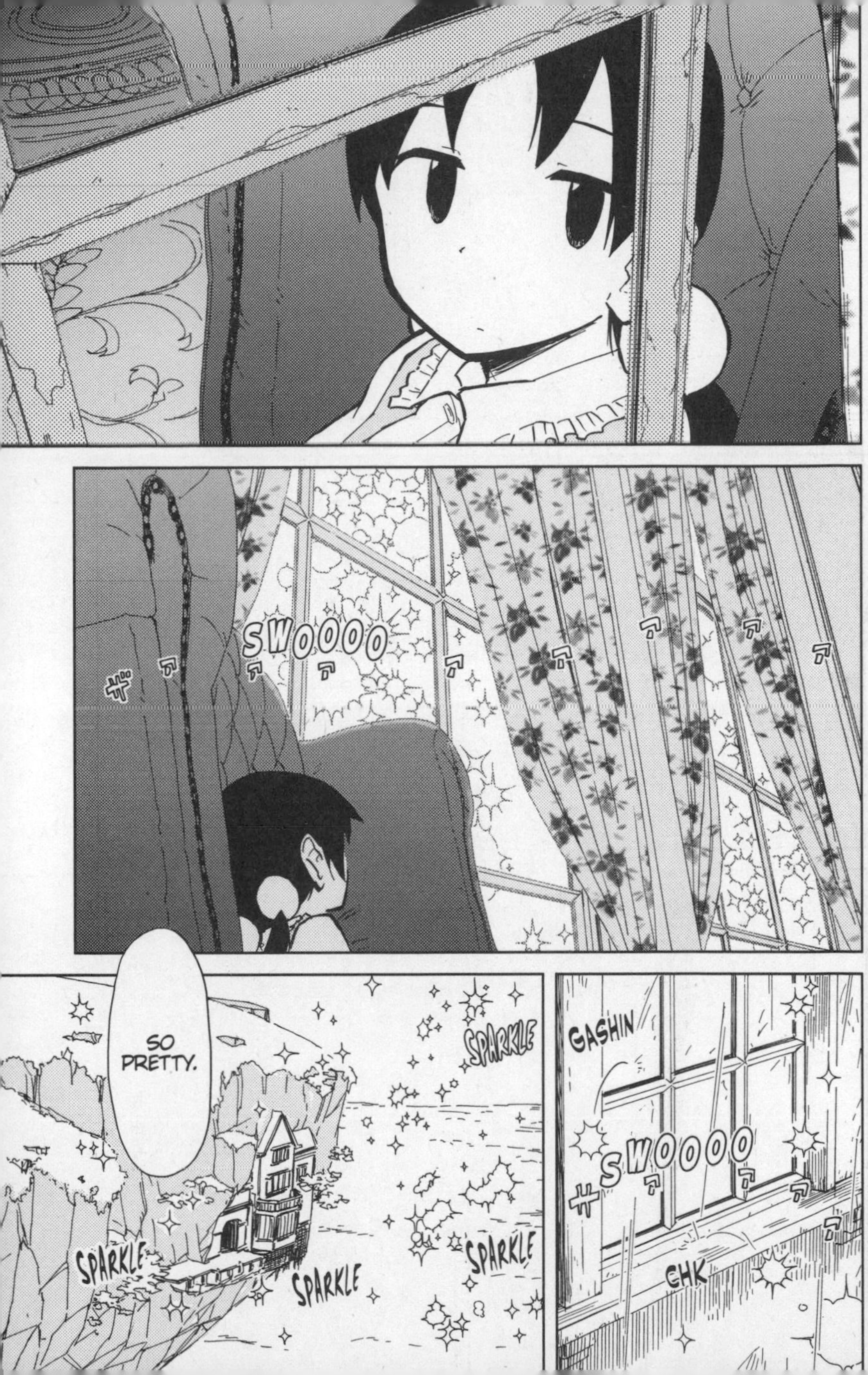
SWOOOO
GASHIN
SWOOOO
CHK
SO PRETTY.
SPARKLE
SPARKLE
SPARKLE
SPARKLE

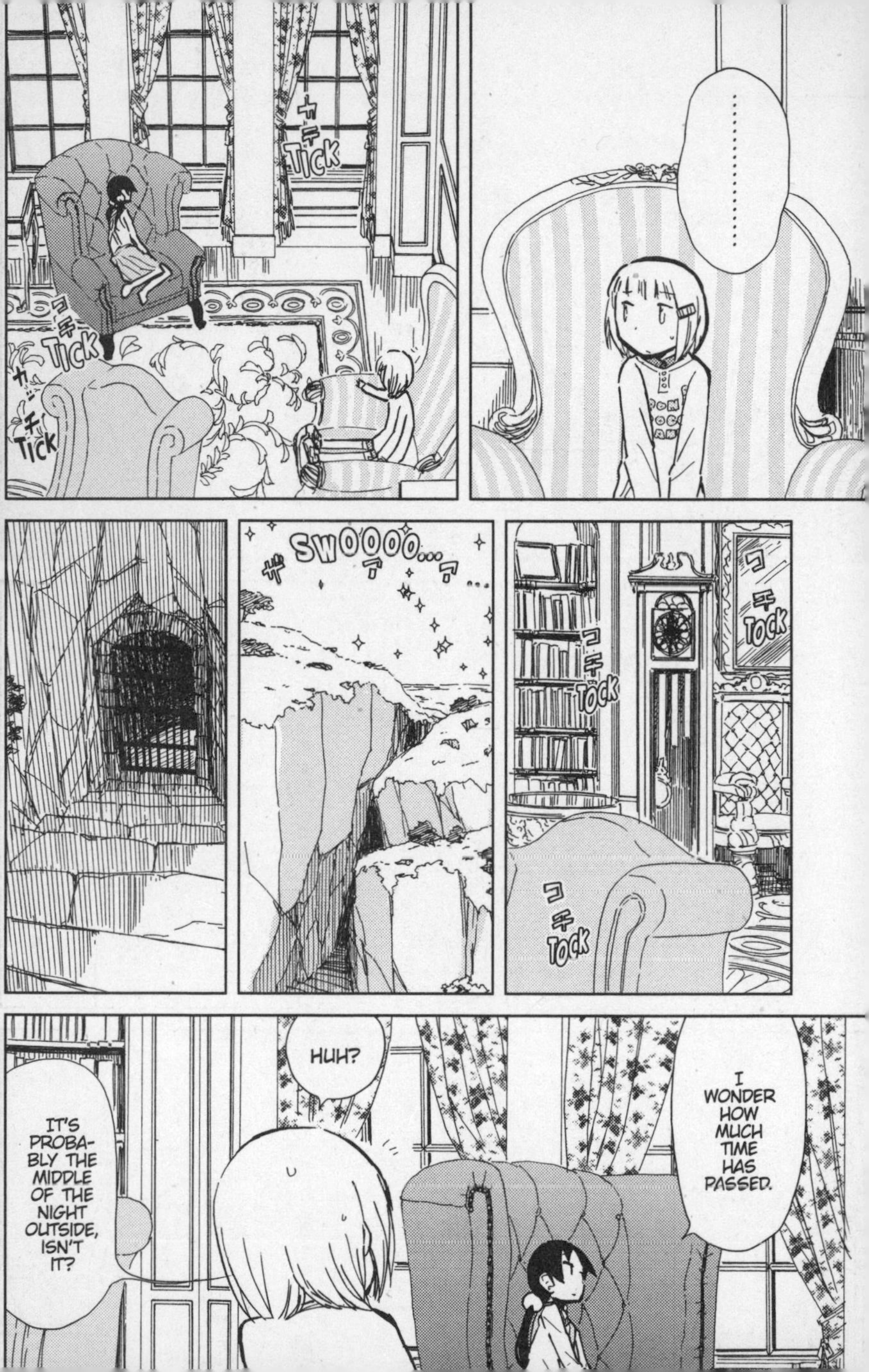
......
TICK
TICK
TICK
TOCK
TOCK
TOCK
SWOOOO...
I WONDER HOW MUCH TIME HAS PASSED.
HUH?
IT'S PROBA-BLY THE MIDDLE OF THE NIGHT OUTSIDE, ISN'T IT?

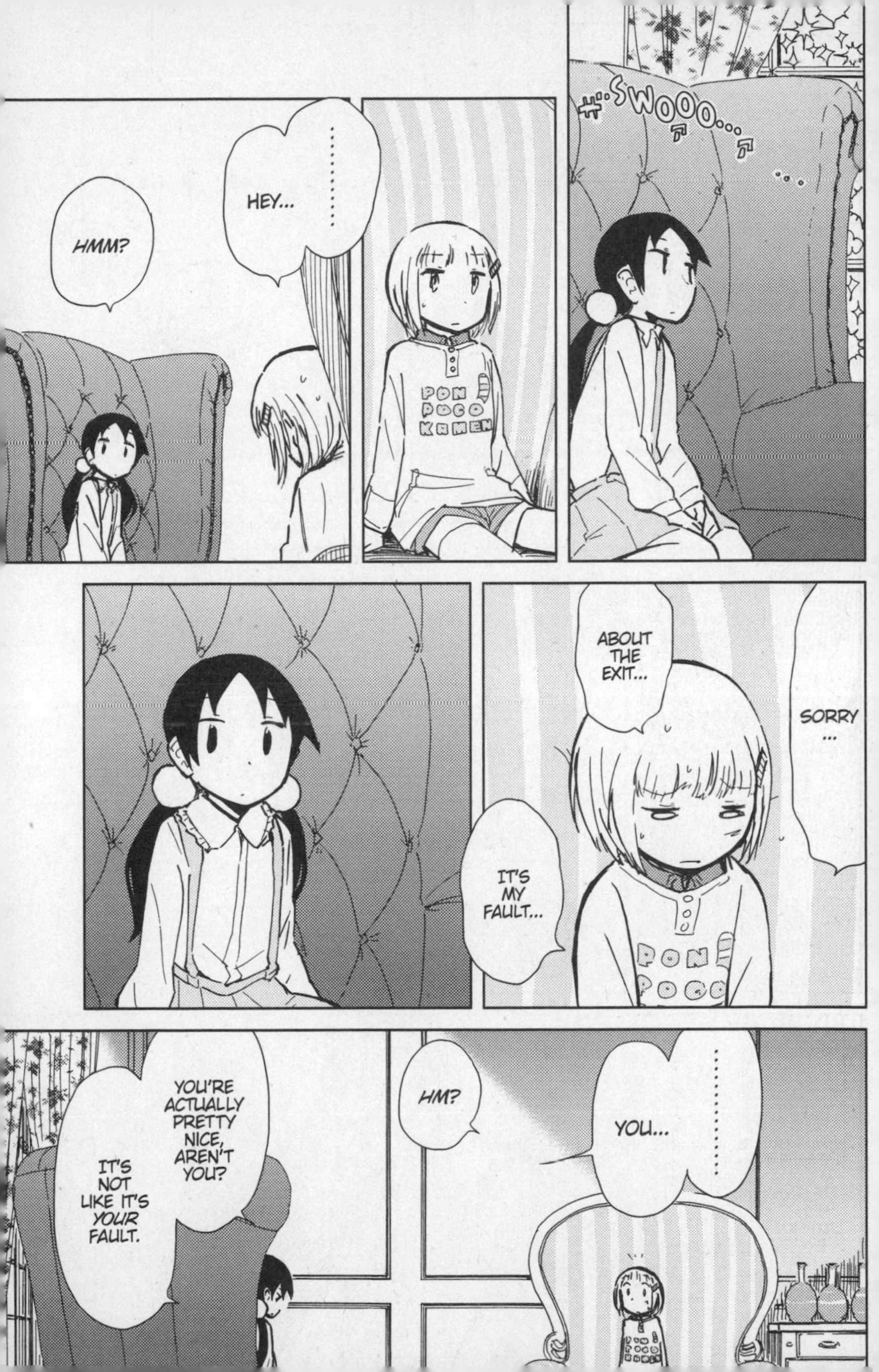
SWOOO...
......
HEY...
HMM?
SORRY...
ABOUT THE EXIT...
IT'S MY FAULT...
......
YOU...
HM?
YOU'RE ACTUALLY PRETTY NICE, AREN'T YOU?
IT'S NOT LIKE IT'S *YOUR* FAULT.

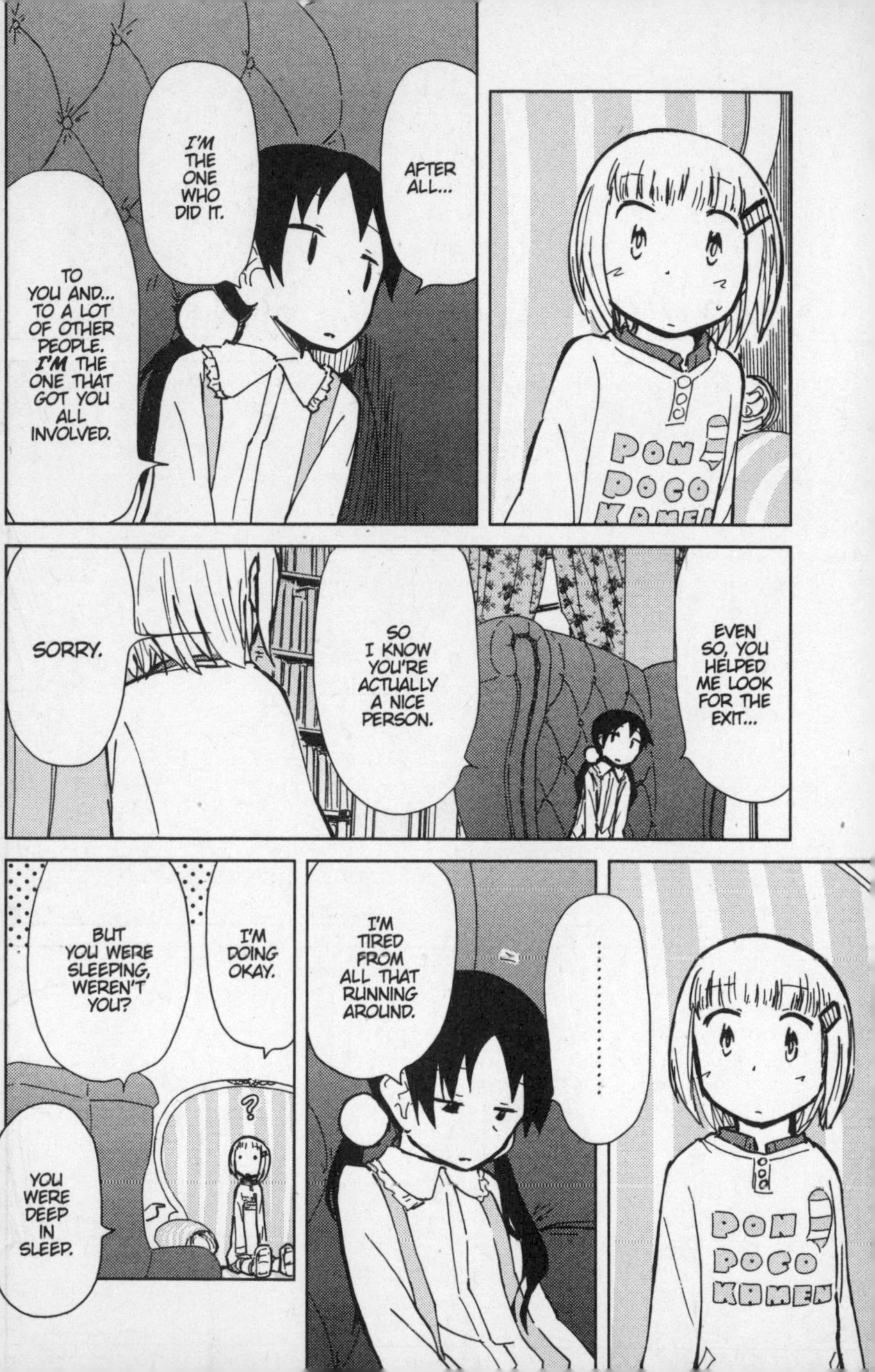
AFTER ALL...
I'M THE ONE WHO DID IT.
TO YOU AND... TO A LOT OF OTHER PEOPLE. *I'M* THE ONE THAT GOT YOU ALL INVOLVED.
EVEN SO, YOU HELPED ME LOOK FOR THE EXIT...
SO I KNOW YOU'RE ACTUALLY A NICE PERSON.
SORRY.
......
I'M TIRED FROM ALL THAT RUNNING AROUND.
I'M DOING OKAY.
BUT YOU WERE SLEEPING, WEREN'T YOU?
?
YOU WERE DEEP IN SLEEP.

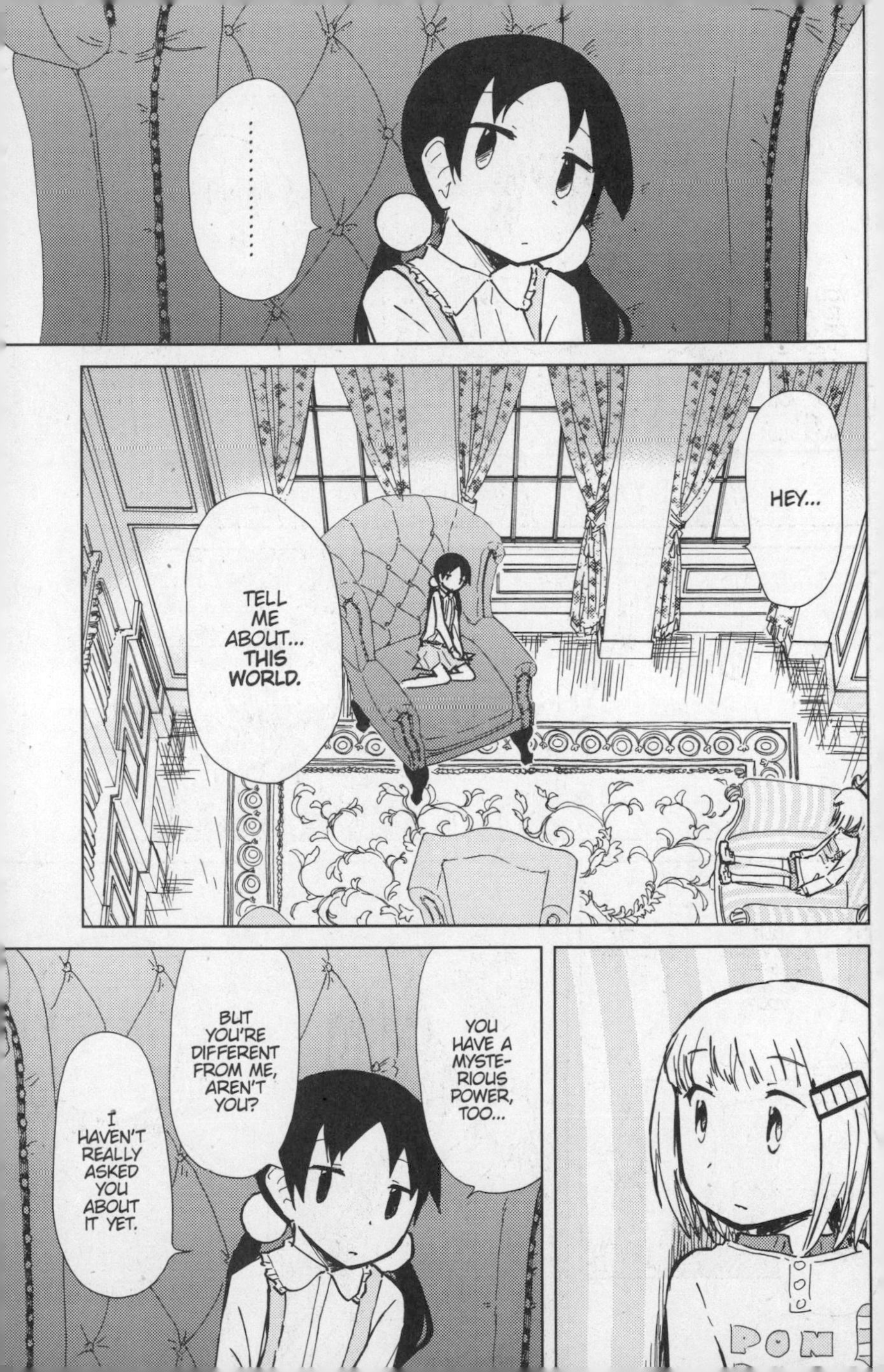
……
HEY...
TELL ME ABOUT... THIS WORLD.
PON
YOU HAVE A MYSTERIOUS POWER, TOO...
BUT YOU'RE DIFFERENT FROM ME, AREN'T YOU?
I HAVEN'T REALLY ASKED YOU ABOUT IT YET.

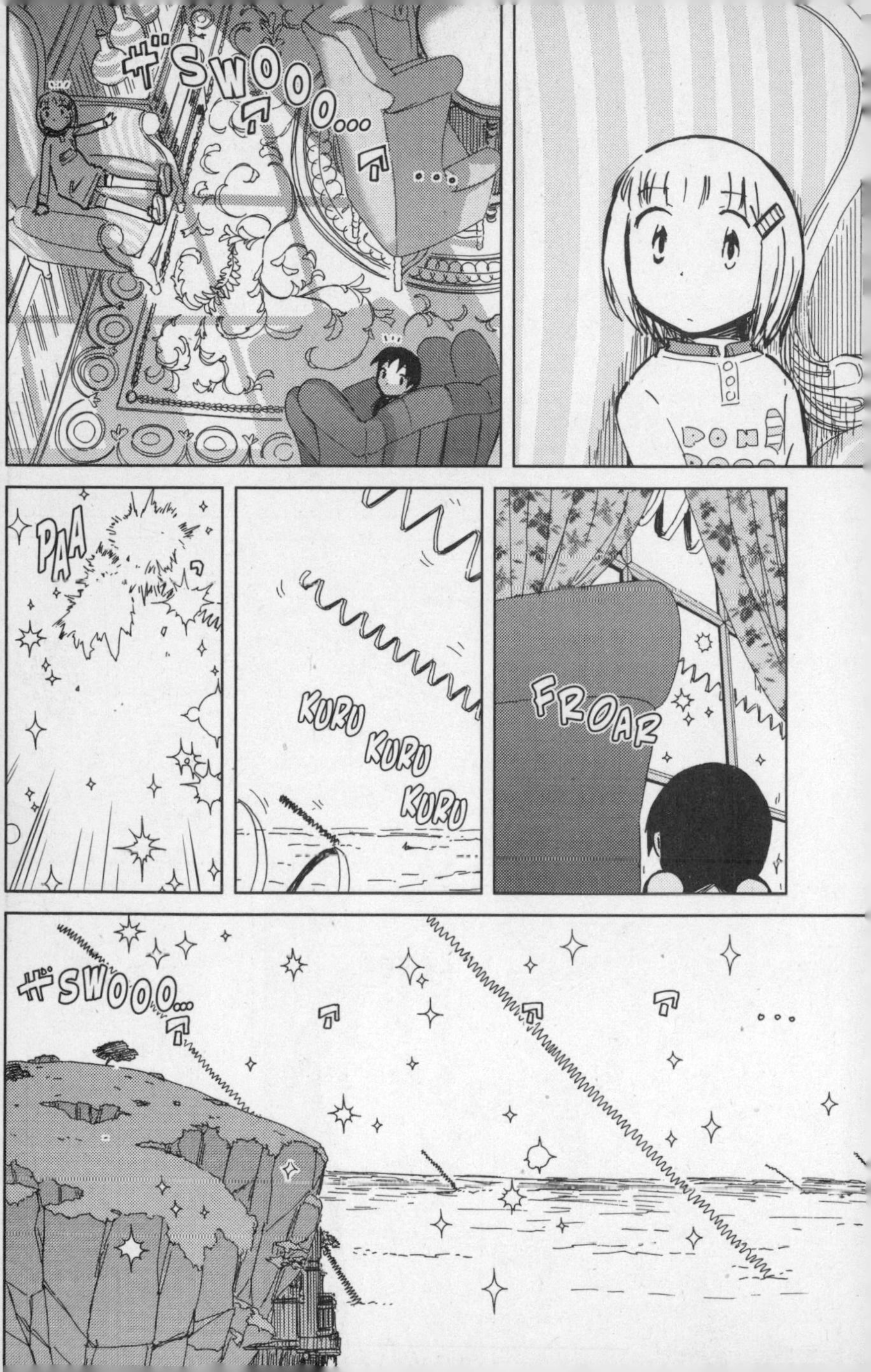
PON
SWOOO...
...
FROAR
KURU KURU KURU
PAA
SWOOO...
...

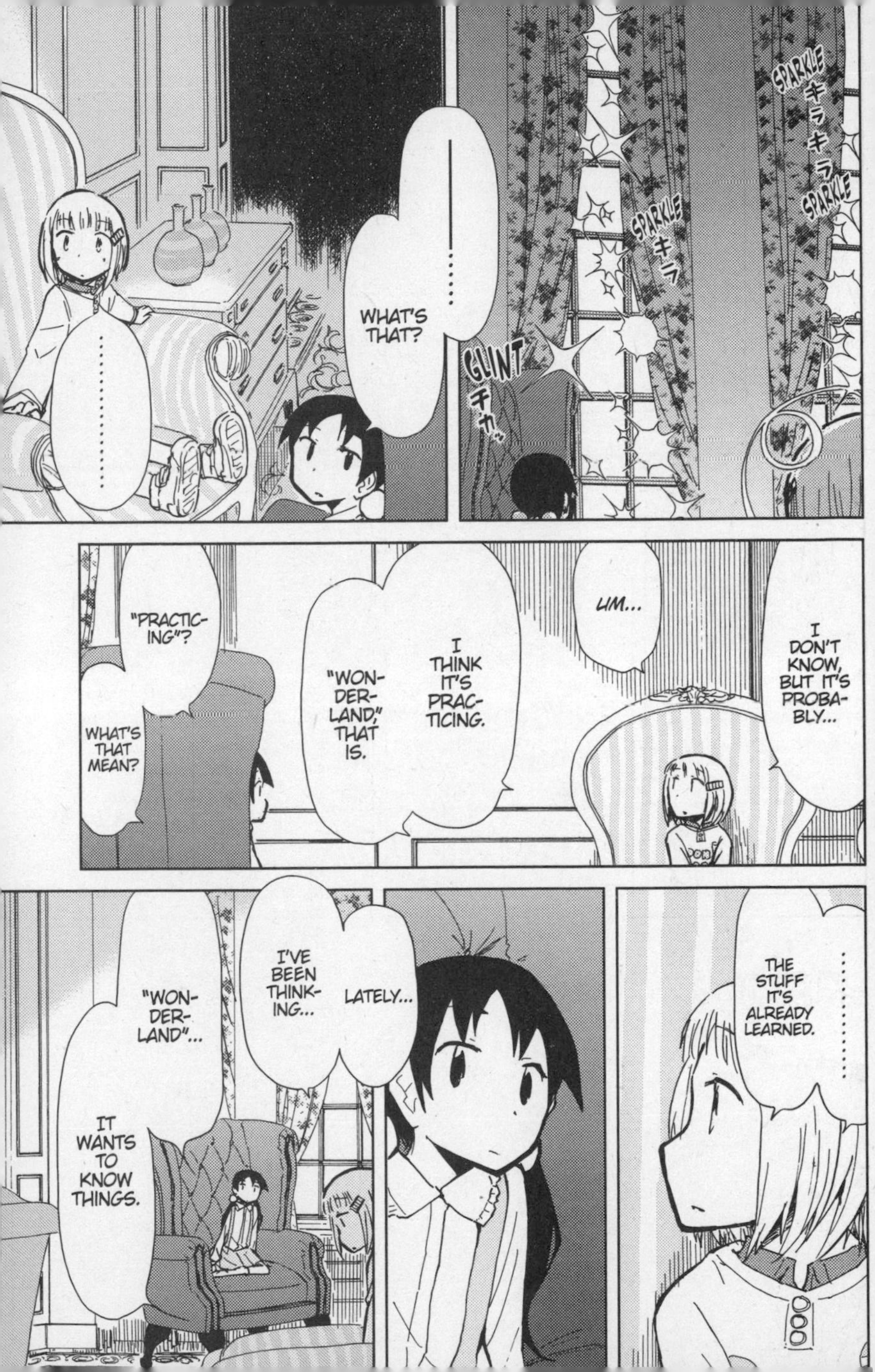
SPARKLE キラキラ SPARKLE
SPARKLE キラ
GLINT チカッ
——......
WHAT'S THAT?
......
I DON'T KNOW, BUT IT'S PROBABLY...
UM...
I THINK IT'S PRACTICING.
"WONDERLAND," THAT IS.
"PRACTICING"?
WHAT'S THAT MEAN?
......
THE STUFF IT'S ALREADY LEARNED.
LATELY...
I'VE BEEN THINKING...
"WONDERLAND"...
IT WANTS TO KNOW THINGS.

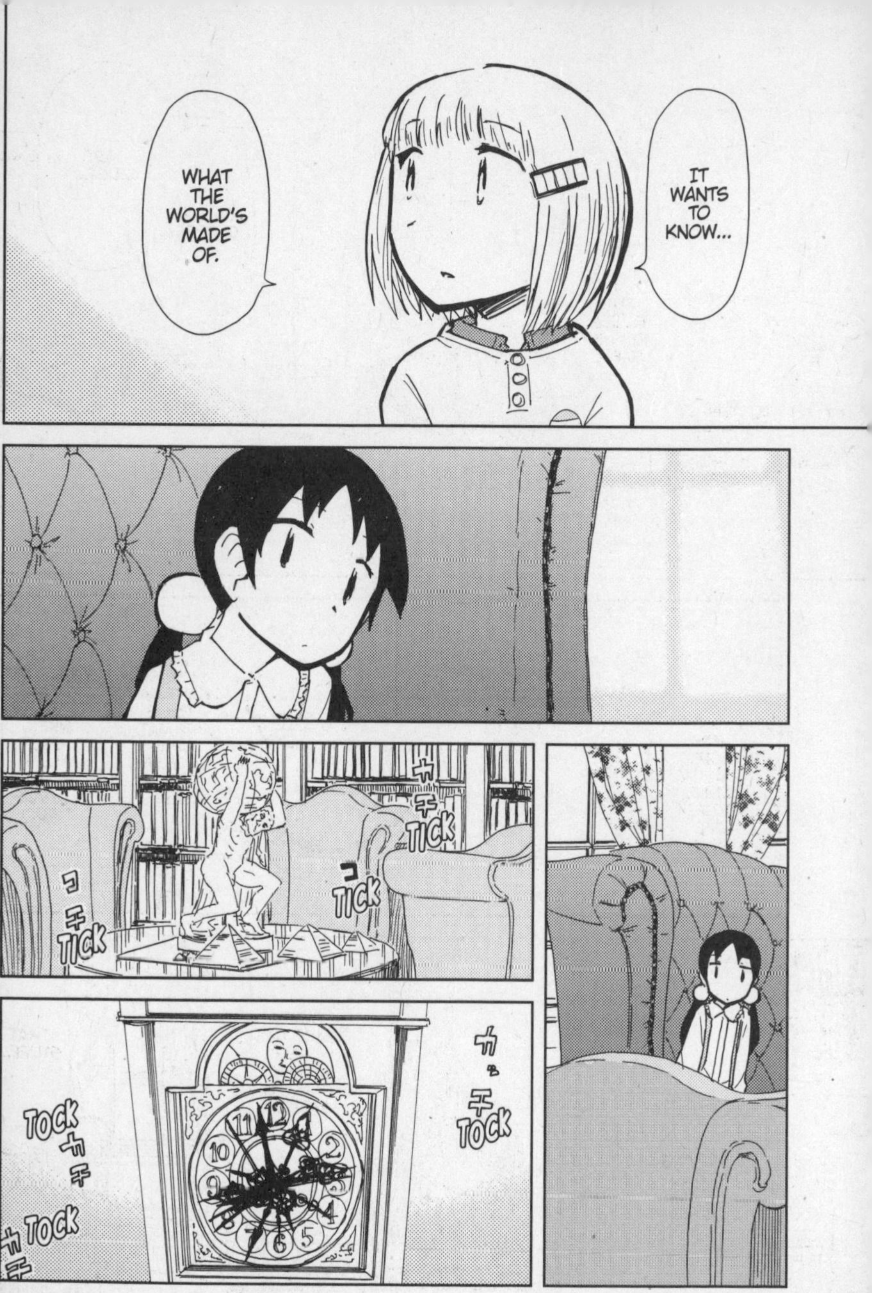
IT WANTS TO KNOW...
WHAT THE WORLD'S MADE OF.
カチ TICK
コ TICK
コチ TICK
カチ TOCK
TOCK カチ
TOCK カチ

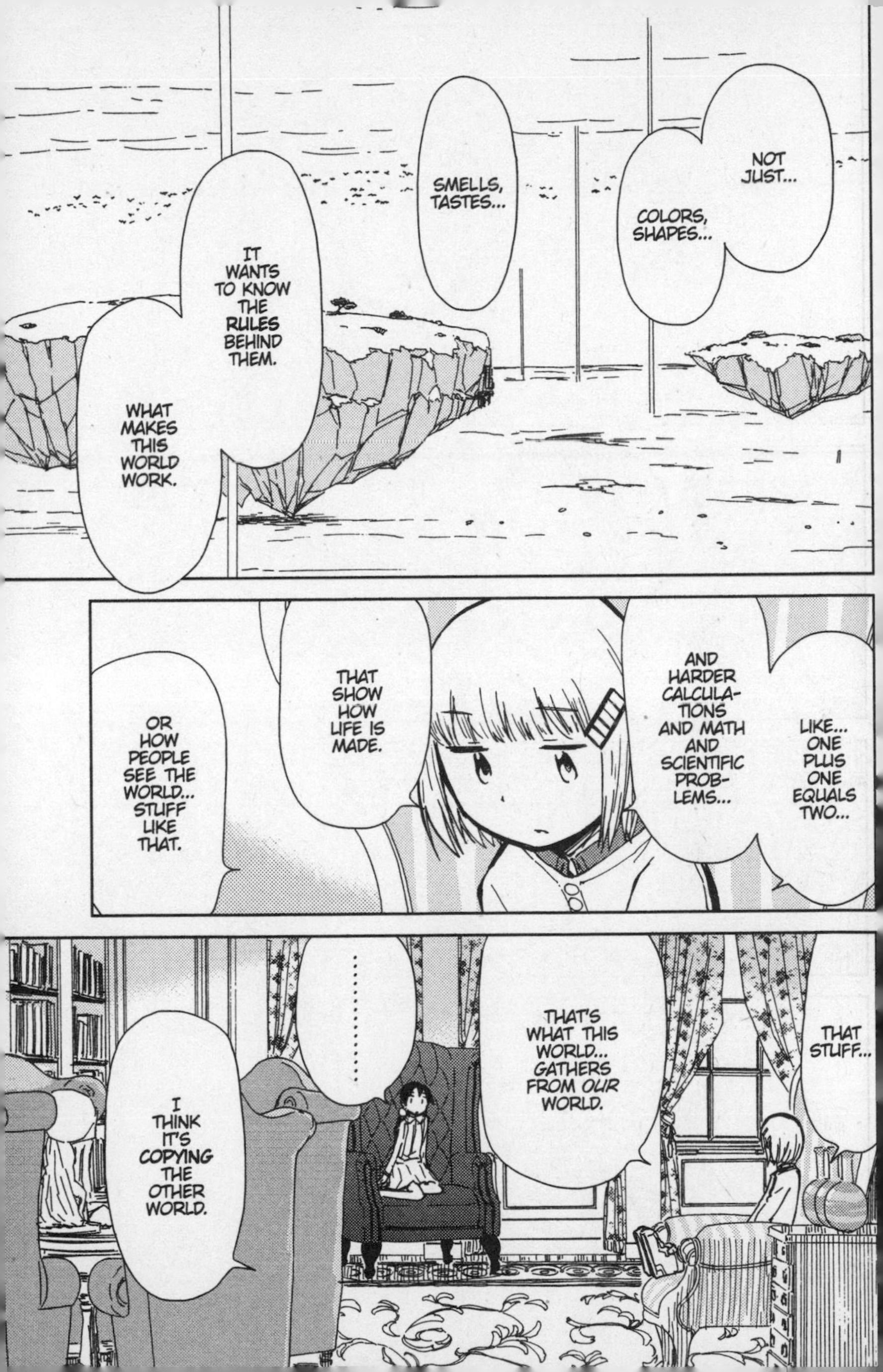
NOT JUST...
COLORS, SHAPES...
SMELLS, TASTES...
IT WANTS TO KNOW THE RULES BEHIND THEM.
WHAT MAKES THIS WORLD WORK.
LIKE... ONE PLUS ONE EQUALS TWO...
AND HARDER CALCULATIONS AND MATH AND SCIENTIFIC PROBLEMS...
THAT SHOW HOW LIFE IS MADE.
OR HOW PEOPLE SEE THE WORLD... STUFF LIKE THAT.
THAT STUFF...
THAT'S WHAT THIS WORLD... GATHERS FROM *OUR* WORLD.
......
I THINK IT'S COPYING THE OTHER WORLD.

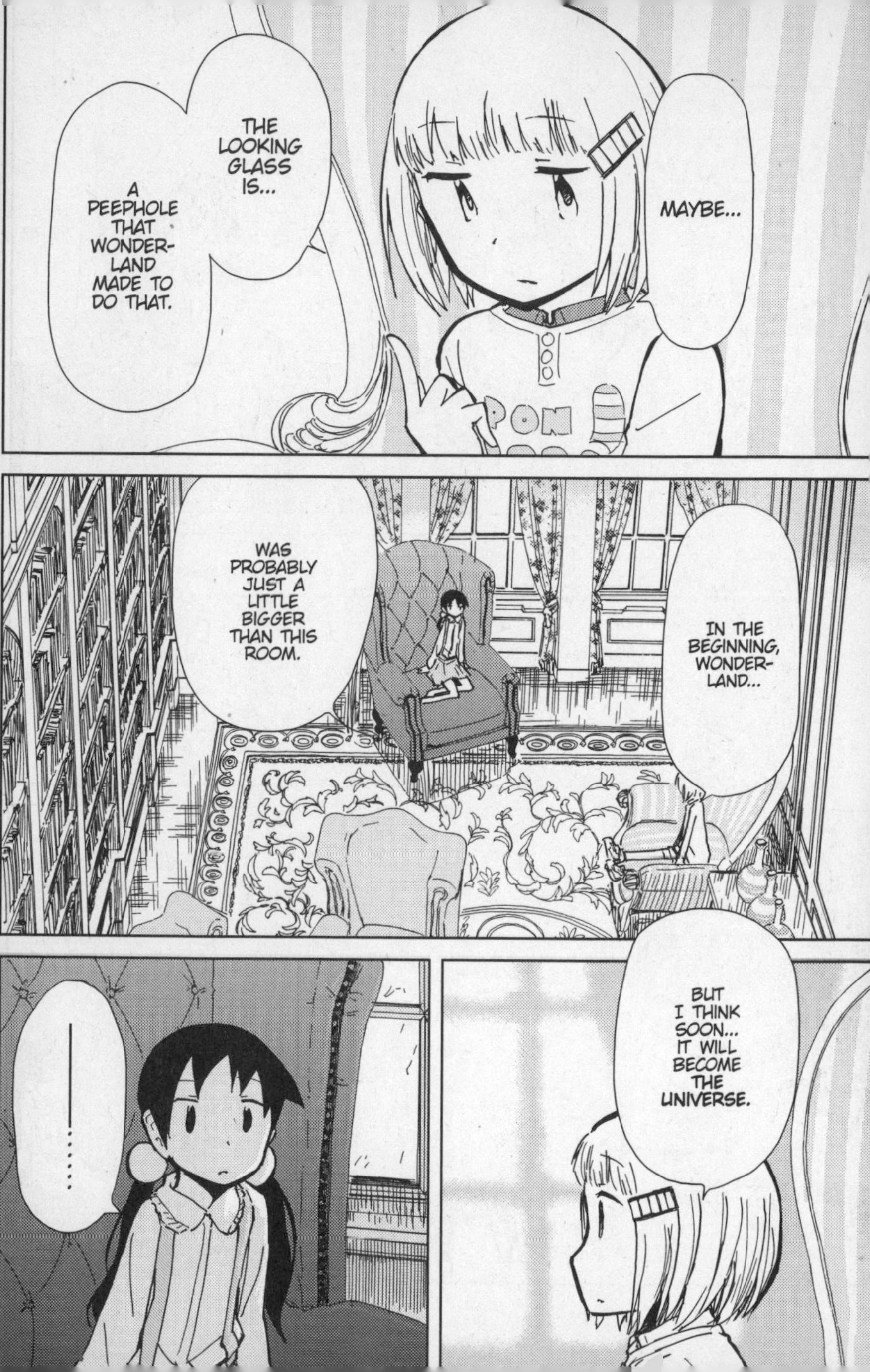
MAYBE...
THE LOOKING GLASS IS...
A PEEPHOLE THAT WONDERLAND MADE TO DO THAT.
PON
IN THE BEGINNING, WONDERLAND...
WAS PROBABLY JUST A LITTLE BIGGER THAN THIS ROOM.
BUT I THINK SOON... IT WILL BECOME THE UNIVERSE.
——......

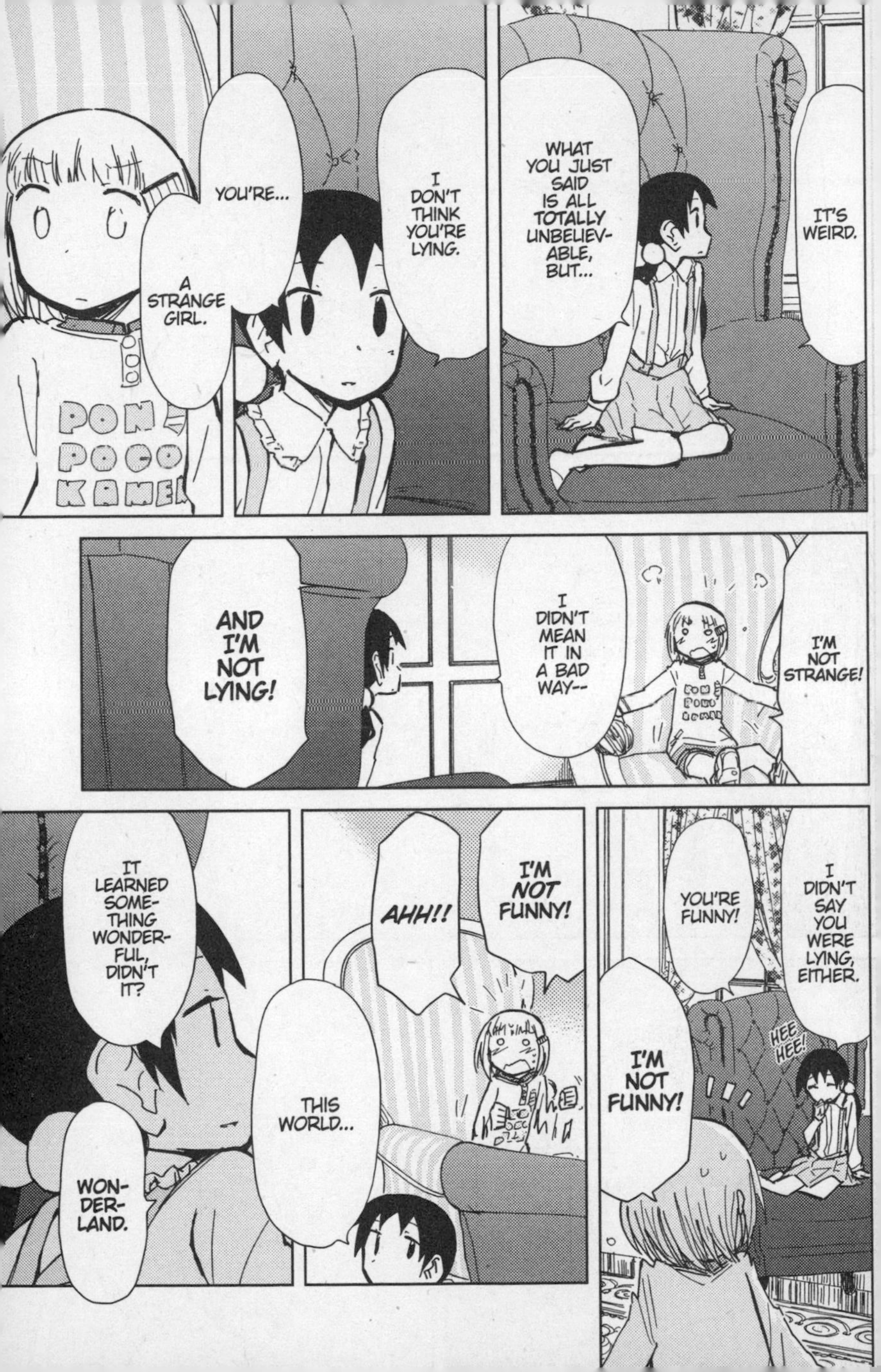
IT'S WEIRD.
WHAT YOU JUST SAID IS ALL TOTALLY UNBELIEVABLE, BUT...
I DON'T THINK YOU'RE LYING.
YOU'RE...
A STRANGE GIRL.
I'M NOT STRANGE!
I DIDN'T MEAN IT IN A BAD WAY--
AND I'M NOT LYING!
I DIDN'T SAY YOU WERE LYING, EITHER.
HEE HEE!
YOU'RE FUNNY!
I'M NOT FUNNY!
I'M *NOT* FUNNY!
AHH!!
THIS WORLD...
IT LEARNED SOMETHING WONDERFUL, DIDN'T IT?
WONDERLAND.

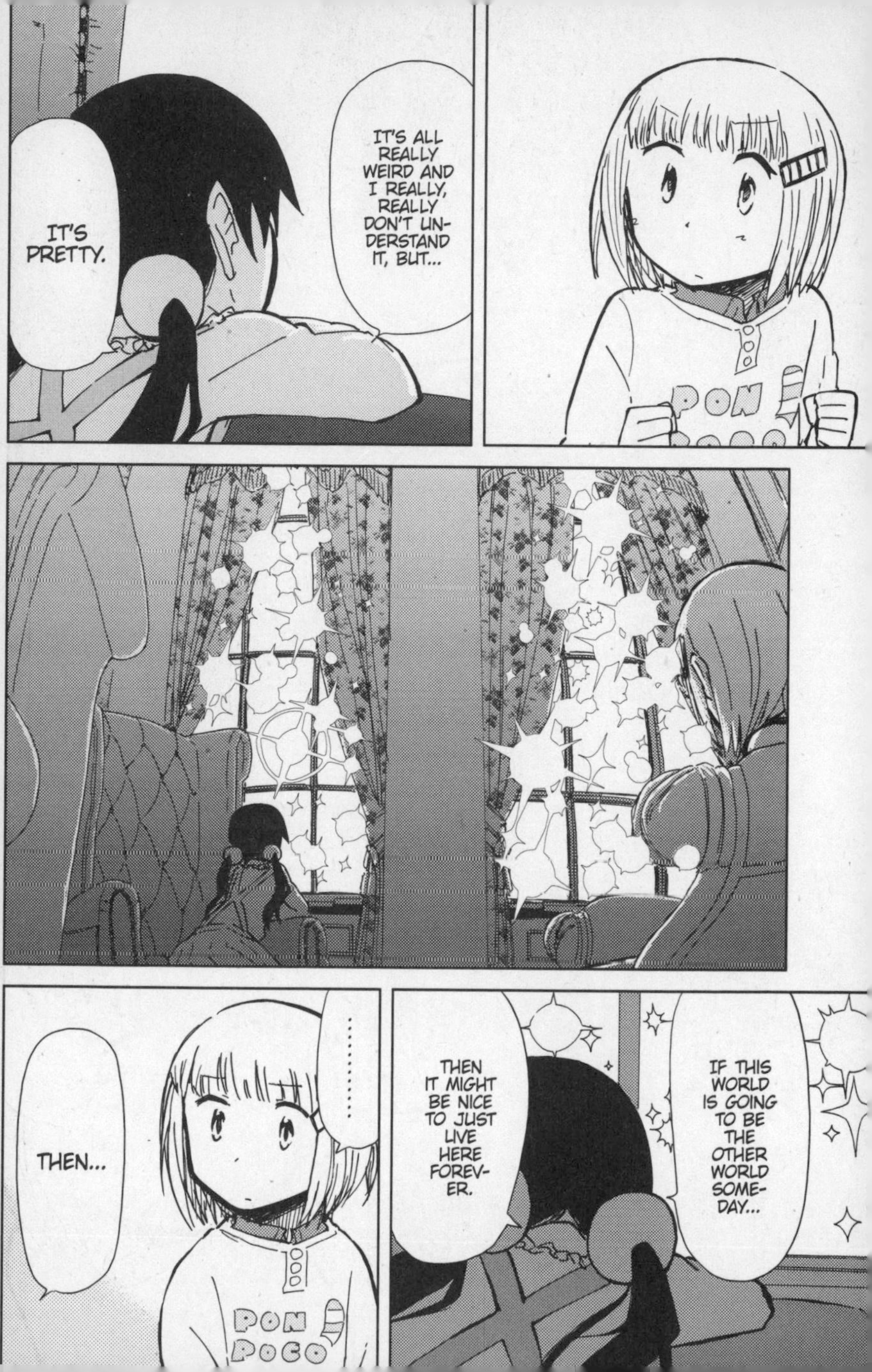
IT'S ALL REALLY WEIRD AND I REALLY, REALLY DON'T UN-DERSTAND IT, BUT...
IT'S PRETTY.
IF THIS WORLD IS GOING TO BE THE OTHER WORLD SOME-DAY...
THEN IT MIGHT BE NICE TO JUST LIVE HERE FOREV-ER.
......
THEN...

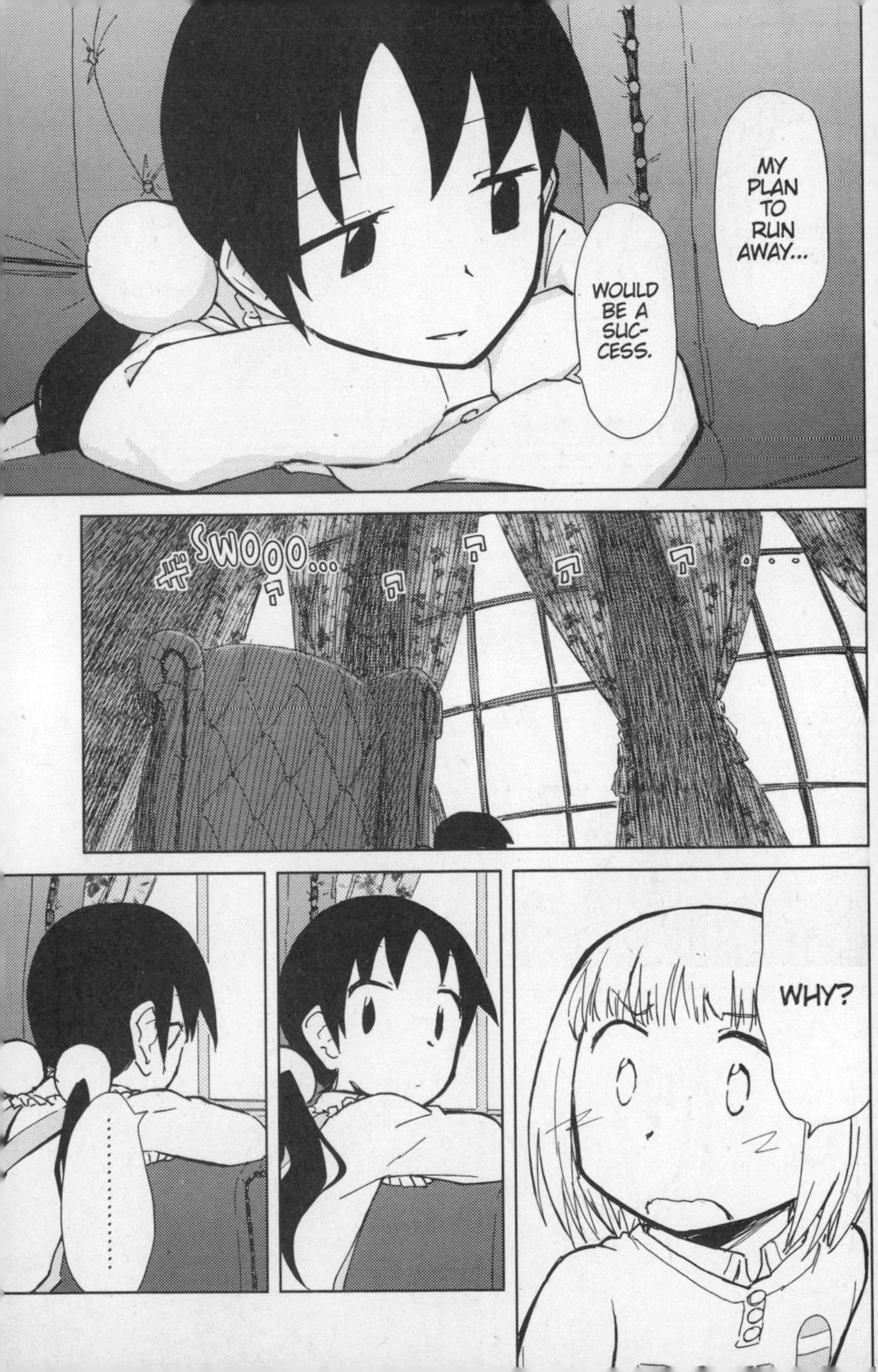

MY PLAN TO RUN AWAY...
WOULD BE A SUC-CESS.
SWOOO...
WHY?

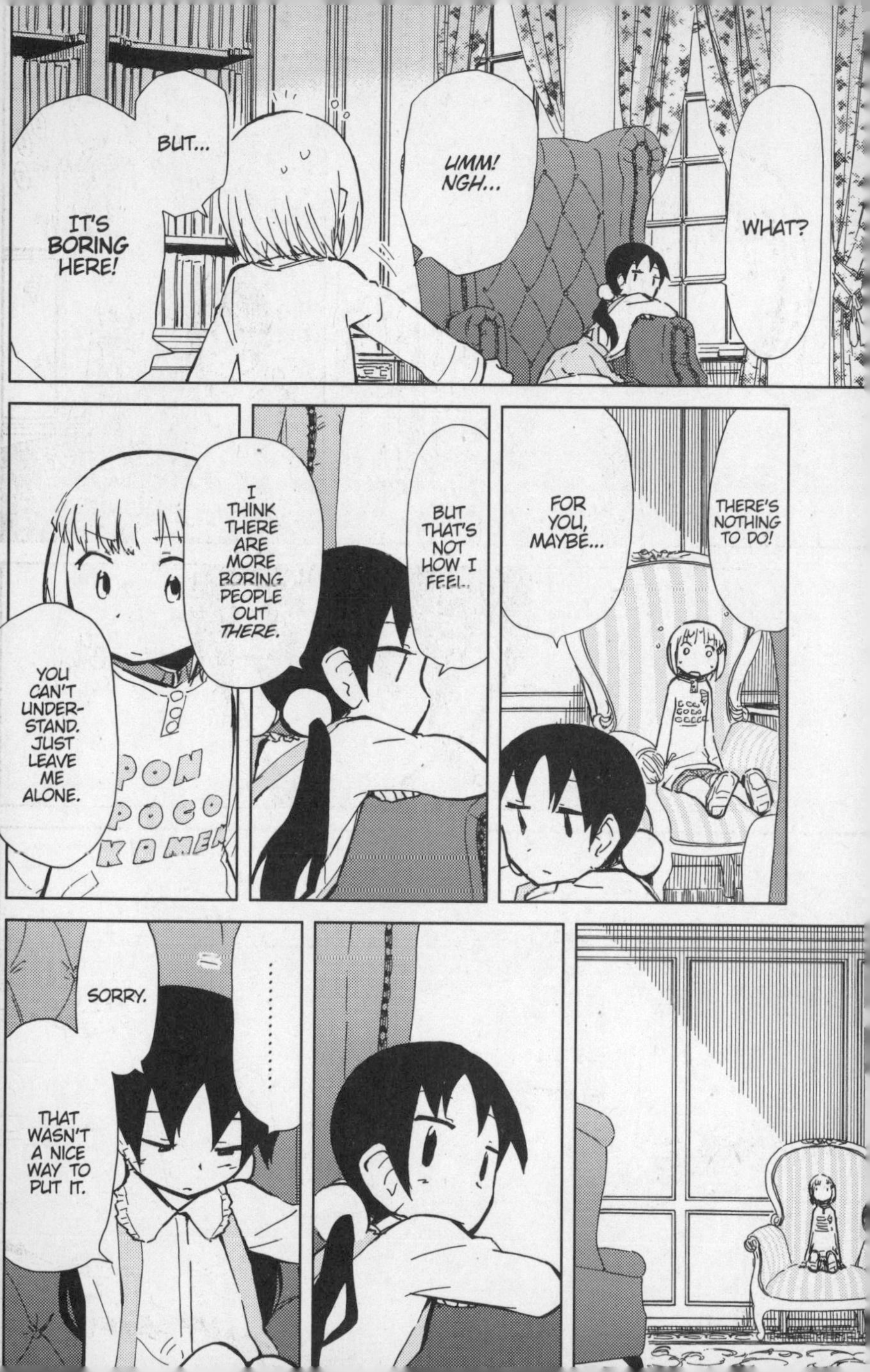
WHAT?
UMM! NGH...
BUT...
IT'S BORING HERE!
THERE'S NOTHING TO DO!
FOR YOU, MAYBE...
BUT THAT'S NOT HOW I FEEL.
I THINK THERE ARE MORE BORING PEOPLE OUT THERE.
YOU CAN'T UNDER-STAND. JUST LEAVE ME ALONE.
......
SORRY.
THAT WASN'T A NICE WAY TO PUT IT.

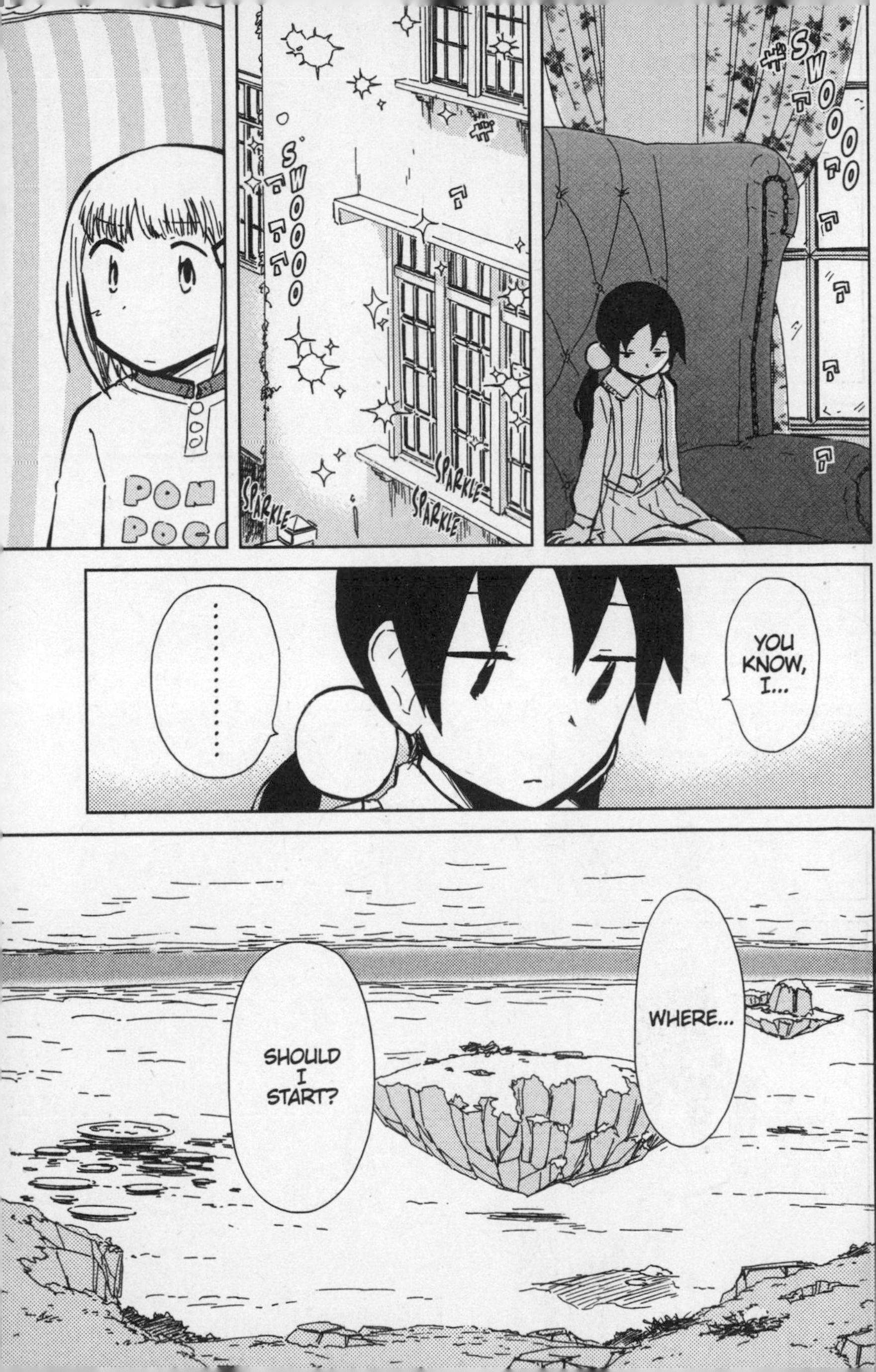
SWOOOO
SWOOOO
SPARKLE
SPARKLE
SPARKLE
PON POCO
YOU KNOW, I...
......
WHERE...
SHOULD I START?

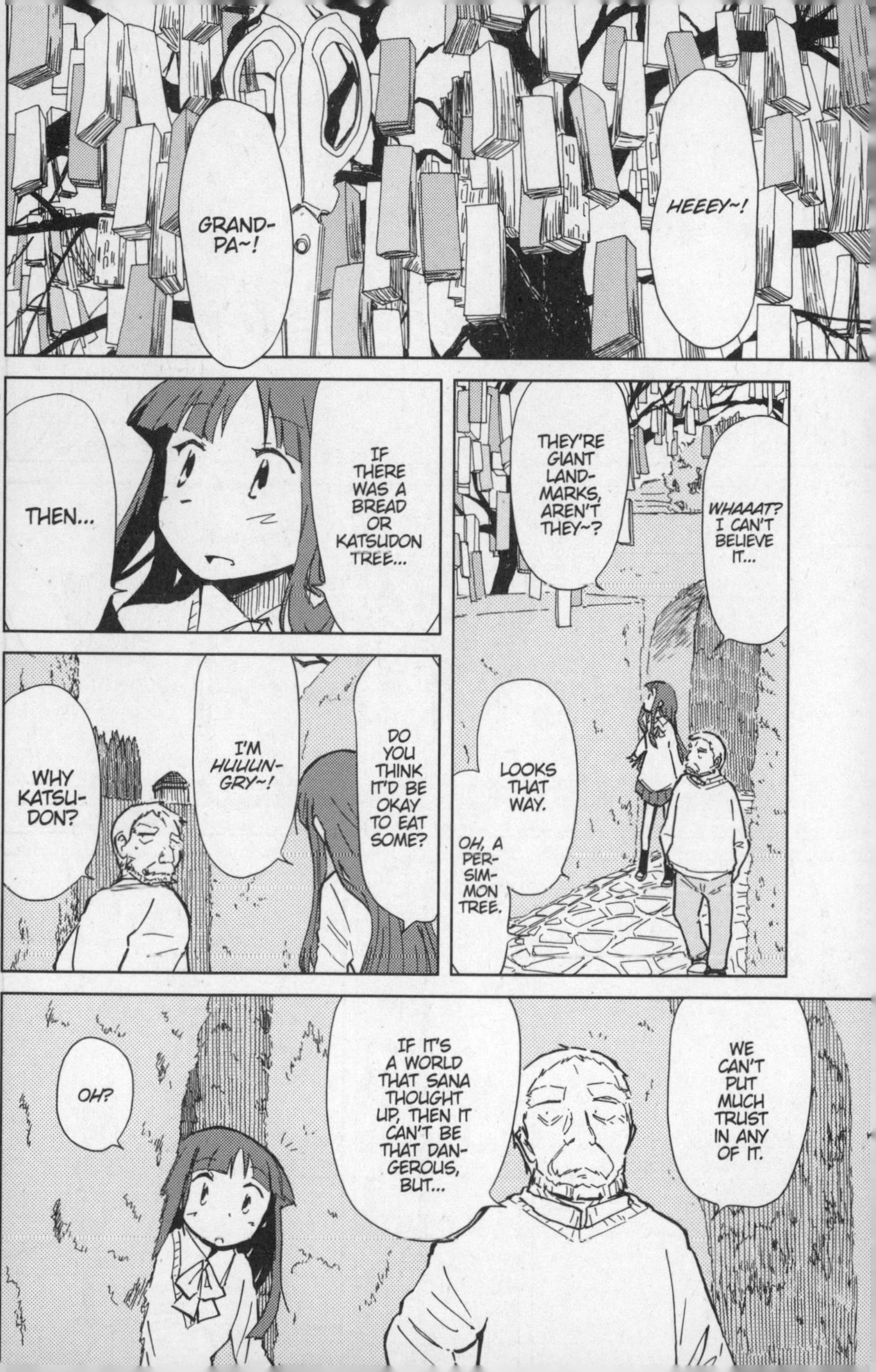
HEEEY~!
GRAND-PA~!
WHAAAT? I CAN'T BELIEVE IT...
THEY'RE GIANT LANDMARKS, AREN'T THEY~?
LOOKS THAT WAY.
OH, A PERSIMMON TREE.
IF THERE WAS A BREAD OR KATSUDON TREE...
THEN...
DO YOU THINK IT'D BE OKAY TO EAT SOME?
I'M HUUUNGRY~!
WHY KATSUDON?
WE CAN'T PUT MUCH TRUST IN ANY OF IT.
IF IT'S A WORLD THAT SANA THOUGHT UP, THEN IT CAN'T BE THAT DANGEROUS, BUT...
OH?

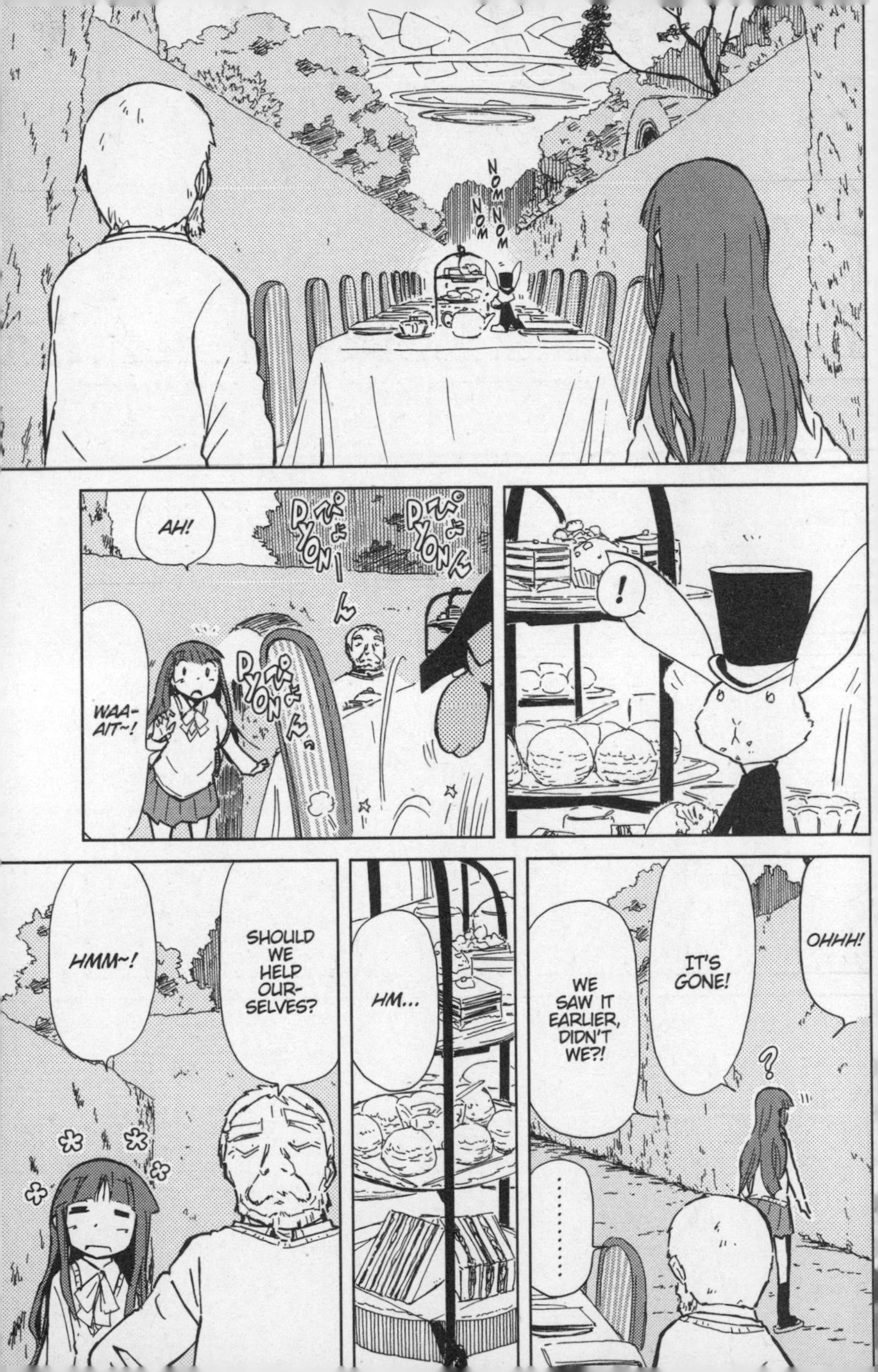
NOM NOM NOM
!
PYON ぴょん
PYON ぴょーん
AH!
PYON ぴょん
WAA-AIT~!
OHHH!
IT'S GONE!
WE SAW IT EARLIER, DIDN'T WE?!
?
......
HM...
SHOULD WE HELP OUR-SELVES?
HMM~!

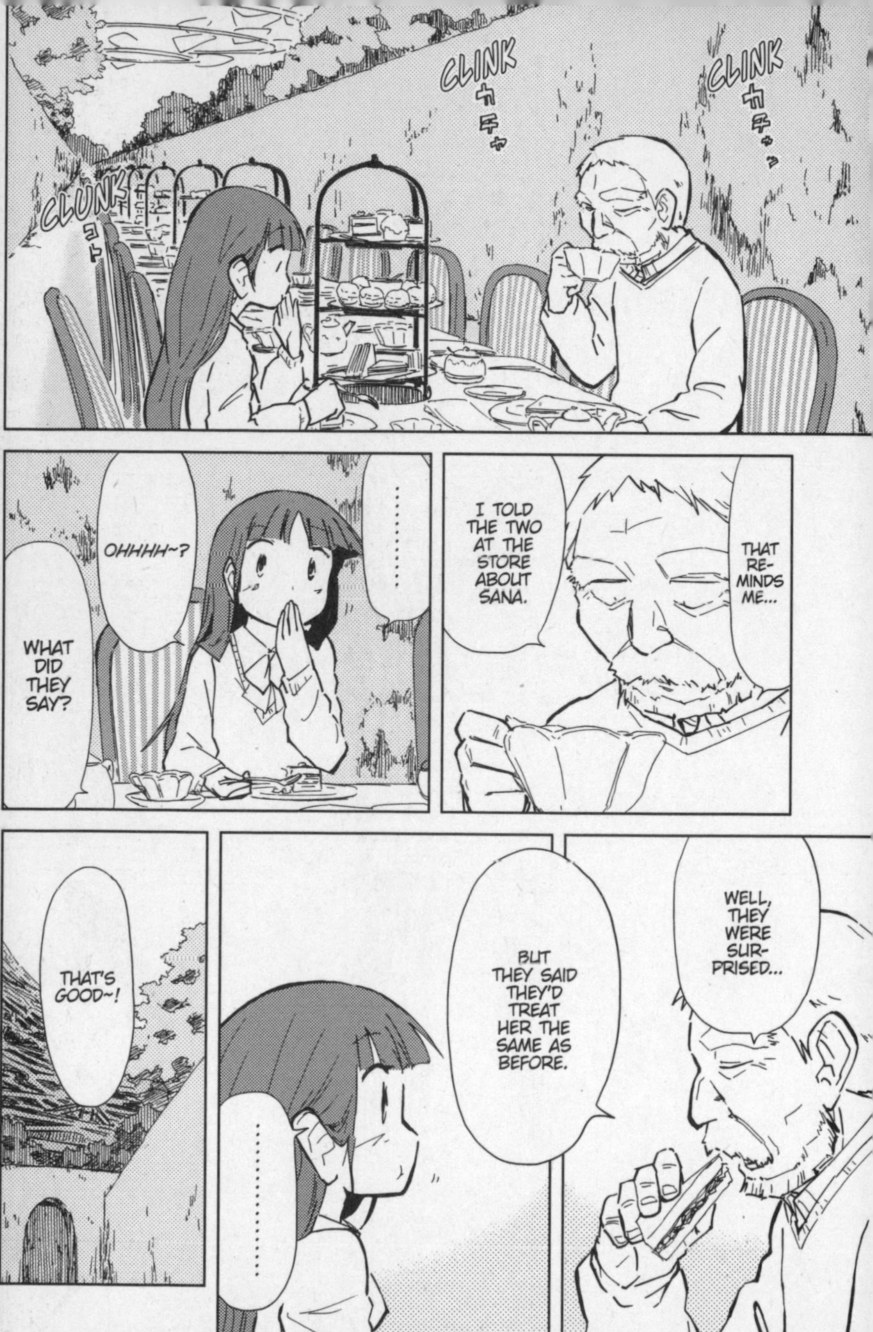
CLINK
カチャ
CLINK
カチャ
CLUNK
コト
THAT RE-MINDS ME...
I TOLD THE TWO AT THE STORE ABOUT SANA.
......
OHHHH~?
WHAT DID THEY SAY?
WELL, THEY WERE SUR-PRISED...
BUT THEY SAID THEY'D TREAT HER THE SAME AS BEFORE.
......
THAT'S GOOD~!

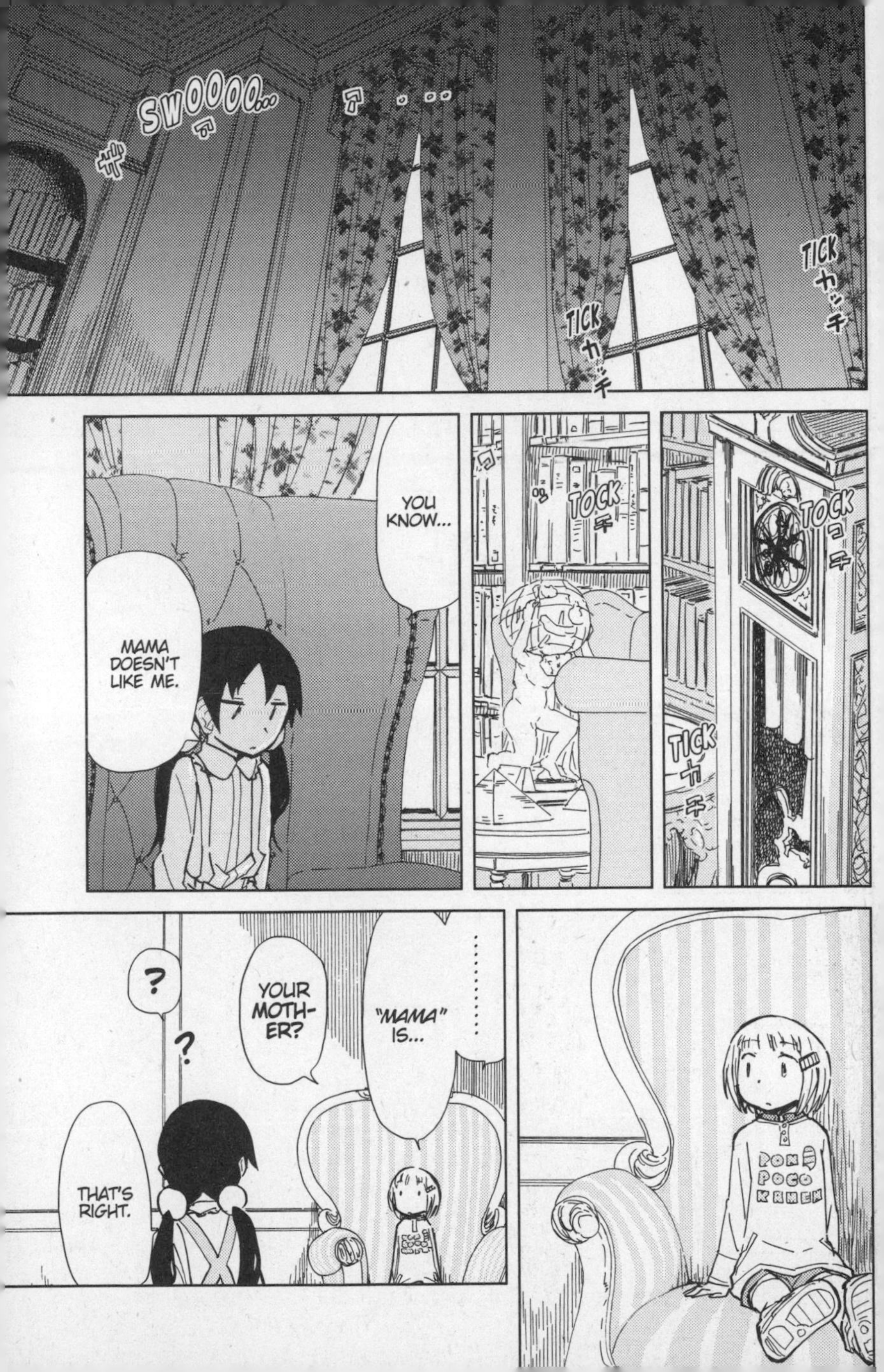
TICK
カッチ
TICK
カッチ
SWOOOO...
TOCK
コッチ
TICK
カッチ
TOCK
コッチ
YOU KNOW...
MAMA DOESN'T LIKE ME.
......
"MAMA" IS...
YOUR MOTHER?
?
?
THAT'S RIGHT.
PON POCO KAMEN

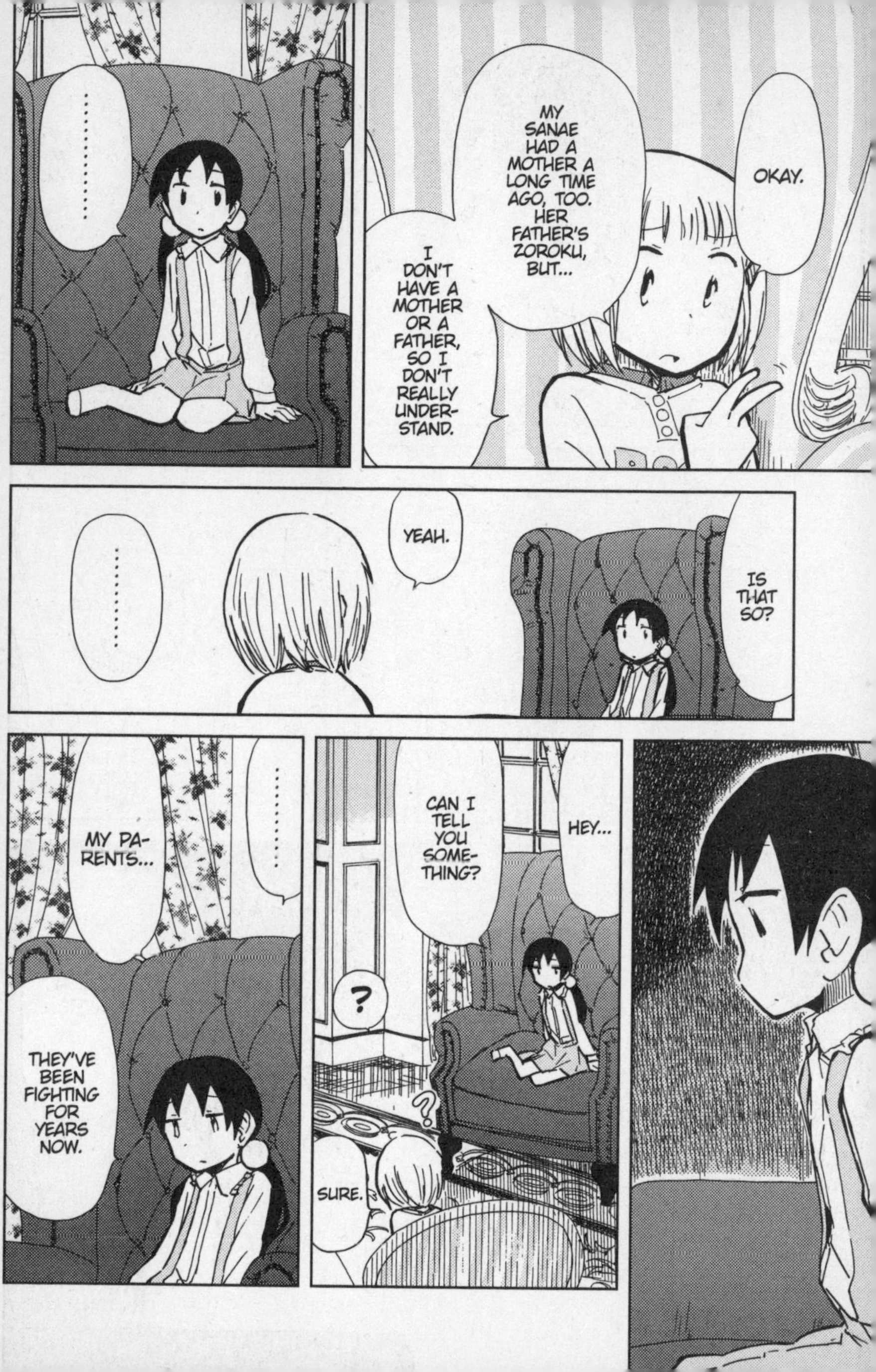
OKAY.
MY SANAE HAD A MOTHER A LONG TIME AGO, TOO. HER FATHER'S ZOROKU, BUT...
I DON'T HAVE A MOTHER OR A FATHER, SO I DON'T REALLY UNDER-STAND.
......
IS THAT SO?
YEAH.
......
HEY...
CAN I TELL YOU SOME-THING?
?
?
SURE.
......
MY PA-RENTS...
THEY'VE BEEN FIGHTING FOR YEARS NOW.

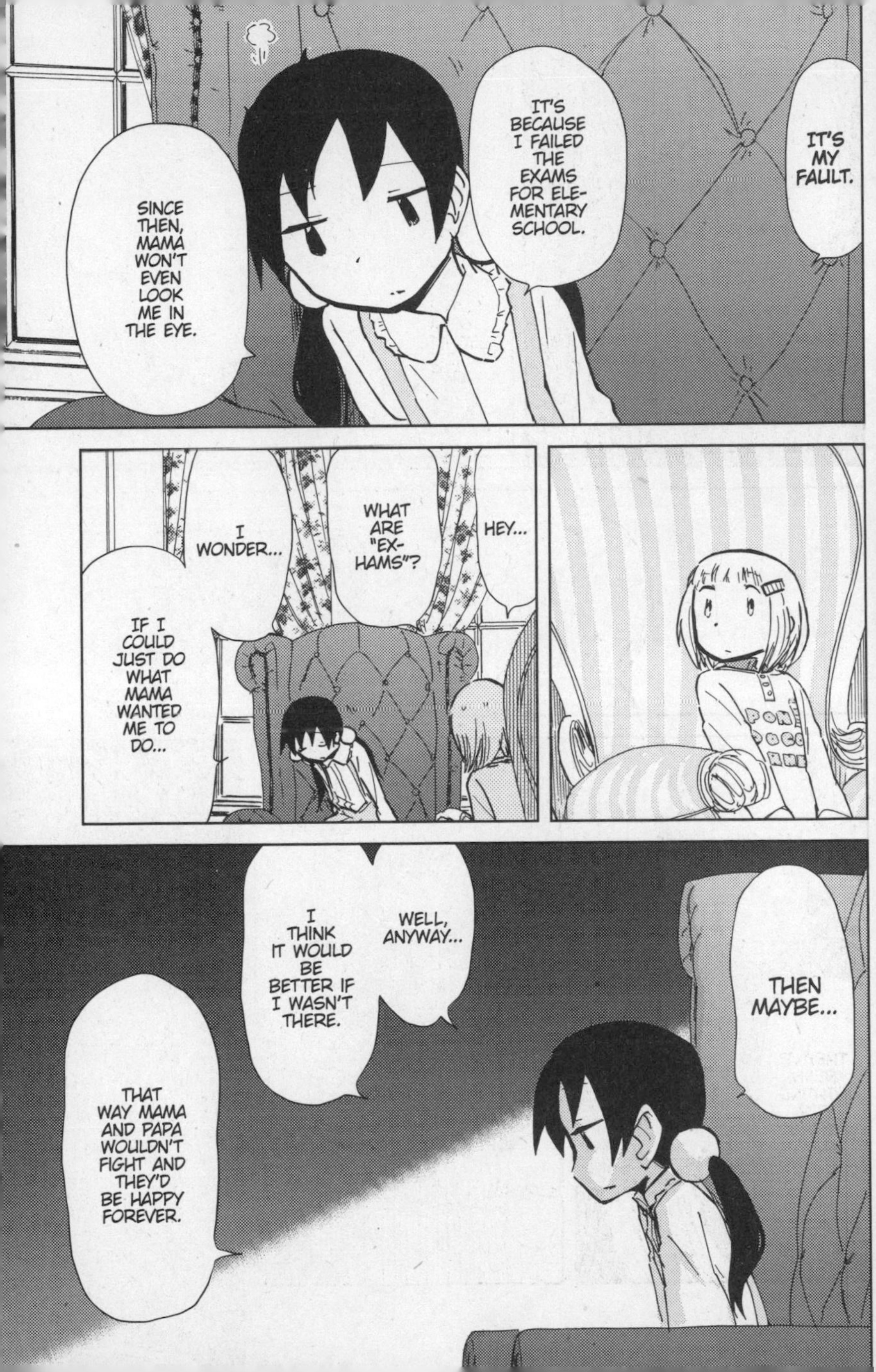
IT'S MY FAULT.
IT'S BECAUSE I FAILED THE EXAMS FOR ELE-MENTARY SCHOOL.
SINCE THEN, MAMA WON'T EVEN LOOK ME IN THE EYE.
HEY...
WHAT ARE "EX-HAMS"?
I WONDER...
IF I COULD JUST DO WHAT MAMA WANTED ME TO DO...
THEN MAYBE...
WELL, ANYWAY...
I THINK IT WOULD BE BETTER IF I WASN'T THERE.
THAT WAY MAMA AND PAPA WOULDN'T FIGHT AND THEY'D BE HAPPY FOREVER.

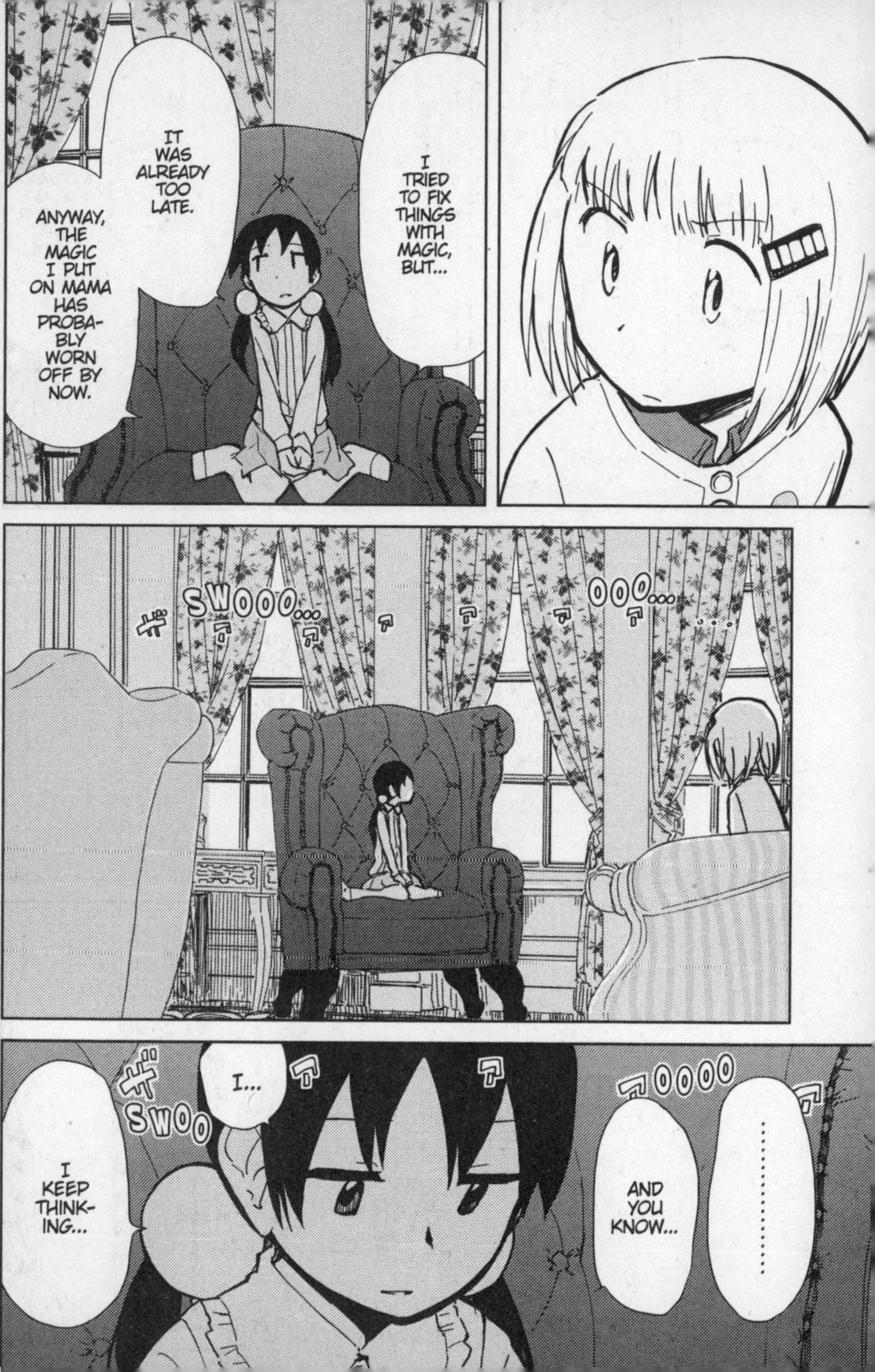
I TRIED TO FIX THINGS WITH MAGIC, BUT...
IT WAS ALREADY TOO LATE.
ANYWAY, THE MAGIC I PUT ON MAMA HAS PROBA-BLY WORN OFF BY NOW.
OOO...
SWOOO...
. . .
......
AND YOU KNOW...
OOOO
I...
SWOO
I KEEP THINK-ING...

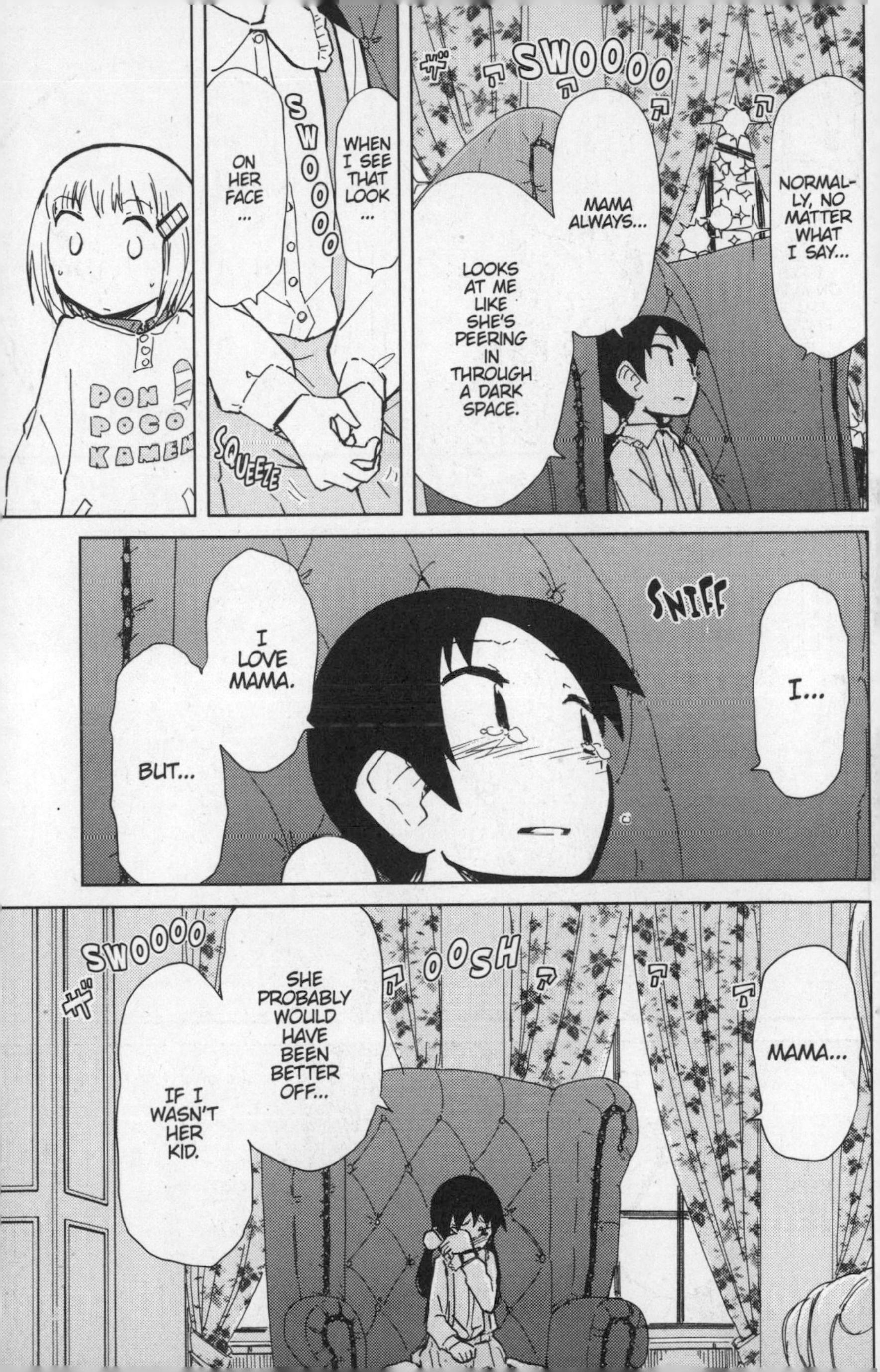
SWOOOO
NORMAL-LY, NO MATTER WHAT I SAY...
MAMA ALWAYS...
LOOKS AT ME LIKE SHE'S PEERING IN THROUGH A DARK SPACE.
SWOOOO
WHEN I SEE THAT LOOK ...
ON HER FACE ...
SQUEEZE
PON POCO KAMEN
SNIFF
I...
I LOVE MAMA.
BUT...
MAMA...
SWOOOO OOSH
SHE PROBABLY WOULD HAVE BEEN BETTER OFF...
IF I WASN'T HER KID.

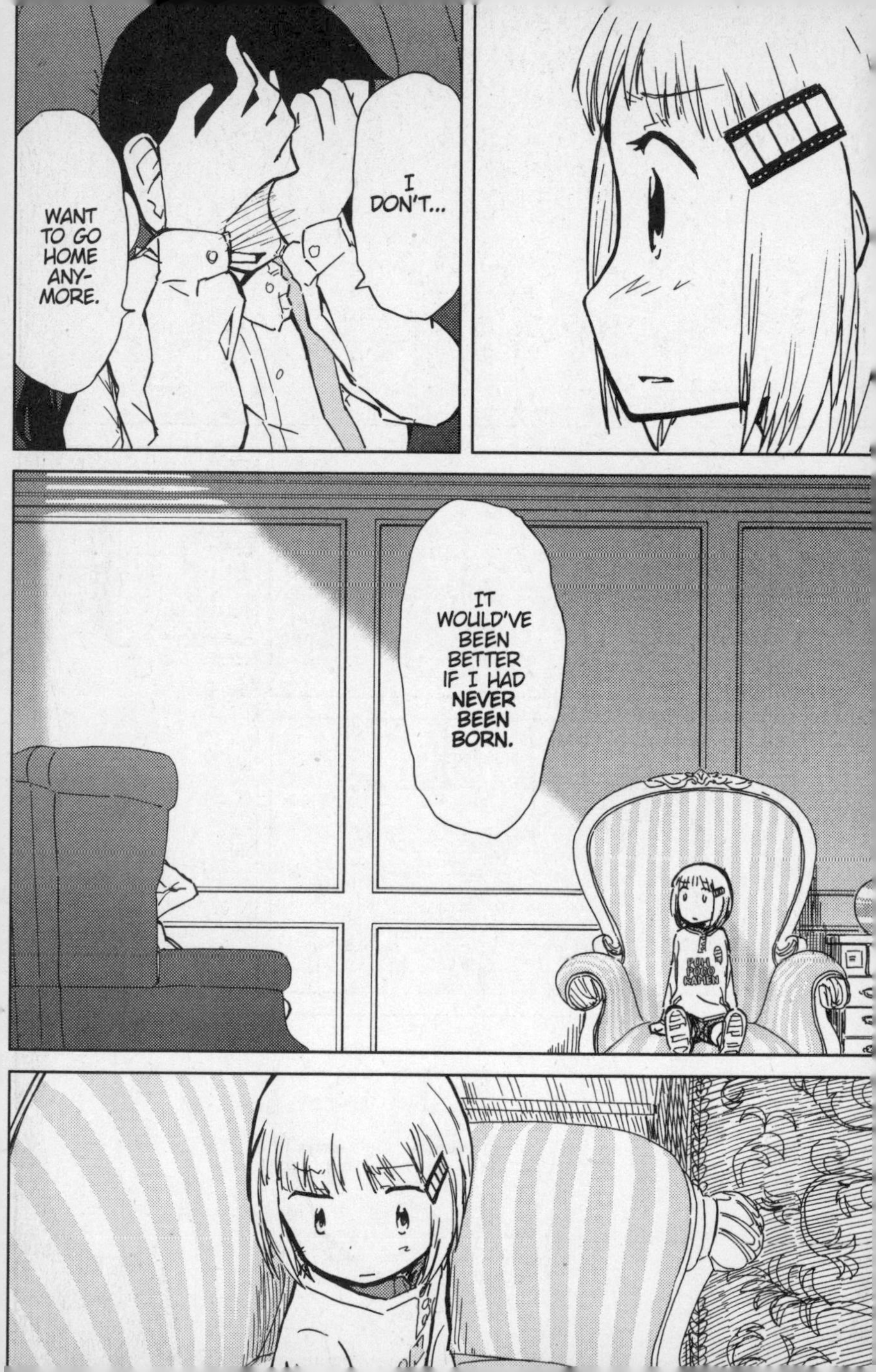
I DON'T...
WANT TO GO HOME ANYMORE.
IT WOULD'VE BEEN BETTER IF I HAD NEVER BEEN BORN.

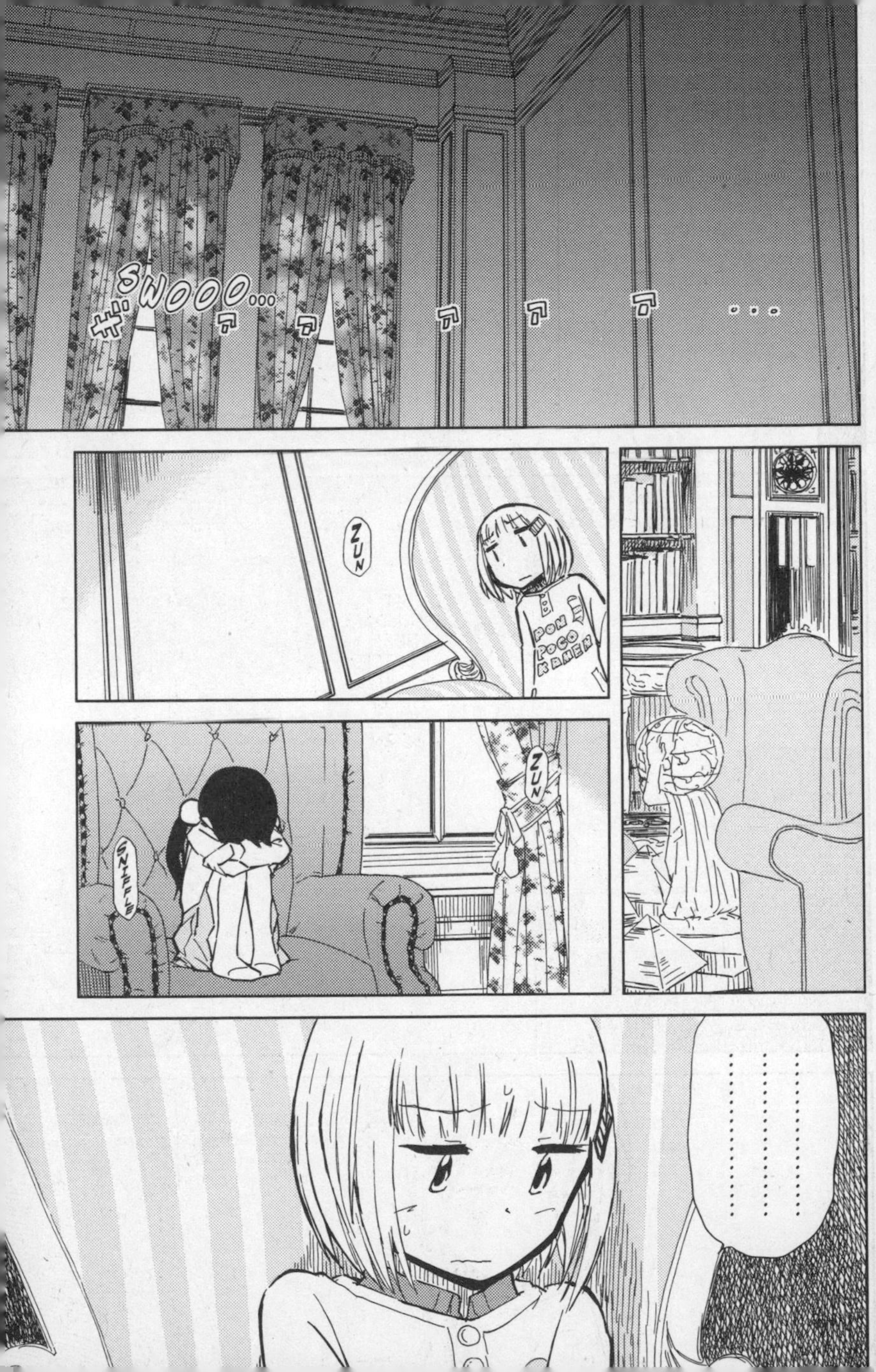
SWOOO...
...
ZUN
ZUN
SNIFFLE
......

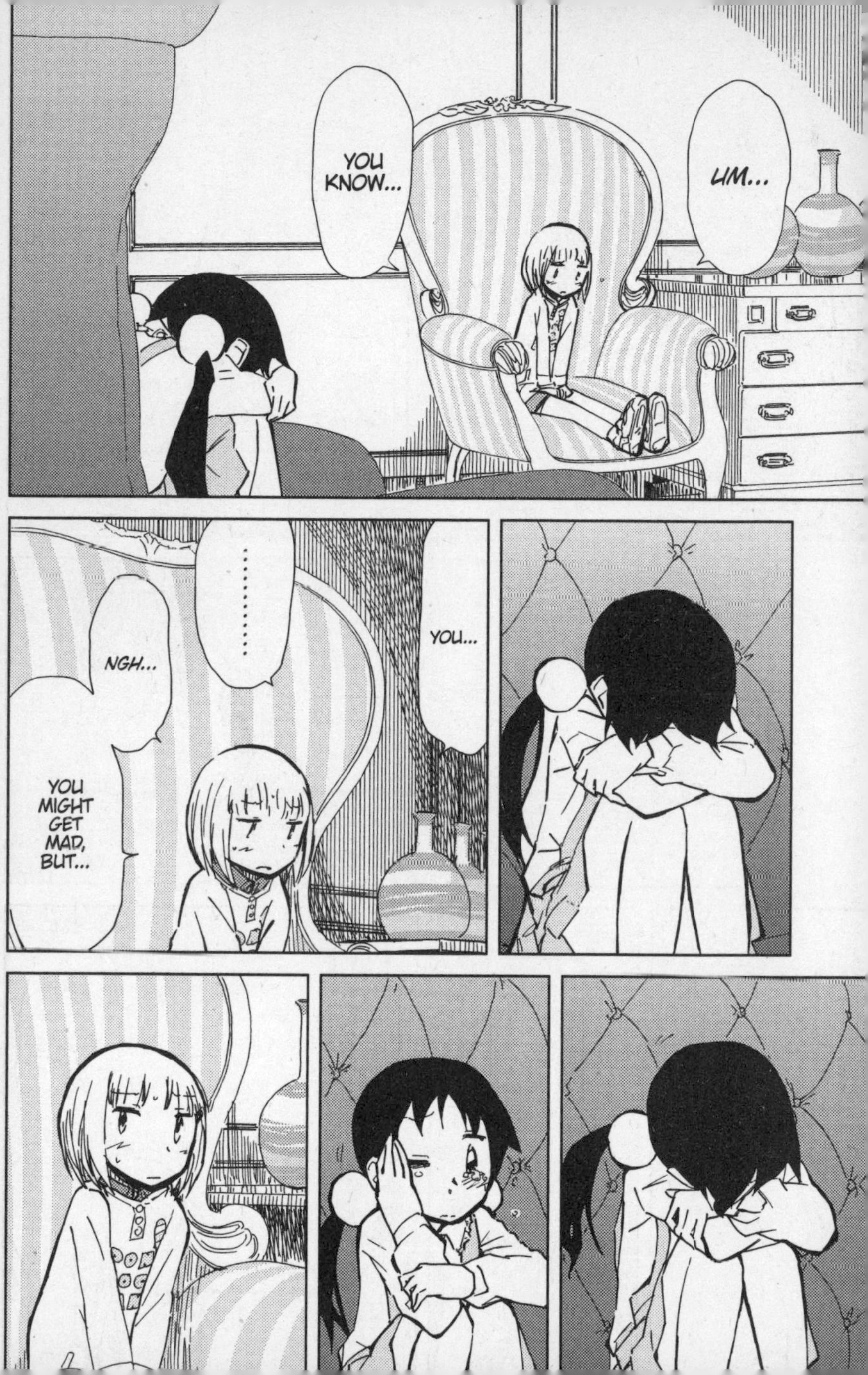
UM...
YOU KNOW...
YOU...
....
NGH...
YOU MIGHT GET MAD, BUT...

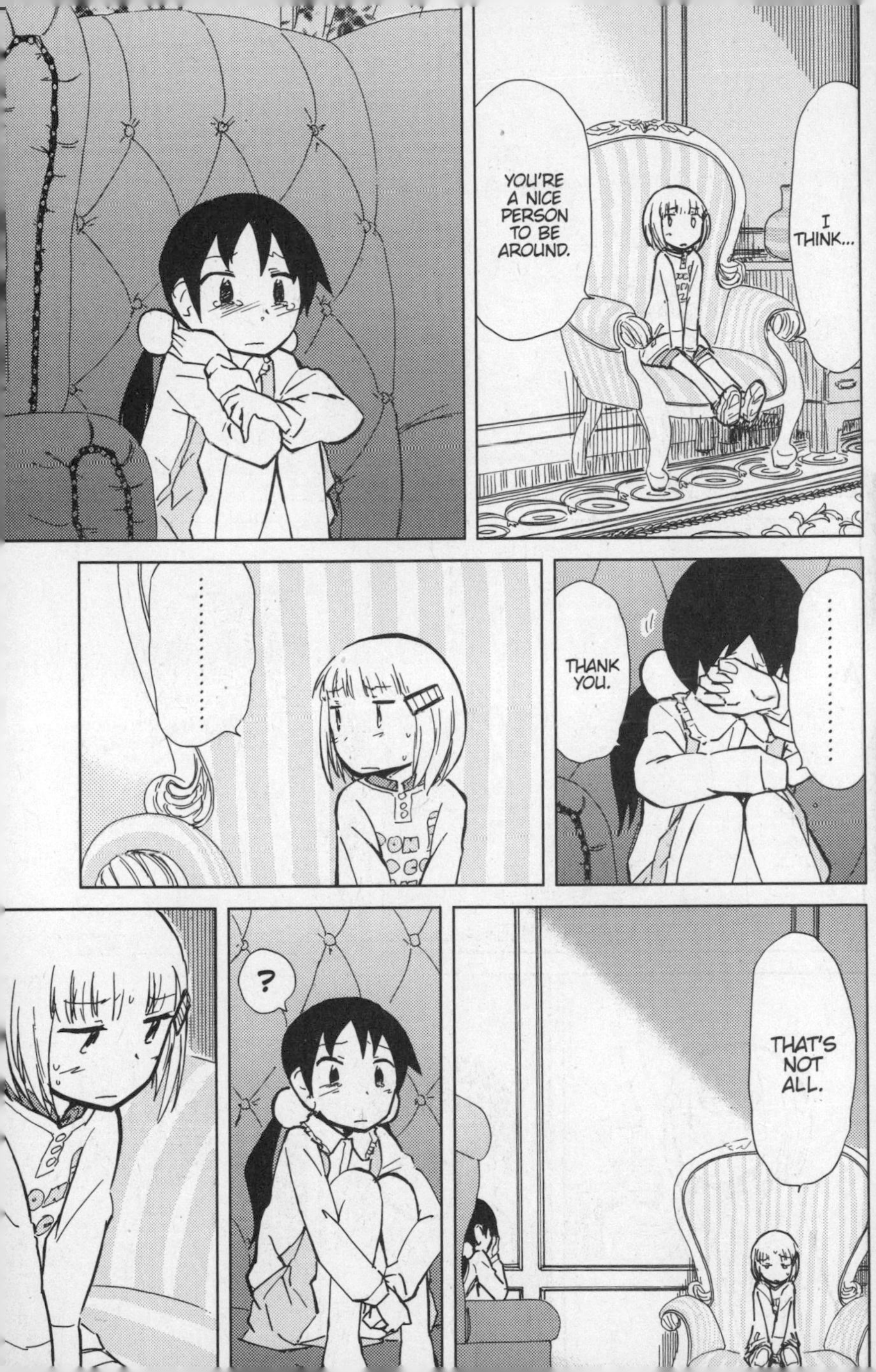
I THINK...
YOU'RE A NICE PERSON TO BE AROUND.
......
THANK YOU.
......
THAT'S NOT ALL.
?

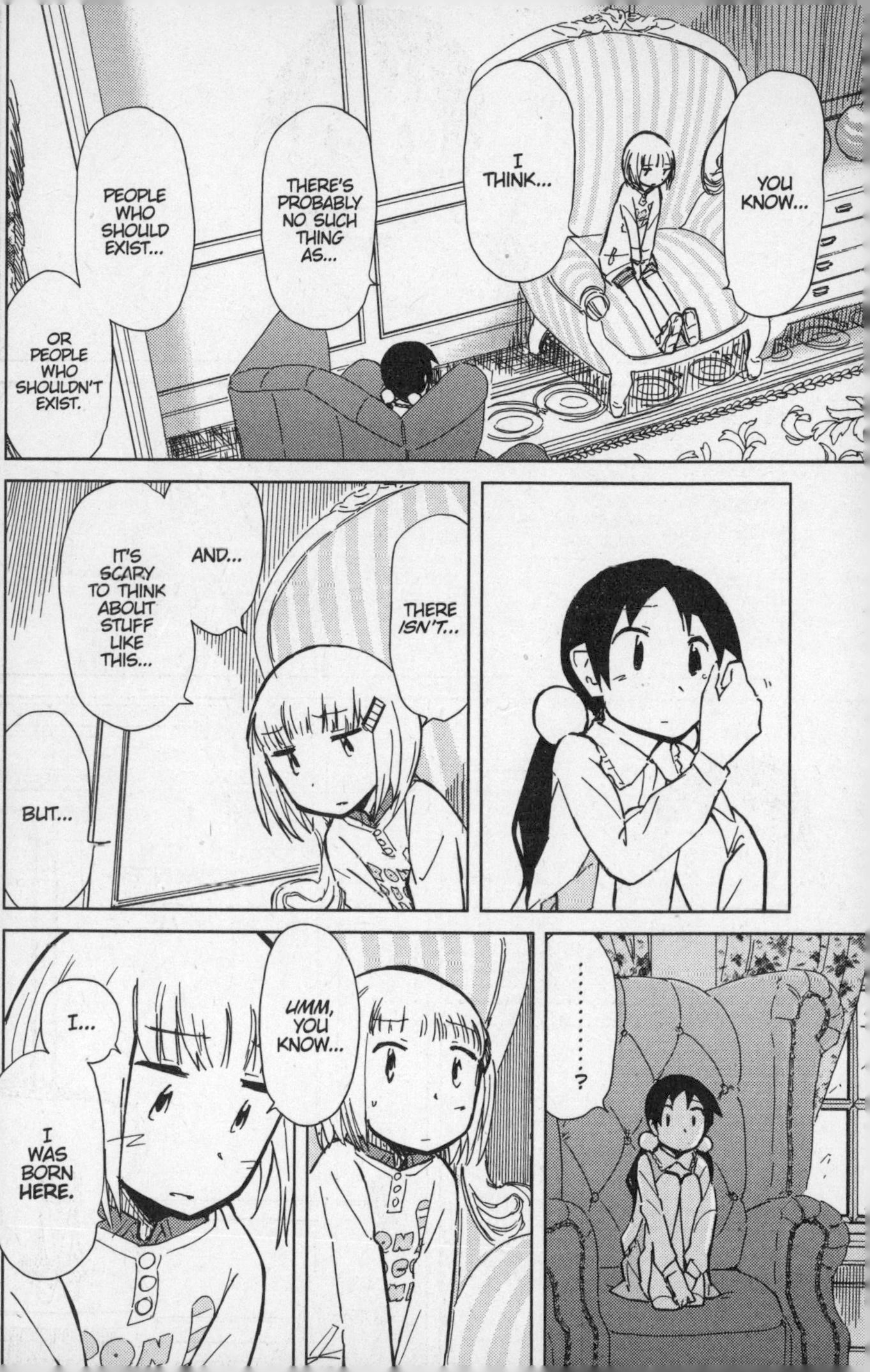
YOU KNOW...
I THINK...
THERE'S PROBABLY NO SUCH THING AS...
PEOPLE WHO SHOULD EXIST...
OR PEOPLE WHO SHOULDN'T EXIST.
THERE ISN'T...
AND...
IT'S SCARY TO THINK ABOUT STUFF LIKE THIS...
BUT...
.........?
UMM, YOU KNOW...
I...
I WAS BORN HERE.

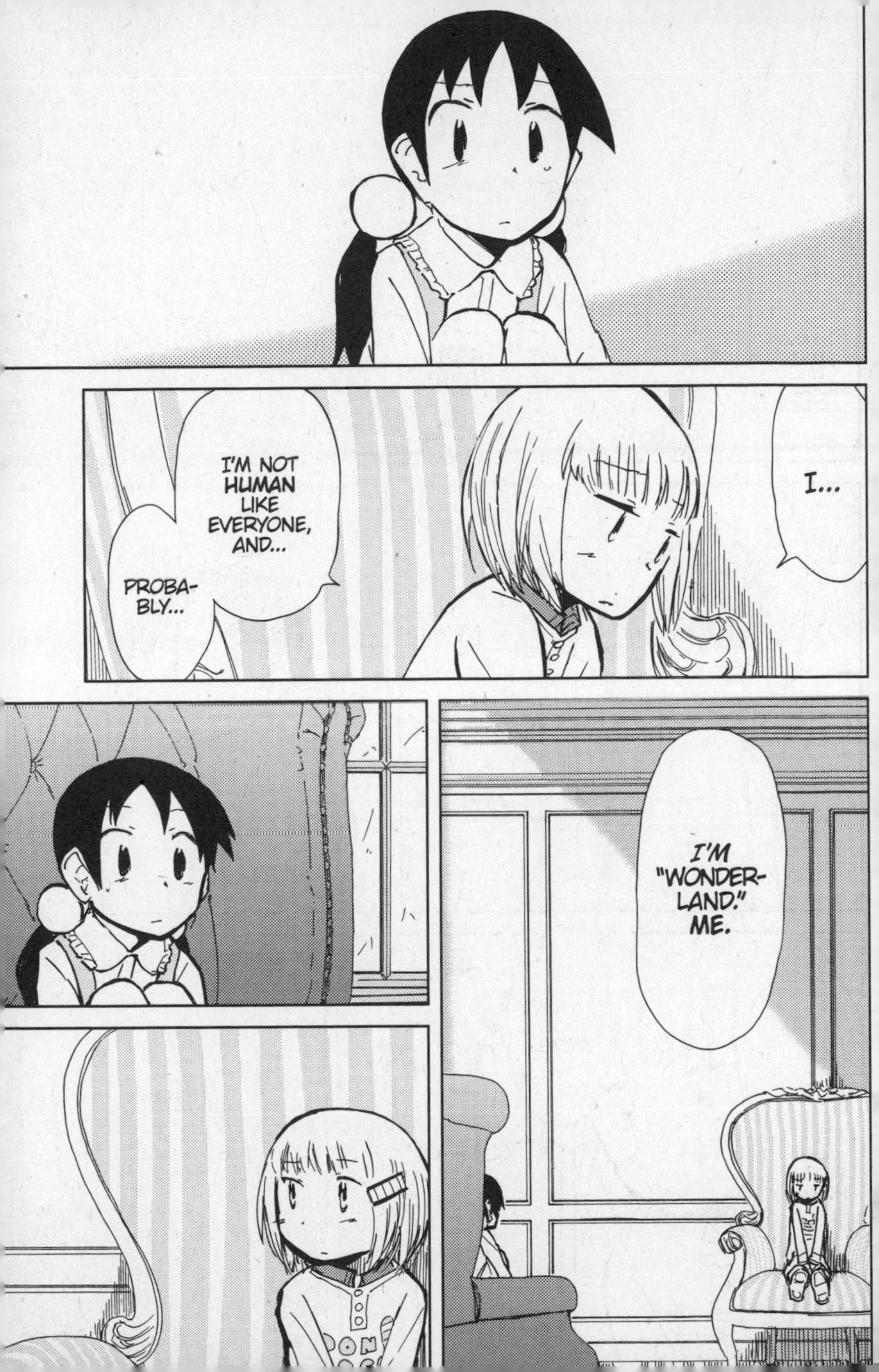
I...
I'M NOT HUMAN LIKE EVERYONE, AND...
PROBA-BLY...
I'M "WONDER-LAND." ME.

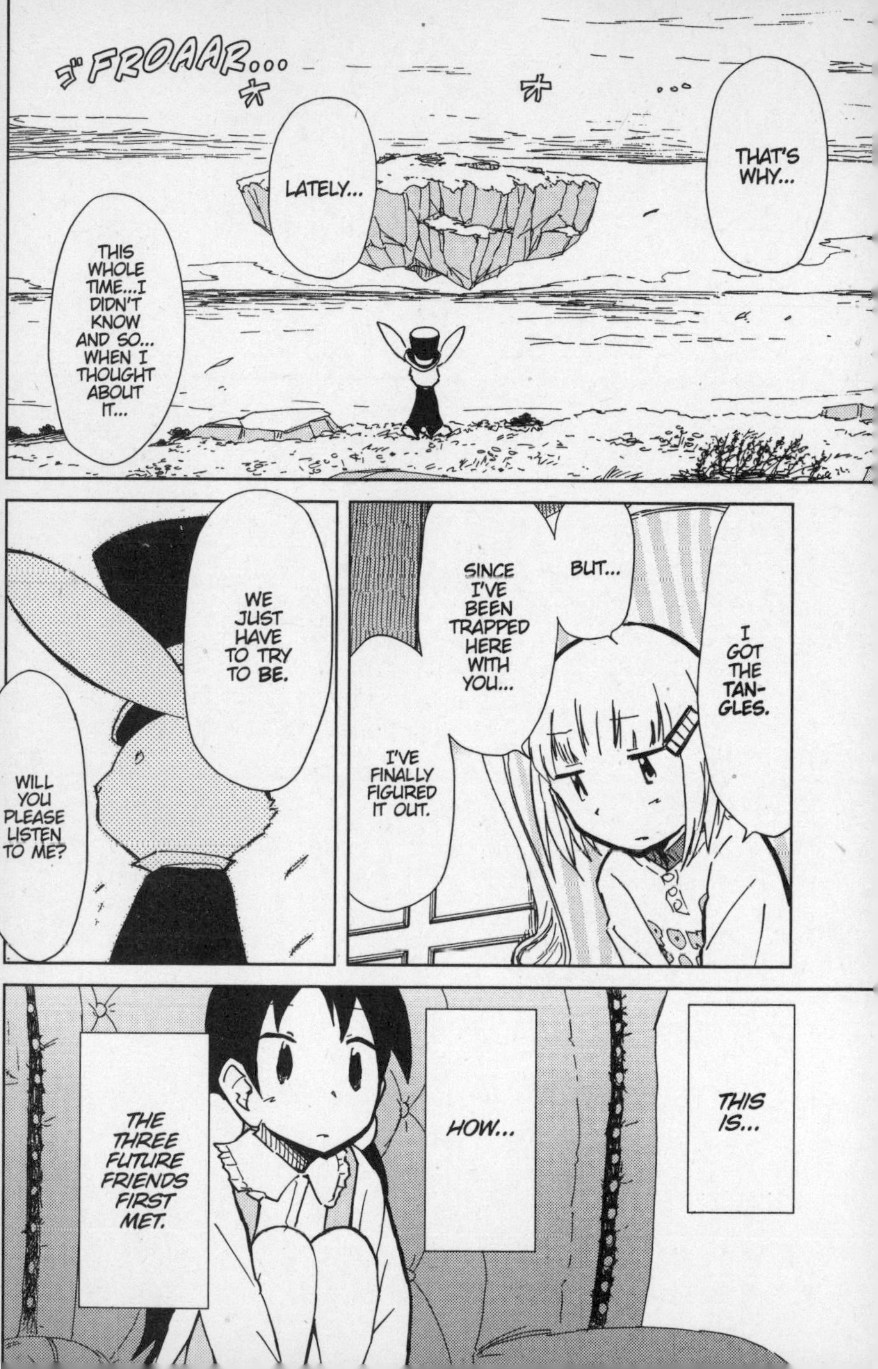
ゴ FROAAR...
THAT'S WHY...
LATELY...
THIS WHOLE TIME...I DIDN'T KNOW AND SO... WHEN I THOUGHT ABOUT IT...
I GOT THE TAN-GLES.
BUT...
SINCE I'VE BEEN TRAPPED HERE WITH YOU...
I'VE FINALLY FIGURED IT OUT.
WE JUST HAVE TO TRY TO BE.
WILL YOU PLEASE LISTEN TO ME?
THIS IS...
HOW...
THE THREE FUTURE FRIENDS FIRST MET.

Alice & Zoroku

INTERLUDE

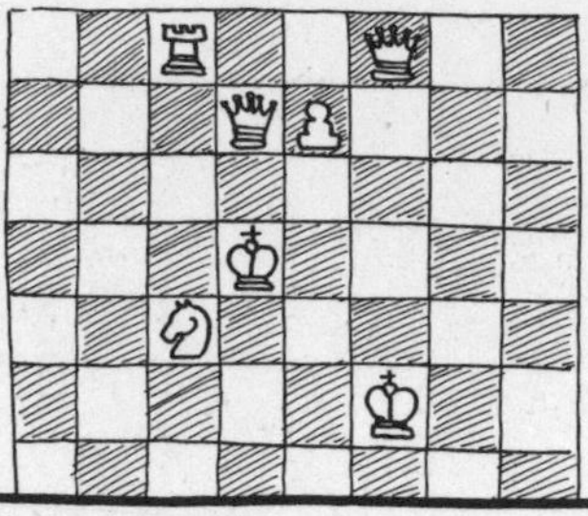

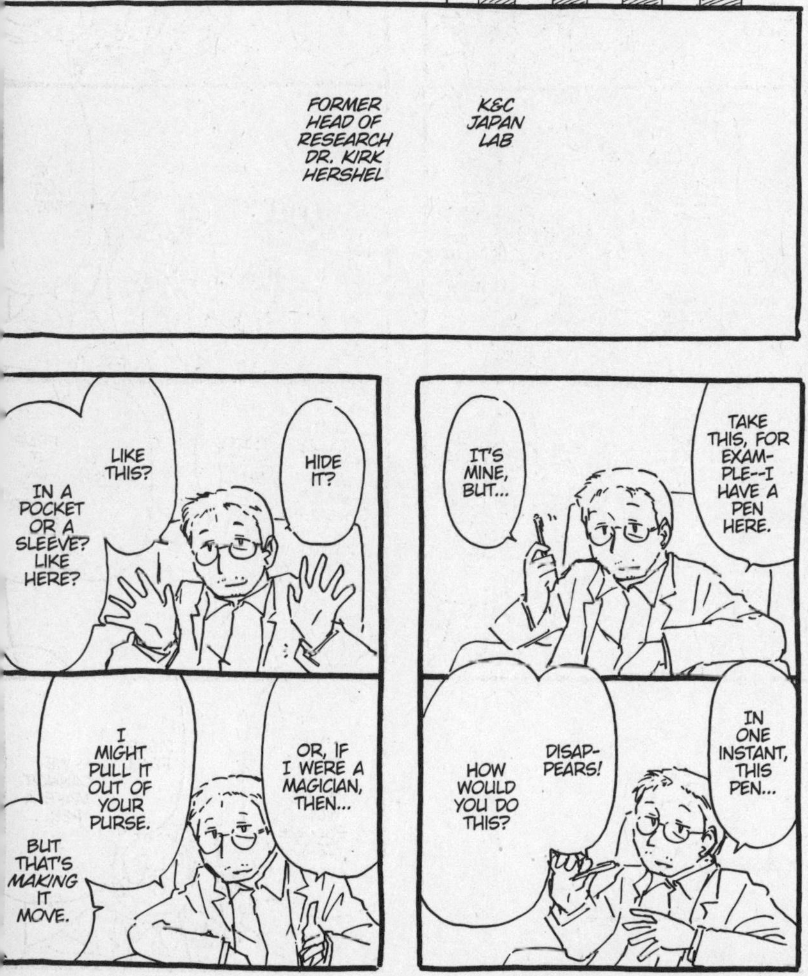
K&C JAPAN LAB
FORMER HEAD OF RESEARCH DR. KIRK HERSHEL
TAKE THIS, FOR EXAM-PLE--I HAVE A PEN HERE.
IT'S MINE, BUT...
HIDE IT?
LIKE THIS?
IN A POCKET OR A SLEEVE? LIKE HERE?
IN ONE INSTANT, THIS PEN...
DISAP-PEARS!
HOW WOULD YOU DO THIS?
OR, IF I WERE A MAGICIAN, THEN...
I MIGHT PULL IT OUT OF YOUR PURSE.
BUT THAT'S *MAKING* IT MOVE.

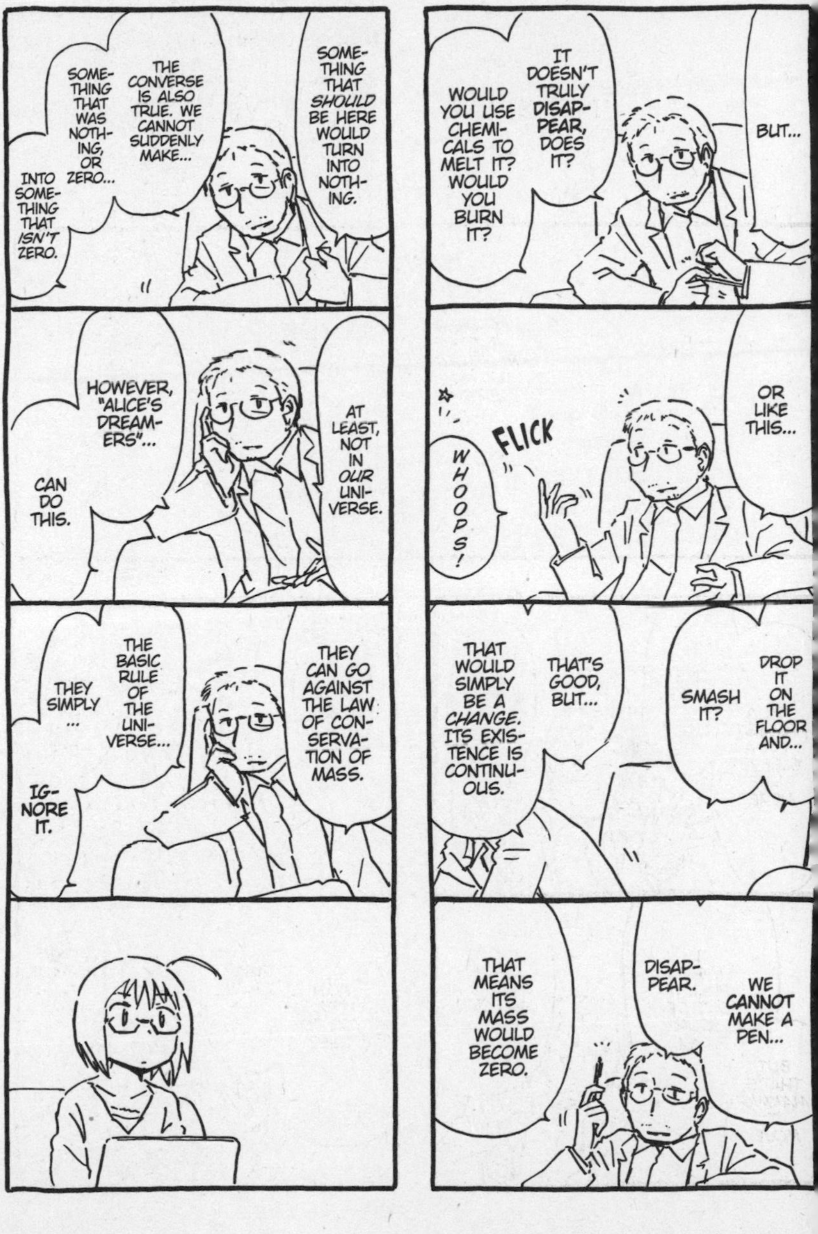
BUT...
IT DOESN'T TRULY DISAPPEAR, DOES IT?
WOULD YOU USE CHEMICALS TO MELT IT? WOULD YOU BURN IT?
OR LIKE THIS...
FLICK
WHOOPS!
DROP IT ON THE FLOOR AND...
SMASH IT?
THAT'S GOOD, BUT...
THAT WOULD SIMPLY BE A *CHANGE*. ITS EXISTENCE IS CONTINUOUS.
WE CANNOT MAKE A PEN...
DISAPPEAR.
THAT MEANS ITS MASS WOULD BECOME ZERO.
SOMETHING THAT *SHOULD* BE HERE WOULD TURN INTO NOTHING.
THE CONVERSE IS ALSO TRUE. WE CANNOT SUDDENLY MAKE...
SOMETHING THAT WAS NOTHING, OR ZERO...
INTO SOMETHING THAT *ISN'T* ZERO.
AT LEAST, NOT IN *OUR* UNIVERSE.
HOWEVER, "ALICE'S DREAMERS"...
CAN DO THIS.
THEY CAN GO AGAINST THE LAW OF CONSERVATION OF MASS.
THE BASIC RULE OF THE UNIVERSE...
THEY SIMPLY...
IGNORE IT.

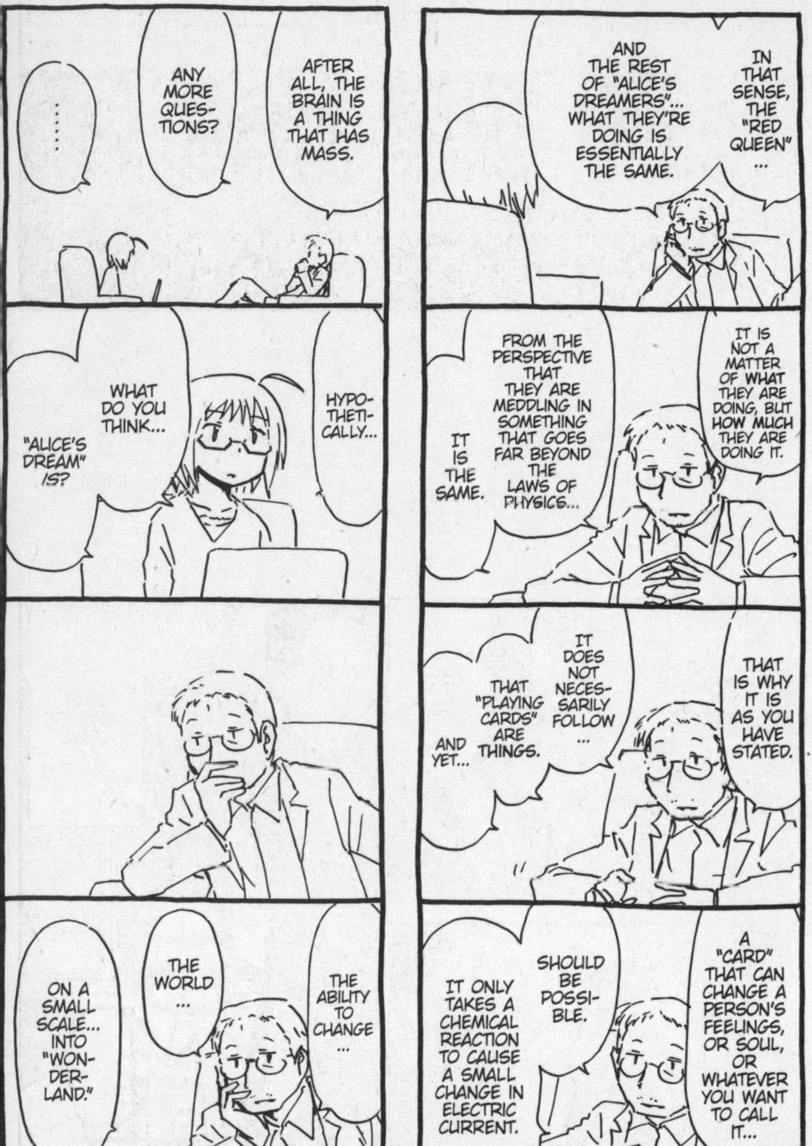
IN THAT SENSE, THE "RED QUEEN"...
AND THE REST OF "ALICE'S DREAMERS"... WHAT THEY'RE DOING IS ESSENTIALLY THE SAME.
IT IS NOT A MATTER OF WHAT THEY ARE DOING, BUT HOW MUCH THEY ARE DOING IT.
FROM THE PERSPECTIVE THAT THEY ARE MEDDLING IN SOMETHING THAT GOES FAR BEYOND THE LAWS OF PHYSICS...
IT IS THE SAME.
THAT IS WHY IT IS AS YOU HAVE STATED.
IT DOES NOT NECES-SARILY FOLLOW...
THAT "PLAYING CARDS" ARE THINGS.
AND YET...
A "CARD" THAT CAN CHANGE A PERSON'S FEELINGS, OR SOUL, OR WHATEVER YOU WANT TO CALL IT...
SHOULD BE POSSI-BLE.
IT ONLY TAKES A CHEMICAL REACTION TO CAUSE A SMALL CHANGE IN ELECTRIC CURRENT.
AFTER ALL, THE BRAIN IS A THING THAT HAS MASS.
ANY MORE QUES-TIONS?
......
HYPO-THETI-CALLY...
WHAT DO YOU THINK...
"ALICE'S DREAM" IS?
THE ABILITY TO CHANGE...
THE WORLD...
ON A SMALL SCALE... INTO "WON-DER-LAND."

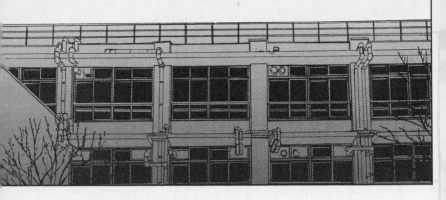

IT'S
BEEN
TEN
DAYS...

SINCE
HAA-CHAN
DISAP-
PEARED.

NGH!

GO,
GO!

THUD

14

IT'S
ALMOST
APRIL.

THUD

BUSTLE
BUSTLE
BUSTLE

WHAP!

NUH-
UH...

?!

INTERLUDE

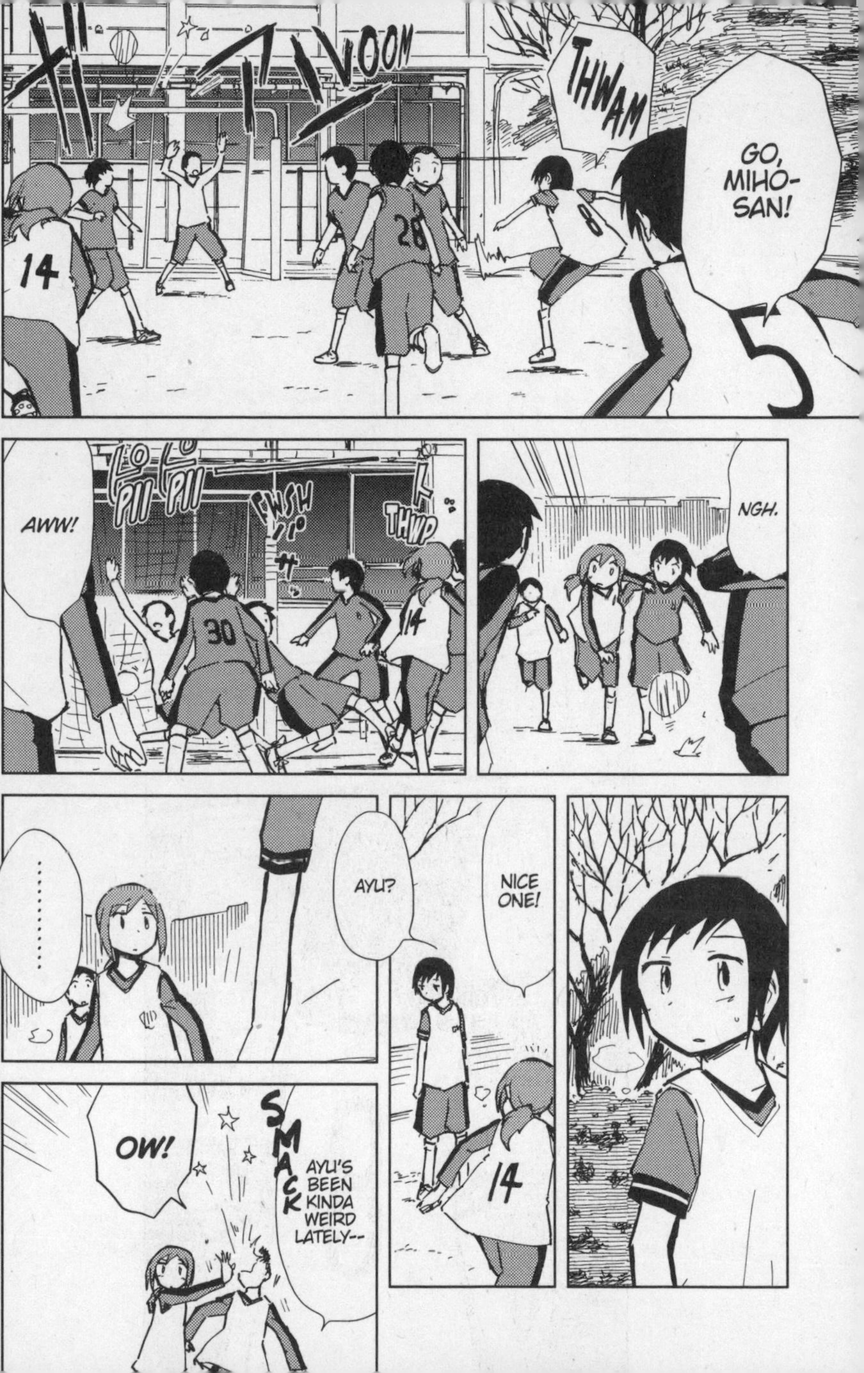
GO, MIHO-SAN!
THWAM
VOOM
NGH.
AWW!
PII PII
FWSH
THWP
NICE ONE!
AYU?
......
OW!
SMACK
AYU'S BEEN KINDA WEIRD LATELY--

INTERLUDE
Downy

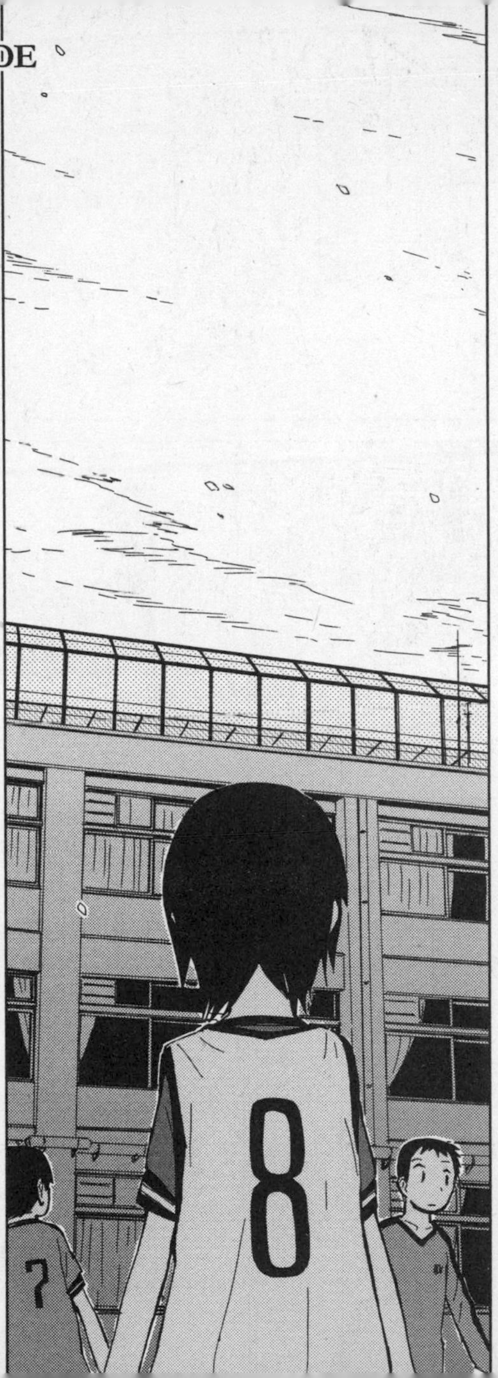

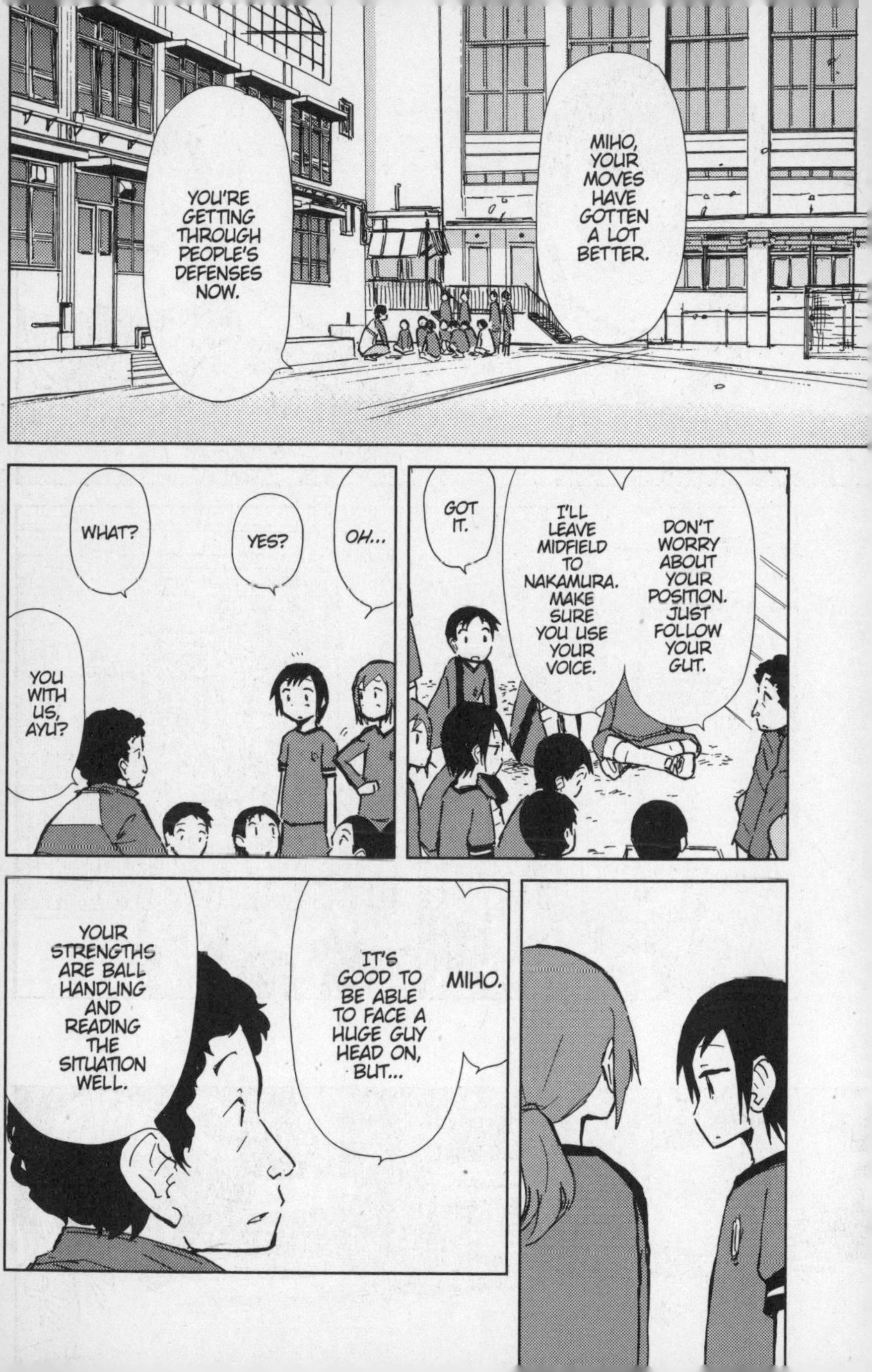
MIHO, YOUR MOVES HAVE GOTTEN A LOT BETTER.
YOU'RE GETTING THROUGH PEOPLE'S DEFENSES NOW.
DON'T WORRY ABOUT YOUR POSITION. JUST FOLLOW YOUR GUT.
I'LL LEAVE MIDFIELD TO NAKAMURA. MAKE SURE YOU USE YOUR VOICE.
GOT IT.
OH...
YES?
WHAT?
YOU WITH US, AYU?
MIHO.
IT'S GOOD TO BE ABLE TO FACE A HUGE GUY HEAD ON, BUT...
YOUR STRENGTHS ARE BALL HANDLING AND READING THE SITUATION WELL.

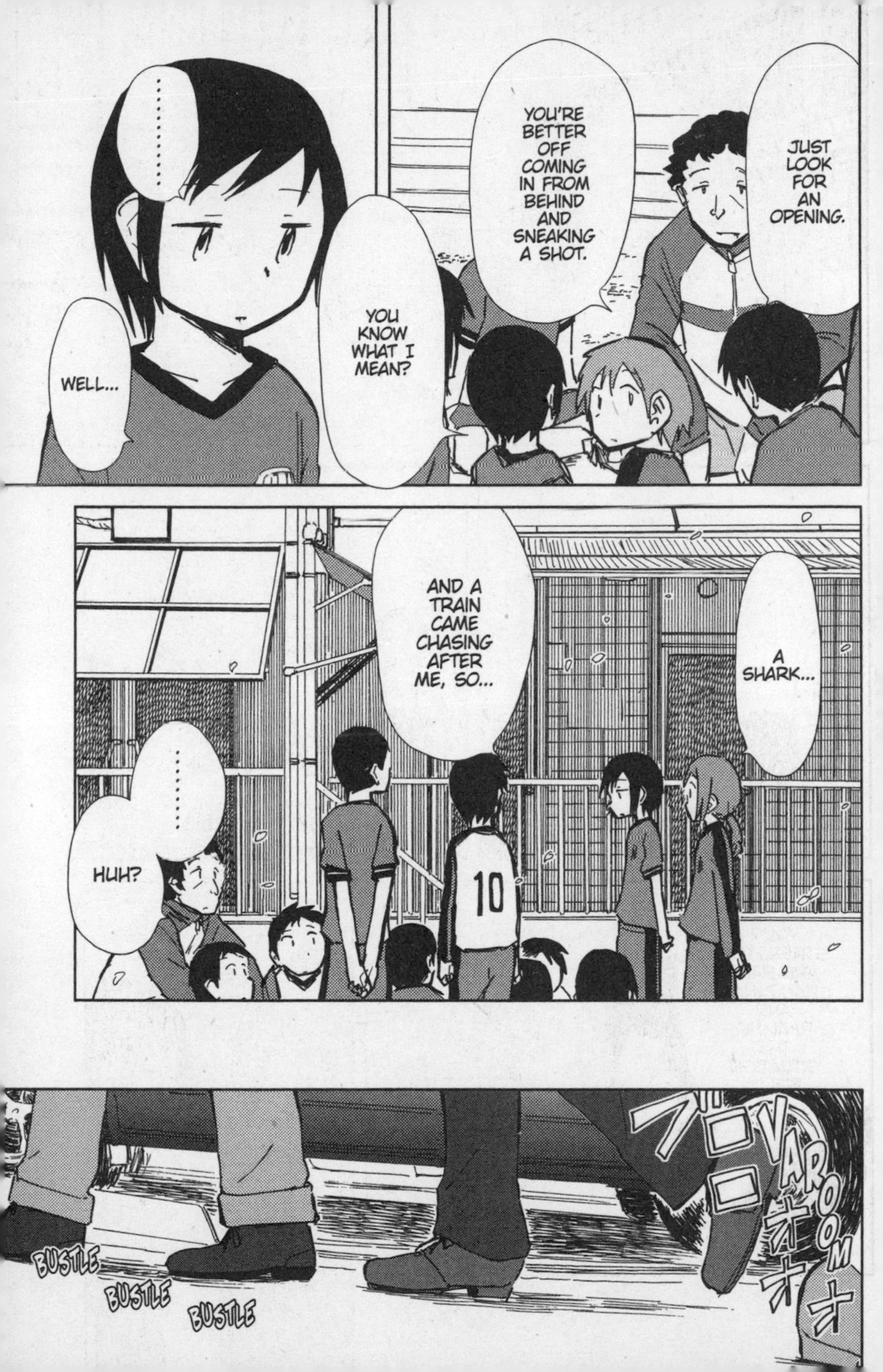
JUST LOOK FOR AN OPENING.
YOU'RE BETTER OFF COMING IN FROM BEHIND AND SNEAKING A SHOT.
YOU KNOW WHAT I MEAN?
……
WELL...
A SHARK...
AND A TRAIN CAME CHASING AFTER ME, SO...
……
HUH?
10
VAROOM
BUSTLE
BUSTLE
BUSTLE

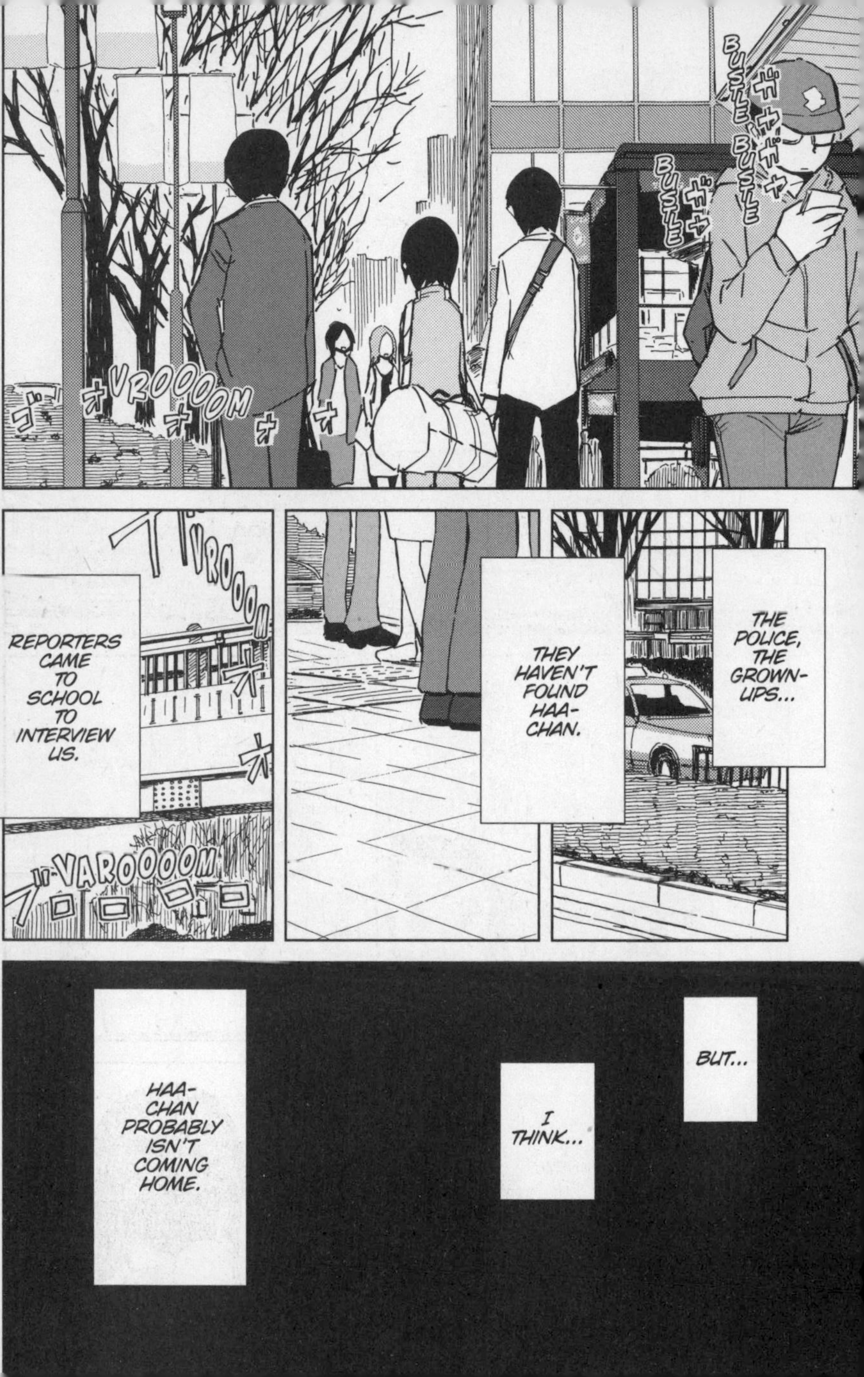

BUSTLE BUSTLE
BUSTLE
VROOOOOM
THE POLICE, THE GROWN-UPS...
THEY HAVEN'T FOUND HAA-CHAN.
REPORTERS CAME TO SCHOOL TO INTERVIEW US.
VROOOOM
VAROOOOM
BUT...
I THINK...
HAA-CHAN PROBABLY ISN'T COMING HOME.

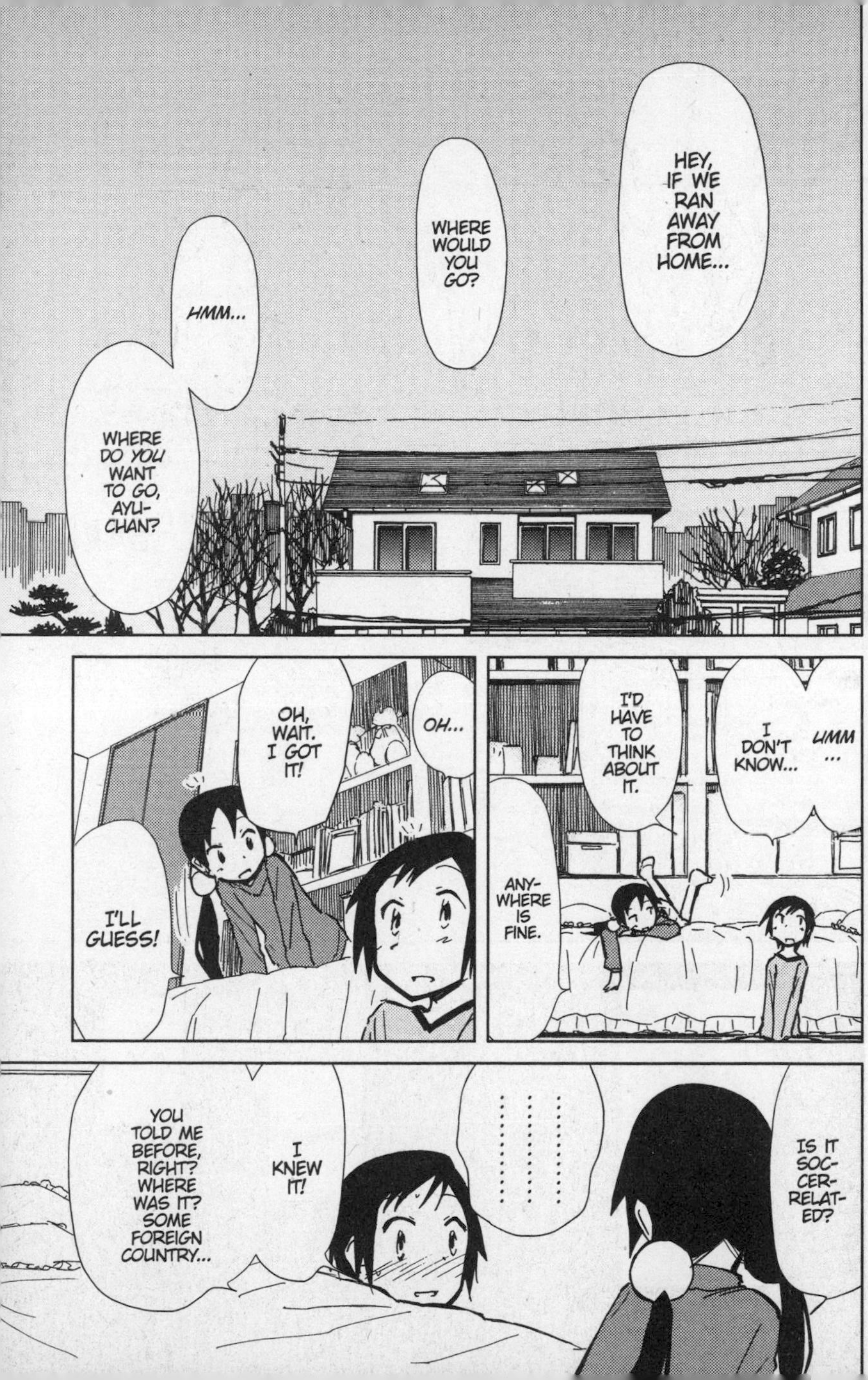
HEY, IF WE RAN AWAY FROM HOME...
WHERE WOULD YOU GO?
HMM...
WHERE DO YOU WANT TO GO, AYU-CHAN?
UMM ...
I DON'T KNOW...
I'D HAVE TO THINK ABOUT IT.
ANY-WHERE IS FINE.
OH...
OH, WAIT. I GOT IT!
I'LL GUESS!
IS IT SOCCER-RELATED?
......
I KNEW IT!
YOU TOLD ME BEFORE, RIGHT? WHERE WAS IT? SOME FOREIGN COUNTRY...

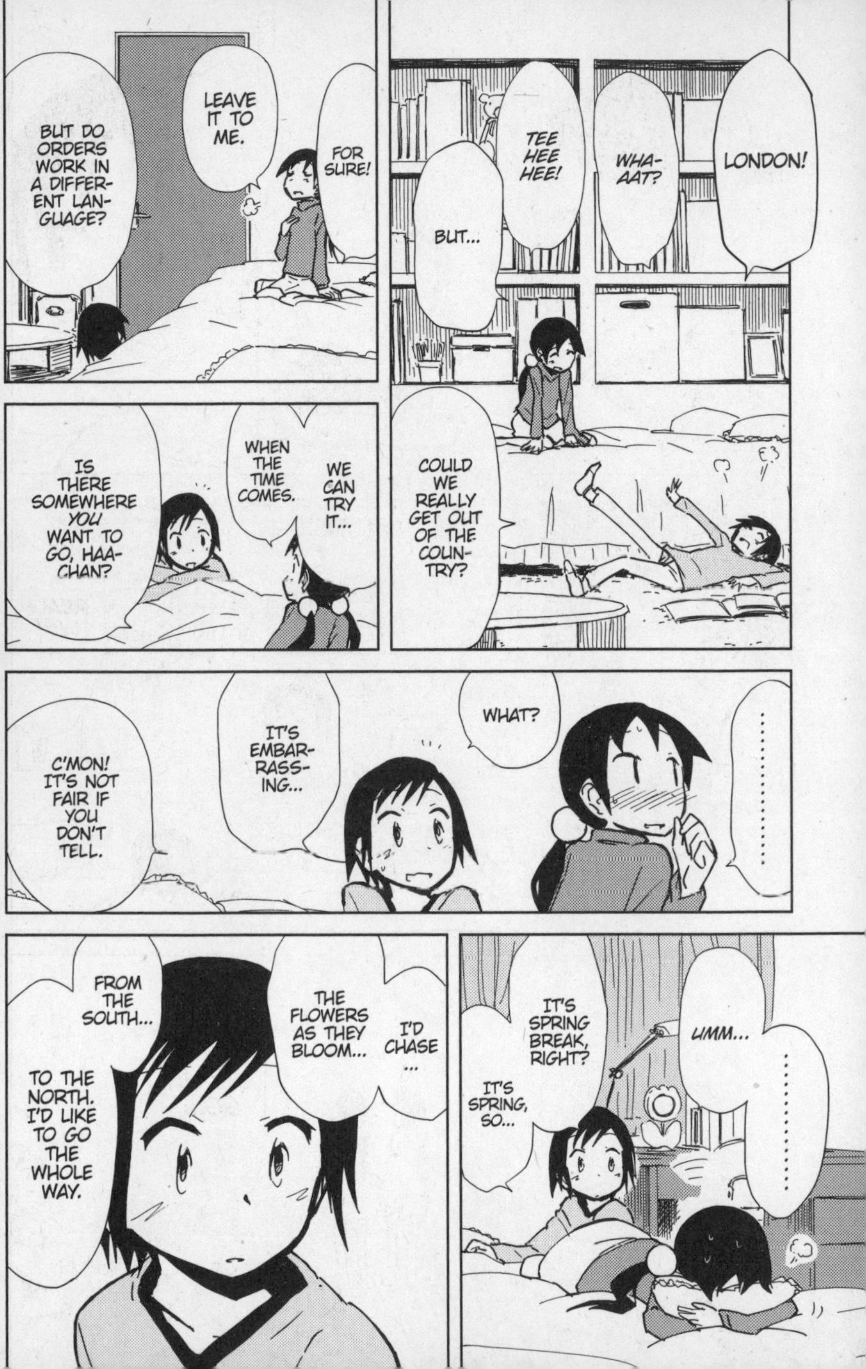
LONDON!
WHA-AAT?
TEE HEE HEE!
BUT...
COULD WE REALLY GET OUT OF THE COUNTRY?
FOR SURE!
LEAVE IT TO ME.
BUT DO ORDERS WORK IN A DIFFERENT LANGUAGE?
WE CAN TRY IT...
WHEN THE TIME COMES.
IS THERE SOMEWHERE *YOU* WANT TO GO, HAA-CHAN?
......
WHAT?
IT'S EMBARRASSING...
C'MON! IT'S NOT FAIR IF YOU DON'T TELL.
......
UMM...
IT'S SPRING BREAK, RIGHT?
IT'S SPRING, SO...
I'D CHASE...
THE FLOWERS AS THEY BLOOM...
FROM THE SOUTH...
TO THE NORTH. I'D LIKE TO GO THE WHOLE WAY.

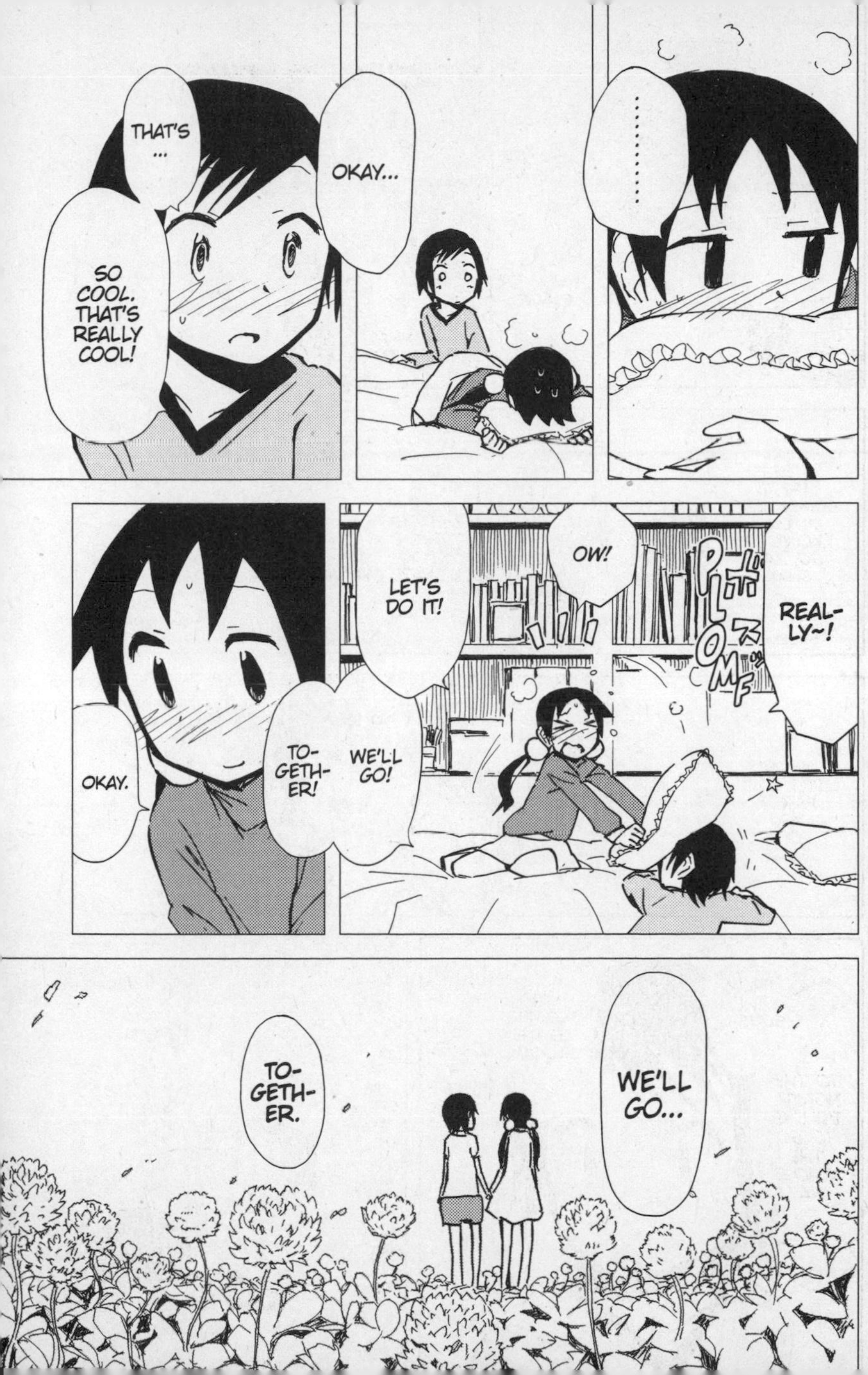
......
OKAY...
THAT'S ...
SO COOL. THAT'S REALLY COOL!
REAL-LY~!
PLOMF
OW!
LET'S DO IT!
WE'LL GO!
TO-GETH-ER!
OKAY.
WE'LL GO...
TO-GETH-ER.

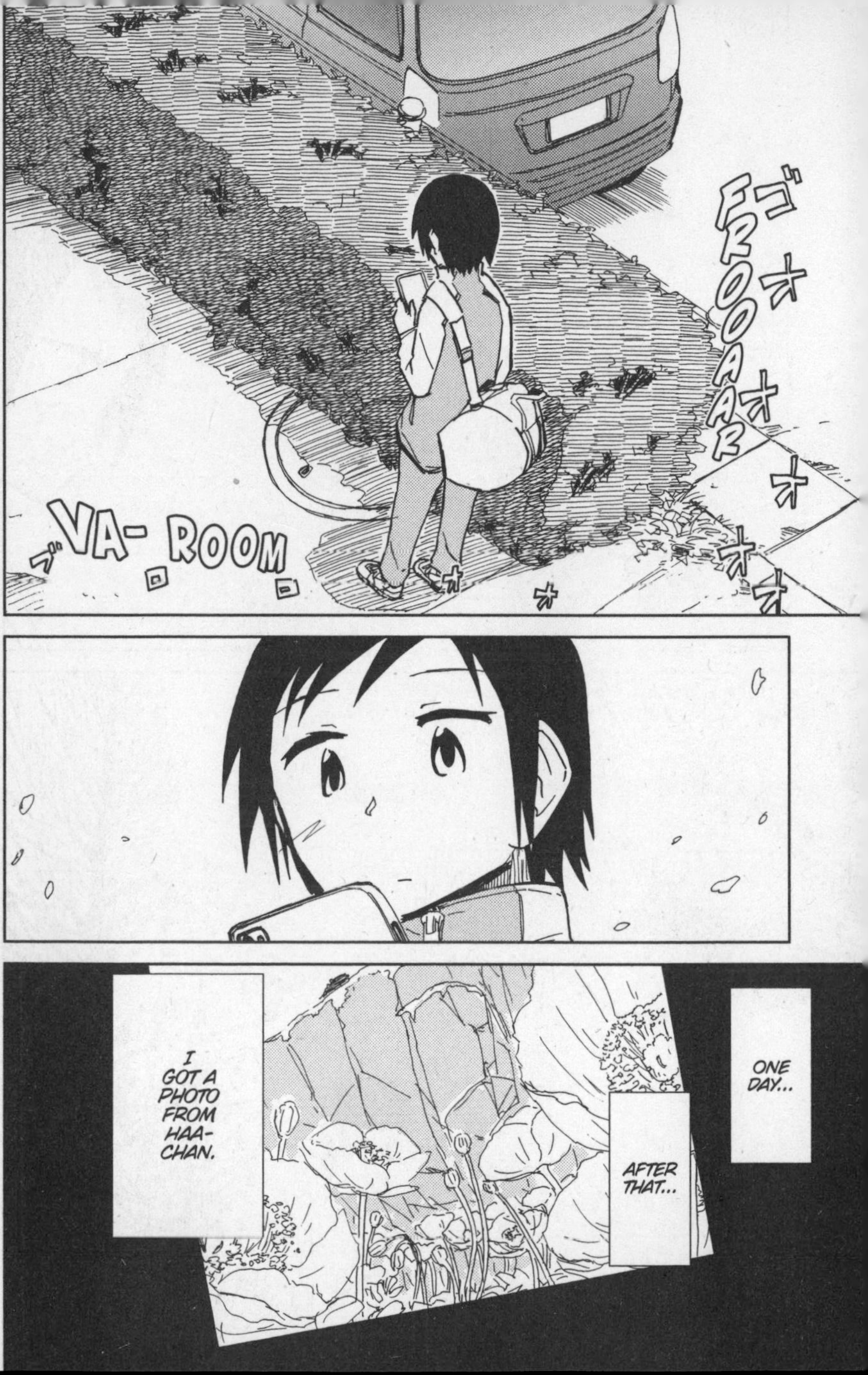
FROOOAAR
VA- ROOM
ONE DAY...
AFTER THAT...
I GOT A PHOTO FROM HAA-CHAN.

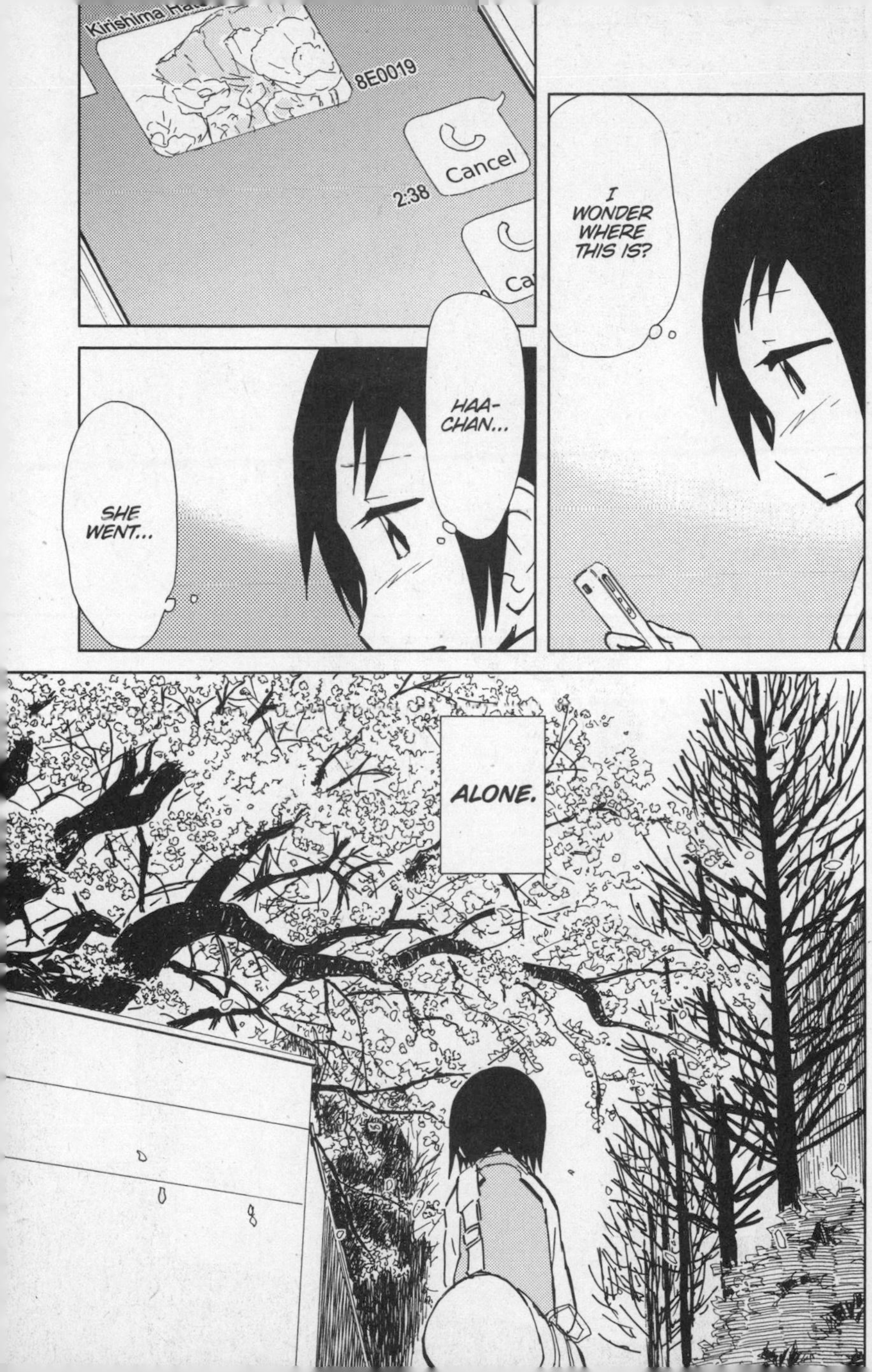
I WONDER WHERE THIS IS?
Kirishima
8E0019
Cancel
2:38
HAA-CHAN...
SHE WENT...
ALONE.

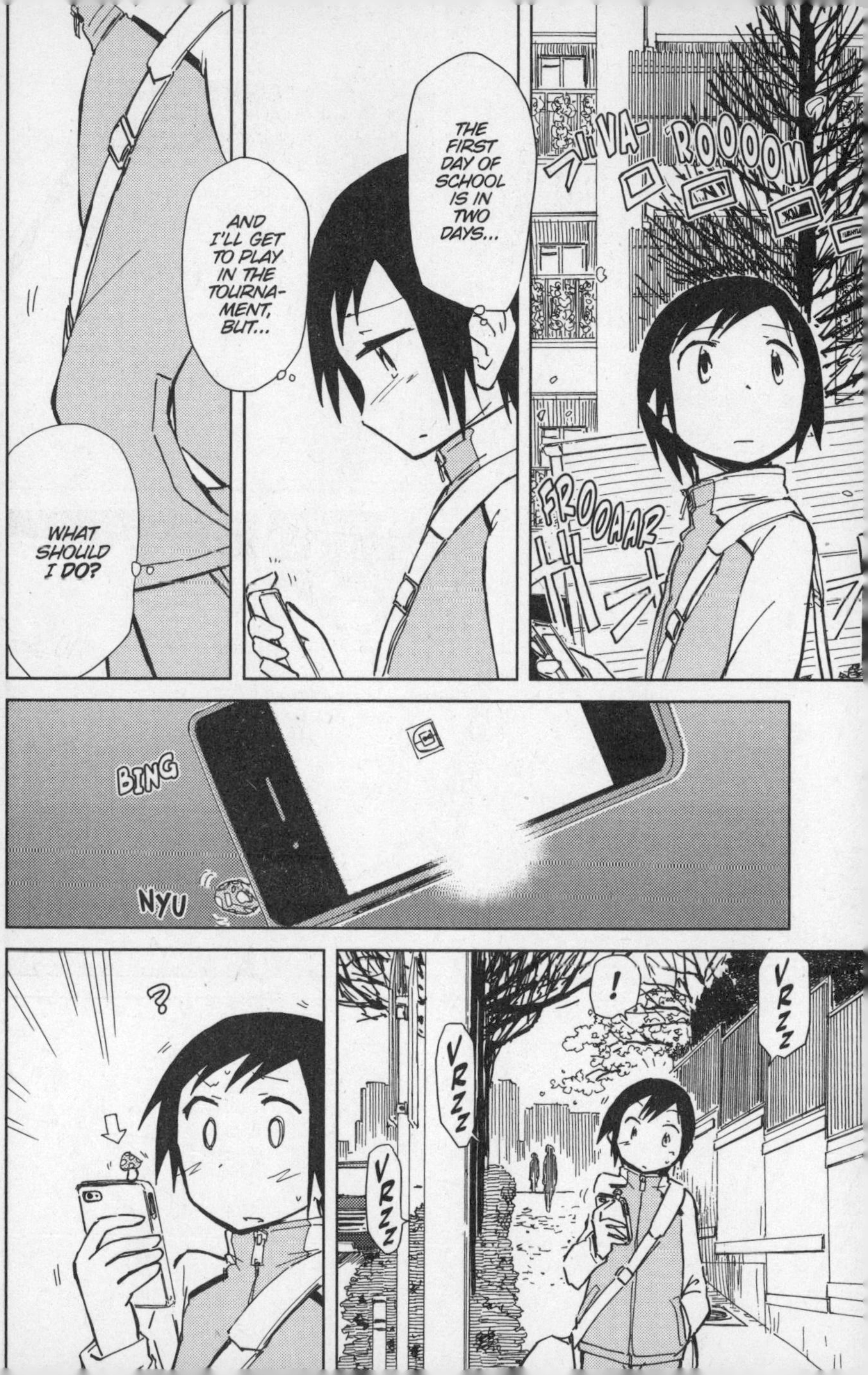
VA-ROOOOM
FROOAAR
THE FIRST DAY OF SCHOOL IS IN TWO DAYS...
AND I'LL GET TO PLAY IN THE TOURNAMENT, BUT...
WHAT SHOULD I DO?
BING
NYU
VRZZ
!
VRZZ
VRZZ
?

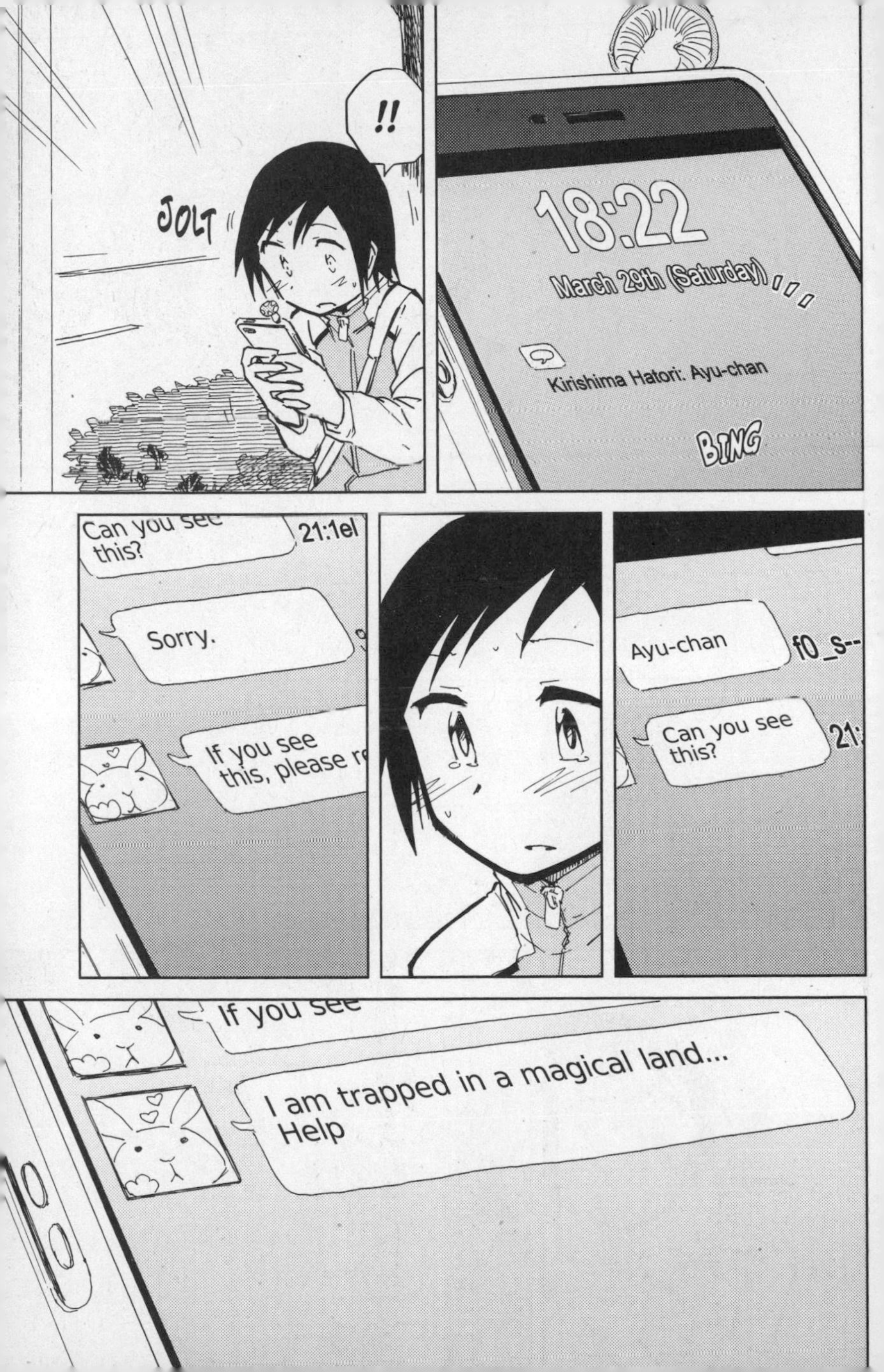
18:22
March 29th (Saturday)
Kirishima Hatori: Ayu-chan
BING
!!
JOLT
Ayu-chan
f0_s--
Can you see this?
21:
Can you see this?
21:1el
Sorry.
If you see this, please r
If you see
I am trapped in a magical land... Help

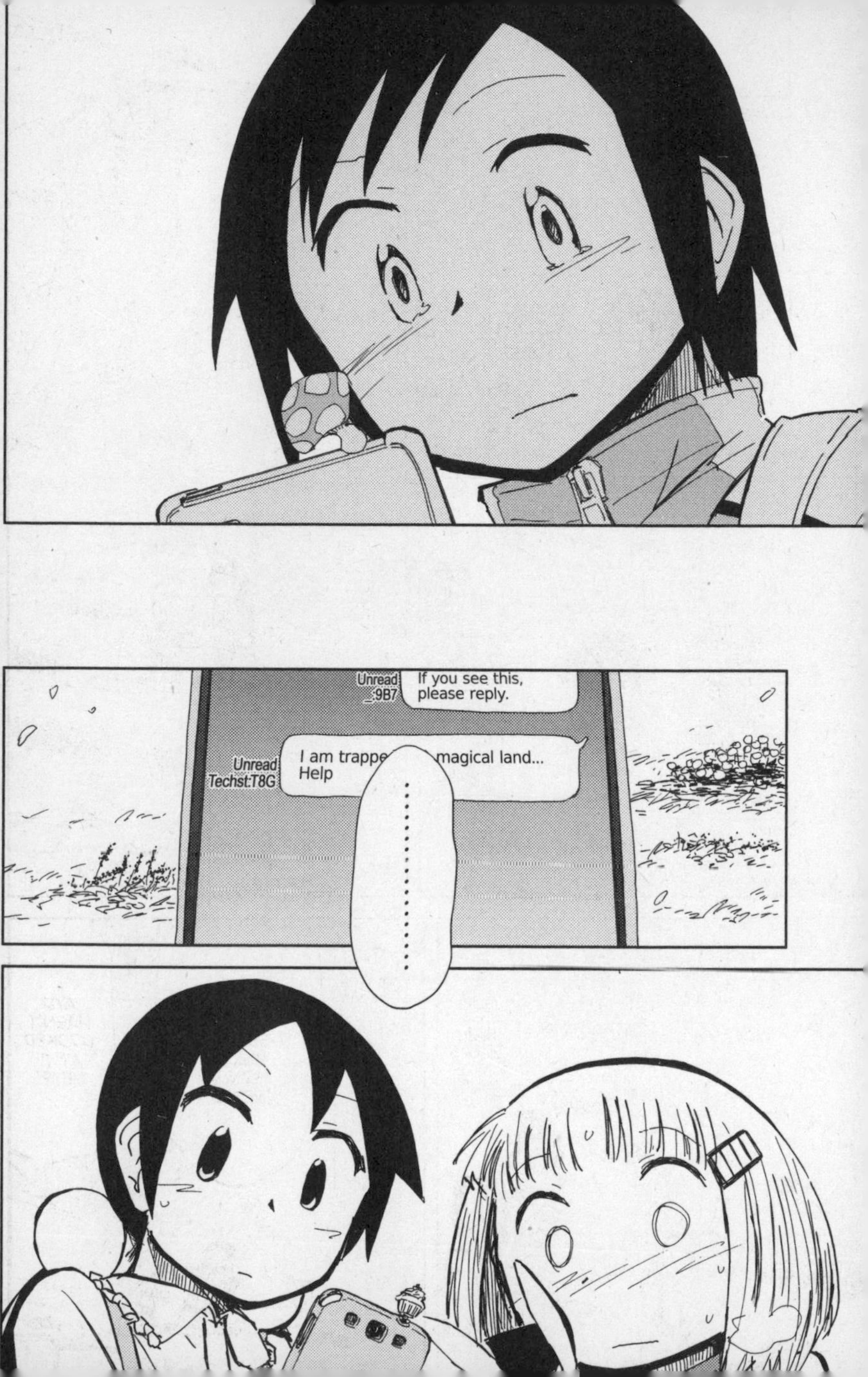
Unread
_:9B7
If you see this, please reply.
Unread
Techst:T8G
I am trappe magical land... Help
......

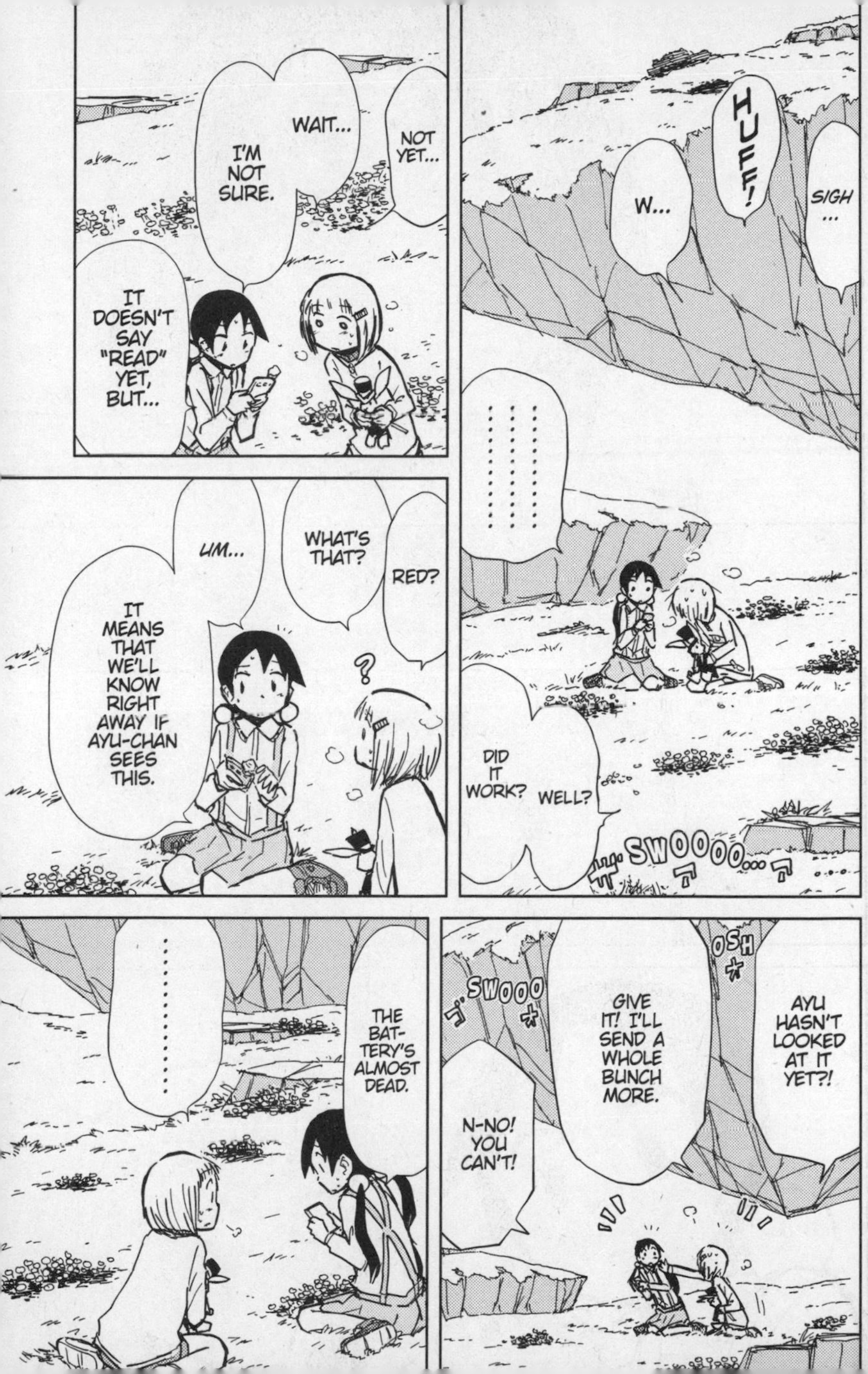
SIGH...
HUFF!
W...
......
WELL?
DID IT WORK?
SWOOOO...
NOT YET...
WAIT... I'M NOT SURE.
IT DOESN'T SAY "READ" YET, BUT...
RED?
WHAT'S THAT?
UM... IT MEANS THAT WE'LL KNOW RIGHT AWAY IF AYU-CHAN SEES THIS.
OSH
AYU HASN'T LOOKED AT IT YET?!
GIVE IT! I'LL SEND A WHOLE BUNCH MORE.
SWOOO
N-NO! YOU CAN'T!
THE BATTERY'S ALMOST DEAD.
......

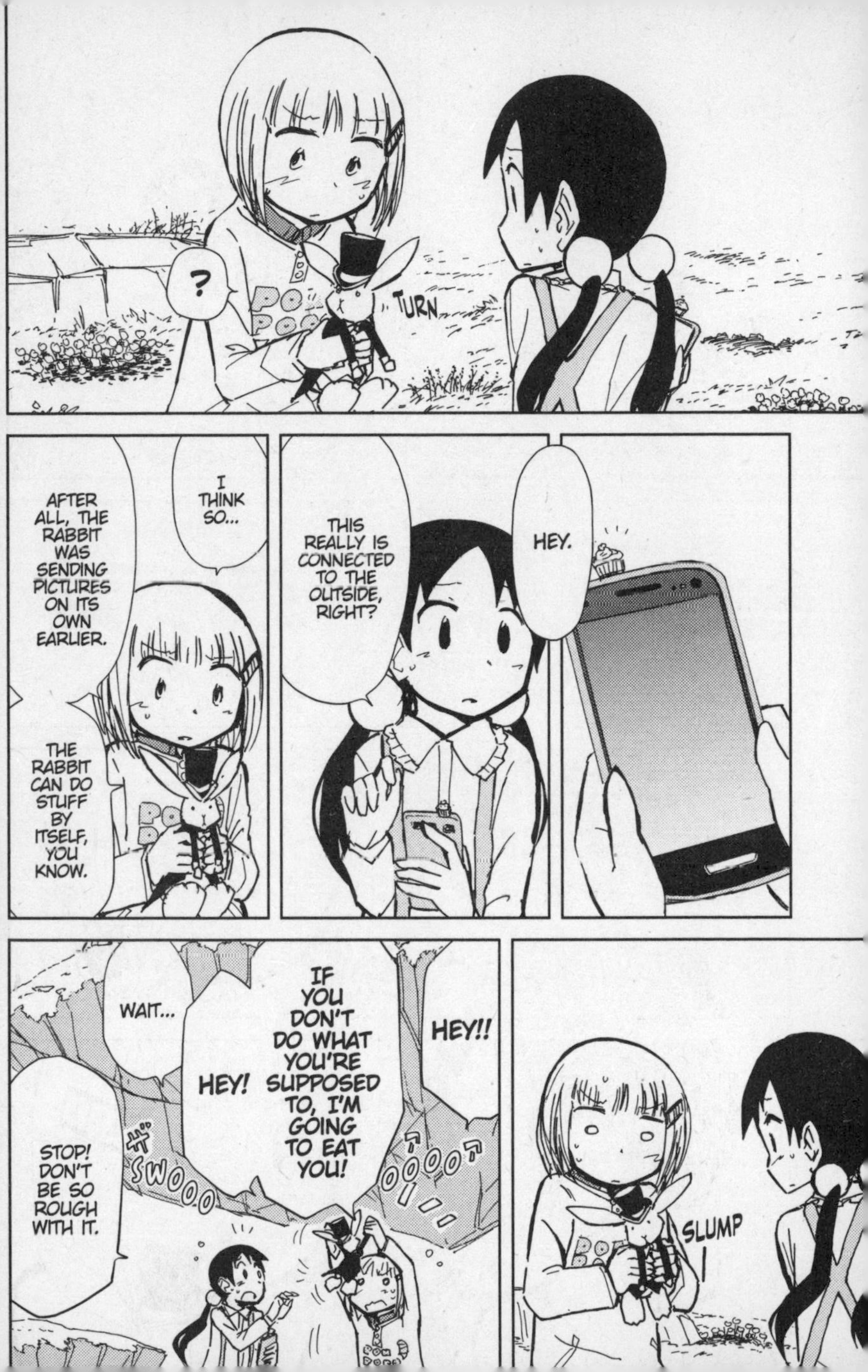
?
TURN
HEY.
THIS REALLY IS CONNECTED TO THE OUTSIDE, RIGHT?
I THINK SO...
AFTER ALL, THE RABBIT WAS SENDING PICTURES ON ITS OWN EARLIER.
THE RABBIT CAN DO STUFF BY ITSELF, YOU KNOW.
SLUMP
HEY!!
IF YOU DON'T DO WHAT YOU'RE SUPPOSED TO, I'M GOING TO EAT YOU!
HEY!
WAIT...
STOP! DON'T BE SO ROUGH WITH IT.
SWOOO

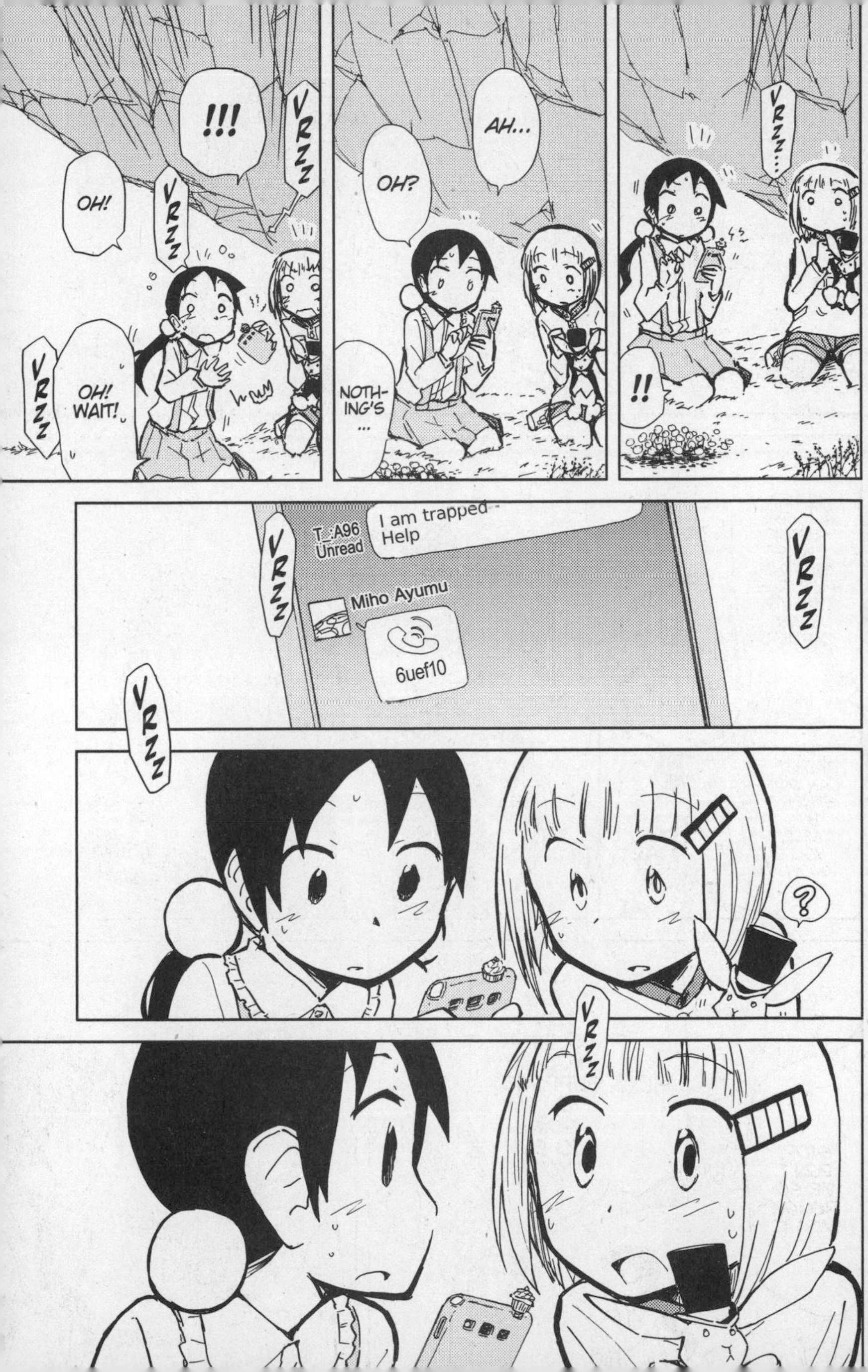
VRZZ...
!!
AH...
OH?
NOTH-ING'S ...
!!!
VRZZ
OH!
VRZZ
OH! WAIT!
VRZZ
VRZZ
T_A96
Unread
I am trapped -
Help
VRZZ
Miho Ayumu
6uef10
VRZZ
?
VRZZ

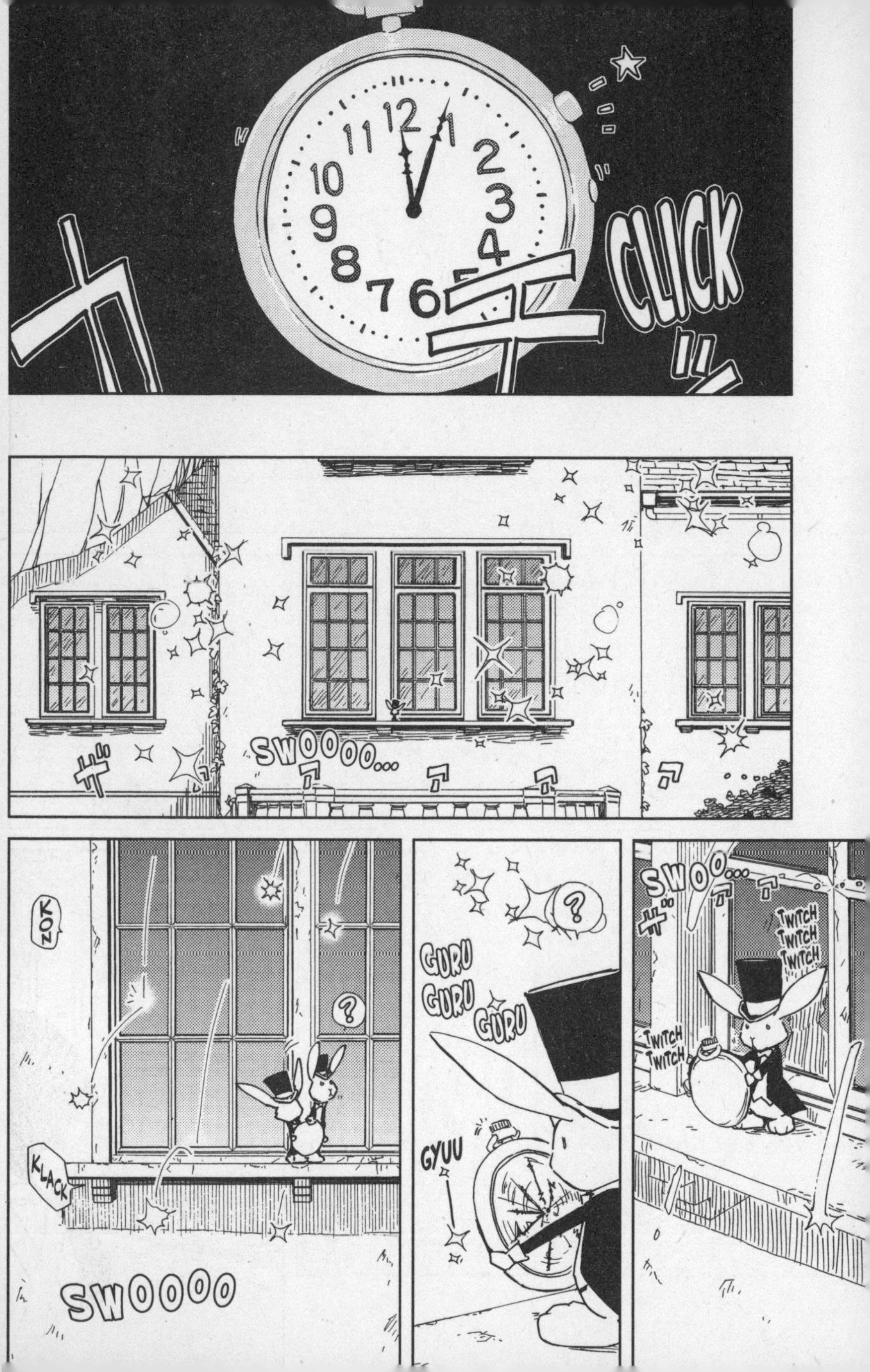
CLICK
SWOOOOO...
SWOO...
TWITCH
TWITCH
TWITCH
TWITCH
TWITCH
GURU
GURU
GURU
GYUU
KON
KLACK
SWOOOO

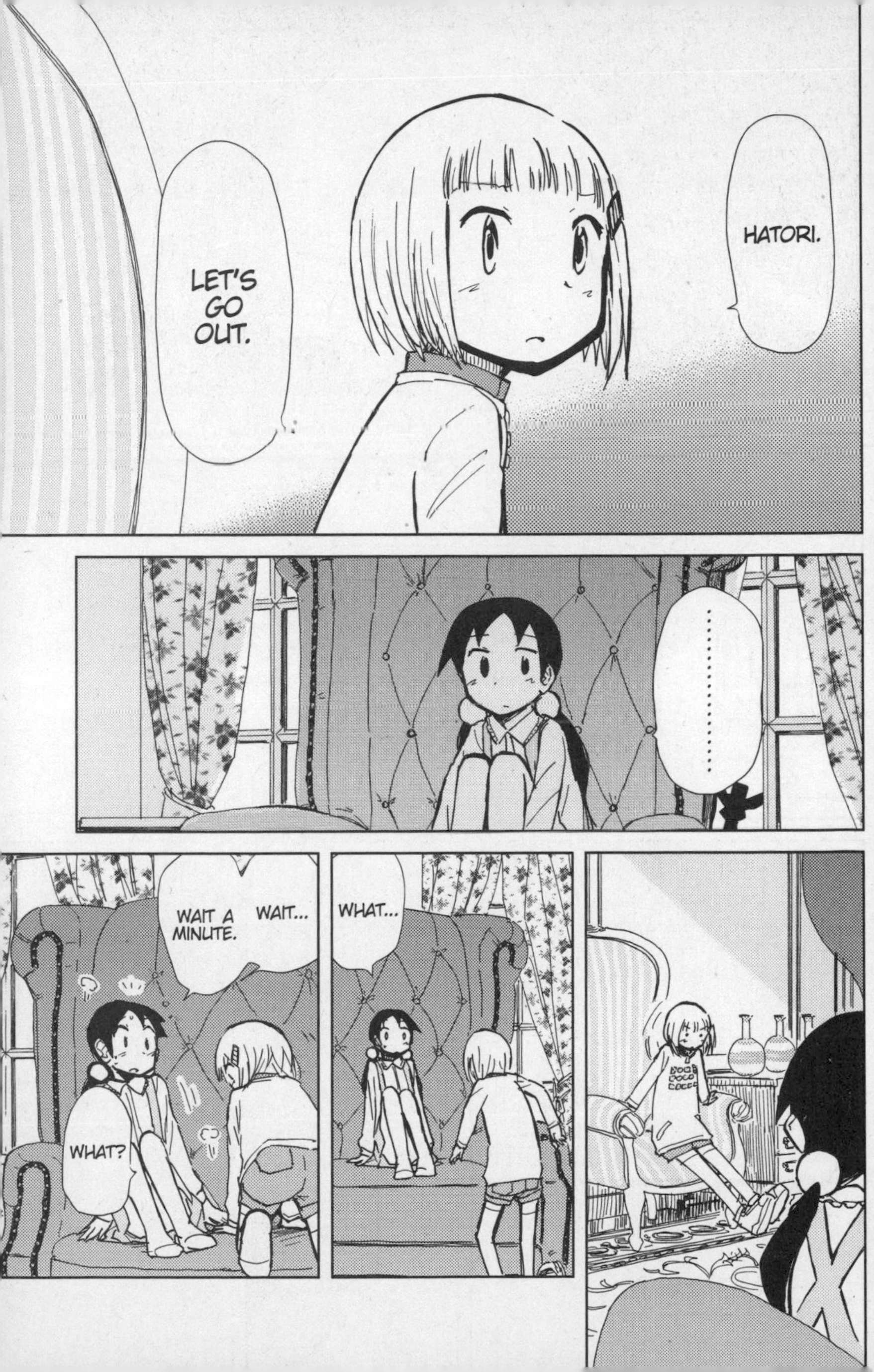
HATORI.
LET'S GO OUT.
......
WHAT...
WAIT... WAIT A MINUTE.
WHAT?

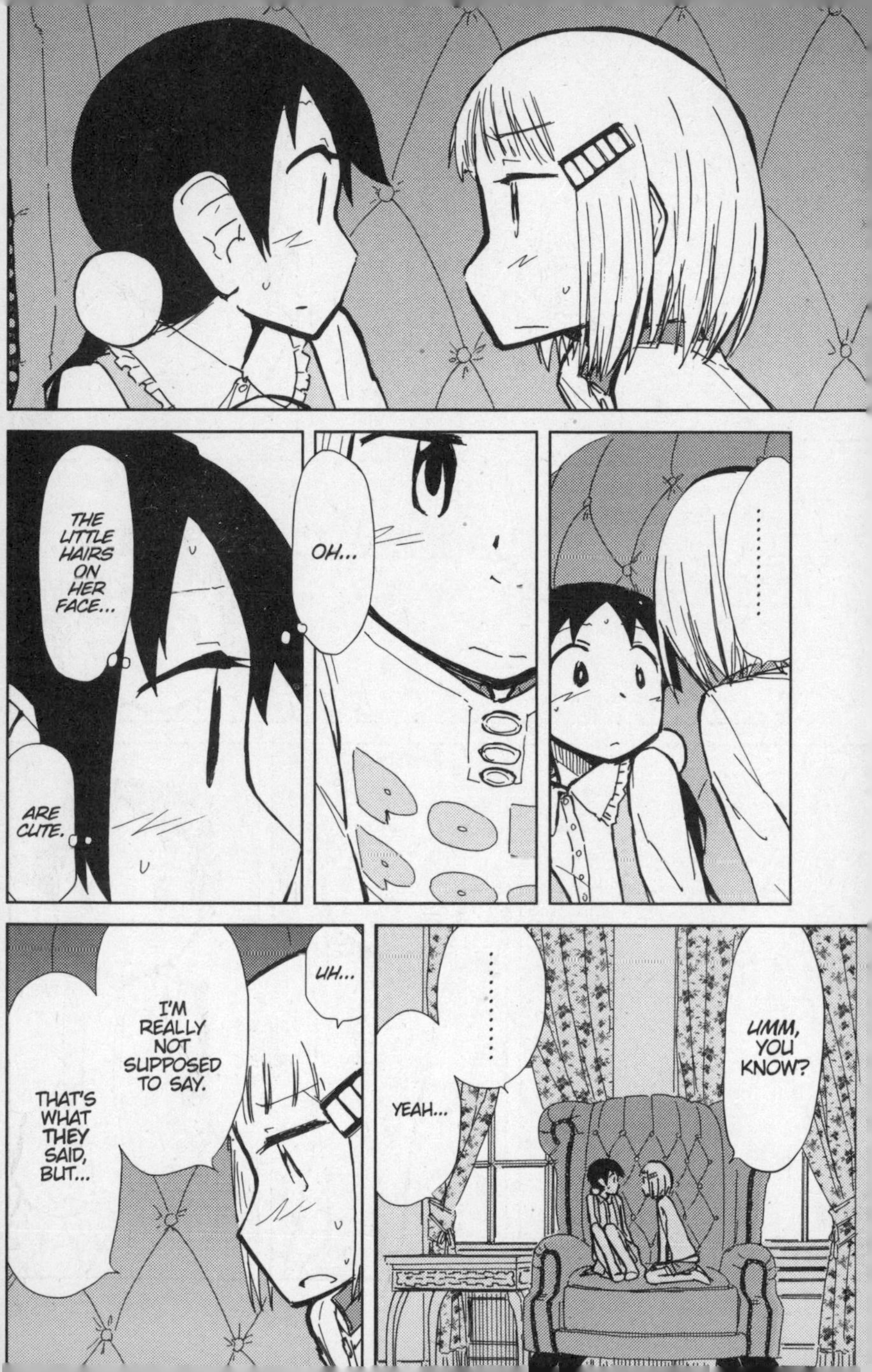
......
OH...
THE LITTLE HAIRS ON HER FACE...
ARE CUTE.
UMM, YOU KNOW?
......
YEAH...
UH...
I'M REALLY NOT SUPPOSED TO SAY.
THAT'S WHAT THEY SAID, BUT...

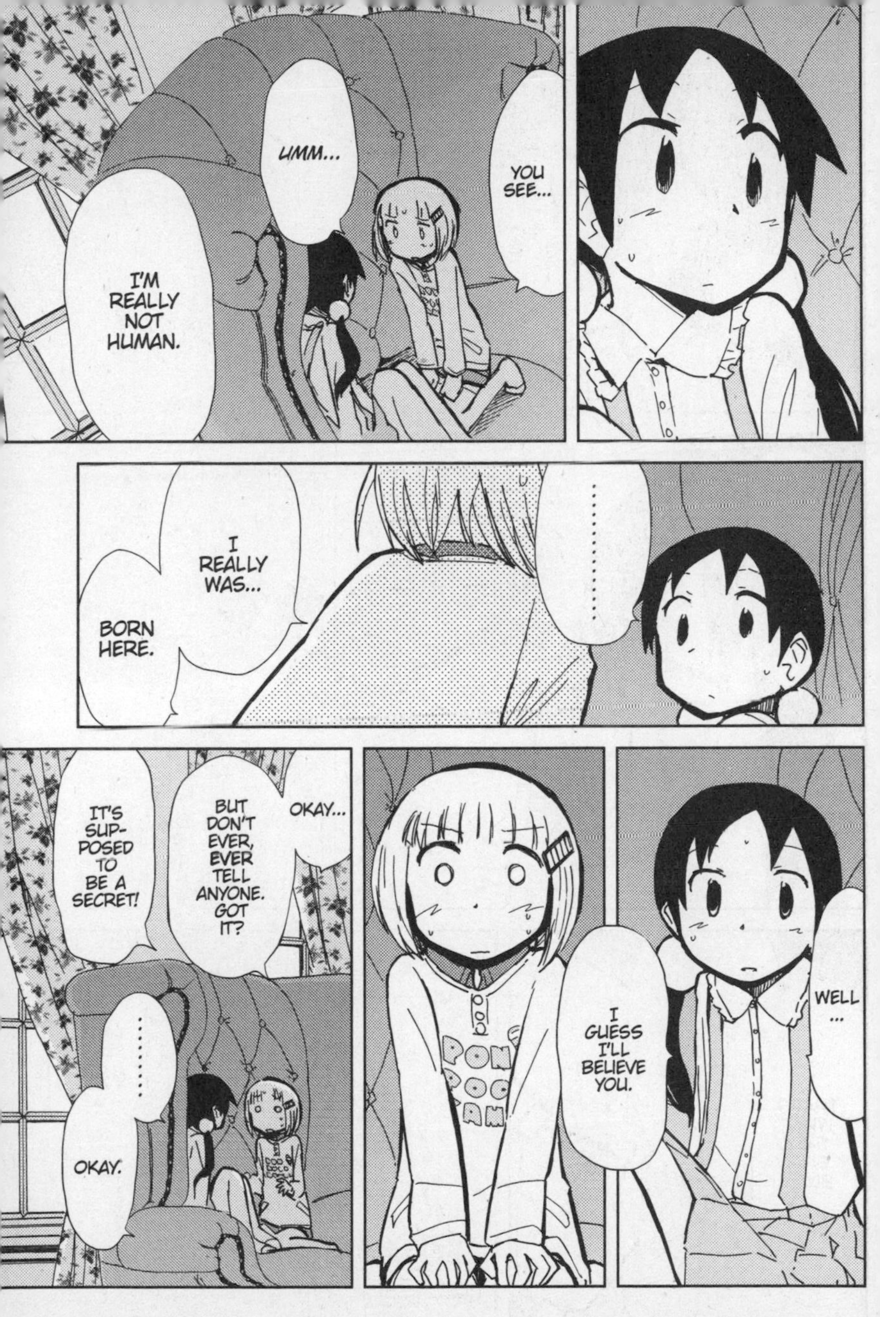
YOU SEE...
UMM...
I'M REALLY NOT HUMAN.
......
I REALLY WAS...
BORN HERE.
WELL...
I GUESS I'LL BELIEVE YOU.
OKAY...
BUT DON'T EVER, EVER TELL ANYONE. GOT IT?
IT'S SUP-POSED TO BE A SECRET!
......
OKAY.

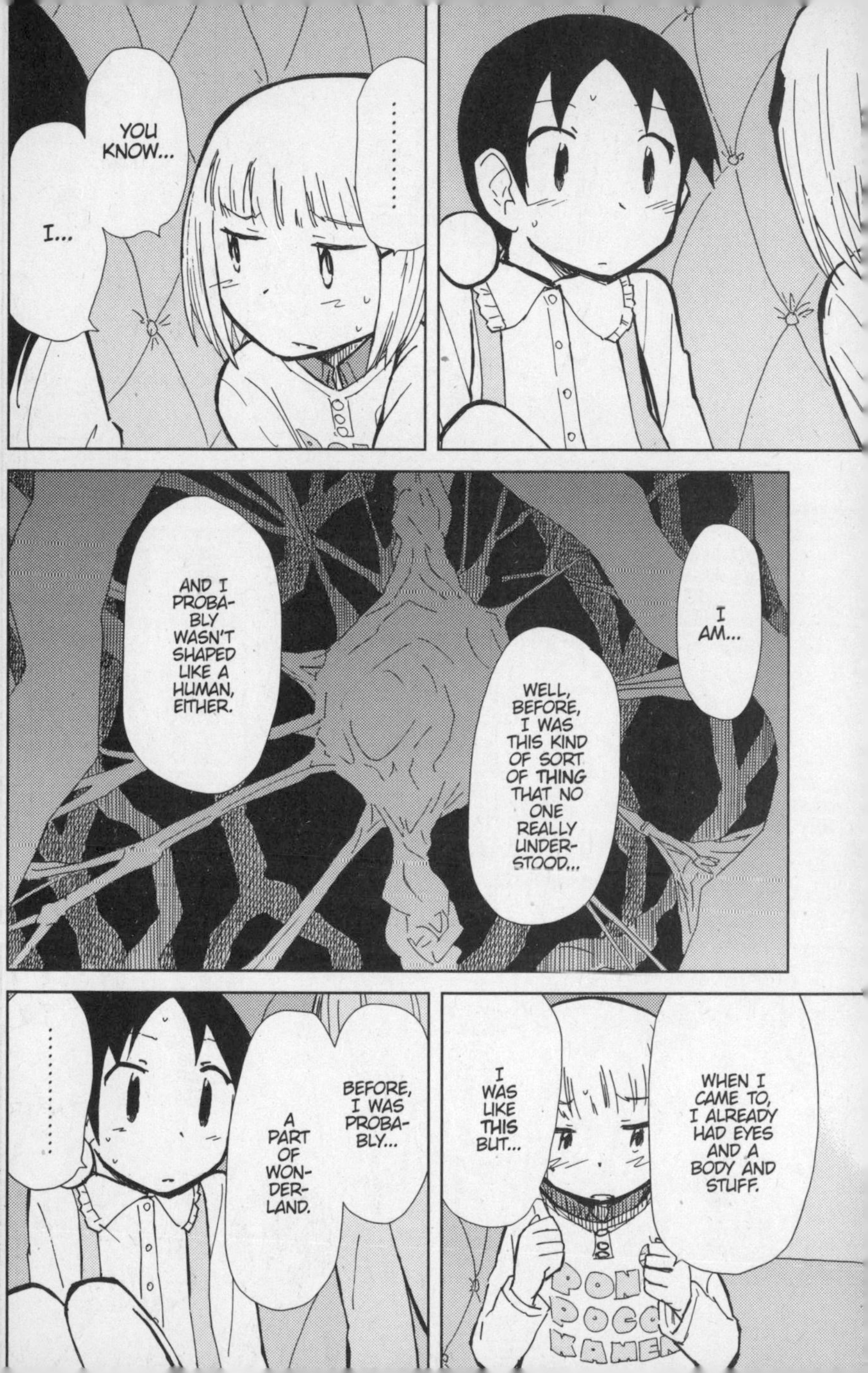
......
YOU KNOW...
I...
I AM...
WELL, BEFORE, I WAS THIS KIND OF SORT OF THING THAT NO ONE REALLY UNDERSTOOD...
AND I PROBABLY WASN'T SHAPED LIKE A HUMAN, EITHER.
WHEN I CAME TO, I ALREADY HAD EYES AND A BODY AND STUFF.
I WAS LIKE THIS BUT...
BEFORE, I WAS PROBABLY...
A PART OF WONDERLAND.
......

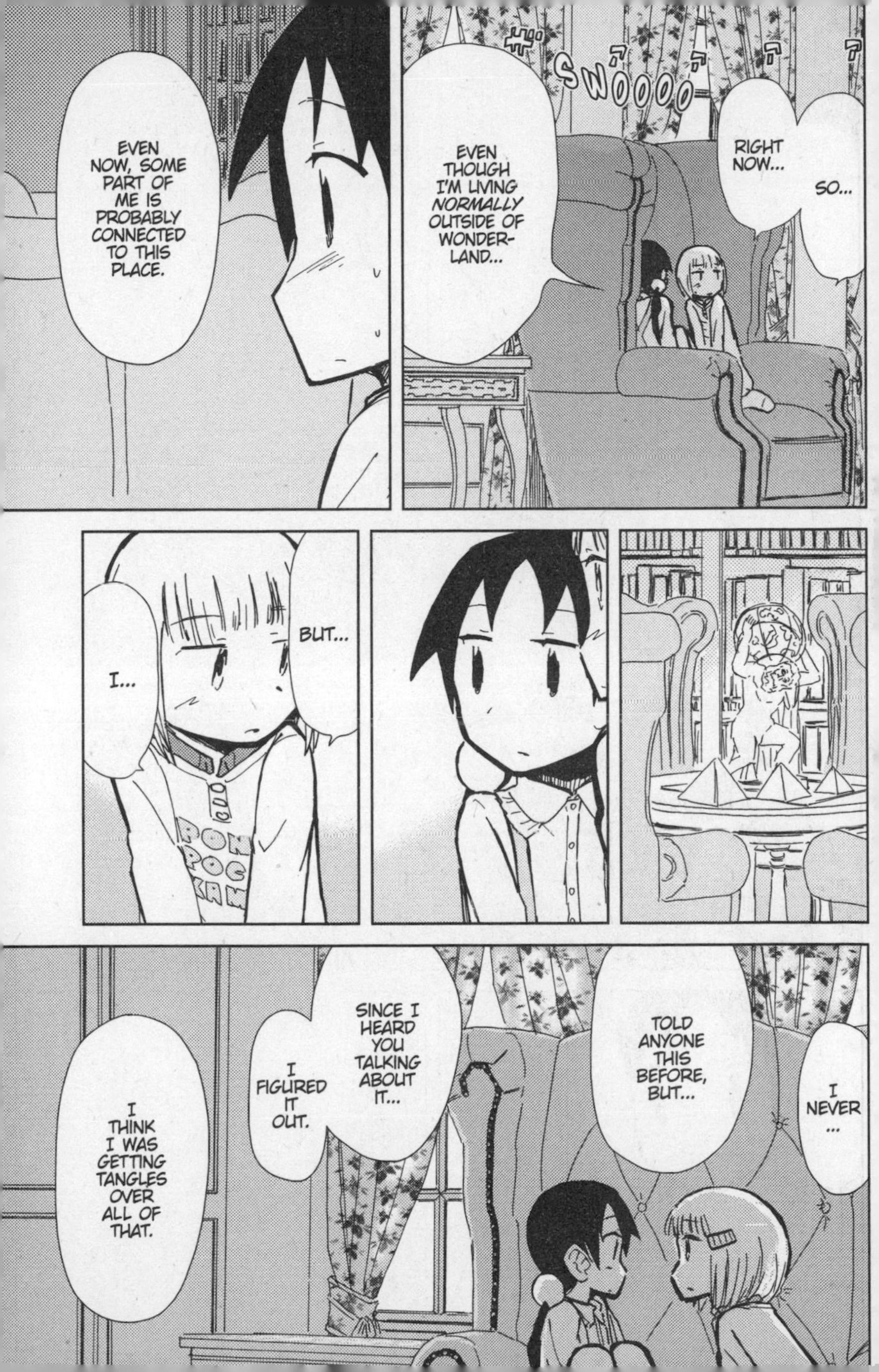
SNOOOO
SO...
RIGHT NOW...
EVEN THOUGH I'M LIVING *NORMALLY* OUTSIDE OF WONDER-LAND...
EVEN NOW, SOME PART OF ME IS PROBABLY CONNECTED TO THIS PLACE.
BUT...
I...
I NEVER...
TOLD ANYONE THIS BEFORE, BUT...
SINCE I HEARD YOU TALKING ABOUT IT...
I FIGURED IT OUT.
I THINK I WAS GETTING TANGLES OVER ALL OF THAT.

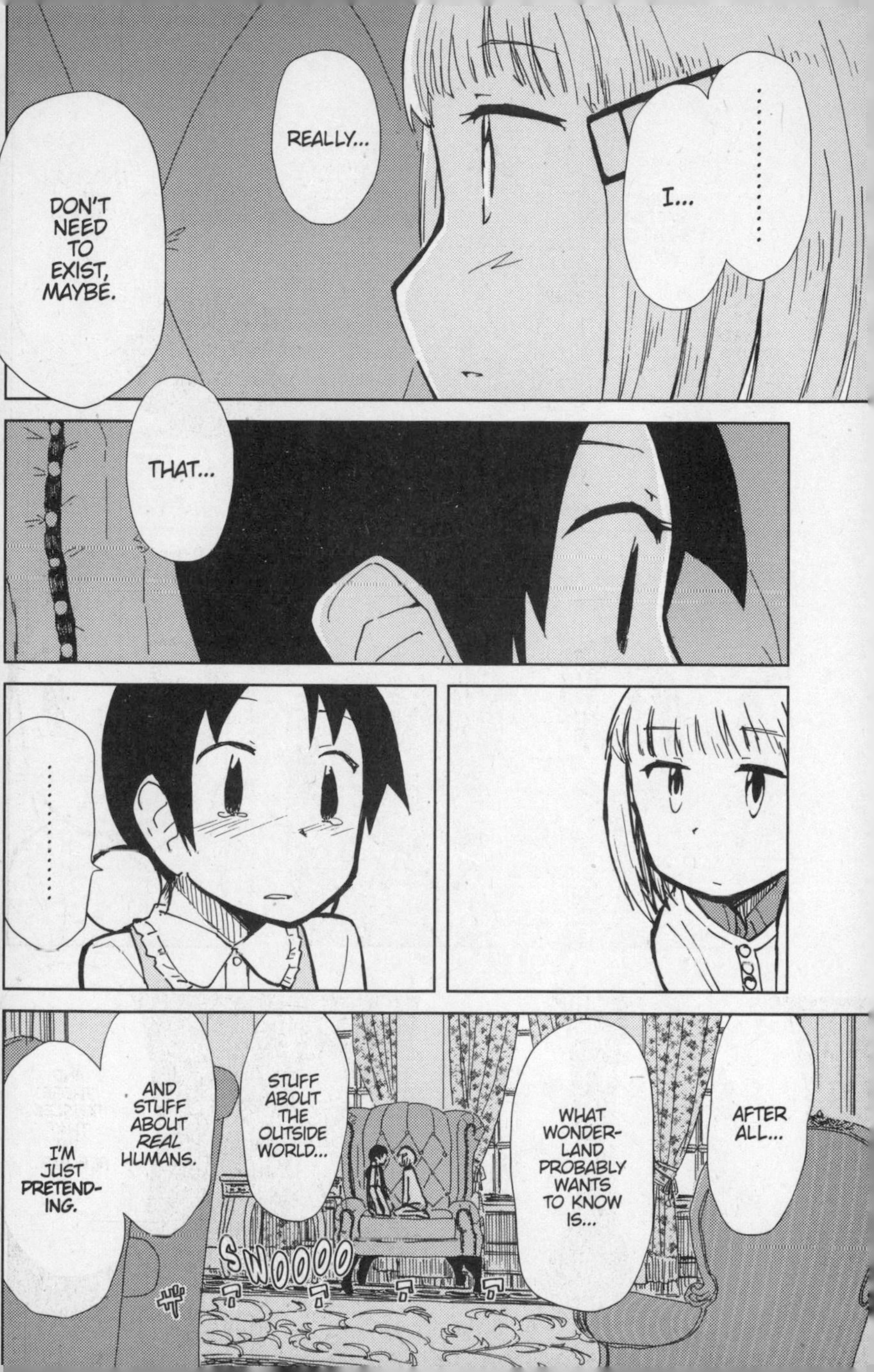
I... ......
REALLY...
DON'T NEED TO EXIST, MAYBE.
THAT...
......
AFTER ALL...
WHAT WONDER-LAND PROBABLY WANTS TO KNOW IS...
STUFF ABOUT THE OUTSIDE WORLD...
AND STUFF ABOUT *REAL* HUMANS.
I'M JUST PRETEND-ING.
SWOOOO
ザ

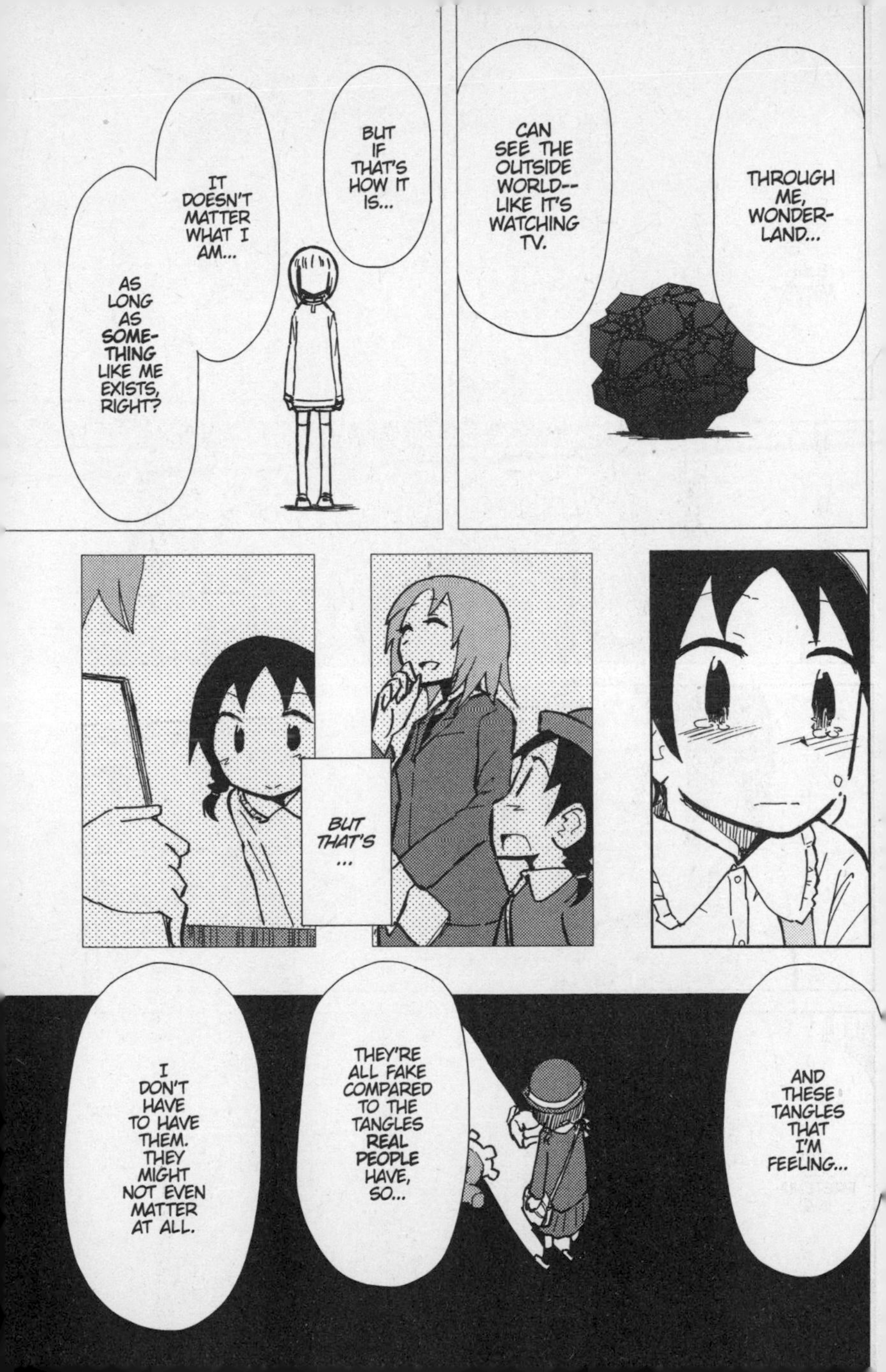
THROUGH ME, WONDERLAND...
CAN SEE THE OUTSIDE WORLD-- LIKE IT'S WATCHING TV.
BUT IF THAT'S HOW IT IS...
IT DOESN'T MATTER WHAT I AM...
AS LONG AS SOMETHING LIKE ME EXISTS, RIGHT?
BUT THAT'S ...
AND THESE TANGLES THAT I'M FEELING...
THEY'RE ALL FAKE COMPARED TO THE TANGLES REAL PEOPLE HAVE, SO...
I DON'T HAVE TO HAVE THEM. THEY MIGHT NOT EVEN MATTER AT ALL.

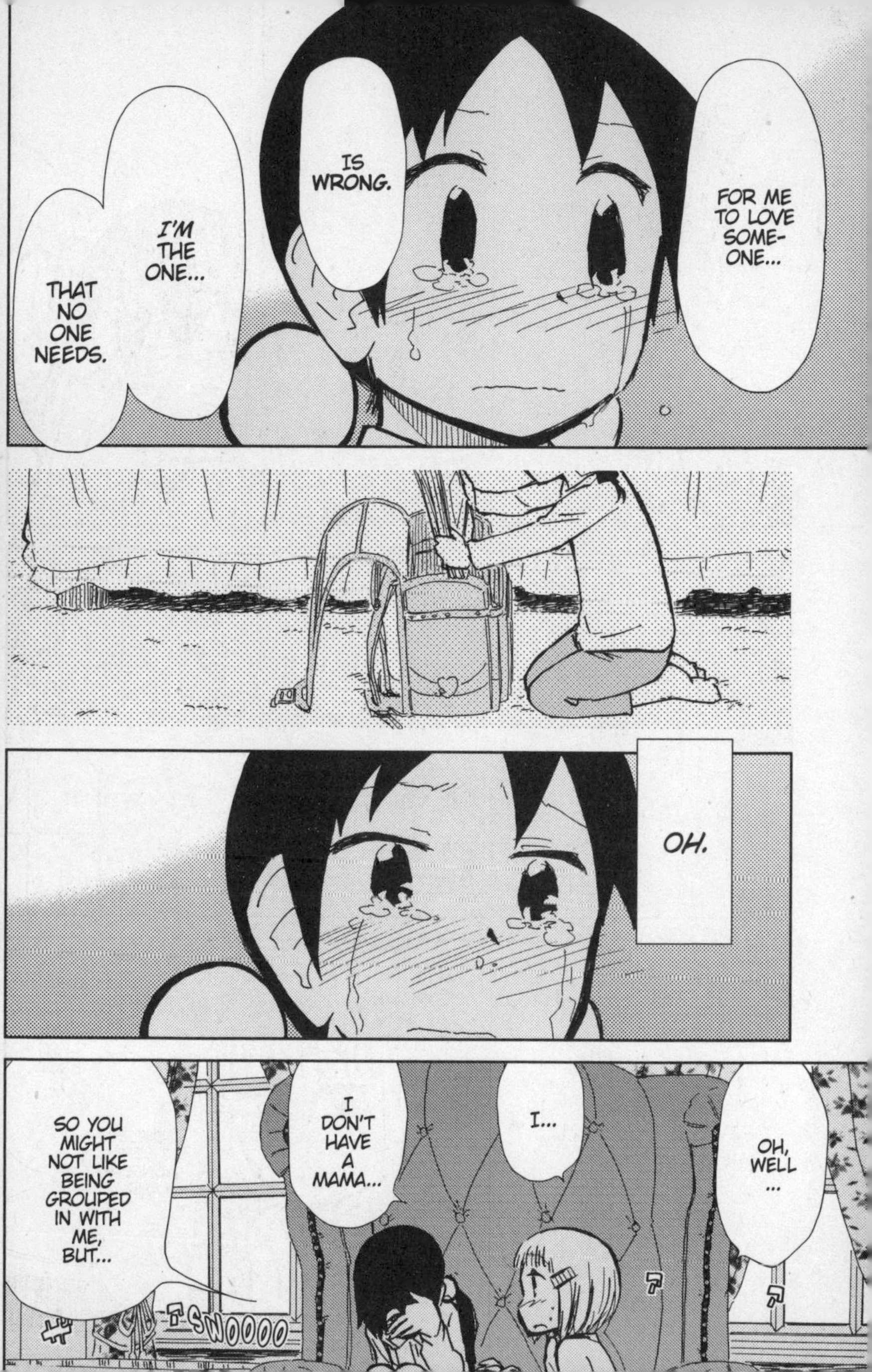
FOR ME TO LOVE SOME-ONE...
IS WRONG.
I'M THE ONE...
THAT NO ONE NEEDS.
OH.
OH, WELL ...
I...
I DON'T HAVE A MAMA...
SO YOU MIGHT NOT LIKE BEING GROUPED IN WITH ME, BUT...
SNOOOO

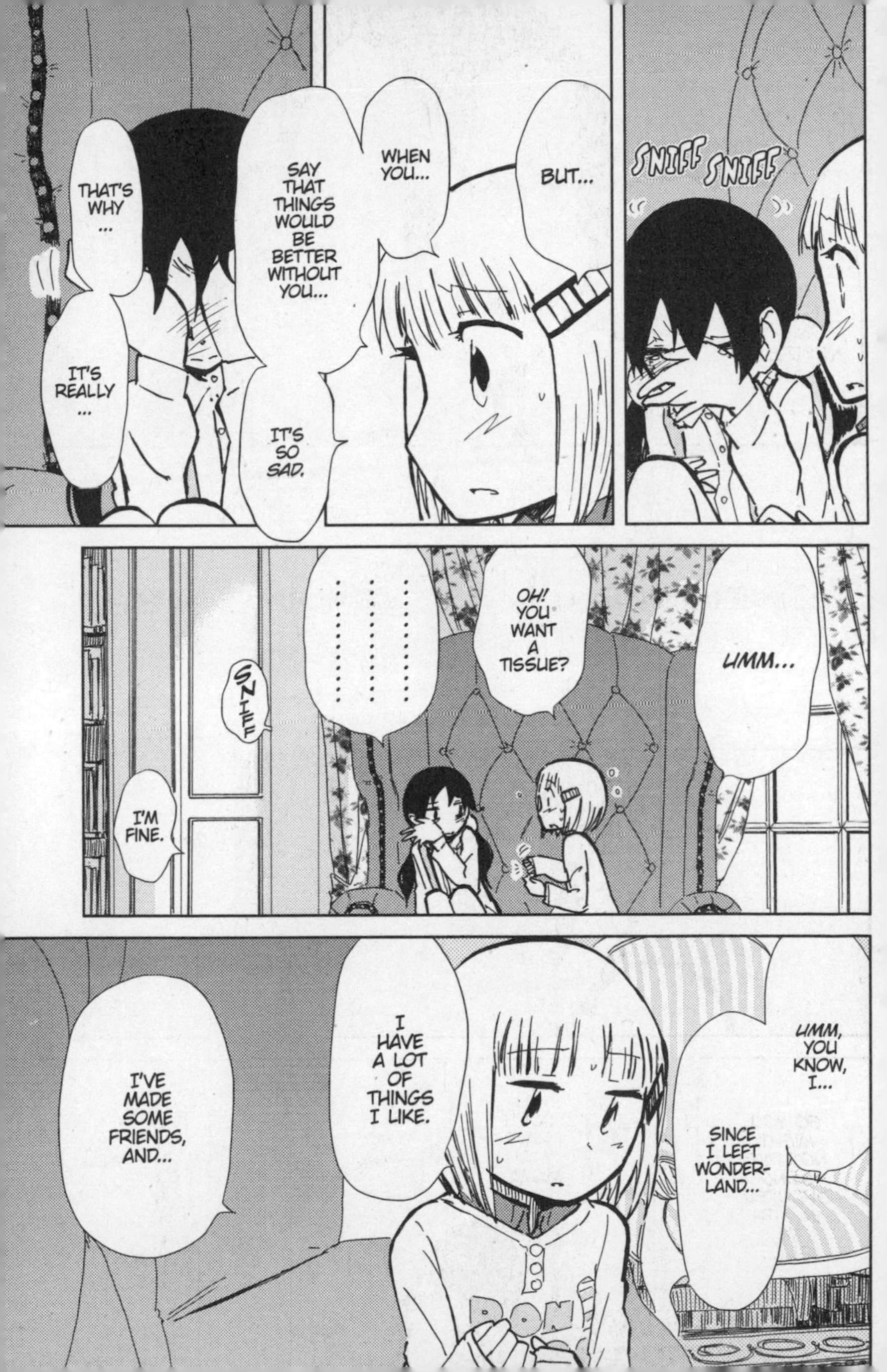
SNIFF SNIFF
BUT...
WHEN YOU...
SAY THAT THINGS WOULD BE BETTER WITHOUT YOU...
IT'S SO SAD.
THAT'S WHY ...
IT'S REALLY ...
UMM...
OH! YOU WANT A TISSUE?
......
SNIFF
I'M FINE.
UMM, YOU KNOW, I...
SINCE I LEFT WONDER-LAND...
I HAVE A LOT OF THINGS I LIKE.
I'VE MADE SOME FRIENDS, AND...

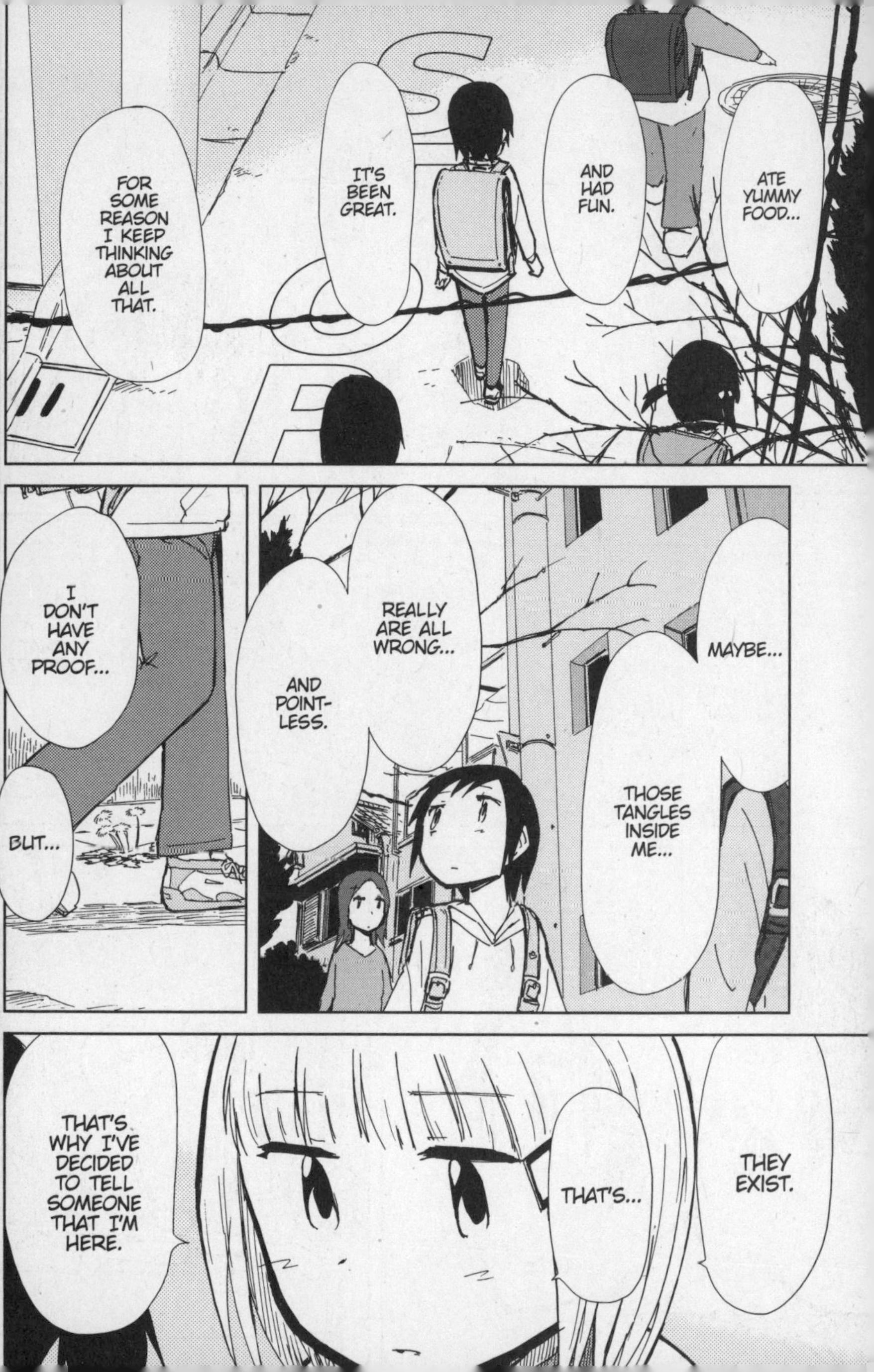
ATE YUMMY FOOD...
AND HAD FUN.
IT'S BEEN GREAT.
FOR SOME REASON I KEEP THINKING ABOUT ALL THAT.
MAYBE...
THOSE TANGLES INSIDE ME...
REALLY ARE ALL WRONG...
AND POINTLESS.
I DON'T HAVE ANY PROOF...
BUT...
THEY EXIST.
THAT'S...
THAT'S WHY I'VE DECIDED TO TELL SOMEONE THAT I'M HERE.

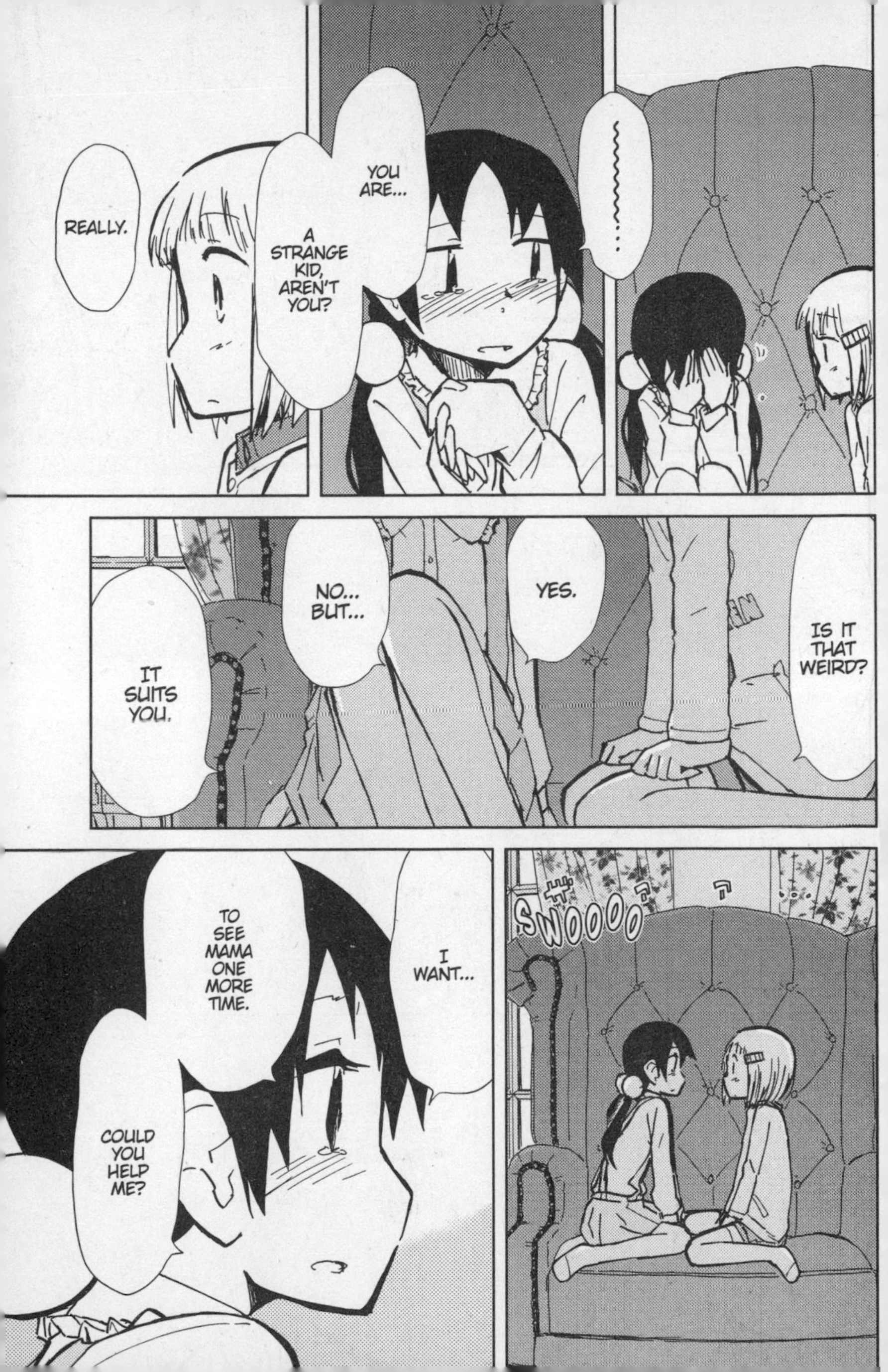

......
YOU ARE...
A STRANGE KID, AREN'T YOU?
REALLY.
IS IT THAT WEIRD?
YES.
NO... BUT...
IT SUITS YOU.
SWOOOO
I WANT...
TO SEE MAMA ONE MORE TIME.
COULD YOU HELP ME?

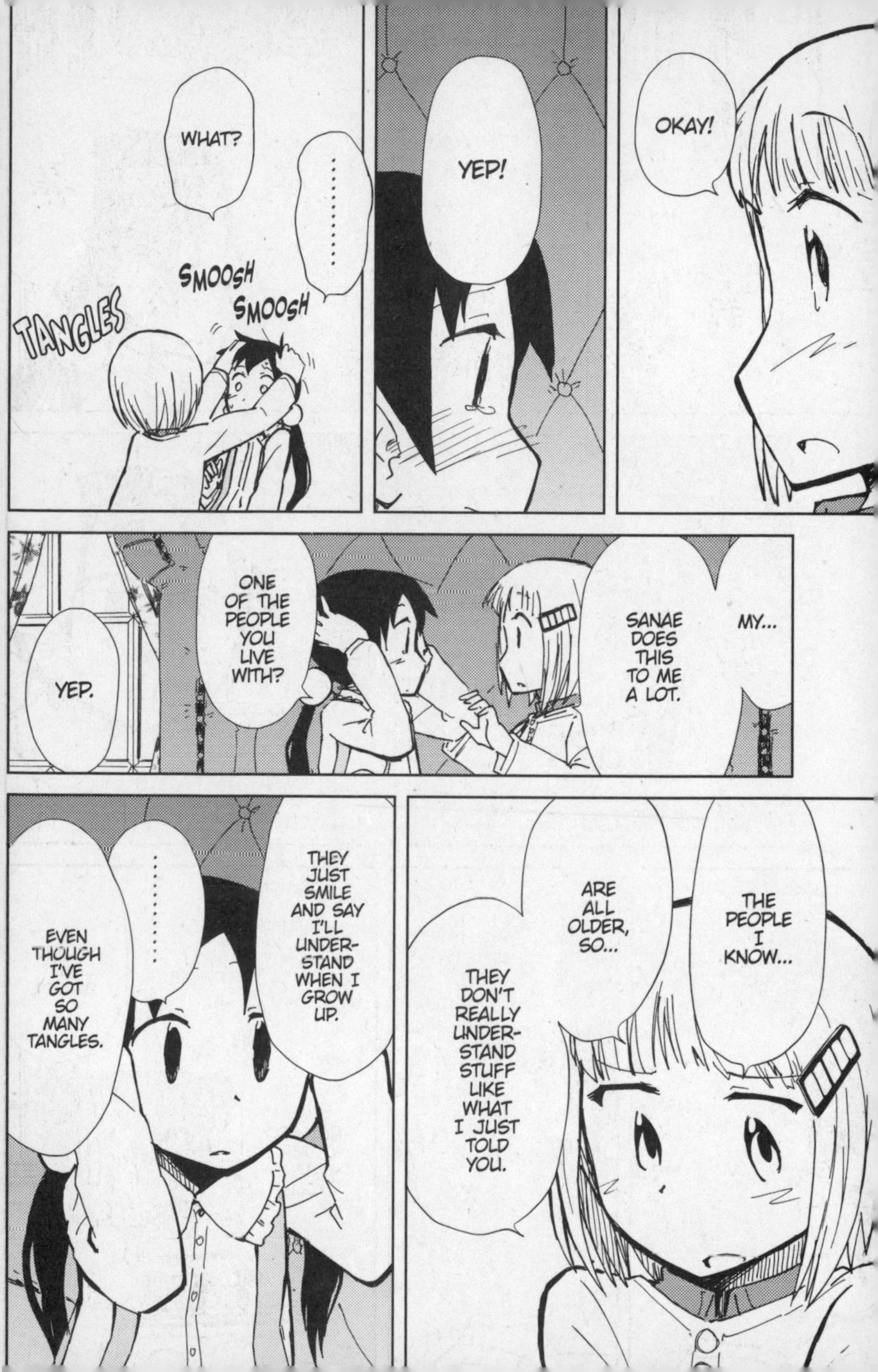
OKAY!
YEP!
......
WHAT?
SMOOSH SMOOSH
TANGLES
MY...
SANAE DOES THIS TO ME A LOT.
ONE OF THE PEOPLE YOU LIVE WITH?
YEP.
THE PEOPLE I KNOW...
ARE ALL OLDER, SO...
THEY DON'T REALLY UNDER-STAND STUFF LIKE WHAT I JUST TOLD YOU.
THEY JUST SMILE AND SAY I'LL UNDER-STAND WHEN I GROW UP.
......
EVEN THOUGH I'VE GOT SO MANY TANGLES.

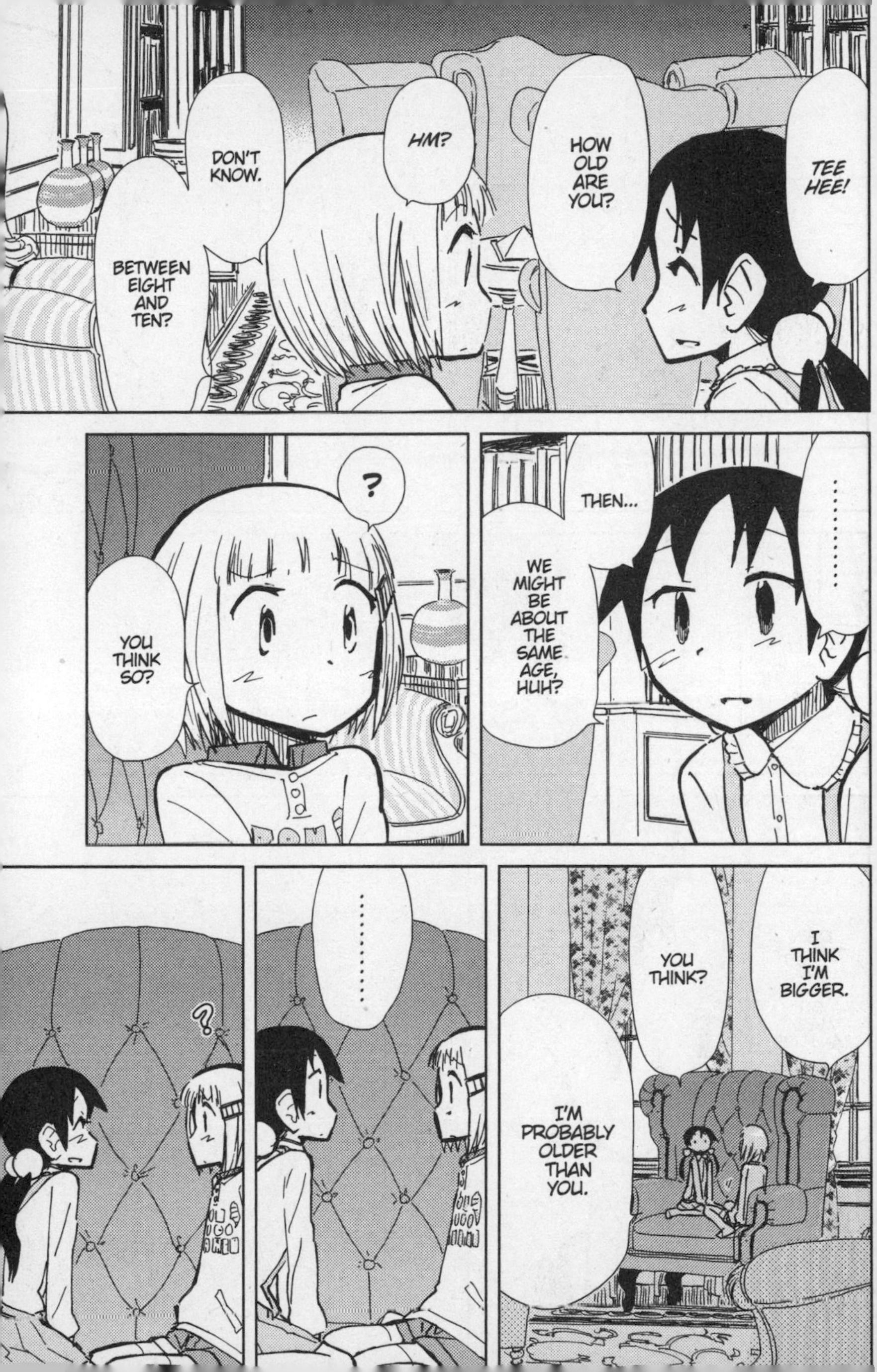
TEE HEE!
HOW OLD ARE YOU?
HM?
DON'T KNOW.
BETWEEN EIGHT AND TEN?
......
THEN...
WE MIGHT BE ABOUT THE SAME AGE, HUH?
?
YOU THINK SO?
I THINK I'M BIGGER.
YOU THINK?
I'M PROBABLY OLDER THAN YOU.
......
?

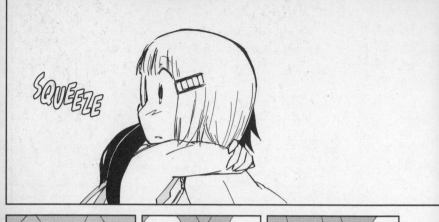

SQUEEZE

SURE...

SHE DOES THIS A LOT.

MY MAMA...

CAN I DO IT FOR A LITTLE BIT?

I CAN HEAR HER HEART-BEAT.

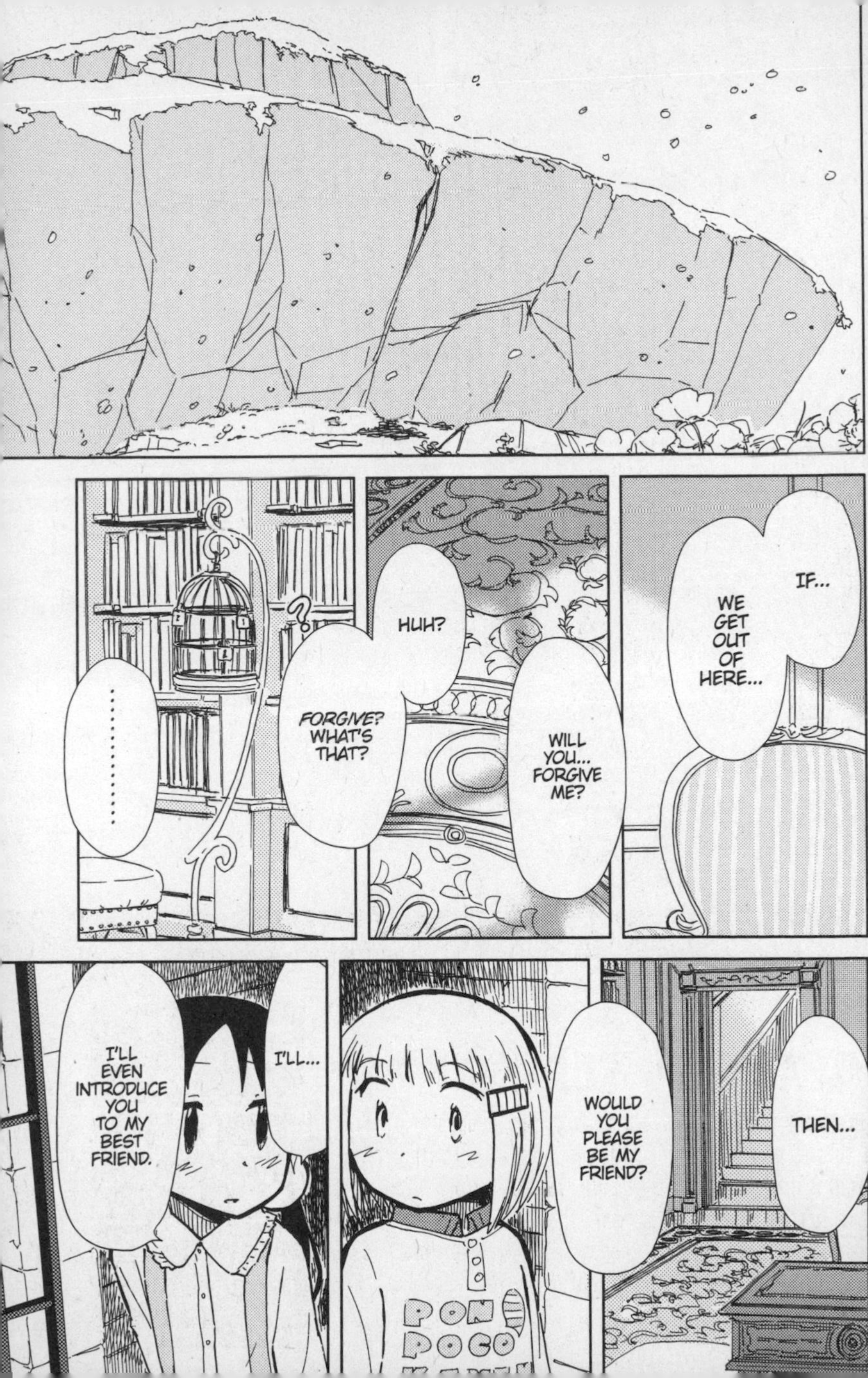
IF...
WE GET OUT OF HERE...
WILL YOU... FORGIVE ME?
HUH?
FORGIVE? WHAT'S THAT?
......
THEN...
WOULD YOU PLEASE BE MY FRIEND?
PON POCO
I'LL...
I'LL EVEN INTRODUCE YOU TO MY BEST FRIEND.

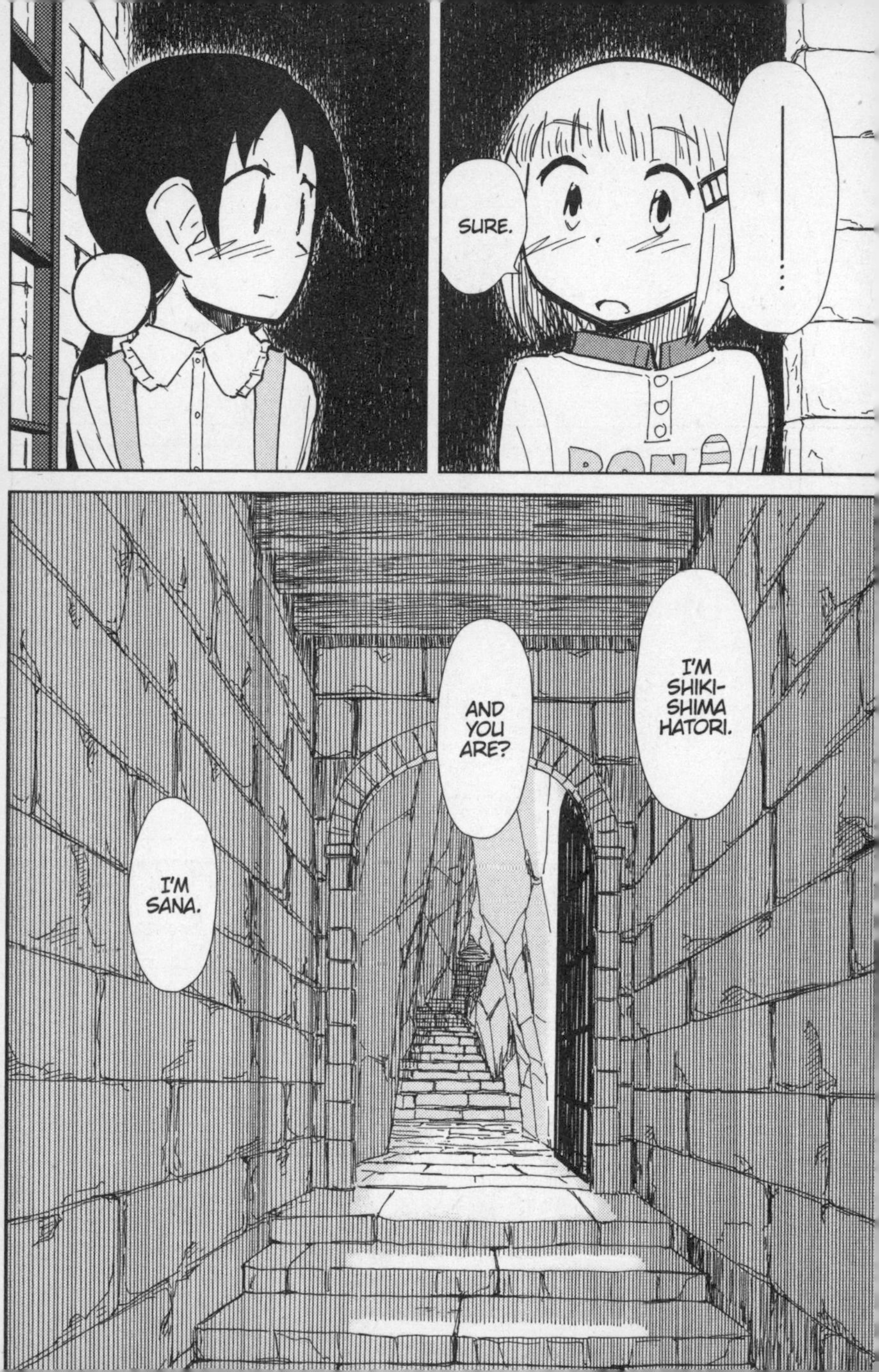
SURE.
I'M SHIKI-SHIMA HATORI.
AND YOU ARE?
I'M SANA.

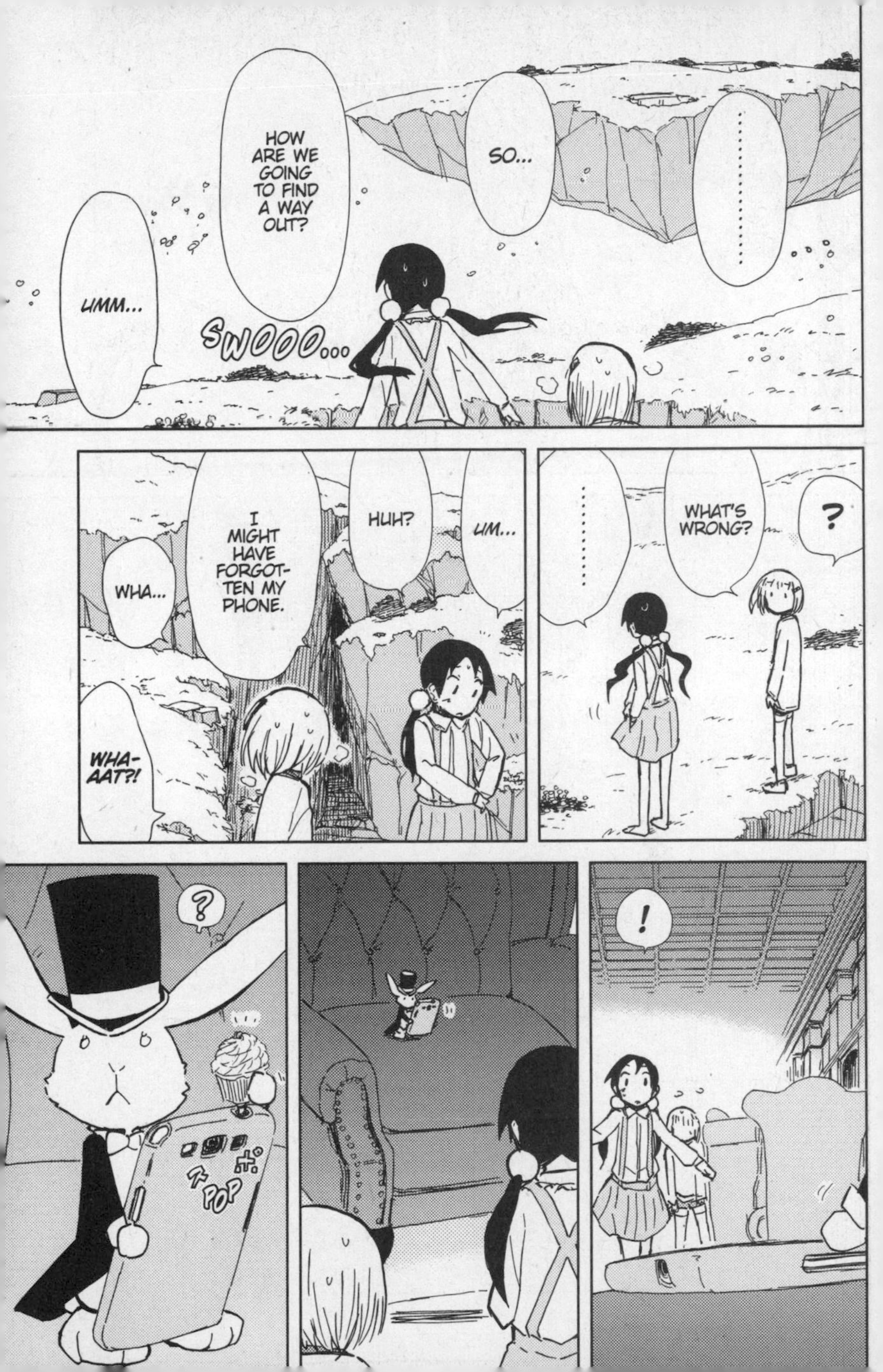
......
SO...
HOW ARE WE GOING TO FIND A WAY OUT?
SWOOO...
UMM...
?
WHAT'S WRONG?
......
UM...
HUH?
I MIGHT HAVE FORGOT-TEN MY PHONE.
WHA...
WHA-AAT?!
!
?
POP

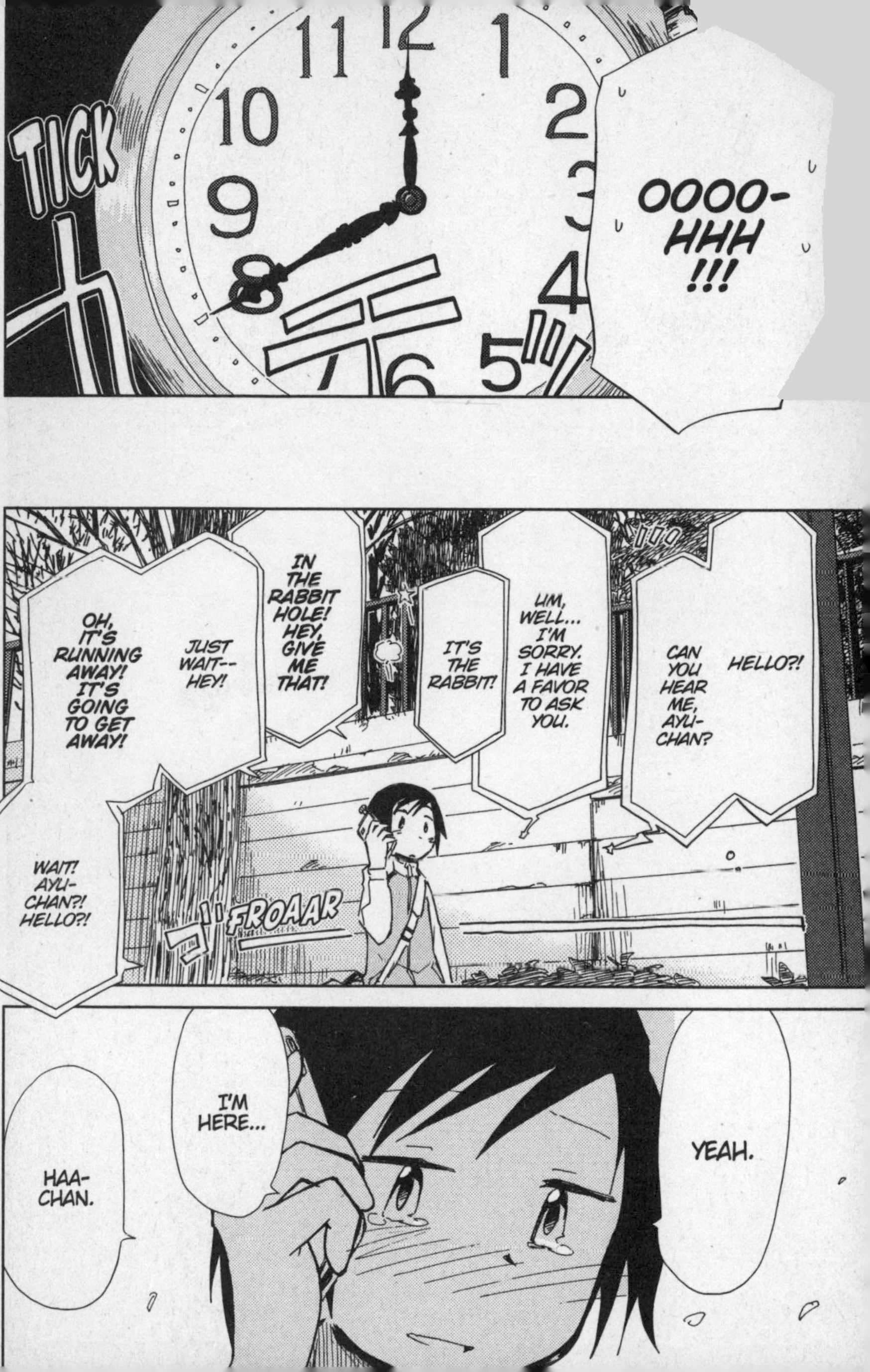
OOOO-HHH!!!
TICK
HELLO?!
CAN YOU HEAR ME, AYU-CHAN?
UM, WELL... I'M SORRY. I HAVE A FAVOR TO ASK YOU.
IT'S THE RABBIT!
IN THE RABBIT HOLE! HEY, GIVE ME THAT!
JUST WAIT-- HEY!
OH, IT'S RUNNING AWAY! IT'S GOING TO GET AWAY!
FROAAR
WAIT! AYU-CHAN?! HELLO?!
YEAH.
I'M HERE...
HAA-CHAN.

Chapter.21
Alice's Adventures in Wonderland (The End)

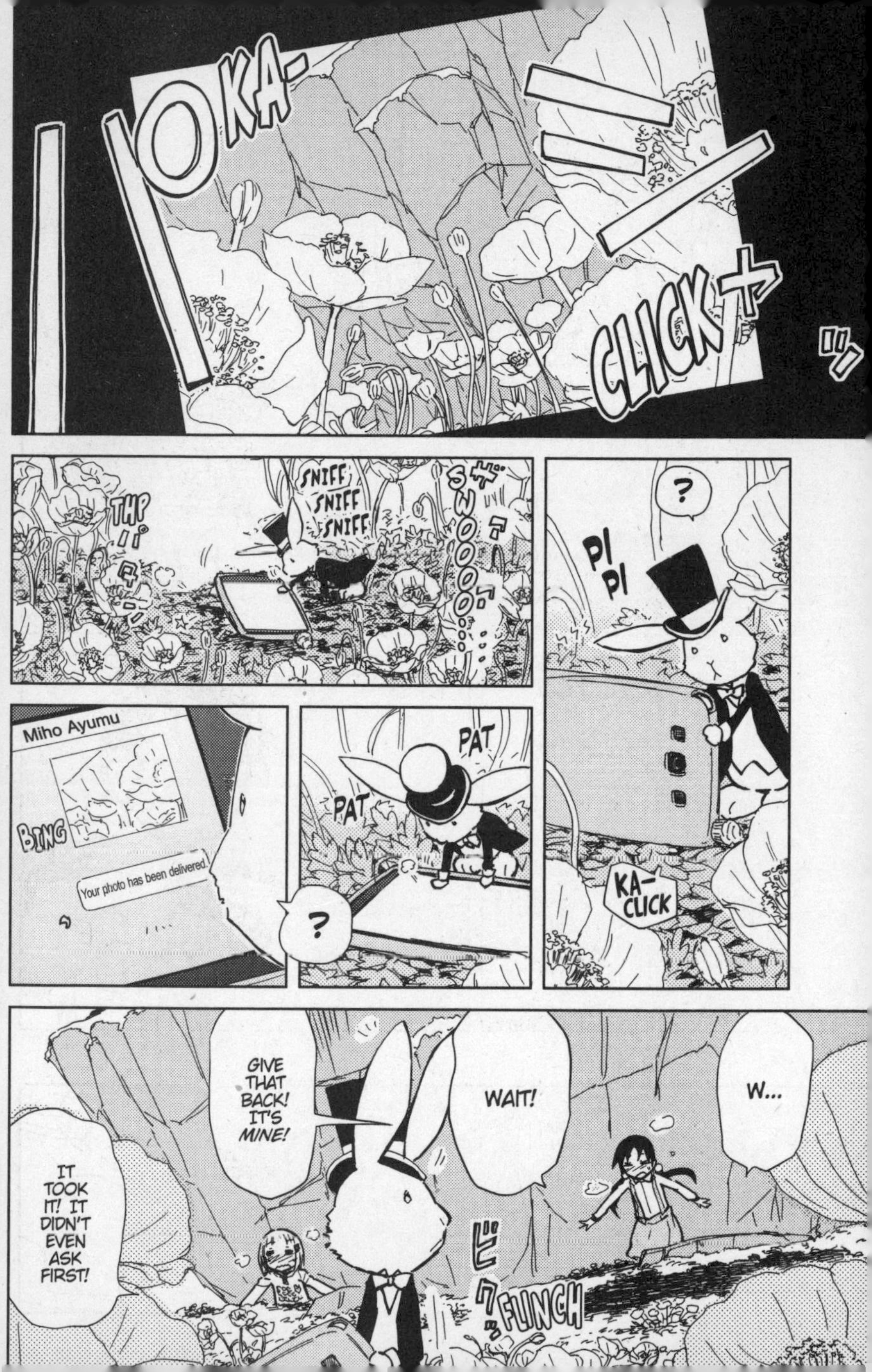

OKA-
CLICK
?
PI PI
KA-CLICK
SNIFF SNIFF SNIFF
SWOOOOO
THP
PAT
PAT
?
Miho Ayumu
BING
Your photo has been delivered.
W...
WAIT!
GIVE THAT BACK! IT'S *MINE!*
FLINCH
IT TOOK IT! IT DIDN'T EVEN ASK FIRST!

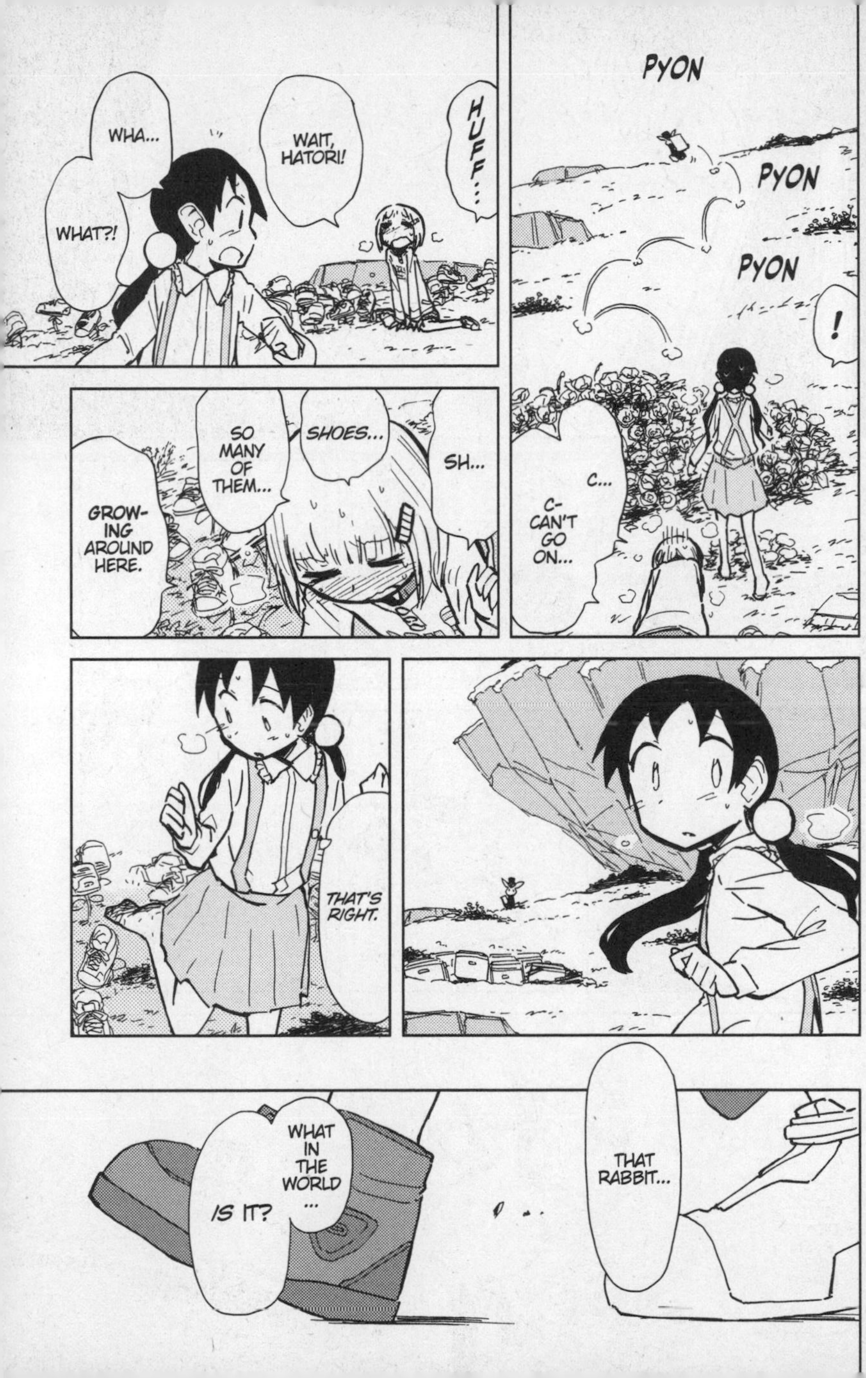
PYON
PYON
PYON
!
C...
C-CAN'T GO ON...
HUFF...
WAIT, HATORI!
WHA...
WHAT?!
SH...
SHOES...
SO MANY OF THEM...
GROWING AROUND HERE.
THAT'S RIGHT.
THAT RABBIT...
WHAT IN THE WORLD ...
IS IT?

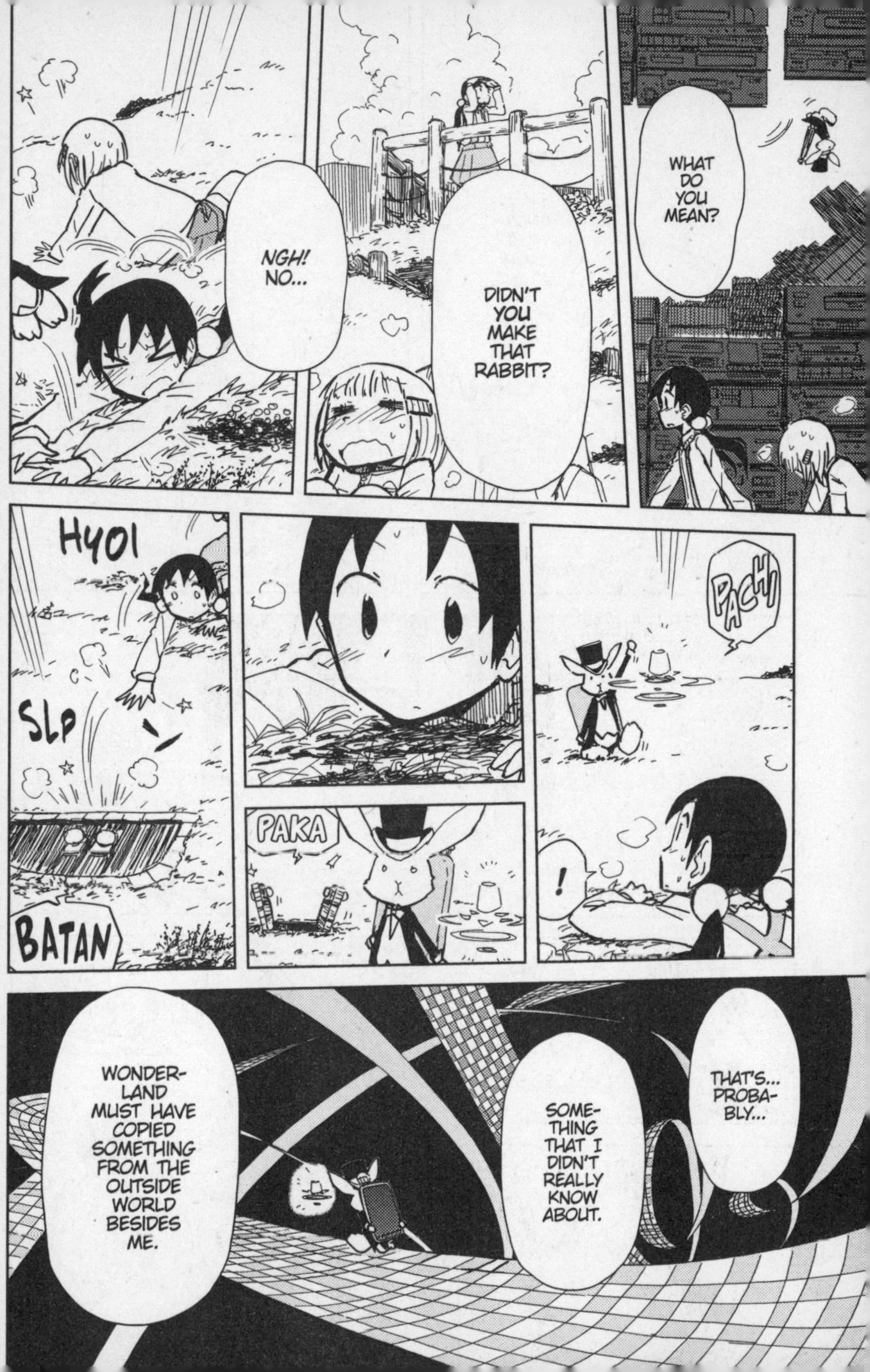
WHAT DO YOU MEAN?
DIDN'T YOU MAKE THAT RABBIT?
NGH! NO...
PACHI
!
PAKA
HYOI
SLP
BATAN
THAT'S... PROBA-BLY...
SOME-THING THAT I DIDN'T REALLY KNOW ABOUT.
WONDER-LAND MUST HAVE COPIED SOMETHING FROM THE OUTSIDE WORLD BESIDES ME.

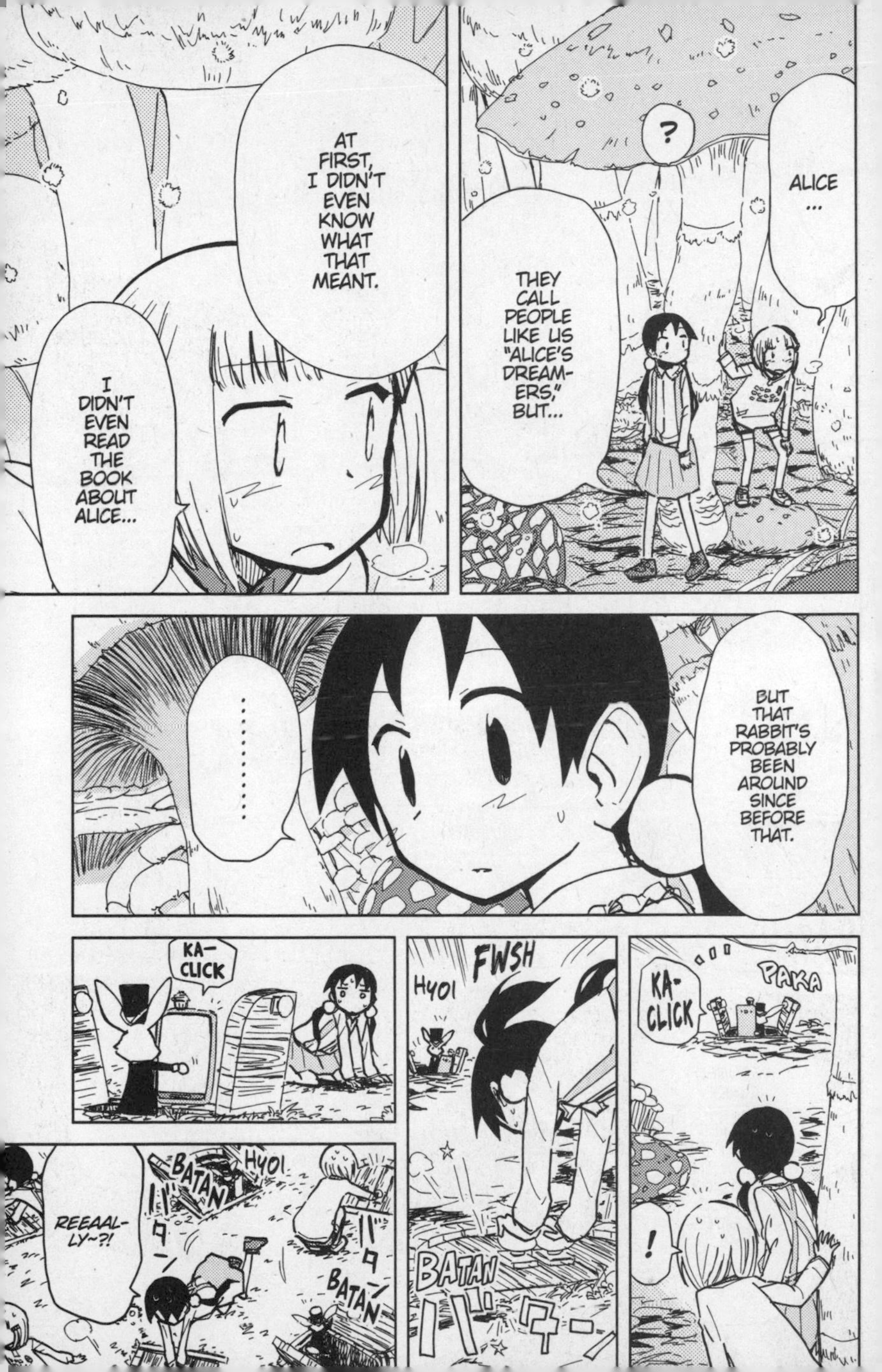
ALICE ...
?
THEY CALL PEOPLE LIKE US "ALICE'S DREAMERS," BUT...
AT FIRST, I DIDN'T EVEN KNOW WHAT THAT MEANT.
I DIDN'T EVEN READ THE BOOK ABOUT ALICE...
BUT THAT RABBIT'S PROBABLY BEEN AROUND SINCE BEFORE THAT.
......
KA-CLICK
PAKA
!
FWSH
HYOI
BATAN
KA-CLICK
HYOI
BATAN
BATAN
REEEALLY~?!

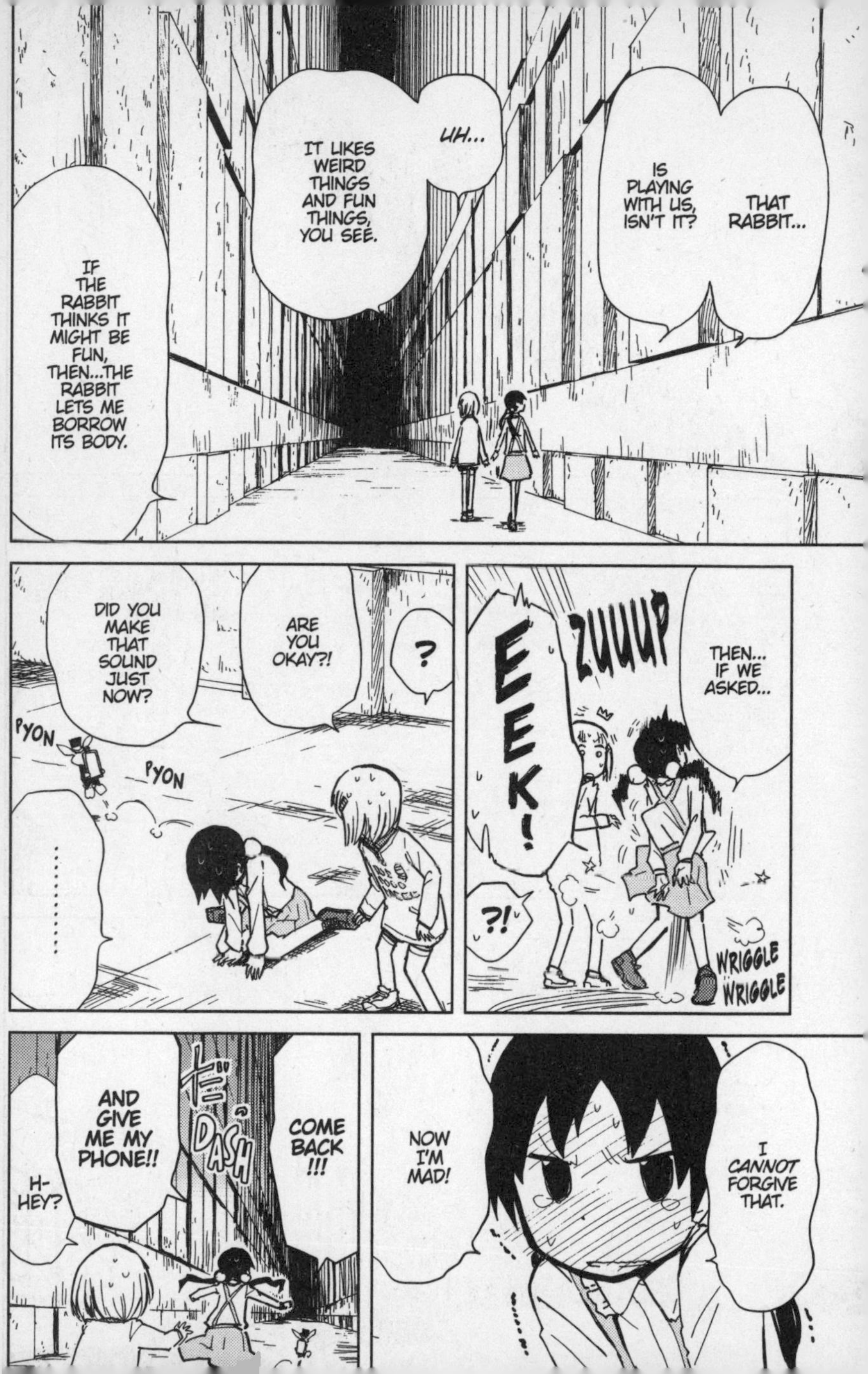
THAT RABBIT...
IS PLAYING WITH US, ISN'T IT?
UH...
IT LIKES WEIRD THINGS AND FUN THINGS, YOU SEE.
IF THE RABBIT THINKS IT MIGHT BE FUN, THEN...THE RABBIT LETS ME BORROW ITS BODY.
THEN... IF WE ASKED...
ZUUUP
EEEK!
?!
WRIGGLE WRIGGLE
?
ARE YOU OKAY?!
DID YOU MAKE THAT SOUND JUST NOW?
PYON
PYON
......
I CANNOT FORGIVE THAT.
NOW I'M MAD!
COME BACK !!!
DASH
AND GIVE ME MY PHONE!!
H-HEY?

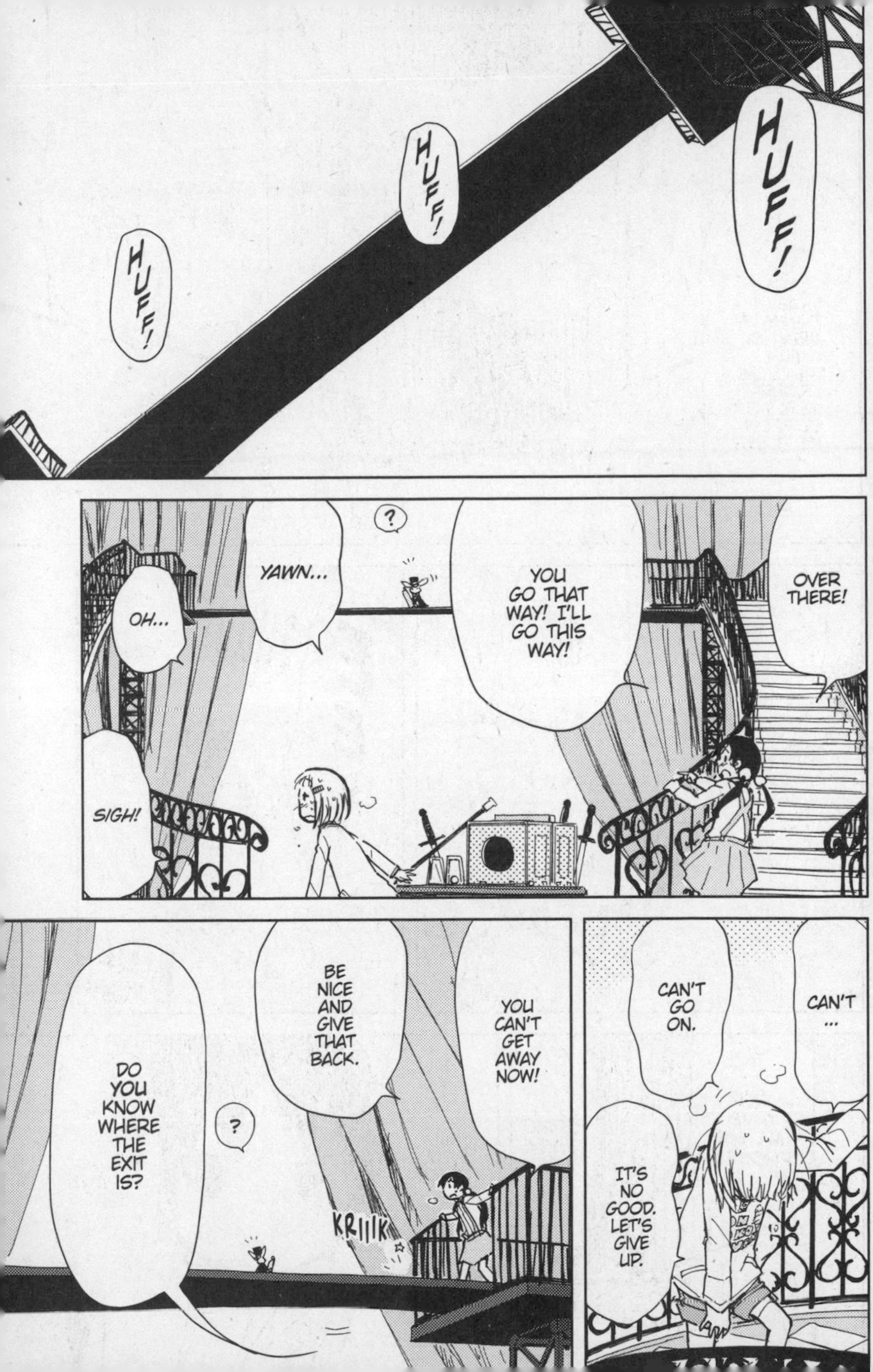
HUFF!
HUFF!
HUFF!
OVER THERE!
YOU GO THAT WAY! I'LL GO THIS WAY!
?
YAWN...
OH...
SIGH!
CAN'T ...
CAN'T GO ON.
IT'S NO GOOD. LET'S GIVE UP.
YOU CAN'T GET AWAY NOW!
BE NICE AND GIVE THAT BACK.
?
KRIIIK
DO YOU KNOW WHERE THE EXIT IS?

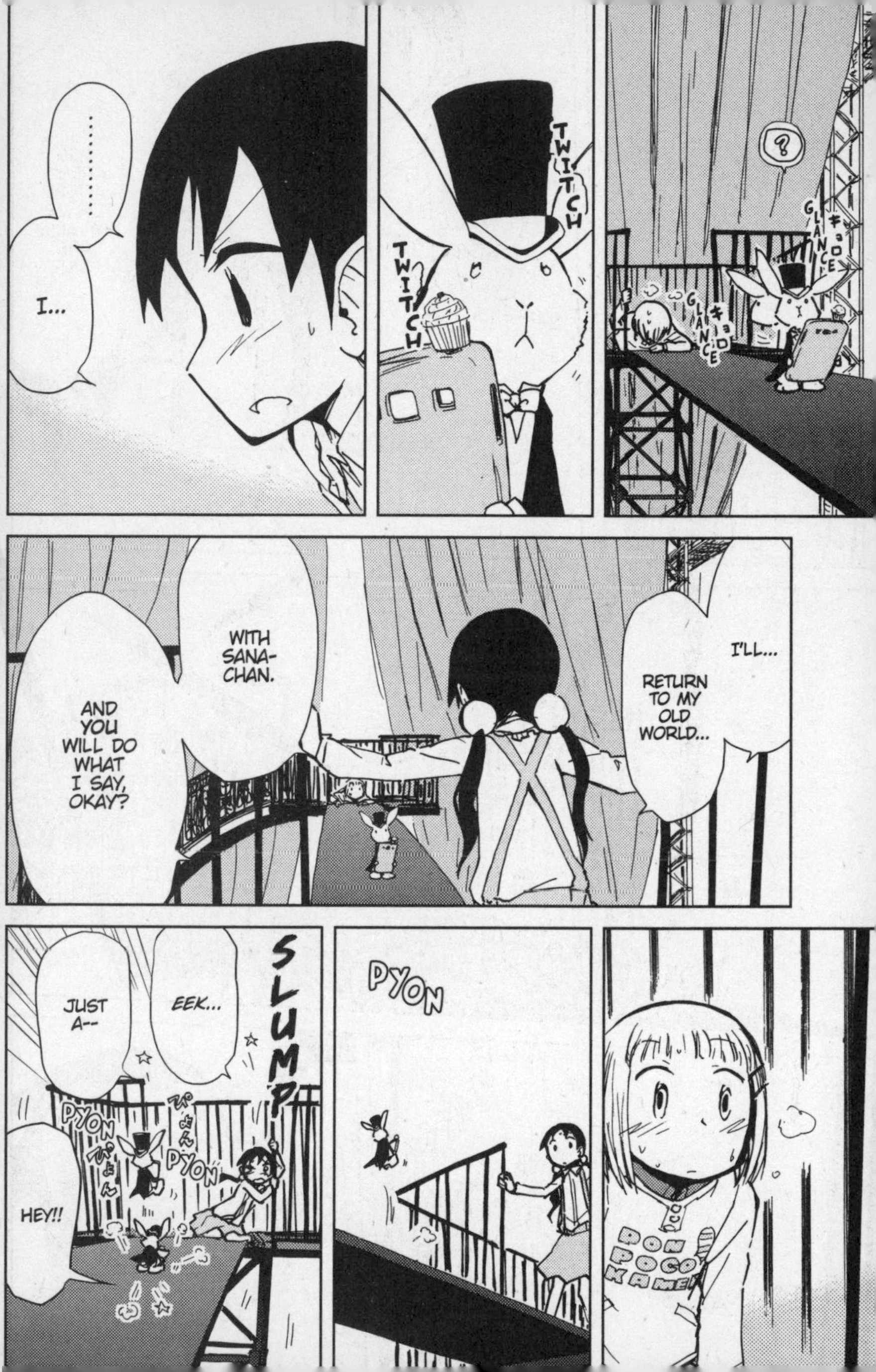
?
GLANCE
キョ
GLANCE
キョ
TWITCH
TWITCH
......
I...
I'LL...
RETURN TO MY OLD WORLD...
WITH SANA-CHAN.
AND YOU WILL DO WHAT I SAY, OKAY?
PYON
SLUMP
EEK...
JUST A--
PYON
ぴょん
PYON
ぴょん
HEY!!
DON POCO KAME

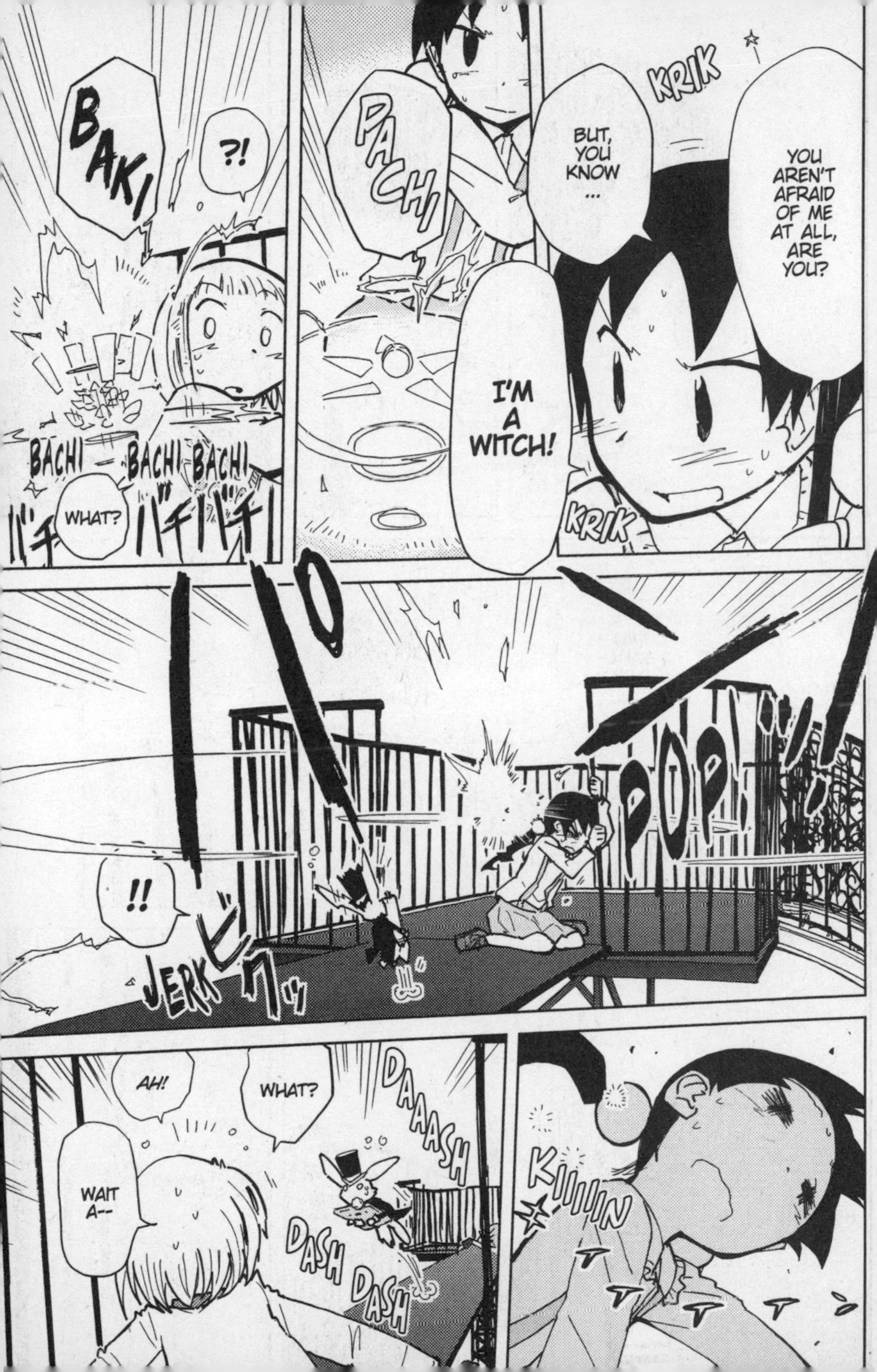
YOU AREN'T AFRAID OF ME AT ALL, ARE YOU?
KRIK
BUT, YOU KNOW ...
I'M A WITCH!
KRIK
PACHI
?!
BAKI
BACHI BACHI BACHI
バチバチ
WHAT?
バチ
POP!
!!
JERK
ビクッ
KIIIIIIN
WHAT?
AH!
DAAAASH
WAIT A--
DASH DASH

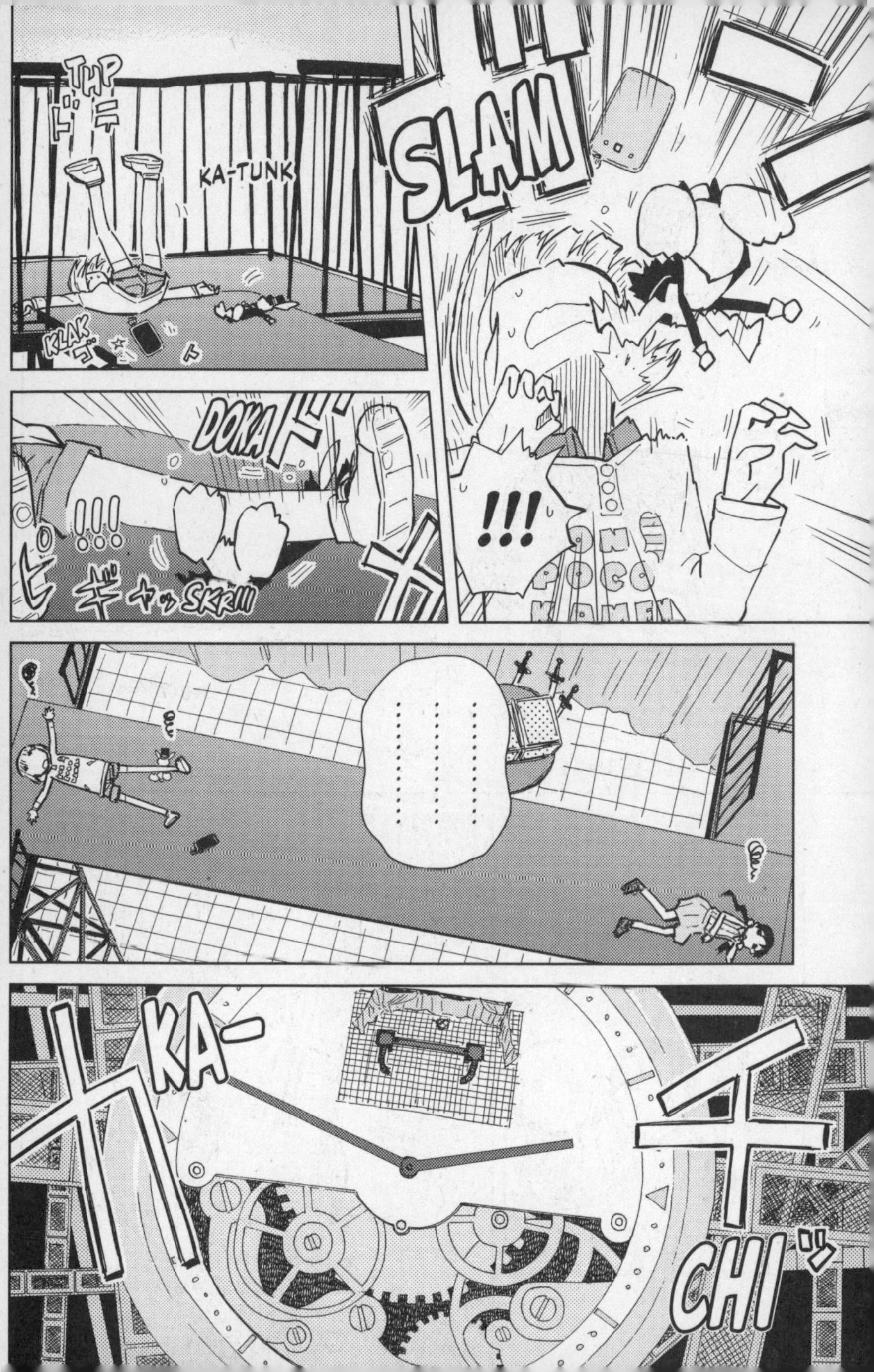

SLAM
!!!
THP
KA-TUNK
KLAK
DOKA
!!!
SKRIII
KA-
CHI

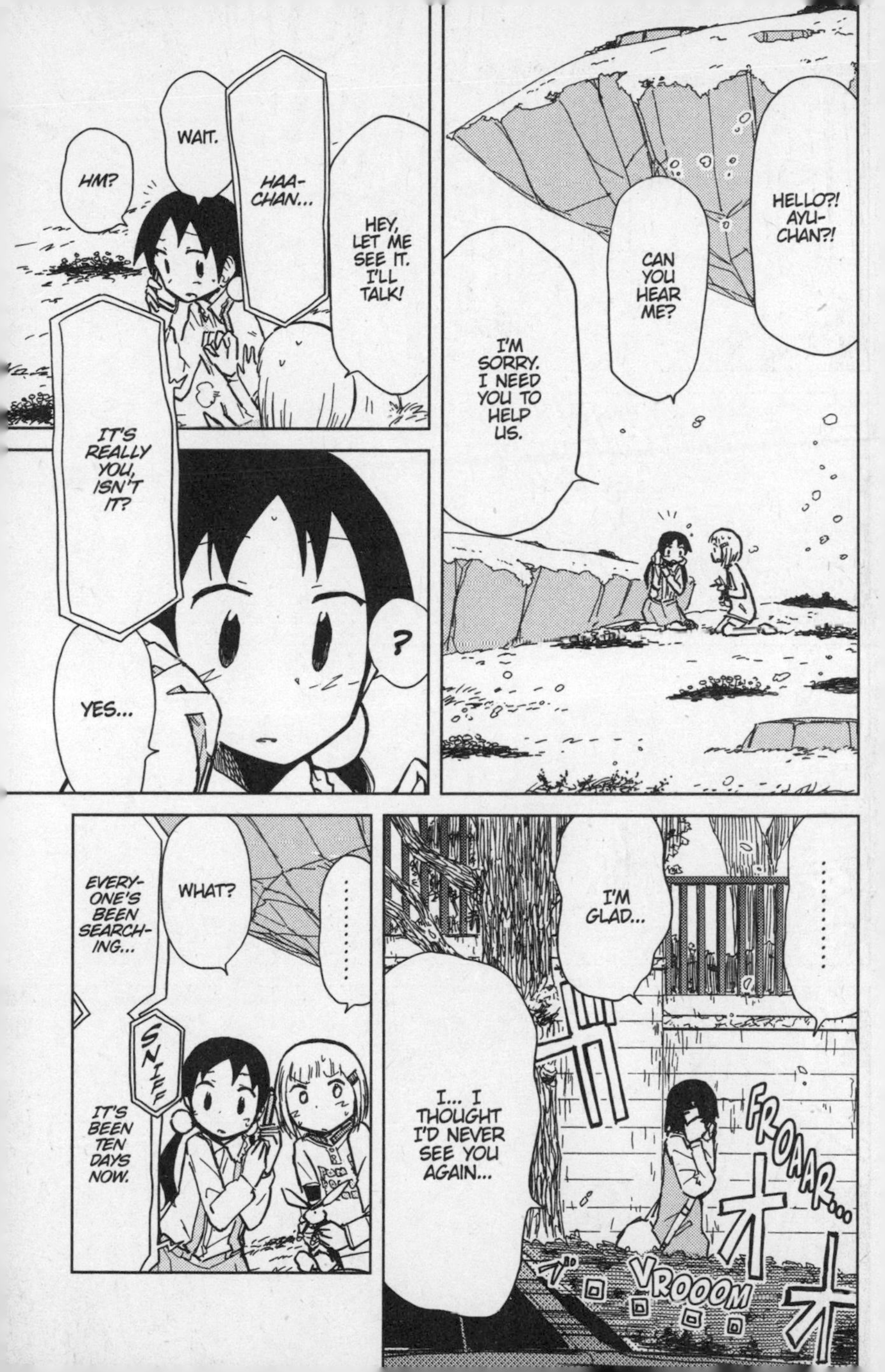
HELLO?! AYU-CHAN?!
CAN YOU HEAR ME?
I'M SORRY. I NEED YOU TO HELP US.
HEY, LET ME SEE IT. I'LL TALK!
HAA-CHAN...
WAIT.
HM?
?
IT'S REALLY YOU, ISN'T IT?
YES...
......
I'M GLAD...
I... I THOUGHT I'D NEVER SEE YOU AGAIN...
FROAAR...
VROOOM
......
WHAT?
EVERY-ONE'S BEEN SEARCH-ING...
SNIFF
IT'S BEEN TEN DAYS NOW.

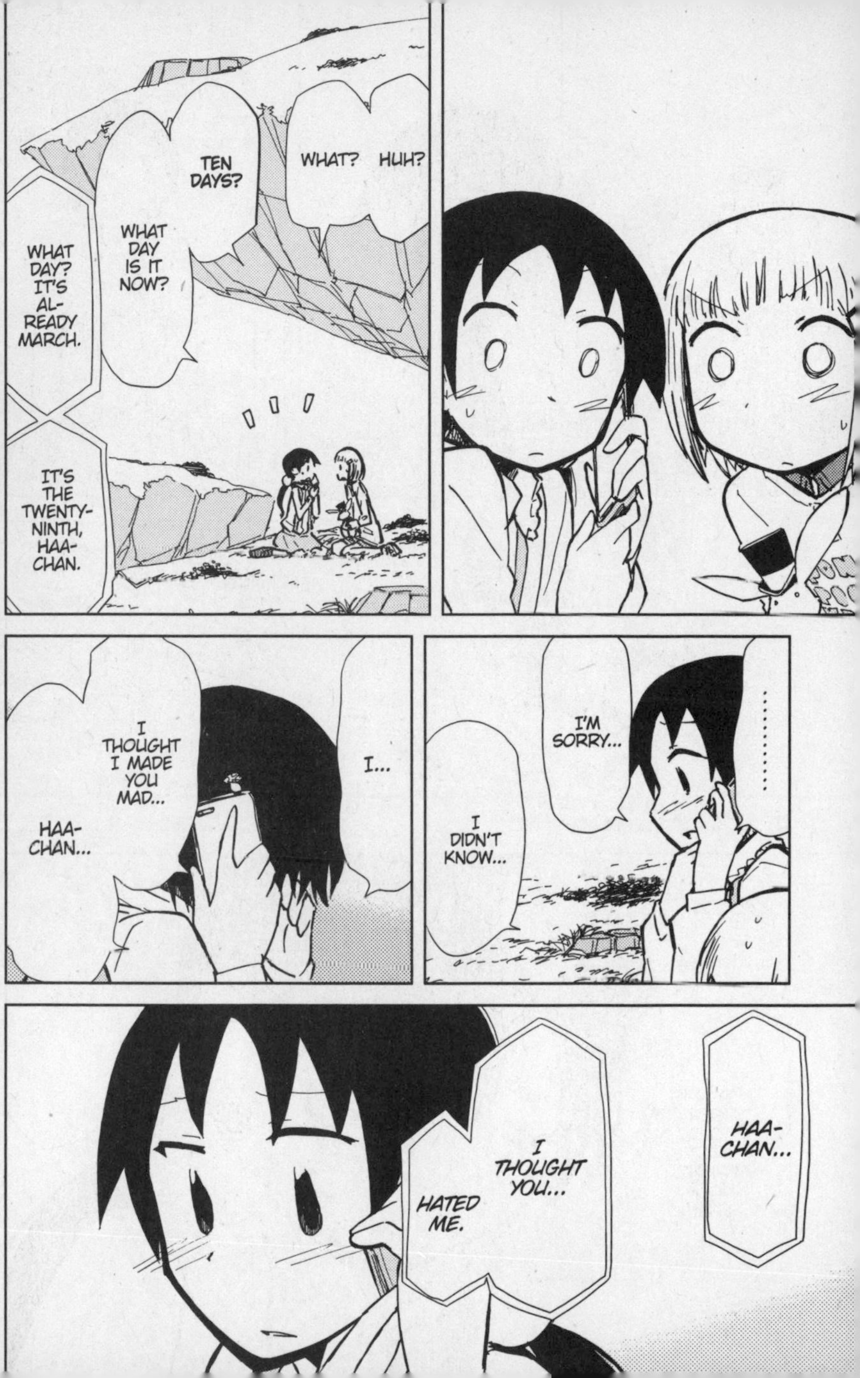
WHAT? HUH?
TEN DAYS?
WHAT DAY IS IT NOW?
WHAT DAY? IT'S AL-READY MARCH.
IT'S THE TWENTY-NINTH, HAA-CHAN.
......
I'M SORRY...
I DIDN'T KNOW...
I...
I THOUGHT I MADE YOU MAD...
HAA-CHAN...
HAA-CHAN...
I THOUGHT YOU...
HATED ME.

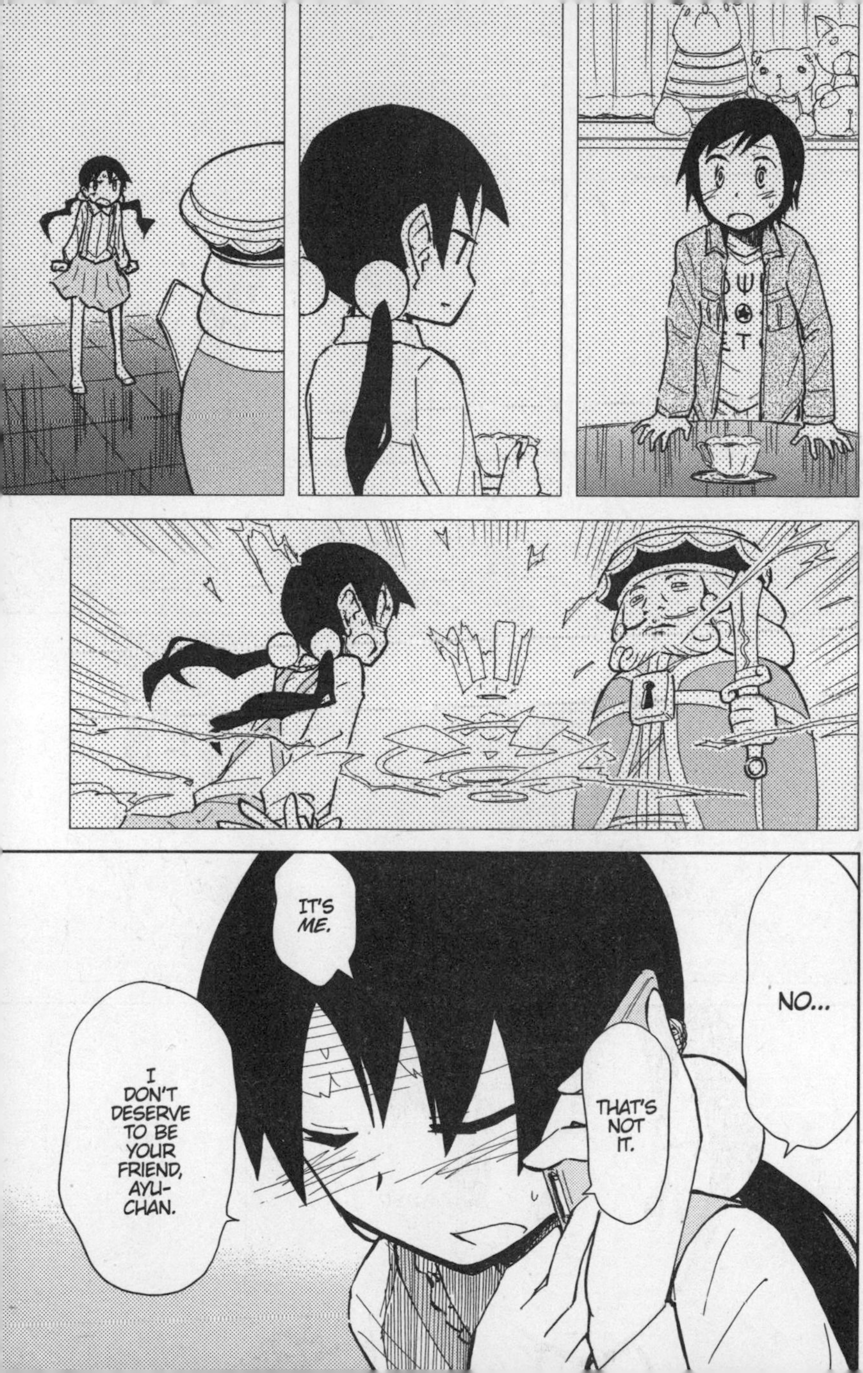
NO...
THAT'S NOT IT.
IT'S ME.
I DON'T DESERVE TO BE YOUR FRIEND, AYU-CHAN.

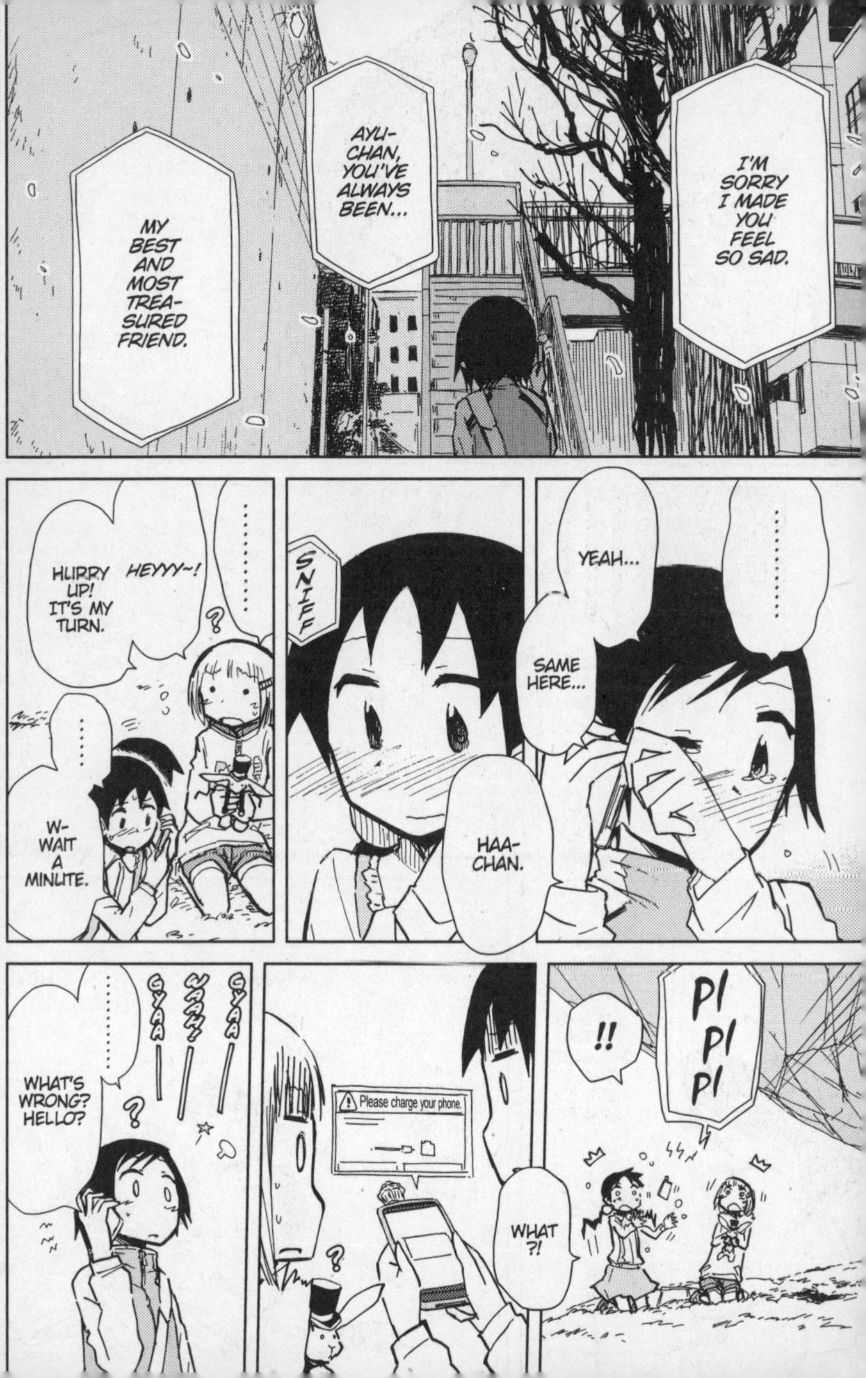
I'M SORRY I MADE YOU FEEL SO SAD.
AYU-CHAN, YOU'VE ALWAYS BEEN...
MY BEST AND MOST TREA-SURED FRIEND.
......
YEAH...
SAME HERE...
SNIFF
HAA-CHAN.
......
HEYYY~!
HURRY UP! IT'S MY TURN.
?
......
W-WAIT A MINUTE.
PI PI PI
!!
Please charge your phone.
?
WHAT ?!
GYAA—
WAAH!
GYAA—
......
WHAT'S WRONG? HELLO?
?

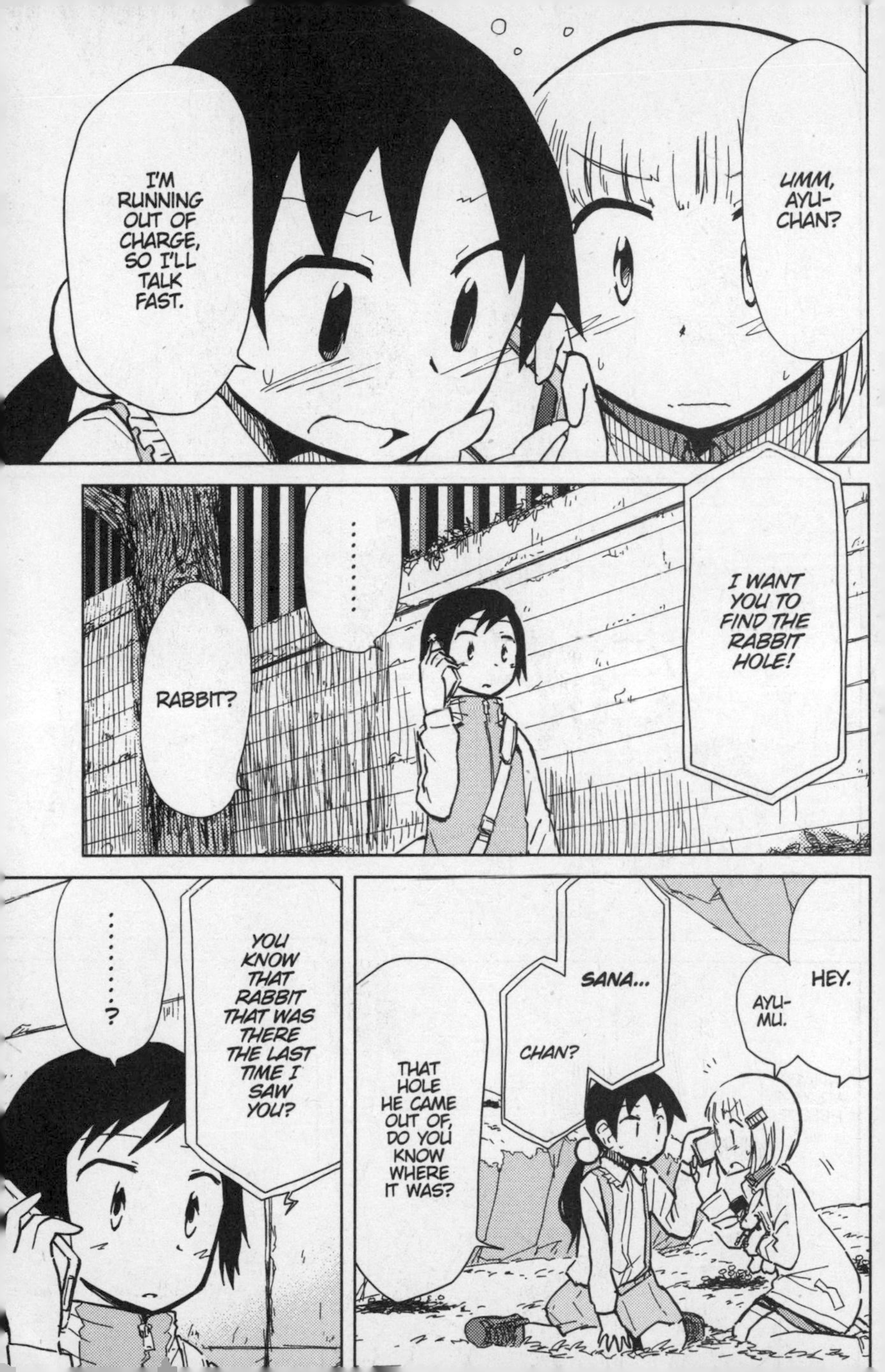

UMM, AYU-CHAN?
I'M RUNNING OUT OF CHARGE, SO I'LL TALK FAST.
I WANT YOU TO FIND THE RABBIT HOLE!
....
RABBIT?
HEY.
AYU-MU.
SANA...
CHAN?
THAT HOLE HE CAME OUT OF, DO YOU KNOW WHERE IT WAS?
YOU KNOW THAT RABBIT THAT WAS THERE THE LAST TIME I SAW YOU?
.......?

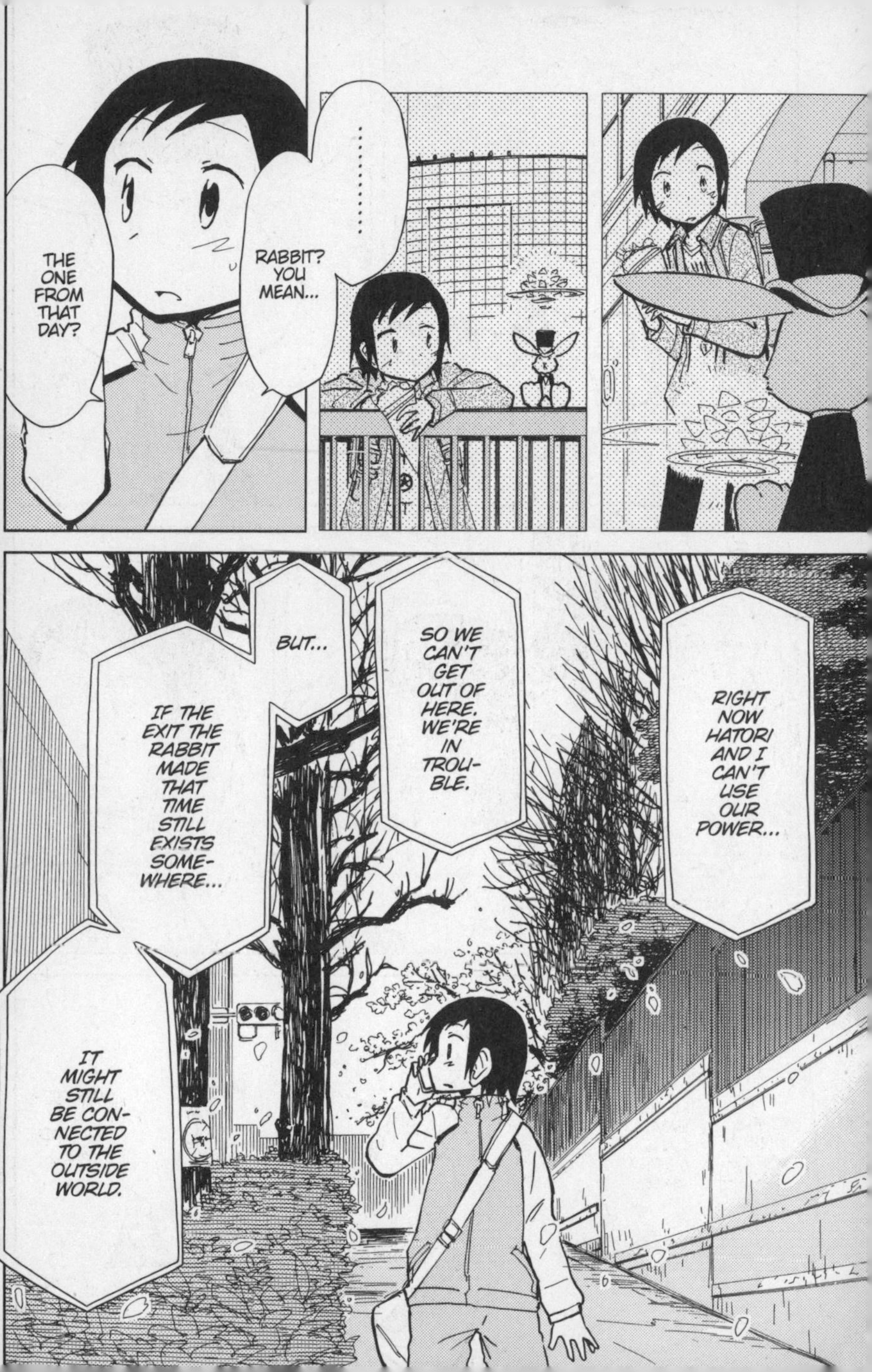
......
RABBIT? YOU MEAN...
THE ONE FROM THAT DAY?
RIGHT NOW HATORI AND I CAN'T USE OUR POWER...
SO WE CAN'T GET OUT OF HERE. WE'RE IN TROUBLE.
BUT...
IF THE EXIT THE RABBIT MADE THAT TIME STILL EXISTS SOME-WHERE...
IT MIGHT STILL BE CONNECTED TO THE OUTSIDE WORLD.

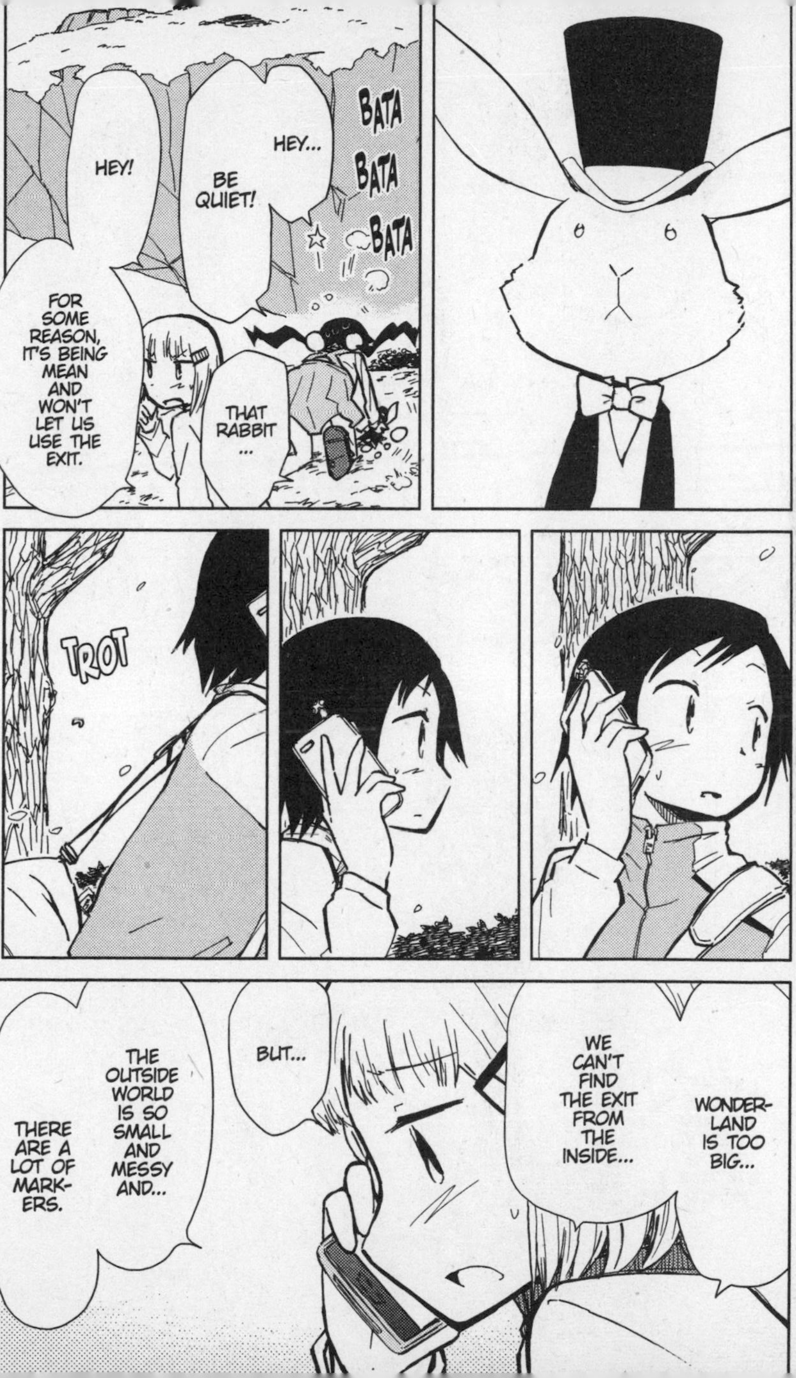
BATA BATA BATA
HEY... BE QUIET!
HEY!
THAT RABBIT ...
FOR SOME REASON, IT'S BEING MEAN AND WON'T LET US USE THE EXIT.
TROT
WONDER-LAND IS TOO BIG...
WE CAN'T FIND THE EXIT FROM THE INSIDE...
BUT...
THE OUTSIDE WORLD IS SO SMALL AND MESSY AND...
THERE ARE A LOT OF MARK-ERS.

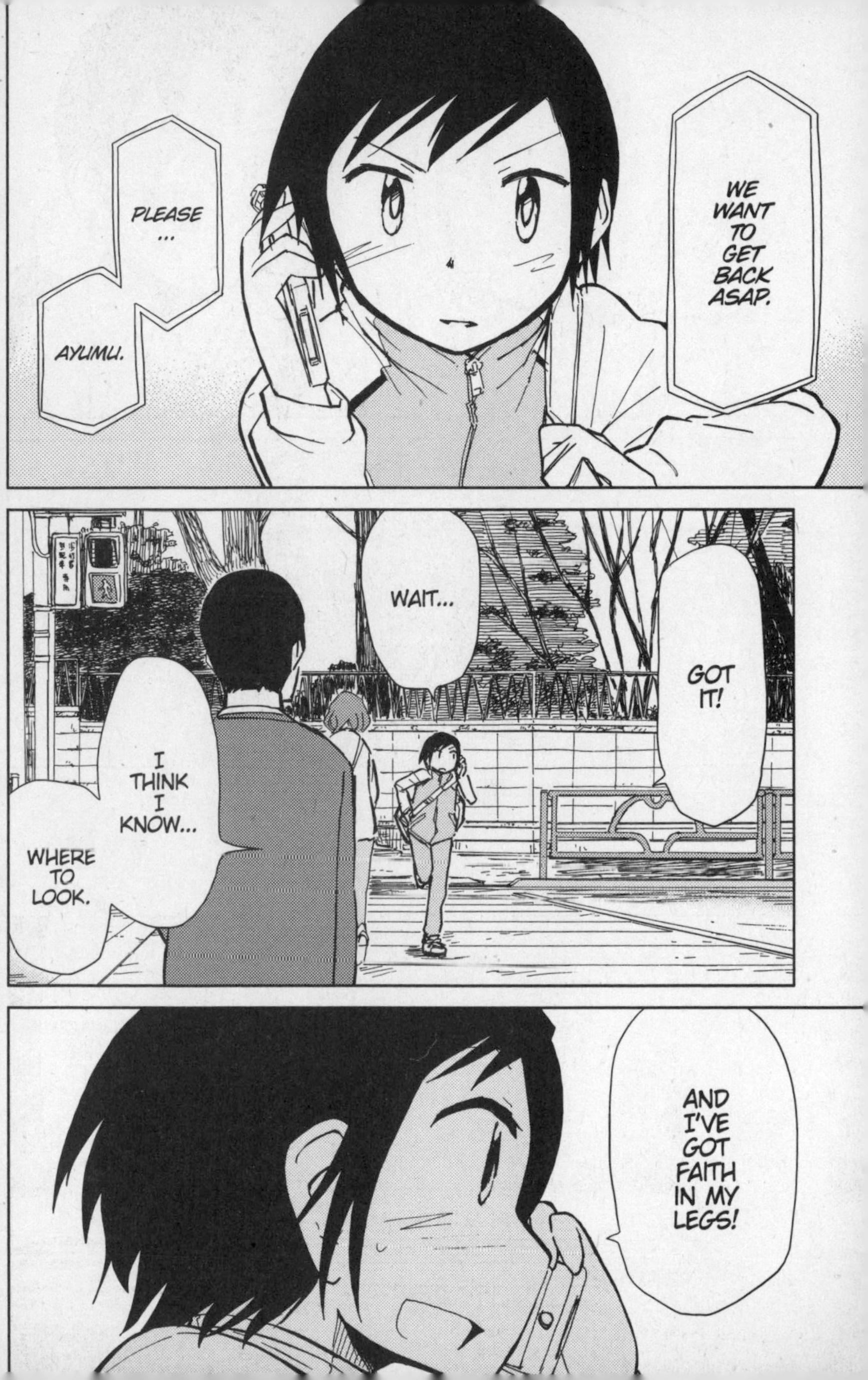
WE WANT TO GET BACK ASAP.
PLEASE... AYUMU.
GOT IT!
WAIT...
I THINK I KNOW... WHERE TO LOOK.
AND I'VE GOT FAITH IN MY LEGS!

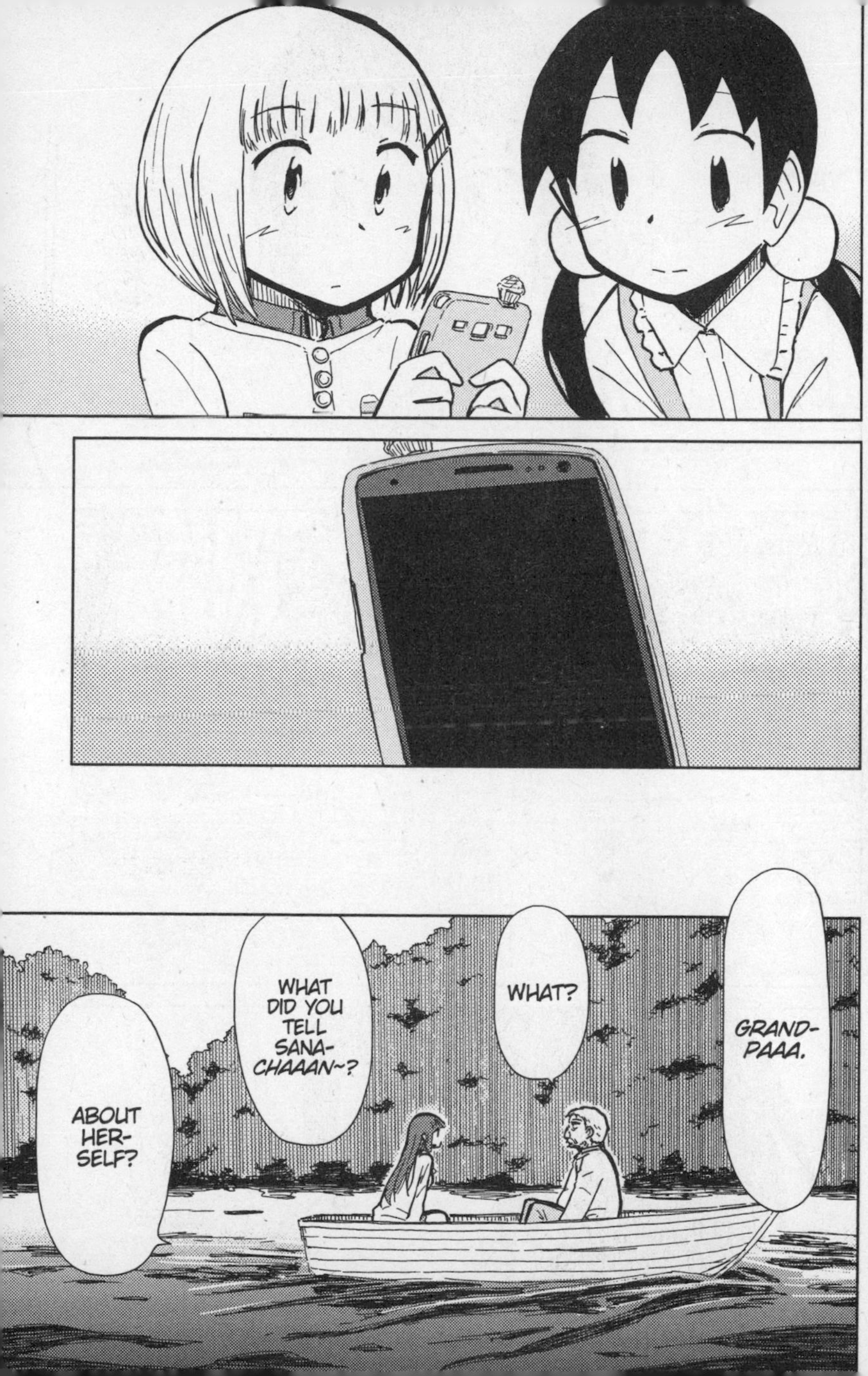
GRAND-PAAA.
WHAT?
WHAT DID YOU TELL SANA-CHAAAN~?
ABOUT HER-SELF?

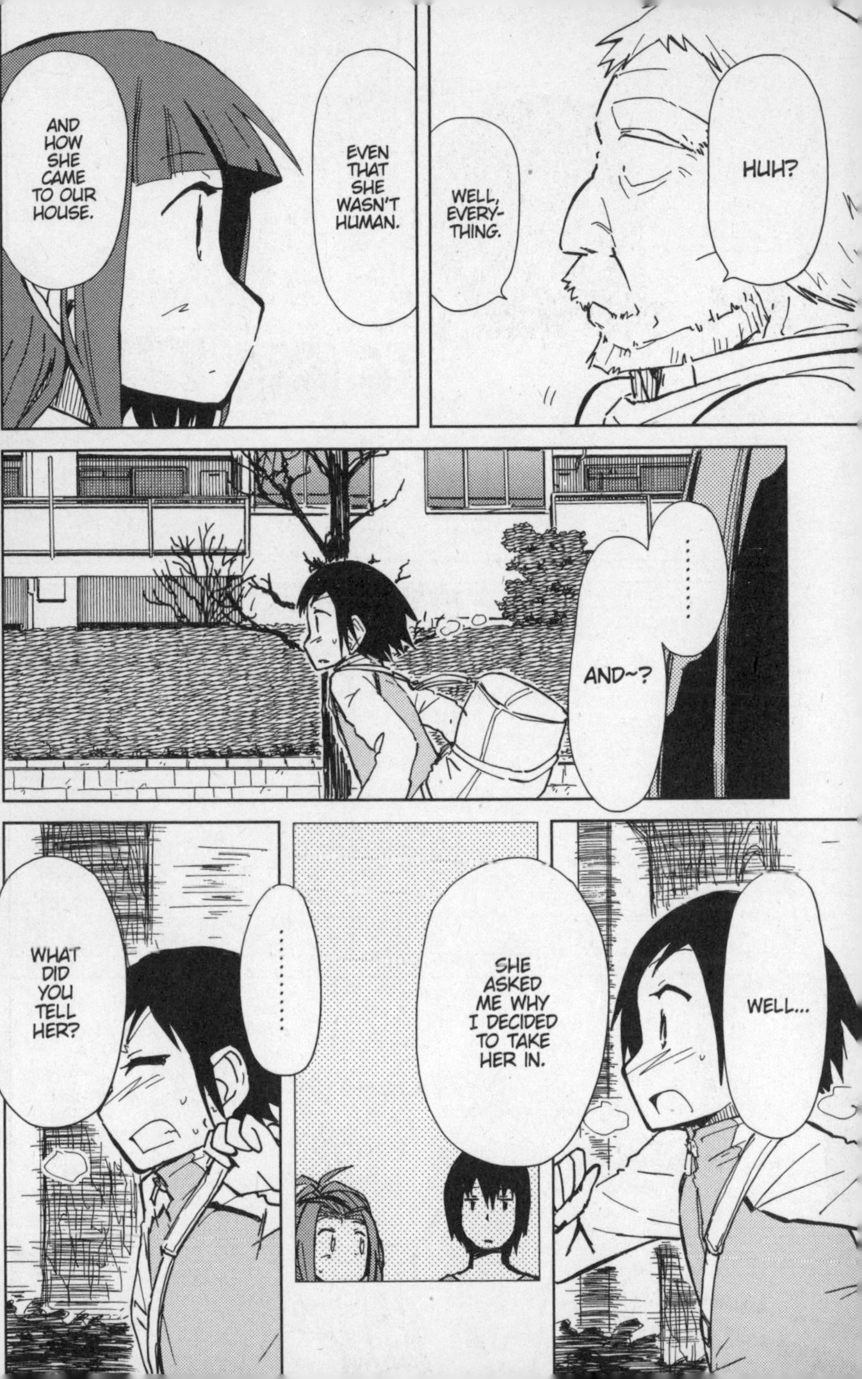
HUH?
WELL, EVERY-THING.
EVEN THAT SHE WASN'T HUMAN.
AND HOW SHE CAME TO OUR HOUSE.
......
AND~?
WELL...
SHE ASKED ME WHY I DECIDED TO TAKE HER IN.
......
WHAT DID YOU TELL HER?

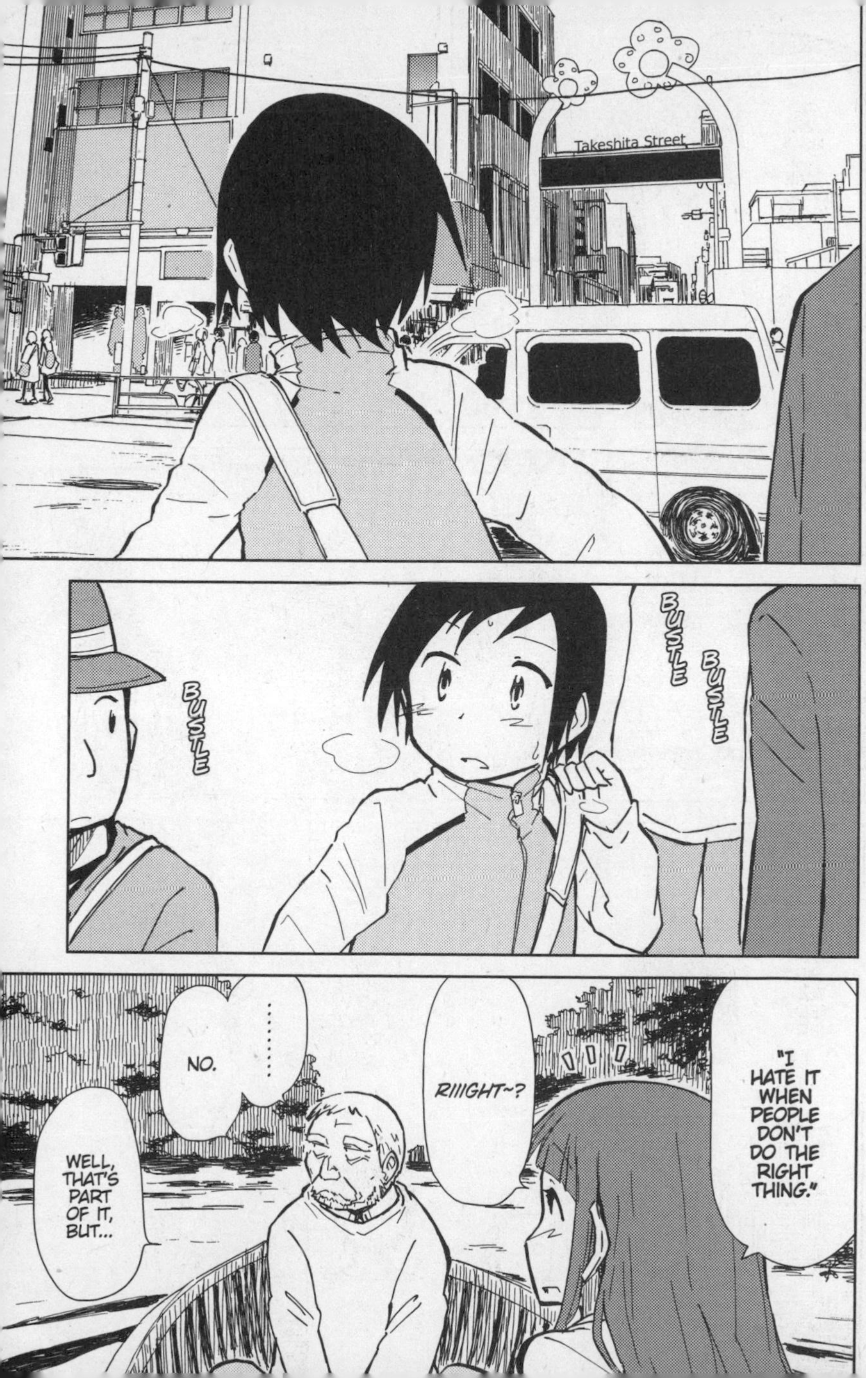
Takeshita Street
BUSTLE
BUSTLE
BUSTLE
"I HATE IT WHEN PEOPLE DON'T DO THE RIGHT THING."
RIIIGHT~?
......
NO.
WELL, THAT'S PART OF IT, BUT...

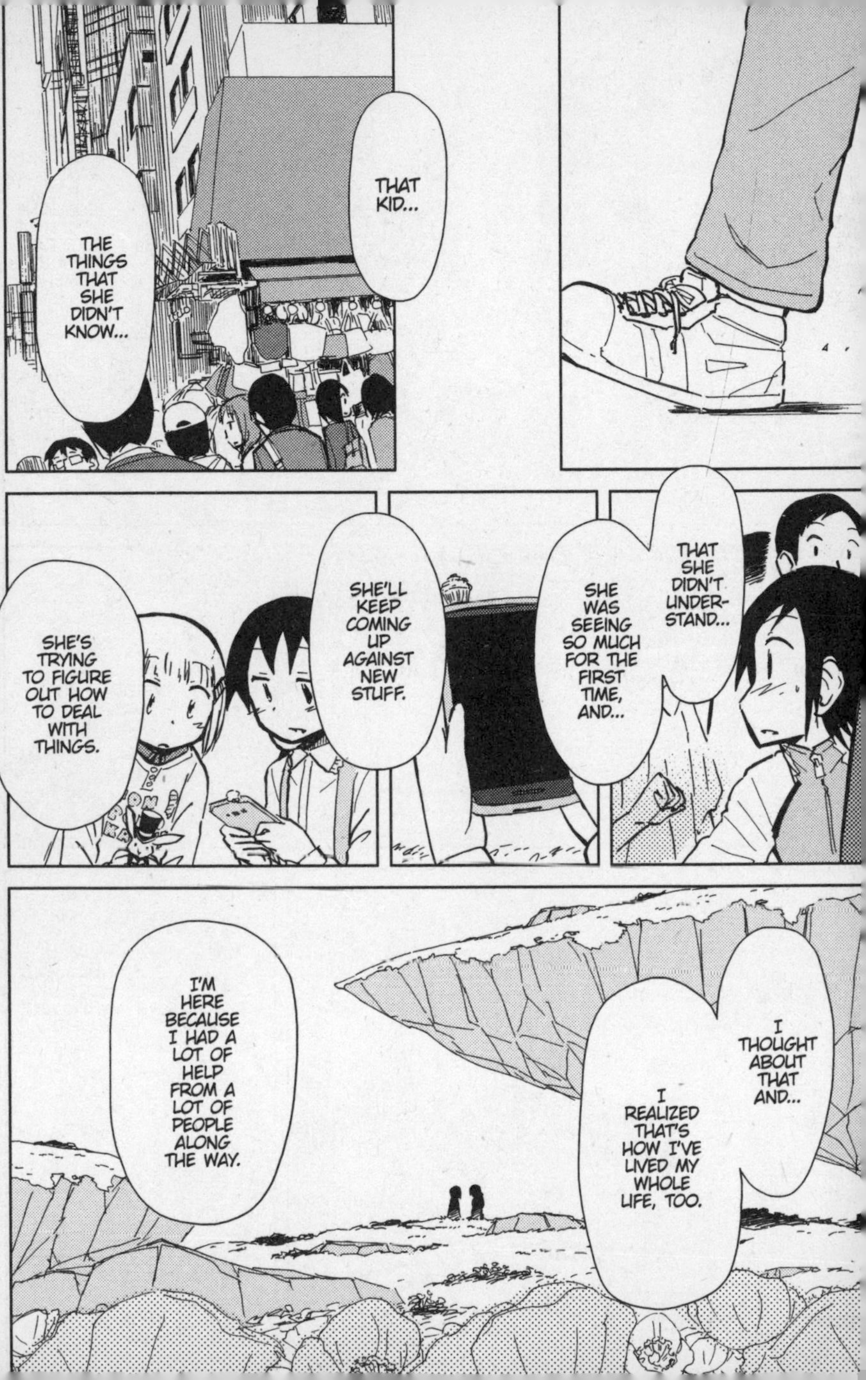
THAT KID...
THE THINGS THAT SHE DIDN'T KNOW...
THAT SHE DIDN'T UNDER-STAND...
SHE WAS SEEING SO MUCH FOR THE FIRST TIME, AND...
SHE'LL KEEP COMING UP AGAINST NEW STUFF.
SHE'S TRYING TO FIGURE OUT HOW TO DEAL WITH THINGS.
I THOUGHT ABOUT THAT AND...
I REALIZED THAT'S HOW I'VE LIVED MY WHOLE LIFE, TOO.
I'M HERE BECAUSE I HAD A LOT OF HELP FROM A LOT OF PEOPLE ALONG THE WAY.

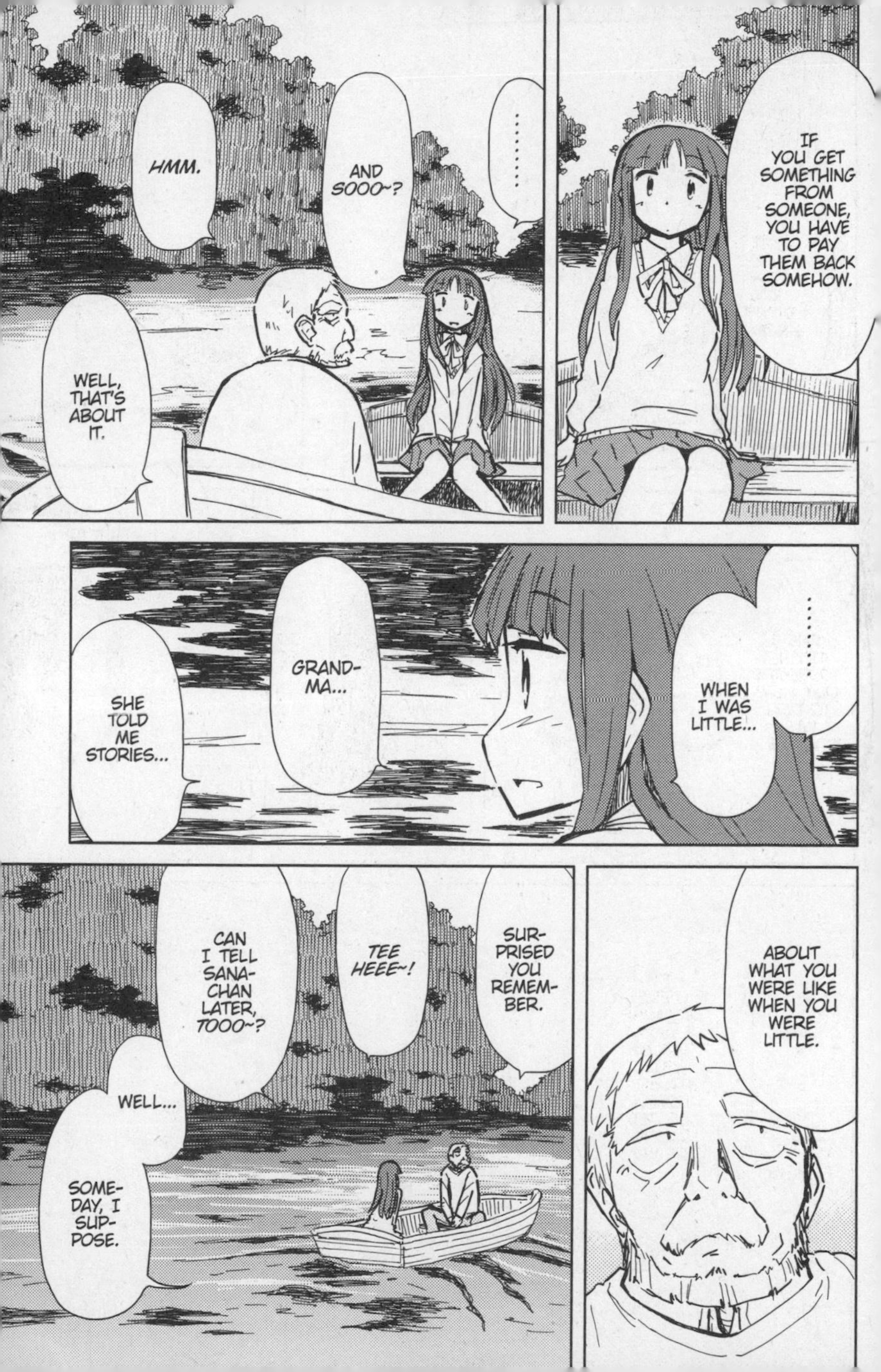
IF YOU GET SOMETHING FROM SOMEONE, YOU HAVE TO PAY THEM BACK SOMEHOW.
......
AND SOOO~?
HMM.
WELL, THAT'S ABOUT IT.
......
WHEN I WAS LITTLE...
GRANDMA...
SHE TOLD ME STORIES...
ABOUT WHAT YOU WERE LIKE WHEN YOU WERE LITTLE.
SURPRISED YOU REMEMBER.
TEE HEEE~!
CAN I TELL SANA-CHAN LATER, TOOO~?
WELL...
SOMEDAY, I SUPPOSE.

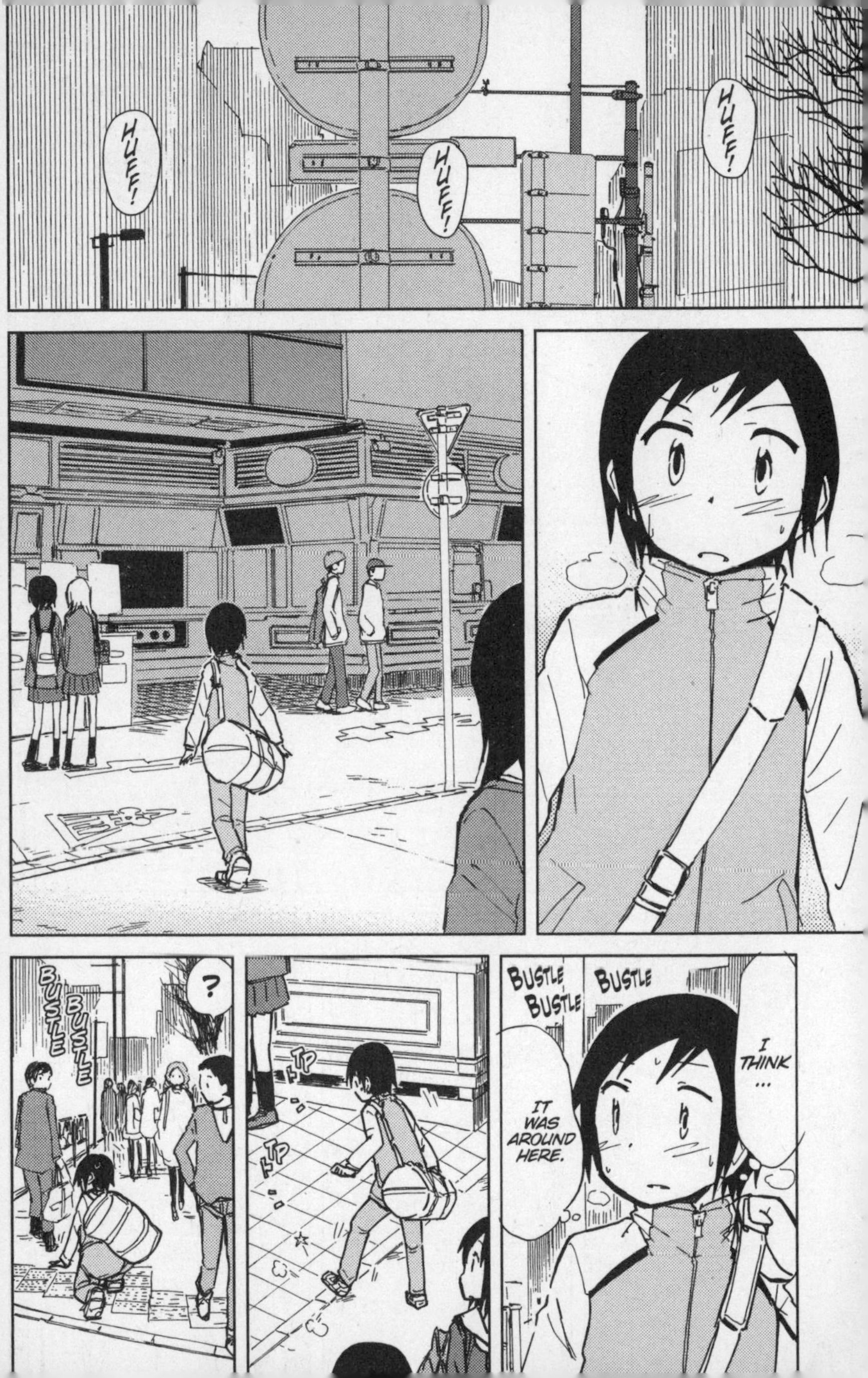
HUFF!
HUFF!
HUFF!
BUSTLE
BUSTLE BUSTLE
I THINK...
IT WAS AROUND HERE.
TP
TP
?
BUSTLE BUSTLE

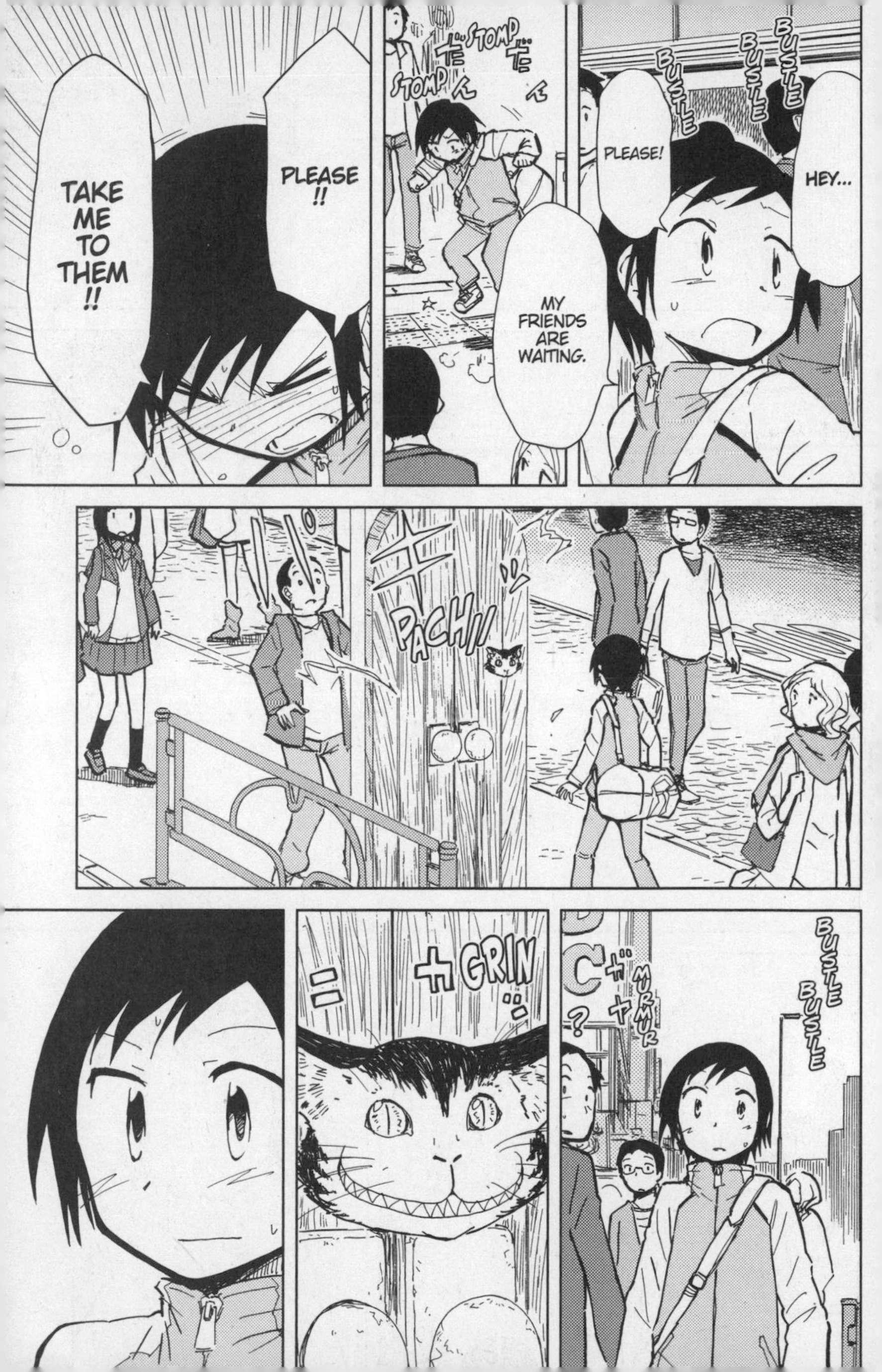
BUSTLE
BUSTLE
BUSTLE
HEY...
PLEASE!
MY FRIENDS ARE WAITING.
STOMP
STOMP
STOMP
PLEASE !!
TAKE ME TO THEM !!
PACHI
BUSTLE
BUSTLE
MURMUR
GRIN

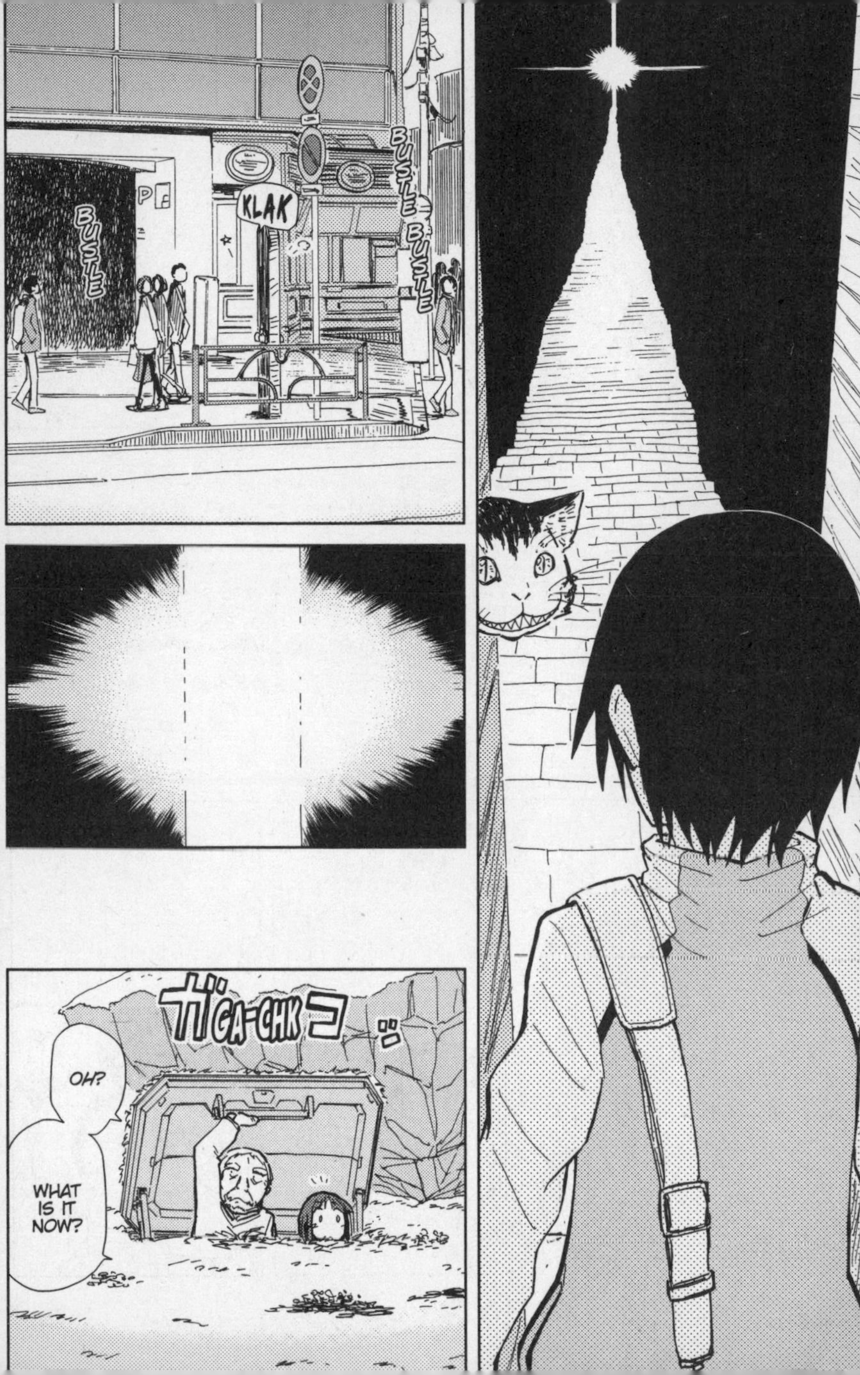
BUSTLE
BUSTLE
KLAK
BUSTLE
GA-CHK
OH?
WHAT IS IT NOW?

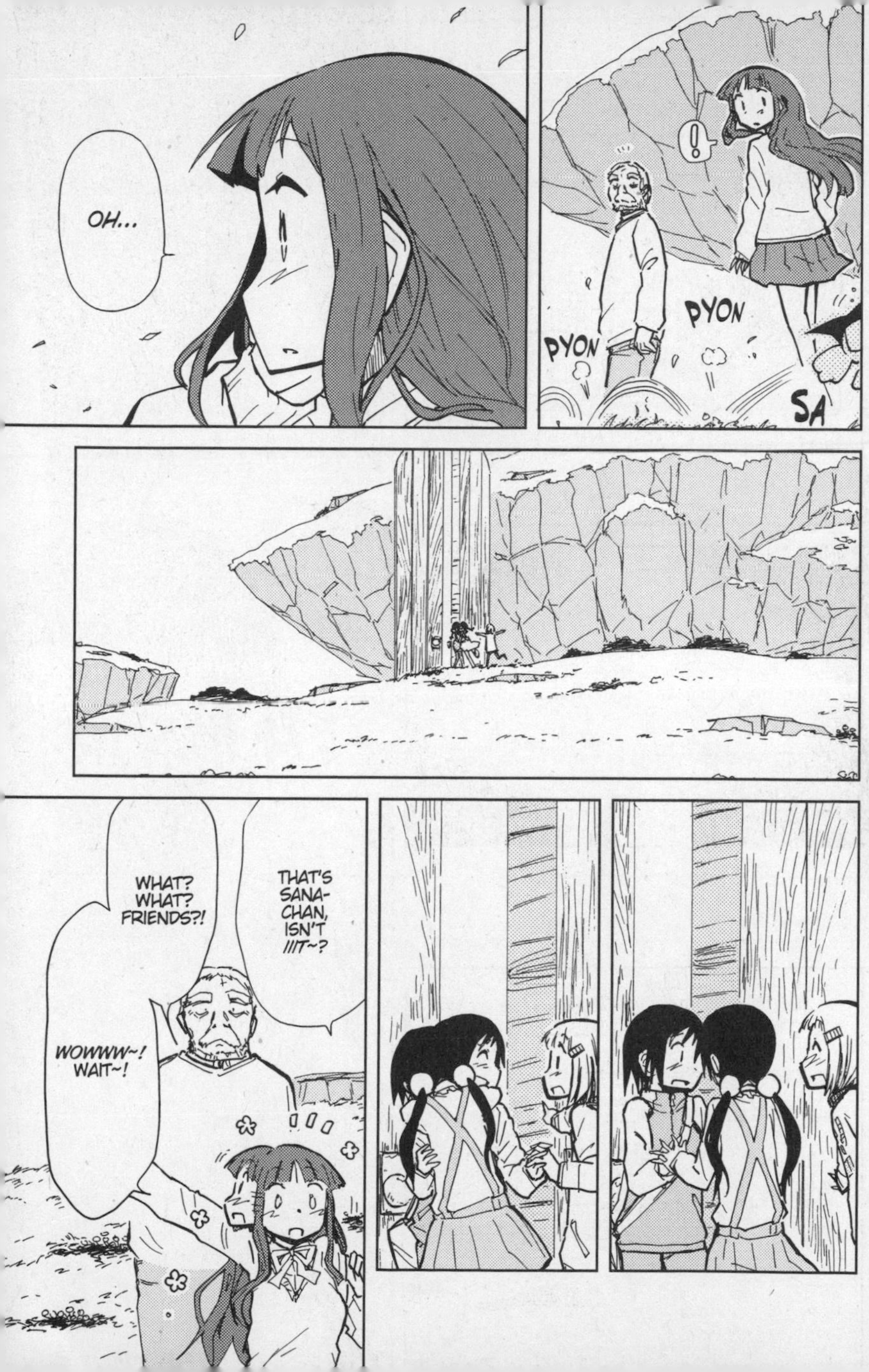
!
PYON
PYON
SA
OH...
THAT'S SANA-CHAN, ISN'T IIIT~?
WHAT? WHAT? FRIENDS?!
WOWWW~! WAIT~!

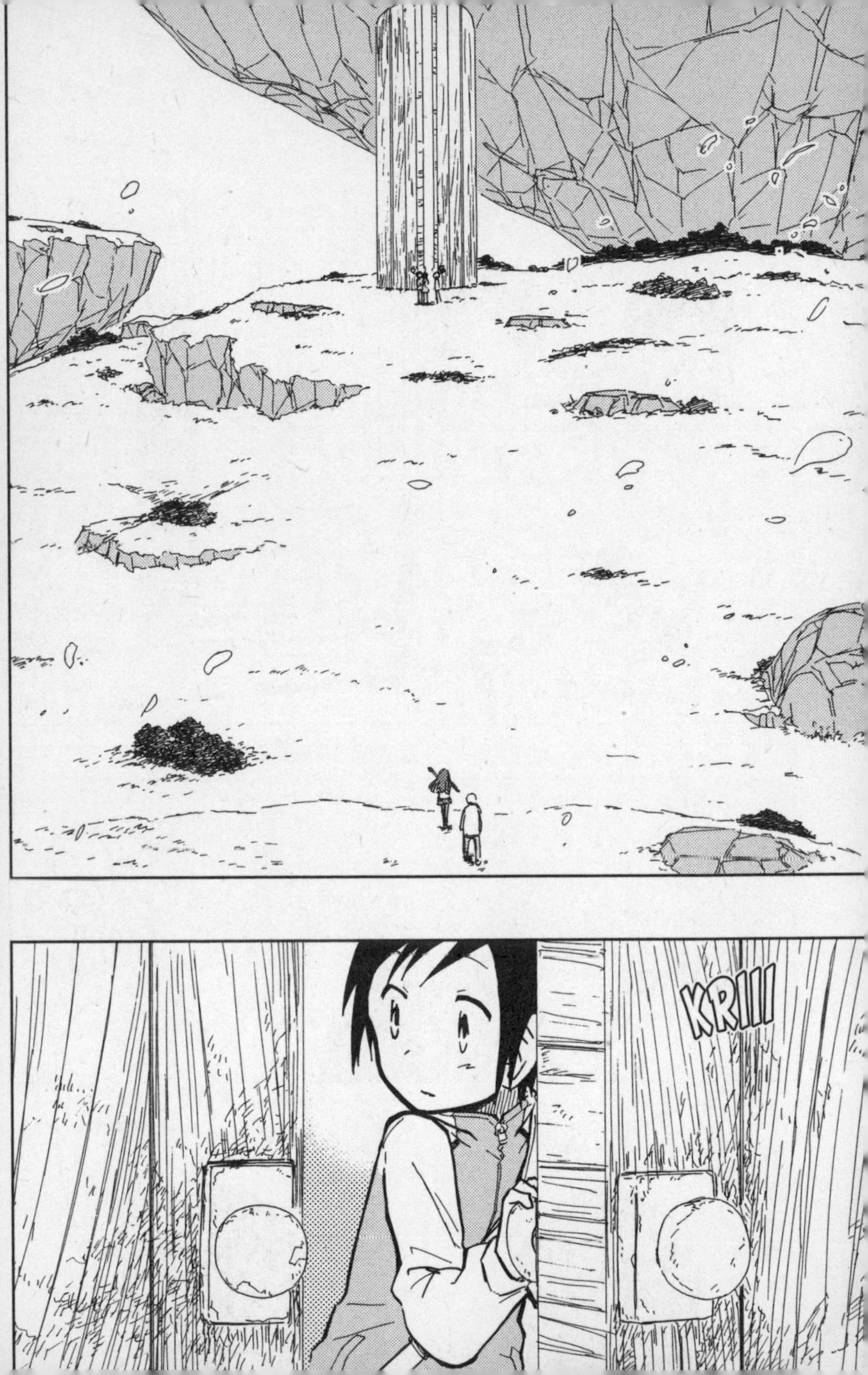
KRIII

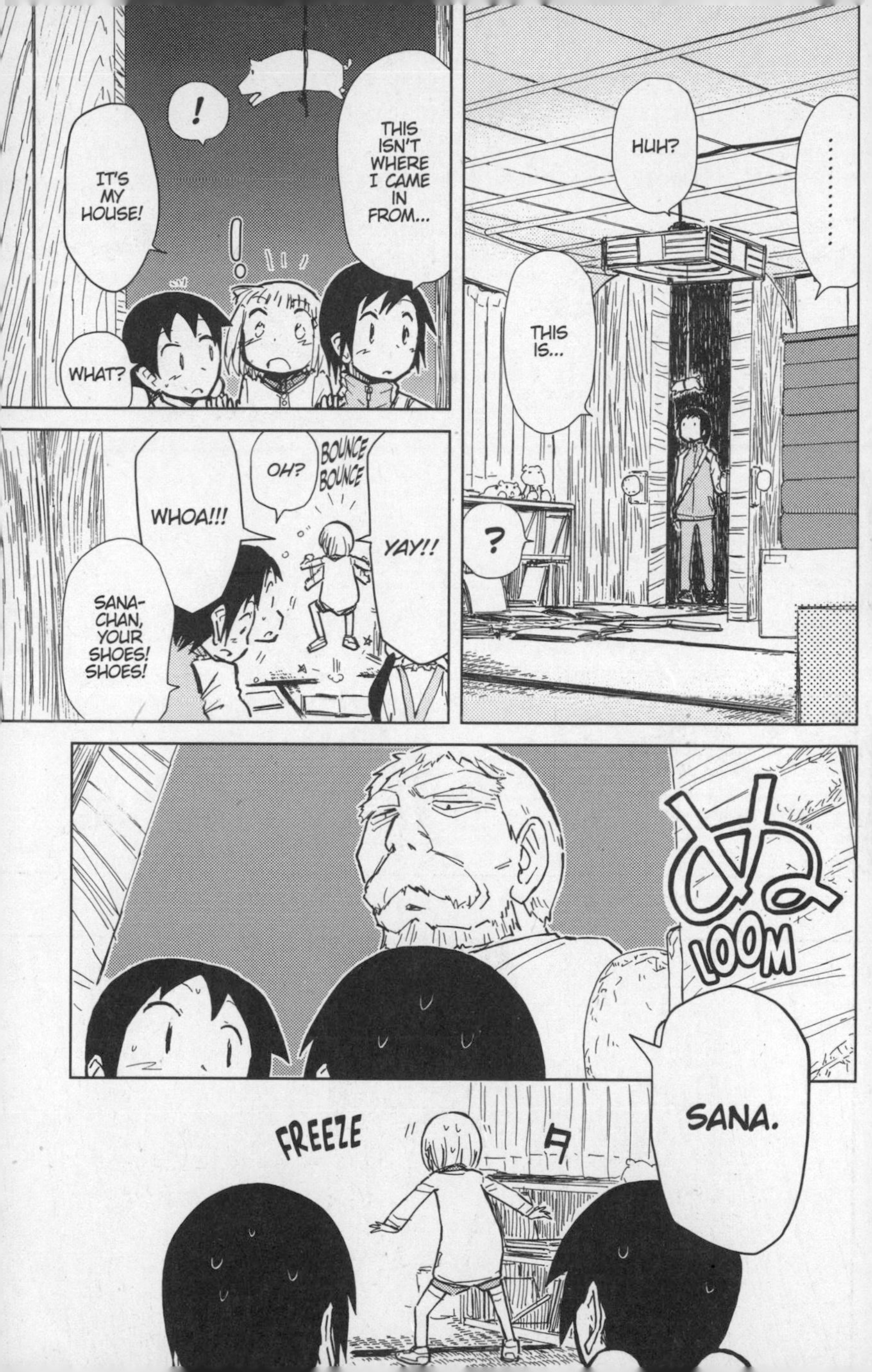
......
HUH?
THIS IS...
?
THIS ISN'T WHERE I CAME IN FROM...
!
IT'S MY HOUSE!
WHAT?
OH?
BOUNCE BOUNCE
YAY!!
WHOA!!!
SANA-CHAN, YOUR SHOES! SHOES!
ぬ
LOOM
SANA.
FREEZE

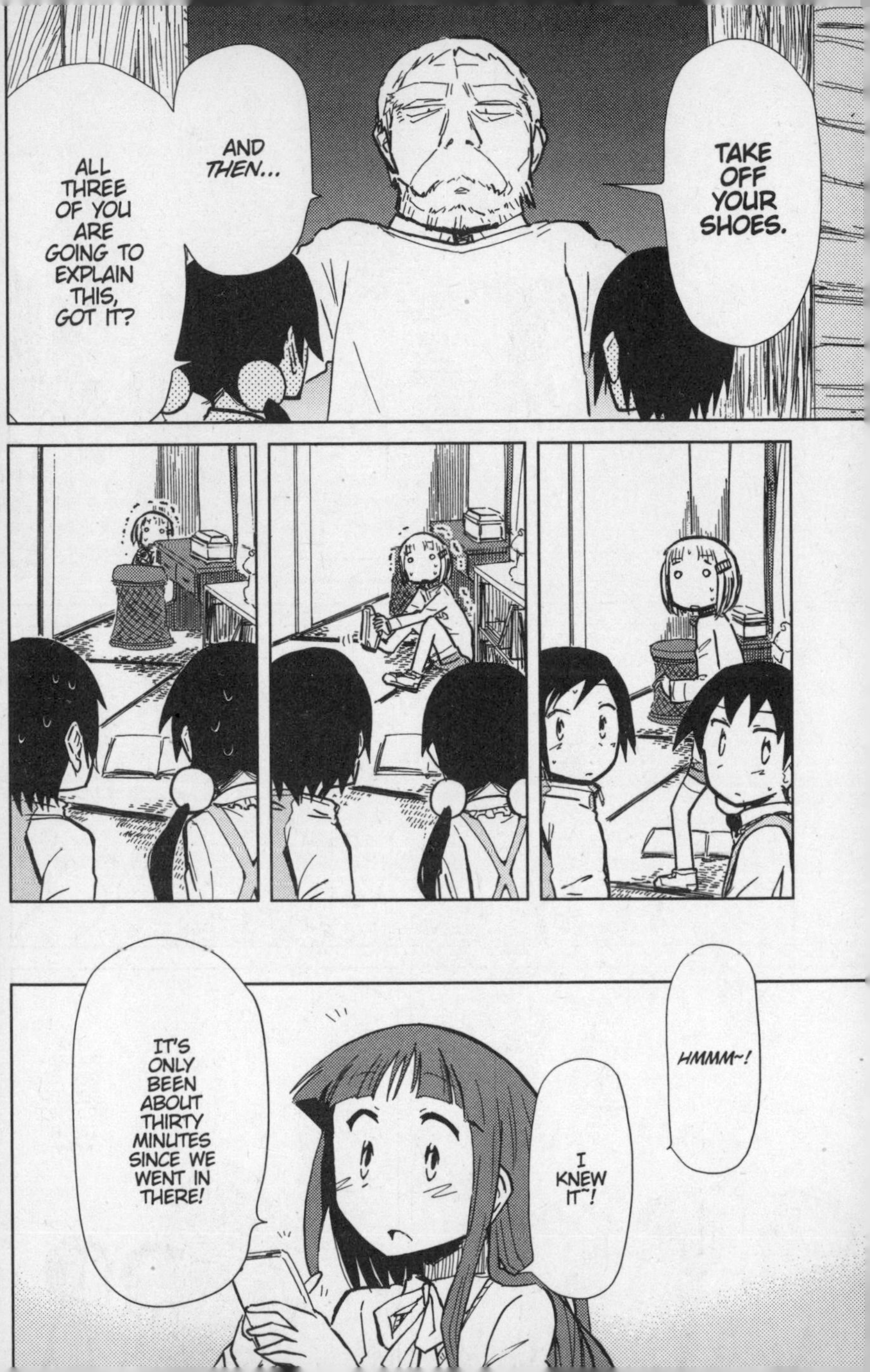
TAKE OFF YOUR SHOES.
AND THEN...
ALL THREE OF YOU ARE GOING TO EXPLAIN THIS, GOT IT?
HMMM~!
I KNEW IT~!
IT'S ONLY BEEN ABOUT THIRTY MINUTES SINCE WE WENT IN THERE!

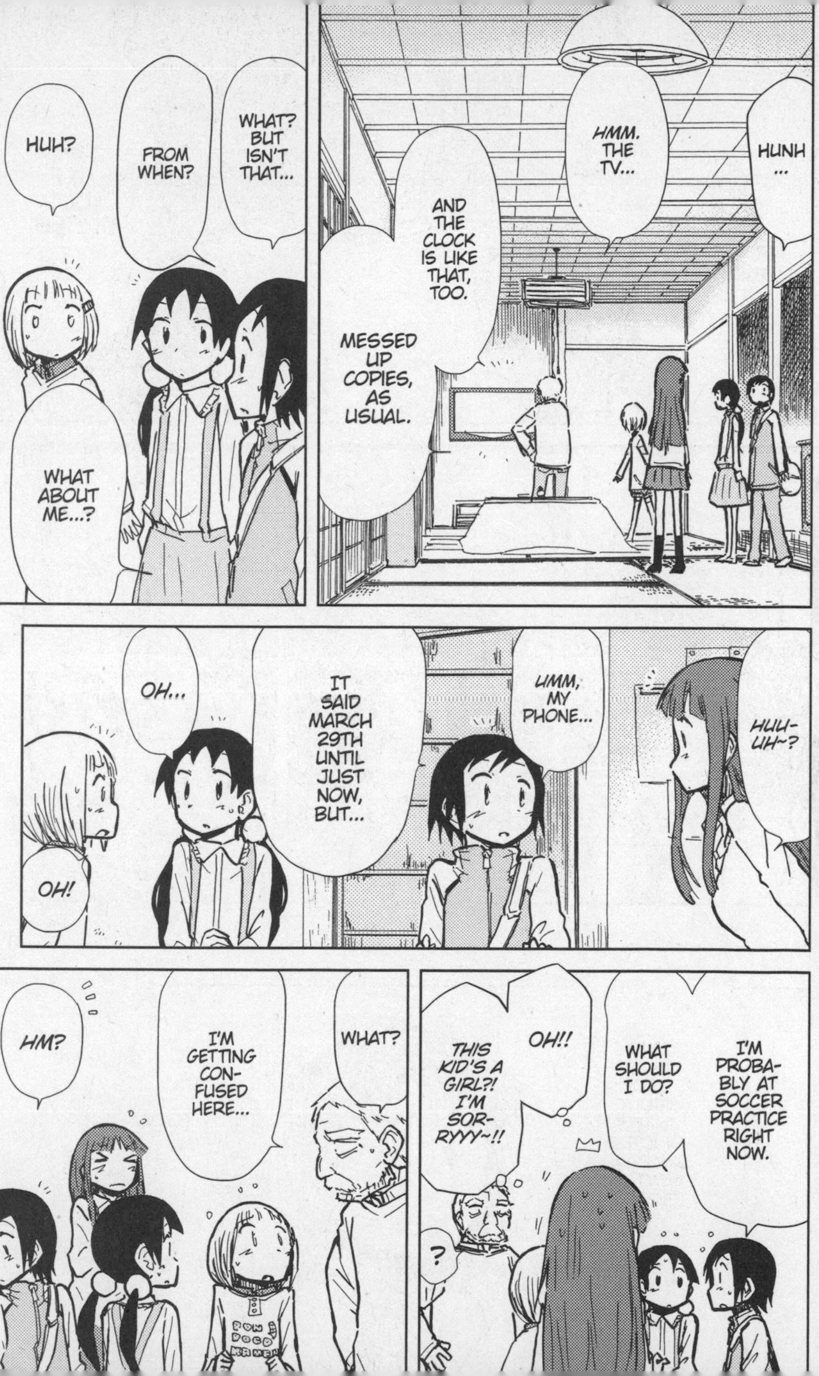
HUNH ...
HMM. THE TV...
AND THE CLOCK IS LIKE THAT, TOO.
MESSED UP COPIES, AS USUAL.
WHAT? BUT ISN'T THAT...
FROM WHEN?
HUH?
WHAT ABOUT ME...?
HUU-UH~?
UMM, MY PHONE...
IT SAID MARCH 29TH UNTIL JUST NOW, BUT...
OH...
OH!
I'M PROBABLY AT SOCCER PRACTICE RIGHT NOW.
WHAT SHOULD I DO?
OH!!
THIS KID'S A GIRL?! I'M SORRYYY~!!
?
WHAT?
I'M GETTING CONFUSED HERE...
HM?

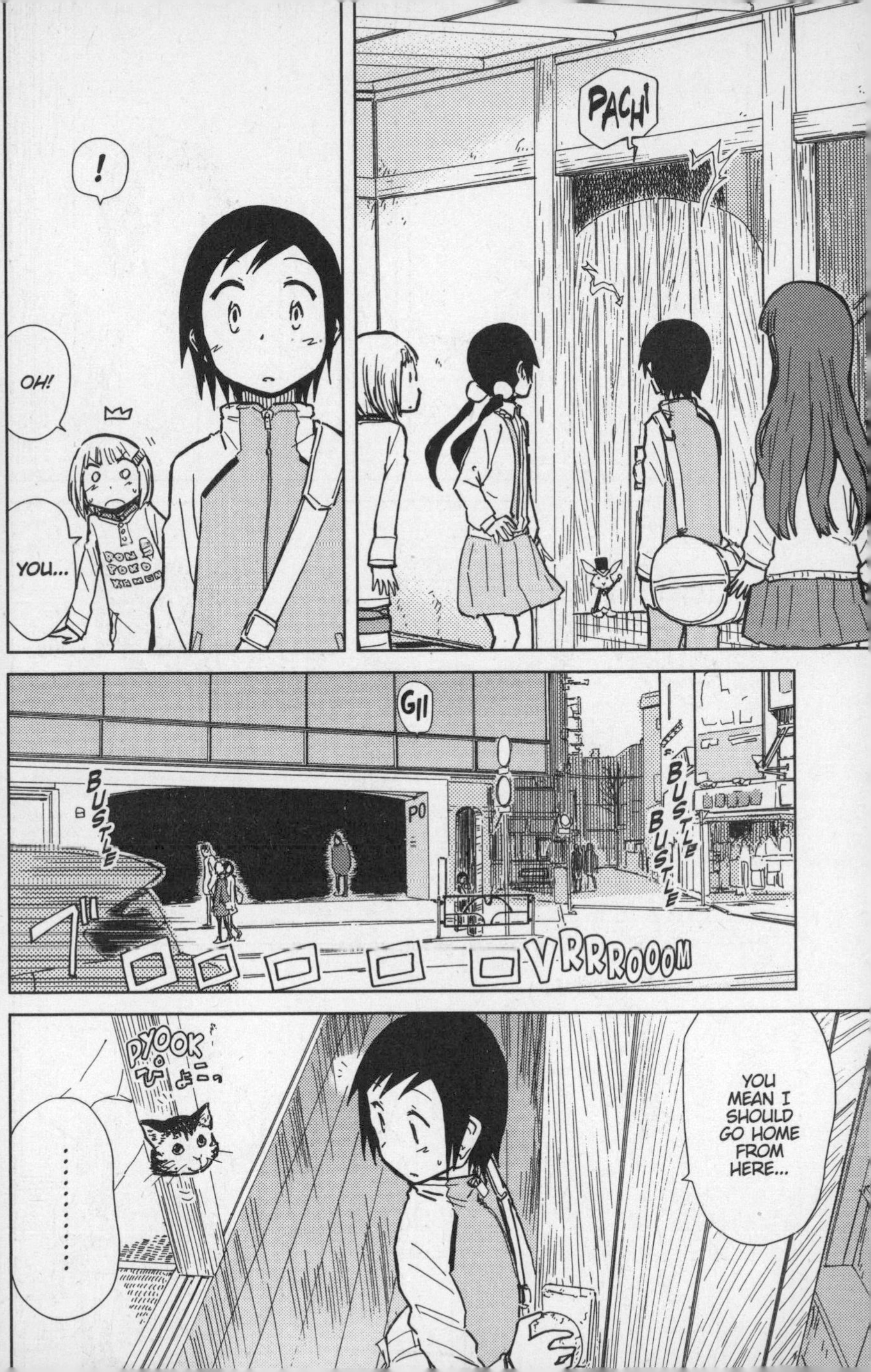
PACHI
!
OH!
YOU...
GII
BUSTLE
BUSTLE
BUSTLE
VRRROOOM
YOU MEAN I SHOULD GO HOME FROM HERE...
DYOOK
......

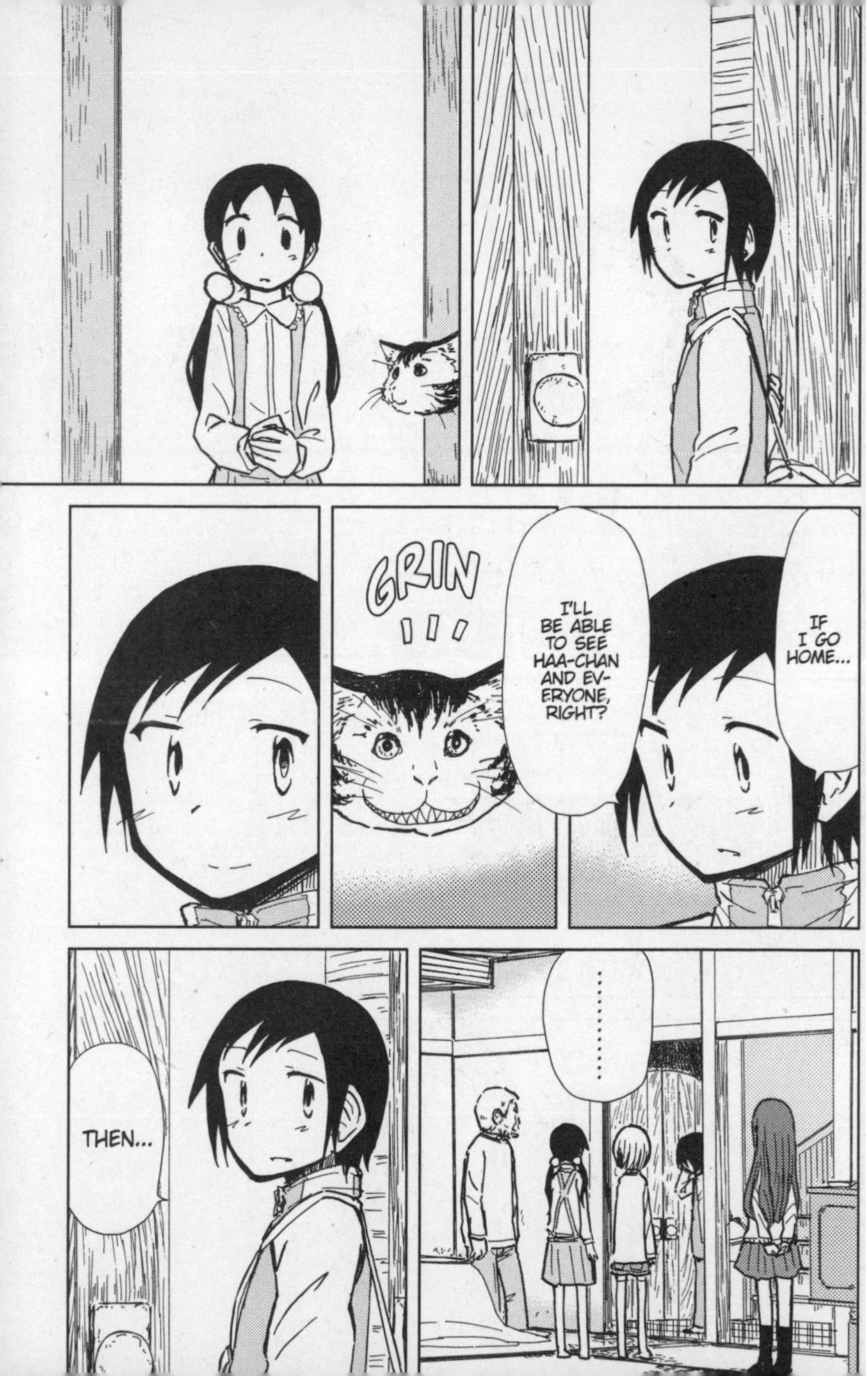
IF I GO HOME...
I'LL BE ABLE TO SEE HAA-CHAN AND EVERYONE, RIGHT?
GRIN
......
THEN...

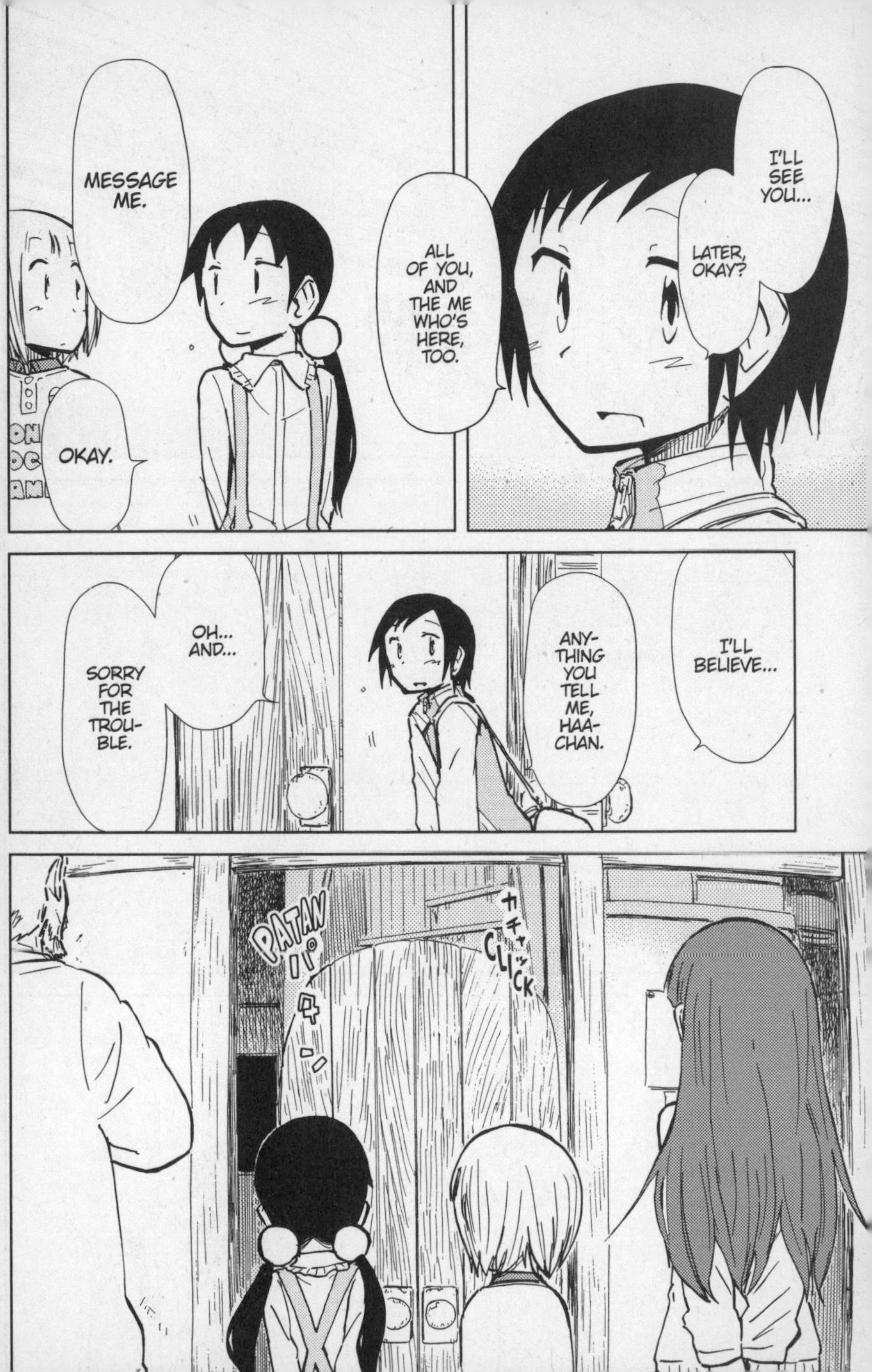
I'LL SEE YOU...
LATER, OKAY?
ALL OF YOU, AND THE ME WHO'S HERE, TOO.
MESSAGE ME.
OKAY.
I'LL BELIEVE...
ANY-THING YOU TELL ME, HAA-CHAN.
OH... AND...
SORRY FOR THE TROU-BLE.
カチャッ
CLICK
パタン
PATAN

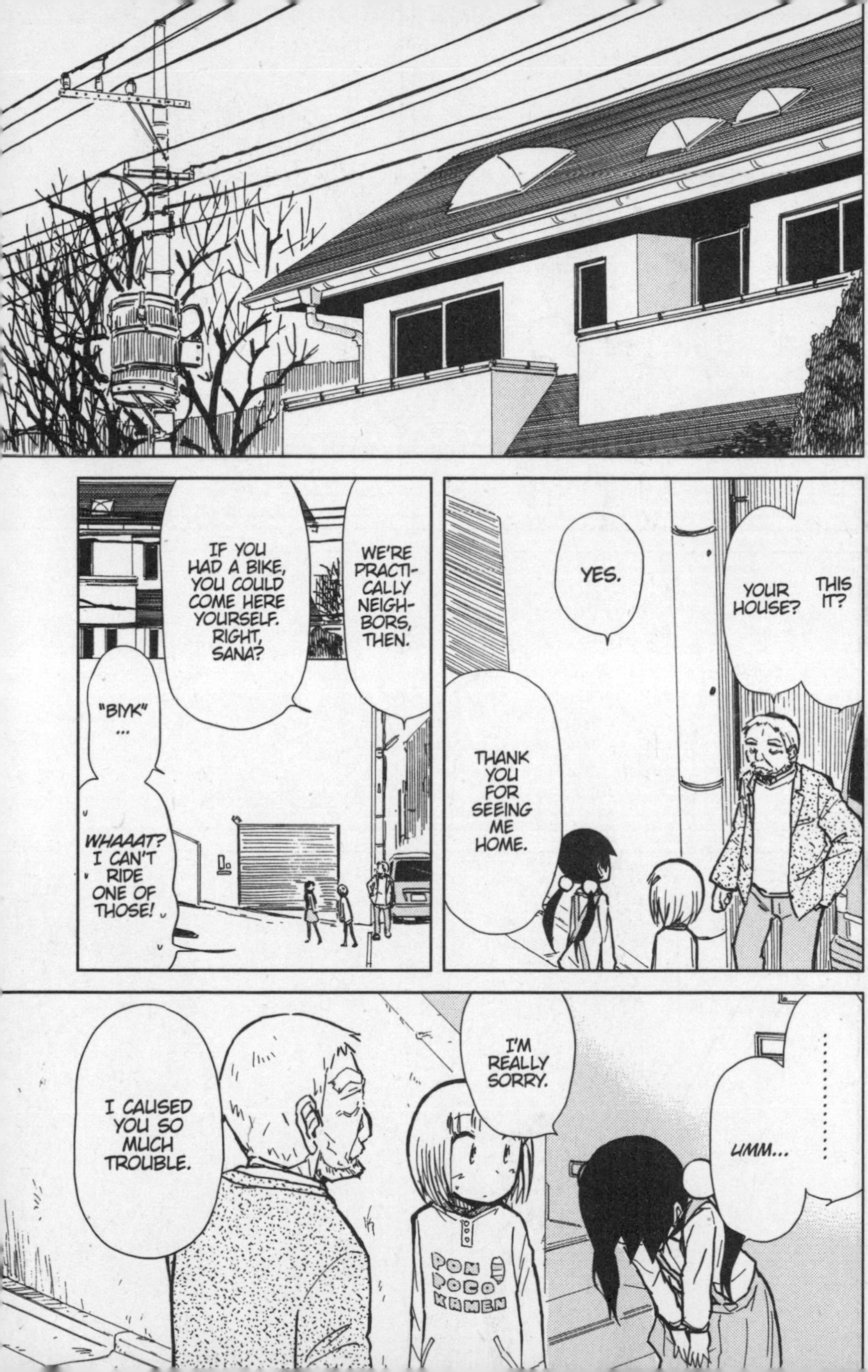
THIS IT? YOUR HOUSE?
YES.
THANK YOU FOR SEEING ME HOME.
WE'RE PRACTI-CALLY NEIGH-BORS, THEN.
IF YOU HAD A BIKE, YOU COULD COME HERE YOURSELF. RIGHT, SANA?
"BIYK" ...
WHAAAT? I CAN'T RIDE ONE OF THOSE!
......
UMM...
I'M REALLY SORRY.
I CAUSED YOU SO MUCH TROUBLE.

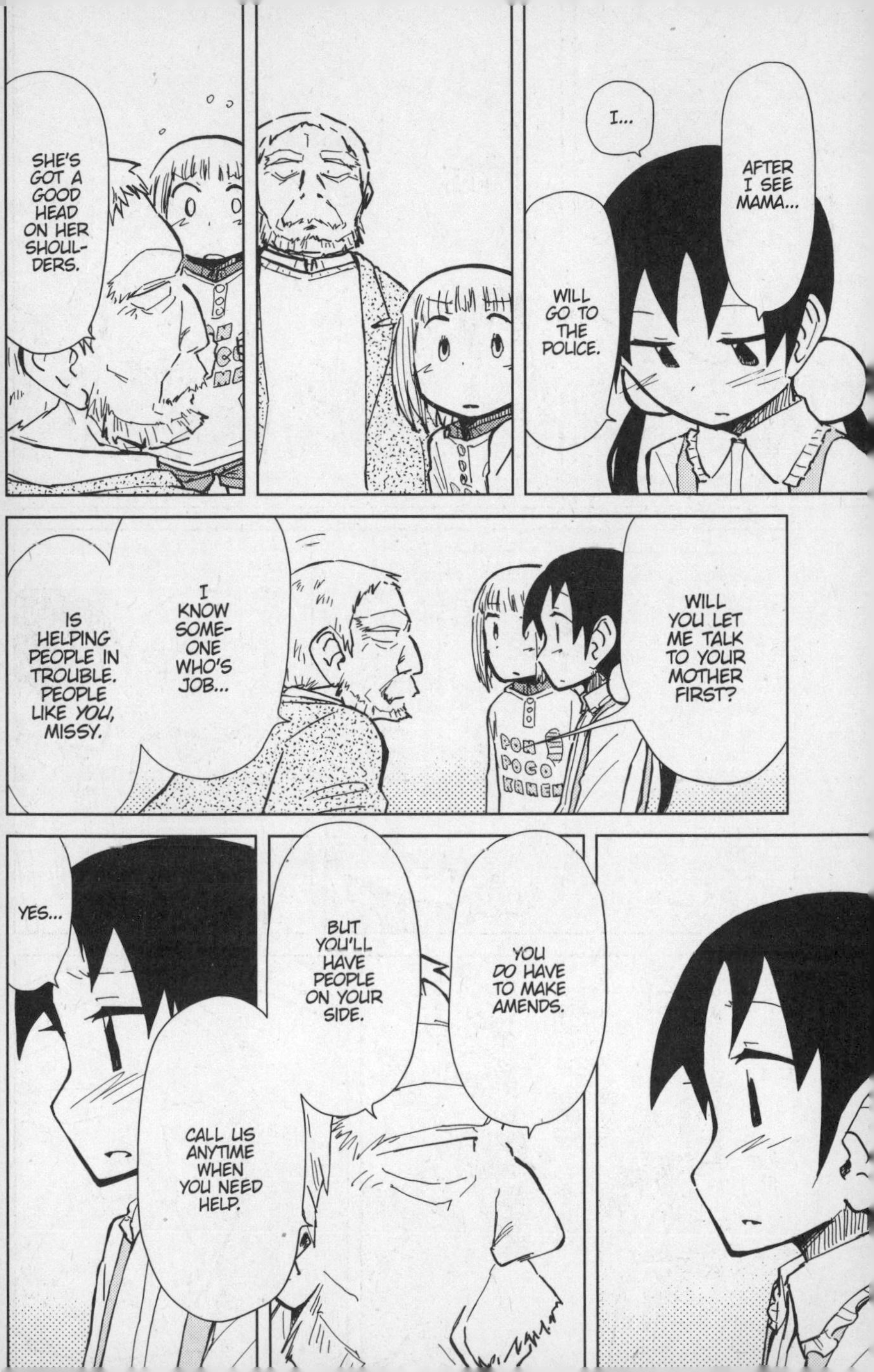
I...
AFTER I SEE MAMA...
WILL GO TO THE POLICE.
SHE'S GOT A GOOD HEAD ON HER SHOULDERS.
WILL YOU LET ME TALK TO YOUR MOTHER FIRST?
PON POGO KAMEN
I KNOW SOMEONE WHO'S JOB...
IS HELPING PEOPLE IN TROUBLE. PEOPLE LIKE *YOU*, MISSY.
YOU DO HAVE TO MAKE AMENDS.
BUT YOU'LL HAVE PEOPLE ON YOUR SIDE.
CALL US ANYTIME WHEN YOU NEED HELP.
YES...

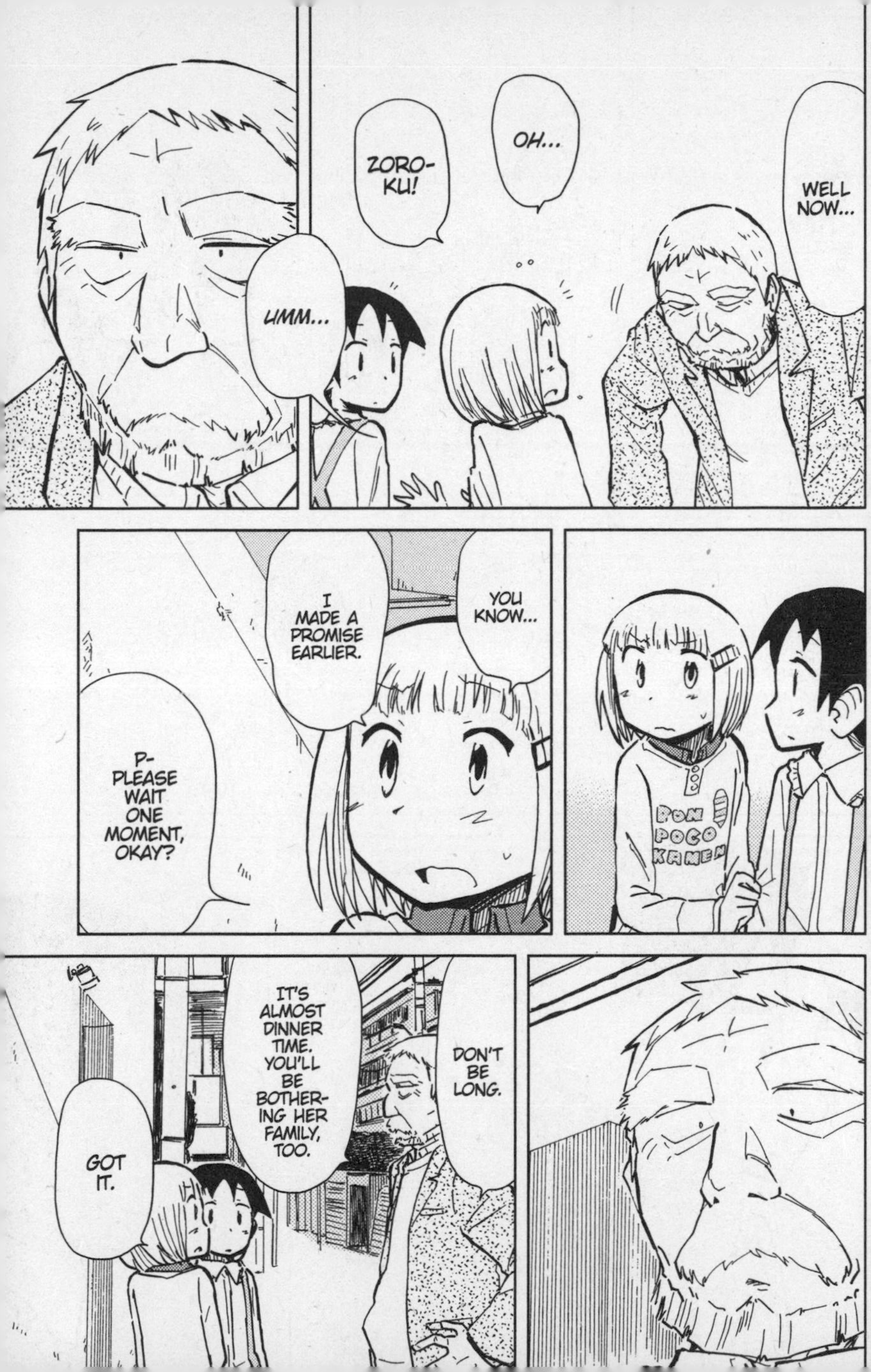
WELL NOW...
OH...
ZORO-KU!
UMM...
PON POCO KAMEN
YOU KNOW...
I MADE A PROMISE EARLIER.
P-PLEASE WAIT ONE MOMENT, OKAY?
DON'T BE LONG.
IT'S ALMOST DINNER TIME. YOU'LL BE BOTHERING HER FAMILY, TOO.
GOT IT.

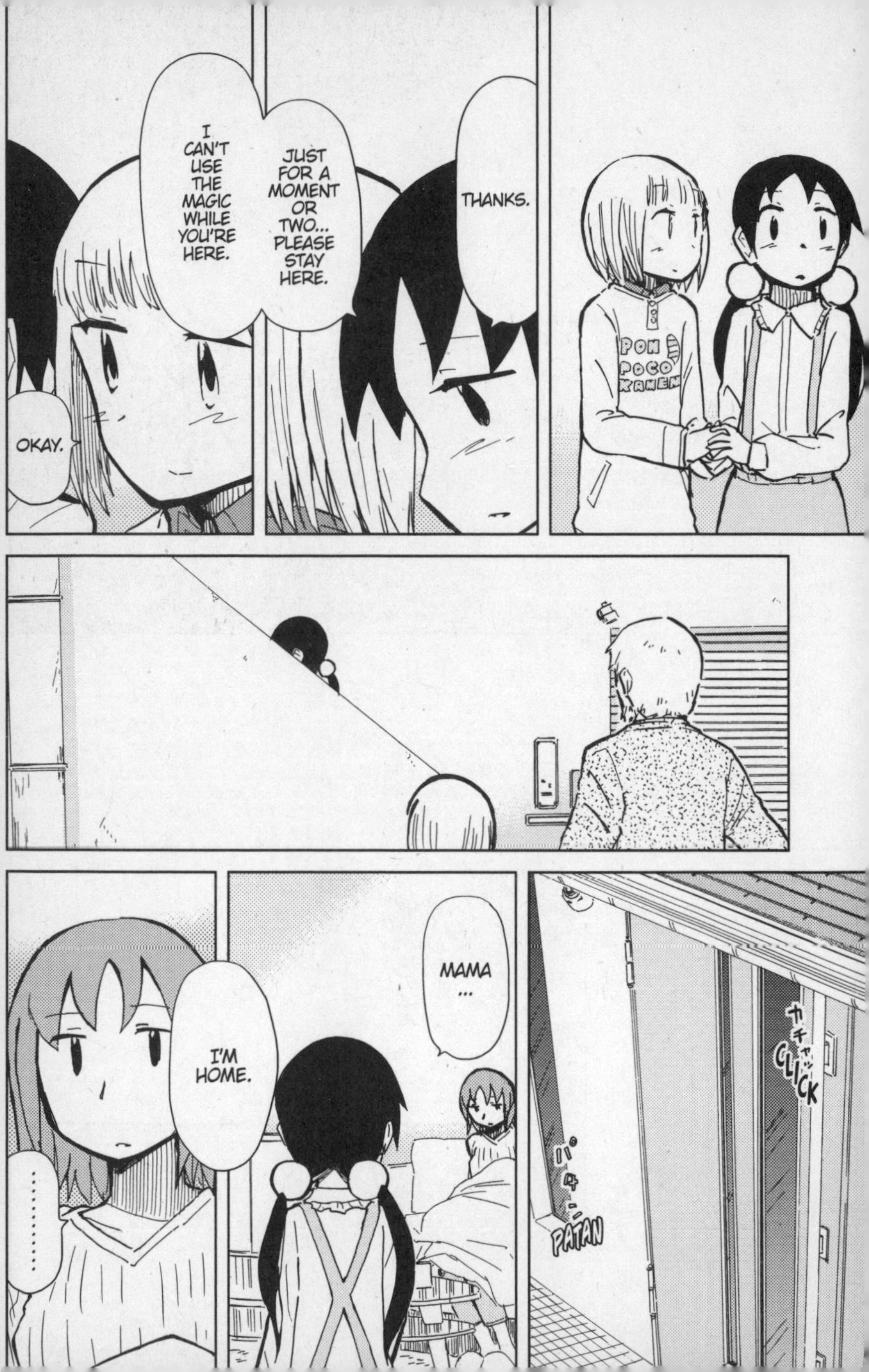
THANKS.
JUST FOR A MOMENT OR TWO... PLEASE STAY HERE.
I CAN'T USE THE MAGIC WHILE YOU'RE HERE.
OKAY.
カチャッ
CLICK
パタン
PATAN
MAMA ...
I'M HOME.
......

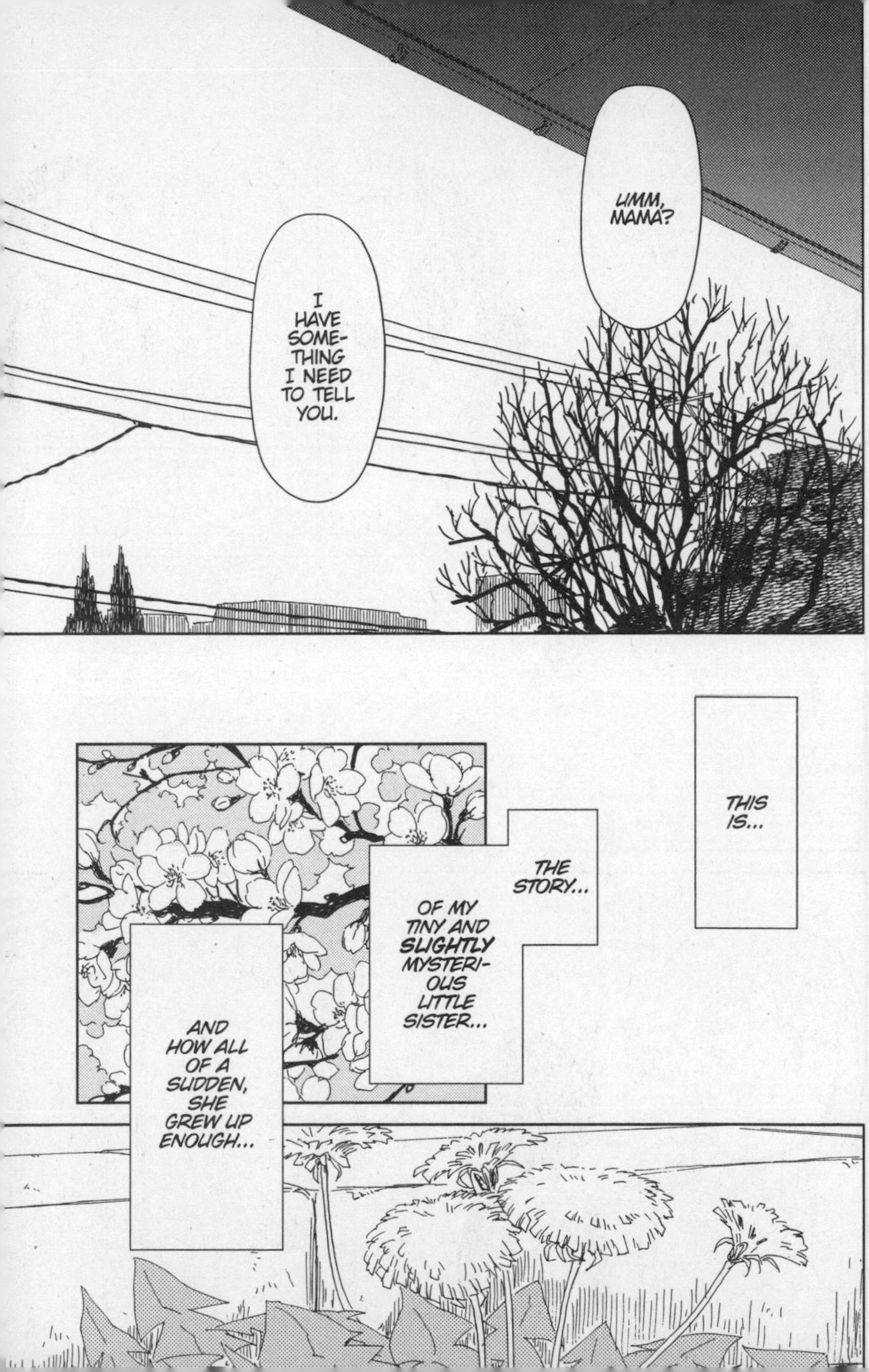
UMM, MAMA?
I HAVE SOME-THING I NEED TO TELL YOU.
THIS IS...
THE STORY...
OF MY TINY AND SLIGHTLY MYSTERI-OUS LITTLE SISTER...
AND HOW ALL OF A SUDDEN, SHE GREW UP ENOUGH...

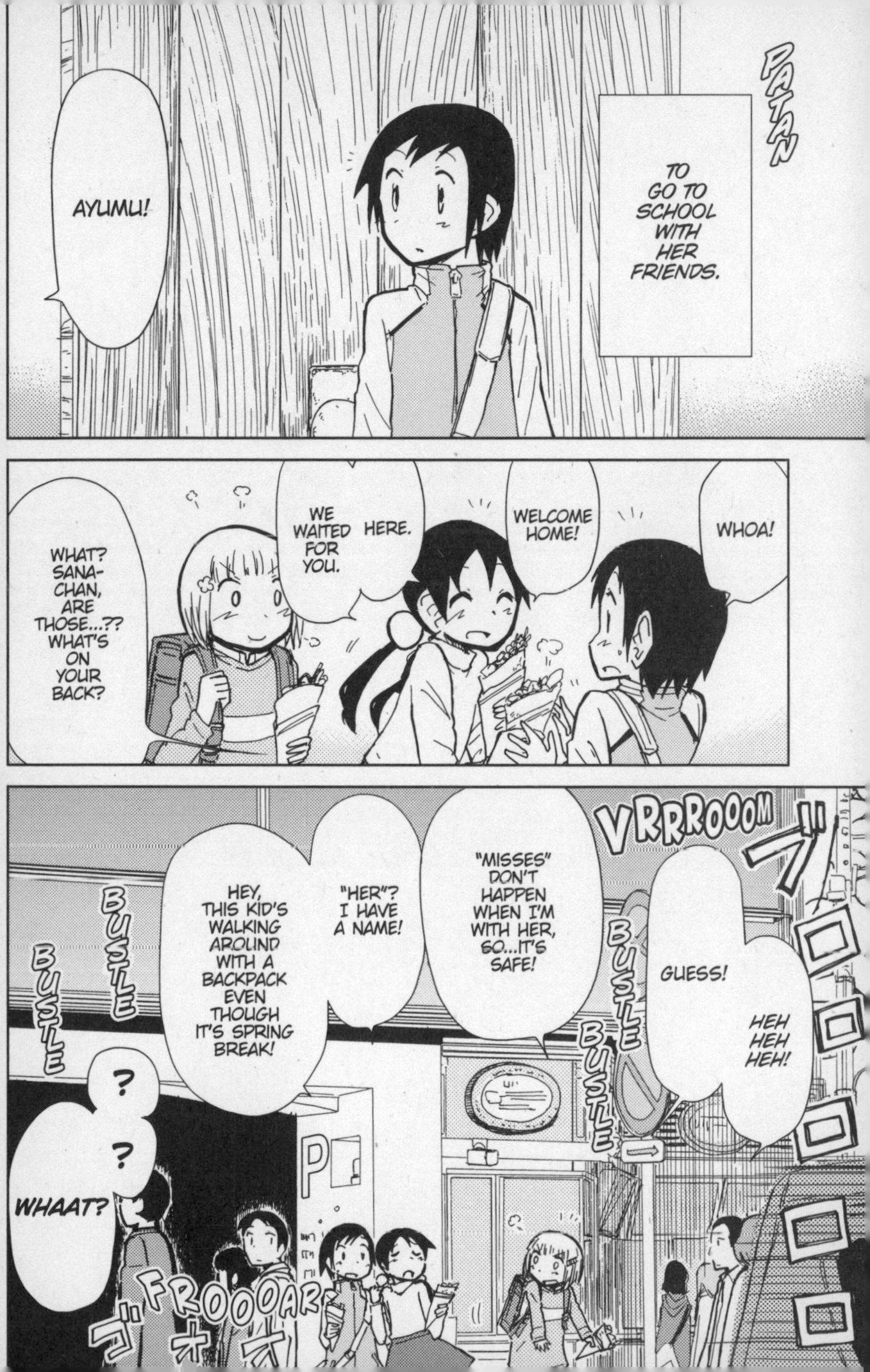
PATAN
TO GO TO SCHOOL WITH HER FRIENDS.
AYUMU!
WHOA!
WELCOME HOME!
WE WAITED HERE. FOR YOU.
WHAT? SANA-CHAN, ARE THOSE...?? WHAT'S ON YOUR BACK?
VRRROOOM
GUESS!
HEH HEH HEH!
BUSTLE
BUSTLE
"MISSES" DON'T HAPPEN WHEN I'M WITH HER, SO...IT'S SAFE!
"HER"? I HAVE A NAME!
HEY, THIS KID'S WALKING AROUND WITH A BACKPACK EVEN THOUGH IT'S SPRING BREAK!
BUSTLE
BUSTLE
?
?
WHAAT?
FROOOAR

Alice & Zoroku

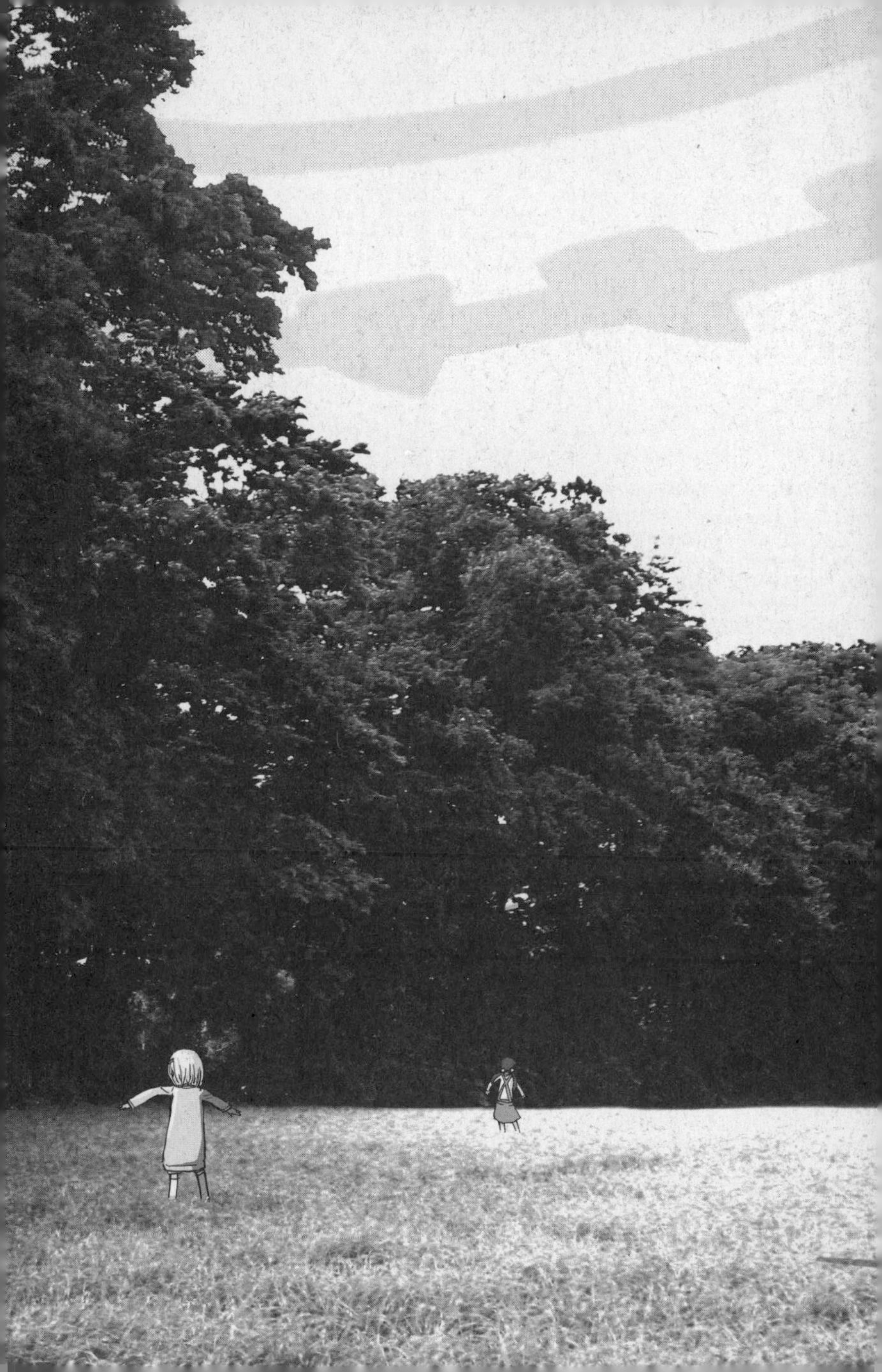

SEVEN SEAS ENTERTAINMENT PRESENTS

Alice & Zoroku

story and art by TETSUYA IMAI

VOLUME 5

TRANSLATION
Beni Axia Conrad

ADAPTATION
Maggie Cooper

LETTERING
Ludwig Sacramento

COVER DESIGN
KC Fabellon

PROOFREADER
B. Lana Guggenheim
Shanti Whitesides

EDITOR
Shannon Fay

PRODUCTION ASSISTANT
CK Russell

PRODUCTION MANAGER
Lissa Pattillo

EDITOR-IN-CHIEF
Adam Arnold

PUBLISHER
Jason DeAngelis

ISBN: 978-1-626928-35-0

Printed in Canada

First Printing: February 2019

10 9 8 7 6 5 4 3 2 1

OLLOW US ONLINE: *www.sevenseasentertainment.com*

READING DIRECTIONS

This book reads from *right to left*, Japanese style.
If this is your first time reading manga, you start
reading from the top right panel on each page and
take it from there. If you get lost, just follow the
numbered diagram here. It may seem backwards at
first, but you'll get the hang of it! Have fun!!

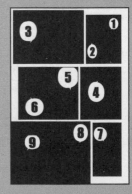